THE NATIONAL SECURITY

THE NATIONAL SECURITY

Its Theory and Practice,
1945–1960

EDITED BY

Norman A. Graebner

New York   Oxford
OXFORD UNIVERSITY PRESS
1986

Oxford University Press

Oxford   New York   Toronto
Delhi   Bombay   Calcutta   Madras   Karachi
Singapore   Hong Kong   Tokyo
Nairobi   Dar es Salaam   Cape Town
Melbourne   Auckland

and associated companies in
Beirut   Berlin   Ibadan   Nicosia

Library of Congress Cataloging-in-Publication Data
Main entry under title:
The national security.
   Includes index.
   1. United States—National securtity—Addresses, essays, lectures.
2. United States—Military policy—Addresses, essays, lectures.
3. Civil-military relations—United States—History—20th century—Addresses, essays, lectures.
I. Graebner, Norman A.
UA23.N275   1986   355′.033073   85–21602
ISBN 0–19–503986–6
ISBN 0–19–503987–4 (pbk.)

Printing (last digit): 9 8 7 6 5 4 3 2 1

Printed in the United States of America

Preface

On April 21–23, 1982, the United States Military Academy at West Point held a symposium "The Theory and Practice of National Security, 1945–1960." This volume comprises the seven essays presented at the symposium, with an introduction and conclusion prepared by the editor. These essays focus essentially on the efforts of the Truman and Eisenhower administrations to come to terms with the consequences of the Allied defeat of the Axis powers and the ensuing failure of the victors to disentangle their interests in a militarily and politically divided world. So thoroughly had the war altered the global balance of power that the United States, under any circumstances, would have responded to the problems of the postwar world with economic and military programs designed to bring some measure of stability and security to both Europe and the Far East. Ultimately it was the burgeoning fears of the U.S.S.R. that determined the character and magnitude of American security policy. In general, the pattern of challenge and response that marked the behavior of the Truman and Eisenhower administrations has continued to dominate the external policies of the United States.

American security policy after 1945 took its initial form from the fact that the United States emerged from the war as the most powerful nation in history, projecting the power of an undamaged productive machine across a world of destroyed economies and collapsing empires. Not in modern times had a country been as predominant industrially, technologically, and militarily as was the United States at its moment of victory. Even as the United States emerged from the war, its leaders were determined to sustain the necessary military power and outposts in the western Pacific and along the western littoral of Europe and North Africa to prevent another war—predictably a much more destructive war—from reaching American shores. Even without any clear postwar perceptions of danger the United States would have maintained a defense structure extending far into the Eastern Hemisphere. What determined the unanticipated size of the national security effort was the assumption of danger after 1948 that permitted no less than a global defense with unprecedented military power. To meet the newly perceived threat of Russian power and expansionism the United States required allies in Europe and Asia, as well as a vast and varied military structure. As early as the Truman years the United States focused on those means where it had the technological advantage—largely atomic and unclear weapons and the means to deliver them. What began as a cautious and contested move toward nuclear power in the Truman years evolved under Eisenhower into a massive nuclear arsenal of almost incomprehensible proportions. In part because of fiscal restraints, the Eisenhower administration, however, did not prepare the nation to fight a limited conventional war in either Europe or Asia. In some measure its doctrine of massive retaliation rendered such a war unlikely.

Those who designed this symposium were concerned with administrative process as well as substantive policy. Recent scholarship, corroborated in these essays, reveals that President Eisenhower performed with great confidence and energy, that he completely dominated his administration, and that his views were instinctively moderate. The new scholarship suggests additionally that Eisenhower's national security apparatus was a model in administrative efficiency. Still these essays demonstrate the profound difficulty in discovering the relationship between process and policy. Process is a means, not an end; the end which any administration pursues is a body of wise decisions. Processes that approach perfection in bureaucratic design may or may not produce ideal policies. What matters in the creation of intelligent policy is the quality of mind behind the effort and the authority of those with the greatest share of historic and political wisdom to dominate the decision-making process. That special and necessary wisdom may be present in a haphazard process of policy-making, yet be absent in one that is bureaucratically efficient. Sound policy does not flow automatically from a commendable administrative structure.

What these essays reveal is the quality of presidential leadership at the level of administration; they leave open for individual judgment the quality of the decisions that the leadership produced as well as the relevance of those decisions to what transpired in the sphere of public policy. For anyone concerned with the broad purposes and the actual record of American foreign policy in the 1950s, it matters little who made the decisions. What statesmen and analysts at home and abroad were compelled to judge was not the private convictions of those in power but the public declarations of policy, characterized less by moderation and admissions of limited power than by purposes aimed at liberation and victory over all the country's Communist enemies. The fact that the Eisenhower administration maintained eight years of peace suggests a high measure of prudence and restraint. Yet that administration vastly extended the country's political and military commitments to friendly governments in the Third World by assuming that all revolutionary pressures emanated not from an assertive nationalism but from a Soviet-based international conspiracy. But, again, if the administration showed little restraint in its Third World involvements, on occasion overthrowing radical regimes and even threatening nuclear war, it avoided an actual conflict. It was not strange that the foreign policies of the Eisenhower years delighted much of the nation and created an almost unshakable national consensus.

This symposium was an ambitious undertaking. It consumed much of the time of Colonel Paul L. Miles, Jr., its director, throughout the 1981–82 academic year. Actually the designing of the symposium and the search for participants began long before that. A generous grant from the Association of Graduates of the United States Academy underwrote the cost of the symposium. (These essays do not necessarily reflect the views of the Association.) Those involved in the symposium are deeply indebted to the Superintendent, Lieutenant General Willard W. Scott, Jr.; to the Dean of the Academic Board, Brigadier General Frederick A. Smith, Jr.; and to the History Department and its efficient secretarial staff headed by Mrs. Sally French. Finally, we owe much to Colonel Roy K. Flint, the Head of the History Department, who helped to execute the symposium in a most effective manner.

Both the essayists and the editor, as well as all who attended the symposium, benefited greatly from the contributions of those scholars who served as moderators and commentators. Henry F. Graff of Columbia University, Ernest R. May of Harvard University, and Gaddis Smith of Yale University moderated the three panels. Those who offered the formal commentary were Thomas H. Etzold of the Naval War College, John Lewis Gaddis of Ohio University, General Andrew J. Goodpaster, Walter LaFeber of Cornell University, Melvyn P. Leffler of Vanderbilt University, and Joan Hoff Wilson of Indiana University.

As Visiting Professor of History at West Point during the 1981–82 academic year, I played a small role in the selection of symposium participants and in the organization of the panels. For the satisfaction that came with a year at the Military Academy, for the opportunity to play an active role in the preparation of the symposium, and for the assignment to edit these essays for publication, I am grateful to those at West Point who made it all possible.

Charlottesville, Virginia   NORMAN A. GRAEBNER
August 10, 1984

Contents

A Note on the Contributors

RICHARD D. CHALLENER is Professor of History at Princeton University, where he has taught continuously since 1949 and has served as departmental chairman in 1970–71 and again from 1973 to 1977. He received his Ph.D. from Columbia University in 1952. His writings in military and diplomatic history include *The French Theory of the Nation in Arms, 1867–1939* (1955) and *Admirals, Generals and American Foreign Policy, 1898–1914* (1973). He has edited various collections of documents on American foreign and military policy.

I. M. DESTLER, Senior Fellow at the Institute for International Economics, completed this essay while a Senior Associate at the Carnegie Endowment for International Peace. His books include *Presidents, Bureaucrats and Foreign Policy* (1972), *Managing an Alliance* (1976), *Making Foreign Economic Policy* (1980), and most recently, *Our Own Worst Enemy: The Unmaking of American Foreign Policy* (1984), co-authored with Leslie H. Gelb and Anthony Lake.

LLOYD C. GARDNER is a professor of history at Rutgers University. He graduated from Ohio Wesleyan University and the University of Wisconsin and has taught at Lake Forest College in Illinois and Rutgers University. His books include *Architects of Illusion* (1970), *Imperial America* (1976), *A Covenant with Power* (1984), and *Safe for Democracy* (1984).

NORMAN A. GRAEBNER is the Randolph P. Compton Professor of History and Public Affairs at the University of Virginia. A graduate of the University of Chicago, he has taught at Iowa State University, the University of Illinois, and, for the past seventeen years, at the University of Virginia. His writings on American foreign relations include *Empire on the Pacific* (1955), *The New Isolationism* (1956), *Ideas and*

Diplomacy (1964), *The Age of Global Power* (1979), and *America As a World Power* (1984), as well as numerous articles and essays.

DOUGLAS KINNARD is Chief of Military History, U.S. Army and Professor Emeritus of Political Science, University of Vermont. He is a graduate of the U.S. Military Academy and received the M.A. and Ph.D. at Princeton. His writings include *President Eisenhower and Strategy Management* (1977), *The War Managers* (1977), and *The Secretary of Defense* (1981), as well as numerous articles and essays.

GARY W. REICHARD teaches United States History at the University of Delaware, where he is also Director of the University Honors Program. He holds degrees from the College of Wooster, Vanderbilt University, and Cornell University, and is author of *The Reaffirmation of Republicanism: Eisenhower and the Eighty-third Congress* (1975), coauthor of *America: Changing Times* (1979, 1982), and co-editor of *Reshaping America: Society and Institutions, 1945–1960* (1982).

DAVID ALAN ROSENBERG is a Senior Fellow at the Strategic Concepts Development Center, National Defense University, Washington, D.C. A graduate of the University of Chicago, he has taught at the University of Houston and the University of Wisconsin-Milwaukee, and has worked on various public history projects. His writings on military and naval history and nuclear strategy have been published in *The Journal of American History*, *The Bulletin of the Atomic Scientists*, *International Security*, *Reviews in American History*, *The Naval War College Review*, and in the books *The Chiefs of Naval Operations*, *Airpower and Warfare*, *The Dictionary of American Military Biography*, and *Strategic Nuclear Targeting*. He prepared the chapter in this volume prior to joining the National Defense University.

MARTIN J. SHERWIN is the Walter S. Dickson Professor of History at Tufts University. A graduate of Dartmouth College and the University of California Los Angeles, he has taught at the University of California Berkeley, Cornell University, Princeton University, the University of Pennsylvania, Dartmouth College, Wellesley College, and Yale University. In addition to numerous articles and essays his publications include a prize-winning study of Hiroshima/Nagasaki and the origins of the nuclear arms race, *A World Destroyed: The Atomic Bomb and the Grand Alliance (1975)*.

THE NATIONAL SECURITY

Introduction: The Sources of Postwar Insecurity

NORMAN A. GRAEBNER

During the triumphal weeks of the spring and summer of 1945 few Americans contemplated the shape of the postwar world or the demands that it would place on the United States. The nation had contributed substantially to the Allied victory of 1918 only to reject Europe's offer of world leadership and withdraw into a utopia of its own. The country's far more extended and costly contribution to victory in the Second World War again did not in itself predict any major foreign involvement beyond the forging of the peace. For its proponents Woodrow Wilson's League of Nations had assured a Europe sufficiently stable to permit an American retreat from it. Similarly countless Americans in 1945 viewed the new United Nations Organization as a promising substitute for power politics. Most Americans harbored only sentiments of appreciation toward the Soviet Union. They viewed the U.S.S.R. as a valiant ally whose costly struggle against Hitler's Germany had made the long-sought victory possible. Diplomats who had dealt with the Russians during the war predicted trouble. But outside official circles their views were unknown and unsuspected. Nothing had occurred to question Franklin D. Roosevelt's assurance to the American people, following his return from the Teheran Conference of December, 1943, that he and Stalin "got along fine" and that in the future the United States was "going to get along very well with him and the Russian people—very well indeed."[1]

Even as Roosevelt maintained cordial relations with the Soviet Union as a military necessity, he, no less than other American and British officials, understood that the Kremlin did not share the Western design for the postwar world as embodied in the principle of self-determination. Americans lauded the magnificent and costly Russian victory at Stalingrad in the spring of 1943, but that victory removed all doubts that the U.S.S.R. would emerge from the war as Europe's dominant power and thus a paramount factor in the postwar international system. By 1944, as the Soviet armies moved into Poland and other regions of Eastern Europe, the Kremlin confronted the West with an inescapable challenge: How did the Kremlin intend to employ its burgeoning land power in the countries soon to come under Russian control? Time alone would clarify Soviet intentions. But the events of 1944 soon demonstrated the limited Soviet respect for the political elements representing Eastern Europe, which had demonstrated, both before and during the war, a pervading animosity toward the U.S.S.R.

Poland became the immediate center of controversy. There, for the first time, the Soviets clarified their determination to rid Eastern Europe of its anti-Soviet proclivities when, in the early autumn of 1944, they refused to support the Warsaw uprising and prevented the United States and Britain from relieving the city. The Polish underground, the Kremlin knew, was tied to the anti-Soviet Polish government-in-exile residing in London; the Nazi destruction of the patriots would eliminate the last body of Polish resistance to Soviet control. Such ambition and conniving troubled United States and British officials in Moscow deeply. Ambassador to Russia Averell Harriman and General John Deane, head of the American Military Mission in Moscow, were, in the words of George Kennan, "shattered by the experience."[2] Harriman reported from Moscow in September that unless the United States confronted Soviet behavior directly, there was "every indication [that] the Soviet Union will become a bully wherever their interests are involved."[3] Thereafter the ambassador reported the Kremlin's growing detachment and secretiveness; no longer, he observed, would Soviet leaders communicate their intentions to Western officials in Moscow.

General Deane expressed his frustration over Soviet duplicity in a letter to General George C. Marshall in December. Deane, like Harriman, did not dislike the Russians; nor did he believe that the United States and the U.S.S.R. had any major interests in conflict. What troubled him, as it did Harriman, was the Kremlin's negative reaction to American expressions of good faith. After each banquet, he wrote, "we send the Soviets another thousand airplanes, and they approve a visa that has been hanging fire for months. We then scratch our heads to see what other gifts we can send, and they scratch theirs to see what else they can ask for." Every show of appreciation met with contempt. "Gratitude," Deane observed, "cannot be banked in the Soviet Union."

The nation that tried to amass it would merely expose itself to endless pressures. Deane advised Washington to demand that the Soviets justify their future requests and insist on a quid pro quo for any assistance not required for winning the war.[4]

Deane's letter, widely circulated in Washington, reaffirmed official doubts regarding the Kremlin's intentions toward Eastern Europe and its total disinterest in European reconstruction on the basis of self-determination. After the Yalta Conference of February 1945, United States–Soviet relations over Eastern Europe quickly disintegrated as the Soviets imposed a Communist government in Rumania and threatened to do so in Poland. After Yalta, Harriman advised Washington to assert its interests in Europe with the same determination displayed by the Soviet Union.[5] Unfortunately American and Soviet interests in Eastern Europe were not symmetrical; nor was the power to render national purposes effective.

In April, Harriman returned from Moscow to remind the new President, Harry S. Truman, that Soviet behavior was intolerable; he urged Washington to adopt a countering policy that would make the Soviets "realize that they cannot continue their present attitude except at great cost to themselves." Harriman feared that Soviet aggression, unless stopped, would not be limited to the regions of Soviet occupation. He warned the President that once the Soviet Union "had control of bordering areas, [it] would attempt to penetrate the next adjacent country."[6] Much of the nation's leadership shared Harriman's preference for a determined anti-Soviet posture. Truman himself caught the new spirit. On April 23 he warned Soviet Foreign Minister V. M. Molotov at the White House that no longer would United States–Soviet cooperation continue "on the basis of a one-way street." When Molotov complained of Truman's language, the President replied, "Carry out your agreements and you won't get talked to like that."[7] Arthur H. Vandenberg of Michigan, the Republican leader in the Senate who placed great faith in words, found enough solace in the President's remarks to confide to his diary, "FDR's appeasement of Russia is over." The United States and Russia could live together in the postwar world, Vandenberg concluded, "if Russia is made to understand that we can't be pushed around."[8] Secretary of the Navy James V. Forrestal led the anti-Soviet contingent in the cabinet. Soviet Communism, he observed in May, was "as incompatible with democracy as was Nazism and Fascism."[9] Forrestal advocated a showdown with the Soviets in the spring of 1945 rather than later.

Within the State Department were high-ranking officers who had become convinced during the interwar years that the Soviet Union was an unreasonable, uninformed, and dangerous enemy of Western society. During the war years, especially after 1942, the necessity of sustaining an effective alliance against Germany had compelled Roosevelt to conduct policy without the advice of the State Department's Soviet experts. Still, that group had remained influential enough to discourage any compromises with Soviet designs on Eastern Europe. With Truman's accession to the presidency in April 1945 the State Department again assumed a dominant role in determining the nature of United States–Soviet relations. Perhaps the most influential official when Truman entered the White House was Under Secretary of State Joseph C. Grew, whose fears of the U.S.S.R. had been evolving for a quarter-century. Assigned to study the Bolsheviks from his Danish listening post after World War I, Grew could discover little that was reassuring in Soviet behavior. Nothing that occurred thereafter, not even the wartime alliance, convinced him that the U.S.S.R. was any less a threat than the Axis had been. In May he predicted that the Soviets would control the states of Eastern Europe after the war. With its stranglehold on those countries, he continued,

> Russia's power will steadily increase and she will in the not distant future be in a favorable position to expand her control, step by step, through Europe. . . . A future war with Soviet Russia is as certain as anything in the world can be certain. . . . The most fatal thing we can do is to place any confidence whatever in Russia's sincerity. . . . She regards and will continue to regard our ethical behavior as a weakness to us and an asset to her.[10]

Other top members of the State Department's hierarchy in 1945 were decidedly anti-Soviet, especially James C. Dunn, Assistant Secretary for European, Asian, Near Eastern, and African Affairs; H. Freeman Matthews, head of the European office; and Loy Henderson, head of the Office of Near Eastern and African Affairs. Henderson, as one of the original Soviet experts in the Foreign Service, had developed a deep animosity toward the U.S.S.R. long before the war. Most of the American ambassadors assigned to the countries of Eastern and Southeastern Europe either entered their posts as Russophobes or at least flooded Washington with increasingly anti-Soviet reports. In considerable measure these reports were not inventions; they revealed in detail the ruthlessness of Soviet officials as they imposed the Kremlin's will on the peoples of the occupied countries and eliminated Western diplomats from an active role in Eastern European affairs. These reports dwelt on Soviet expansionism as well as Soviet repression.[11] George F. Kennan's warning from Moscow was characteristic of many: "The endless, fluid pursuit of power is a habit of Russian statesmanship, ingrained not only in the traditions of the Russian State but also in the ideology of the Communist Party. . . ."[12] For many government officials the great wartime collaboration had never created the foundations for a friendly, successful postwar Soviet-American relationship.

I

Pearl Harbor had demonstrated that the United States, however limited its interest in war, was vulnerable to attack from afar. Marquis Childs, the noted American journalist, expressed the convictions of countless Americans in his reponse to the attack:

> No Americans who lived through that Sunday will ever forget it. It seared deeply into the national consciousness, shearing away illusions that had been fostered for generations. And with the first shock came a sort of panic. This struck our deepest pride. It tore at the myth of our invulnerability. Striking at the precious legend of our might, it seemed to leave us suddenly naked and defenseless.

The approaching victory over Germany and Japan three years later removed the immediate threat to American security, but it did not convince numerous leaders, in Congress and the armed services, that the new weapons of war would permit any country to escape destruction in another war. Senator Vandenberg, a leading prewar proponent of isolationism, warned the Senate on January 10, 1945: "I do not believe that any nation hereafter can immunize itself by its own exclusive action. . . . Our oceans have ceased to be moats which automatically protect our ramparts. Flesh and blood now compete unequally with winged steel. War has become an all-consuming juggernaut."[13]

Military leaders such as Chief of Staff George C. Marshall had been haunted throughout the war by America's profound military weakness in 1939. Sharing the conviction that every nation had become vulnerable to attack, Marshall feared that the United States, should it return to a state of military impotence, would again invite war. He warned an audience of chaplains in April 1945:

> If the history of our post war procedures means anything it would seem clearly to indicate that we must expect an intolerance of military proposals and requirements, along with powerful opposition to all military appropriations. We know what follows, that is, the tragedy of war, which I believe might be avoided, with attendant colossal appropriations and subsequent debts and interest charges.[14]

Marshall deplored the feast or famine pattern in American defense; no limit on expenditures in time of war, no interest in preparedness in time of peace. That pattern had left the United States military structure so limited in the 1930s that it could frighten no one. During the last two years of the war military leaders such as Marshall feared that a sudden end of hostilities would compel a general demobilization and again lessen American influence in world affairs.

In June 1943 the United States Army, on General Marshall's advice, organized the Project Planning Division to plan the postwar American military structure, one sufficiently awesome to preserve world stability after the final conclusion of the war. The assignment was difficult because no one could name the enemy. Still, for military planners, the issue was not that of designating the next enemy but of anticipating the nature of the war that the enemy would unleash. In that war, it seemed clear, the safety of all countries would be precarious. Forrestal phrased the danger in May 1943: "There is no such thing as security, and the word should be stricken from our dictionary. We should put in every school book the maxim that power like wealth must be either used or lost."[15] All service chiefs agreed by 1944 that the next enemy would be, like Germany and Japan, a military colossus, probably totalitarian, prepared to unleash a lightning attack over great distances. War, ran the general prediction, would be total. One intelligence officer described it in February:

> There can be no future war for great powers that is not total war—and "total" in a sense never before experienced. Under the circumstances there is nothing that a foresighted nation can do but make its plans so all-encompassing, so flexible, so adaptable to continually changing conditions that it would enter any new struggle fully prepared to win under the new conditions as they might exist. A war in the future cannot be measured on a fixed historical yardstick but only on one projected into the future on the experience of the past.[16]

To avoid destruction, the country would require a military structure capable of meeting aggression before it could reach the United States.

The need to counter aggression far from American shores rendered the entire globe an area of potential strategic concern. "It no longer appears practical," observed Marshall, "to continue what we once conceived a hemisphere defense as a satisfactory base for our security. We are now concerned with the peace of the entire world." United States security would require no less than a system of bases that would command the Atlantic and Pacific oceans. Air Force General H. H. Arnold argued in February, 1945, that the "potentialities for production of weapons capable of sudden and overpowering attack are such . . . that the air power on which we must rely for protection against them must have available to it and under our control a system of air bases extending far beyond our domestic shores and not limited to our present insular possessions."[17] Naval planners emphasized the need for a ring of bases around the Western Hemisphere, which might permit the United States, in time of crisis, to concentrate force effectively in outlying regions. Should aggression actually occur, the United States could launch strikes at the enemy's offensive power and thereby limit further damage.

To preserve its strategic hegemony in the western Pacific the United States pressed the allies for permanent rights to the islands mandated to Japan under the League of Nations. In 1944 the Joint Chiefs of Staff advocated outright annexation, arguing that the islands properly belonged to the United States as the victor in the Pacific. Secretary of War Henry L. Stimson, on February 20, 1945, requested the President to prevent countries without legitimate security interests in the Pacific from interfering with the disposition of the mandated islands; it was unthinkable, he said, that the United States would give up any of its bases in the Pacific. In April, Forrestal urged President Truman to negotiate for permanent bases in the Philippines as well. At the San Francisco Conference in June the United States secured control of the Japanese bases through a trusteeship arrangement.[18] Following the defeat of Japan in August, Washington quickly converted Okinawa into a powerful military base off the Asian coast.

To counter an attack from the east and south the Joint Chiefs sought bases in Canada, Greenland, Iceland, and the Caribbean, as well as the west coast of Africa, including the Canaries and the Azores. Within Latin America itself they prepared to defend six areas regarded especially significant. These included the Panama Canal and its surrounding waters, the Straits of Magellan, Northeast Brazil, Mexico, the Estuary of the River Plate and its approaches, and the west coast of South America, especially Peru and Chile. These outlying areas in Latin America and the Atlantic, added to the distant Pacific bases, comprised an extensive sphere of influence. Lacking effective allies, the United States could assume that its preeminence as a military power and its contribution to victory—added to its role as the special protector of the peace—gave it claims to strategic frontiers, transit rights, and world resources, which it did not need to concede to others, especially to its potential adversaries.[19]

Even as they planned the country's extended defense system, military leaders, in general, did not share the State Department's fears of Soviet aggression. Until the autumn of 1945 defense planners had little interest in contemplating a future war against Russia. Air Force officers foresaw an enemy with high technological competence; that could be only Germany or Japan. The Navy discounted the Soviet danger because the Kremlin displayed little interest in naval power. The U.S.S.R. possessed great land forces, but Army leaders could visualize no future conflict with the Russians across Europe.[20] Military officers, with some notable exceptions, were not prepared emotionally to view the nation that carried the major burden of the war as a potential enemy. General Marshall continued to discredit the reports of Russian duplicity and argued that Russia had good reasons for maintaining tight security. Goldthwaite Dorr, Stimson's adviser in the War Department, challenged Forrestal's appeal for a showdown with Russia. He complained to John J. McCloy in early June 1945: "I do not know how we can expect to receive from the Russians a tolerance for the existence of the capitalist system . . . , if we cannot feel the same tolerance with regard to the socialist form of economy."[21] Dorr was more apprehensive of the misperceptions and possible miscalculations of Western leaders than of Soviet aggressiveness. That Soviet actions might give Americans pause he readily admitted, but, he added, United States behavior might frighten the Soviets no less. McCloy agreed overwhelmingly with Dorr's analysis of the Soviet problem.

Already such views were receding before the pressure of events. An intelligence report of July 6 insisted that the Soviets were bent on world domination. "The limit has been reached," the writer warned, "to which the United States can subscribe to Soviet expansion."[22] Earlier, Stimson had favored a policy aimed at coexistence with the U.S.S.R., but during the final months of the war he became increasingly troubled by Russia's apparent aggressiveness. He observed at Potsdam in late July: "I believe that we must not accept the present situation as permanent for the result will then almost inevitably be a new war and the destruction of our civilization." General Arnold recalled that by the time of Potsdam he believed that "our next enemy would be Russia."[23] By 1946 American military leaders had adopted views of the Soviet Union which varied little from those of the State Department. Navy and Air Force officers who favored large defense budgets had a vested interest in the official perceptions of Russian aggressiveness. Eventually, Army leaders agreed. Thus, by early 1946 the Joint Chiefs of Staff could declare that

the consolidation and development of the power of Russia is the greatest threat to the United States in the foreseeable future. . . . United States foreign policy should continually give consideration to our immediate capabilities for supporting our policy by arms if the occasion should demand, rather than to our long term potential, which, owing to the length of time required for mobilization of the nation's resources, might not be sufficient to avert disaster in another war.[24]

For military planners the surest defense against destruction from such an enemy lay in the country's capacity to deter aggression. Secretary Stimson, for example, revealed little concern in the country's preparation for victory in another war. "I prefer," he informed the cabinet in September 1945, "to look at it from another angle. I do not want war to come. I want to prevent it from ever coming."[25] The prevention of war, Forrestal assured members of Congress, required a military structure that no nation could defeat, and the willingness to employ that power against aggression anywhere. Service chiefs then and later would not agree on the shape of the ideal military structure. Still, during the war, air power had gained a major role in the country's strategy. General Arnold, as commander of United States bomber forces in Europe, dominated air planning largely because of the special relevance of strategic air power to the nation's technological leadership. For Air Force spokesmen the airplane was not merely another weapon; it was the ultimate weapon for global peacekeeping. Even Marshall agreed that air power would be the country's first line of defense and the major source of its deterrent power. Air Force officers, convinced that they could command postwar military budgets, anticipated the perpetuation of the military-industrial-scientific complex which had achieved the amazing wartime triumphs in technology and production. Ultimately the atomic bomb, in its capacity to underwrite the American quest for an effective deterrent, assured the success of the nation's endeavor to manage the peace. Yet some wondered how the United States could render even an atomic strategy effective against aggressive behavior that threatened the peace, but not American security.

Behind the burgeoning expectations of a postwar global strategy was the country's absolute economic superiority. The war had brought ruin to every major power of Europe and Asia, destroying countless cities, factories, and rail lines. In France one-fifth of all buildings were damaged or destroyed; in Britain almost a third; in Germany, Russia, and Japan far more. By contrast the United States emerged from the war unscathed. Its undamaged industrial capacity matched that of the rest of the industrialized world. It possessed an atomic monopoly and two-thirds of the world's capital wealth. Its technological supremacy, enhanced by the war, was so obvious that the world assumed its existence and set out to use or copy American products. During the immediate postwar years the United States reached the highest point of world power achieved by any nation in modern times. British writer Harold J. Laski wrote in November 1947:

> America bestrides the world like a colossus; neither Rome at the height of its power nor Great Britain in the period of its economic supremacy enjoyed an influence so direct, so profound, or so pervasive. . . . Today literally hundreds of millions of Europeans and Asiatics know that both the quality and the rhythm of their lives depend upon decisions made in Washington. On the wisdom of those decisions hangs the fate of the next generation.[26]

So excessive was American power that the country did not require allies to protect its clear and vital interests. What contributed to the easy extension of American power to distant corners of the world, aside from the wartime destruction of Germany and Japan, was the assured demise of the European empires that had once established the traditional boundaries of American influence in Africa, Asia, and the Pacific. When the United States, during the presidency of Harry Truman, assumed the role of stabilizing a world of shattered economies and disintegrating empires, it undertook obligations that far exceeded the normal political and military commitments of the past.

Despite the unprecedented pace of its overseas expansion, the United States after 1945 was so commanding in its economic and military power that it could preserve its tradition of unilateralism in its relations with other countries. Whether in the name of internationalism or collective security, American leaders sought above all to guarantee the country's historic freedom of action. Even on a global scale they pursued external purposes with little regard for the will and preference of other countries unless the proclaimed interests of the United States seemed to demand a high level of cooperation and compliance. So completely had the war destroyed Europe's historic position at the center of world politics, so reliant was Europe on the United States for both the means of rehabilitation and its postwar security, that Western leaders could scarcely question, much less influence, the decisions that poured out of Washington. United States officers refused to share with Europeans the control of the American arsenal or the possible manner of its use. What enhanced the capacity of strong American leaders to pursue expensive, global objectives unilaterally was the overwhelming support which they received from all segments of American society.[27]

II

War had come to the United States at Pearl Harbor. Thereafter, the country succeeded in keeping war far from its own soil; it hoped to do so in the future by maintaining distant bases and sufficiently high levels of military power to protect itself against another unwanted war. No less would the U.S.S.R. attempt to exploit the advantages of victory in an effort to prevent the recurrence of what appeared unacceptably dangerous or destructive to it. Unlike the United States, the Soviet Union entered the war by contesting the greatest military invasion in history. That German assault on Russian territory ultimately forced the U.S.S.R. to bear a disproportionate share of the war's costs. Recounting the price of defeating Germany, Winston Churchill declared before Parliament in February 1945:

> One must regard these 30 years or more of strife, turmoil and sufferings in Europe as part of one story. . . . In its main essentials it seems to me to be one story of a 30 years' war, or more than a 30 years' war, in which British, Russians, Americans and French have struggled to their utmost to resist German aggression at a cost most grievous to all of them, but to none more frightful than to the Russians, whose country has twice been ravaged.[28]

In the course of World War II the U.S.S.R. had lost more than 2000 towns and cities. The Nazi invaders had demolished 31,000 Russian factories and slaughtered 20 million hogs and 17 million cattle—altogether one-fourth of Russia's capital supply. The Soviet Union had suffered some 20 million deaths. Its 7.5 million dead soldiers numbered about one in every twenty-two Russians. By contrast, the 292,100 military deaths of the United States numbered one in every 450 persons. To defend itself from a repetition of such disaster, the U.S.S.R. would not seek distant bases for its non-existent aircraft and naval vessels, but control of the avenues of invasion from the west—and that, through the insistence that the governments along its periphery be pro-Soviet in their external orientation. Despite its greater wartime suffering, the U.S.S.R. defined its postwar security needs in less expansive terms than did the United States. Fortunately the basic security zones of the two powers did not intersect.

Still, United States officials resisted any arrangement with the Soviet Union based on spheres of influence. For most Americans the future of Eastern Europe was not a matter of personal or national concern. Some who recognized the significance of Russian policy in Rumania and Poland doubted that the United States could influence developments in the regions under Russian occupation. But Americans of Eastern European origin, organized most effectively in the Polish American Congress, were understandably distraught over Soviet behavior. The administration understood that this minority would view any negotiation over spheres of influence as a desertion of the wartime principle of self-determination. During the war many State Department officers had become equally committed to the precepts of the Atlantic Charter and recognized no need to compromise them through formal agreements with the Kremlin. The record of Soviet repression in Eastern Europe reinforced the conviction in Washington that any recognition of the Soviet political hegemony, itself the creation of that repression, would be totally reprehensible.

Perhaps the more pervading motive for denying the legitimacy of Soviet political encroachments in Europe was the assumption of State Department officers that Soviet ambitions reached far beyond Eastern Europe. For those who shared these fears any recognition of the Soviet sphere would merely stabilize the base of Russian power and encourage further aggression. No longer was there any semblance of the old European equilibrium. In both France and Italy, Communist parties with close ties to Moscow were members of coalition governments. Britain, historically the protector of the Ottoman Empire, the eastern Mediterranean, and the Indian Ocean, could no longer defend those important regions against suspected Russian expansionism. During the final year of the war Moscow's apparent interest in Iran, Turkey, and Greece had become a matter of serious concern in Washington and London alike. So extensive were the fears and animosities of some Washington officials that any Soviet pressures outside the areas of military occupation would produce an exaggerated reaction.

Iran emerged as the immediate postwar point of conflict. The armistice with Japan in early September, 1945, established the date of March 2, 1946, for the final evacuation of all foreign troops from Iran. One day before the deadline for withdrawal Moscow announced that it would remove a portion of its forces but leave some behind until it had come to terms with the Teheran government. In subsequent days Iran protested to the Soviet Union, Britain, and the United States. Reports indicated that the Soviets had dispatched additional armies and other heavy equipment across the Russian border toward Turkey and Iraq as well as Teheran. It seemed apparent that the Russians were determined to obtain concessions to Iranian oil. In September 1944, when the British and Americans were negotiating for oil concessions in Teheran, a Soviet delegation demanded mineral and oil rights in Iran's northern provinces. The Iranian government now terminated all oil negotiations. In leaving Teheran the Soviet Vice Commissar for Foreign Affairs denounced the Iranian government for refusing to negotiate. Shortly thereafter the Soviets supported an effort of local Communists to take control of autonomous Azerbaijan. In late 1945 a revolution in this northern province, supported by Russian troops, established Communist control. In Washington the Iranian ambassador warned State Department officials that Azerbaijan was only the initial move "in a series which would include Turkey and other countries in the Near East." If the Russians held Azerbaijan, he added, "the history of Manchuria, Abyssinia, and Munich would be repeated and Azerbaijan would prove to have been the first shot fired in [the] third world war." In mid-January 1946, the Iranian delegation to the United Nations accused the Soviet Union of interfering in Iran's internal affairs and requested that the Security Council institute an investigation. The Security Council admonished the Iranians and Russians to negotiate a settlement. By March the negotiations had failed.[29]

Meanwhile the evacuation date of March 2 passed, forcing the Security Council to take up the Iranian issue directly on March 25. Within a day the Soviets accepted Iran's modified demands, permitting Andrei Gromyko, the Soviet representative at the United Nations, to announce that the Soviets would withdraw from Iran within five or six weeks. Behind that decision were British Foreign Minister Ernest Bevin's strong warning to the Kremlin before the House of Commons on February 21, and Secretary of State James Byrnes's speech before the Overseas Press Club of New York a week later. At Fulton, Missouri, on March 5, Winston Churchill warned the West of Soviet expansionism and recommended a new British-American union to discourage Soviet aggression. Not even the Soviet announcement of March 26 brought peace to Iran. Widespread rioting, led by the Communist-controlled Tudeh Party, threatened the oil region of southwest Iran dominated by the Anglo-Iranian Oil Company. British forces moved into Basra across the Iraqi border from Abadan. The Iranian government demanded the withdrawal of the British forces even as it turned on the Tudeh leaders in Teheran, driving them from the cabinet. Iranian troops invaded Azerbaijan and overthrew the revolutionary government. At last, in December 1946, the Iranian government had regained control of the entire country. Western leaders viewed Soviet behavior in Iran as evidence of Soviet expansionism, and Soviet withdrawal as a successful exertion of Western resistance.[30]

Again the Kremlin appeared to demonstrate Middle Eastern ambitions when, on March 19, 1945, it announced that it would terminate its 20-year-old treaty with Turkey. On June 7 the Soviets informed the

Turkish ambassador in Moscow that they wanted a new treaty that would (1) convey to Russia some border districts in the Caucasus, which the Russians had taken in 1878 and returned to the Turks after World War I; (2) revise the Montreux Convention (1936) governing the straits which connected the Black Sea with the Mediterranean; and (3) lease to Russia strategic bases in the Straits for joint defense. Turkey rejected the demands outright. Frustrated by their inability to gain the concessions to which they believed their recent victories and new international status entitled them, the Russians turned on the Turkish government by claiming superior rights to several Turkish districts around the Black Sea. Washington officials regarded the Soviet pressure on Turkey as renewed evidence of Russia's insatiable ambitions in the Middle East. When the Soviets, in October 1945, asked for a mandate to Libya, Secretary Byrnes argued that the Soviets wanted to "facilitate their access right down to the Belgian Congo." In December, Loy Henderson noted that the Kremlin seemed determined to destroy Britain's historic position in the Middle East "so that Russian power can sweep unimpeded across Turkey through the Dardanelles into the Mediterranean, and across Iran and through the Persian Gulf into the Indian Ocean. . . ."[31]

In August 1946 the Soviet Union addressed notes to Turkey, the United States, and Great Britain to arrange a new Straits settlement. The United States responded by dispatching a large naval vessel to the eastern Mediterranean. Acting Secretary of State Acheson and the Chiefs of Staff, with the advice of Middle East experts from the State Department, prepared a memorandum which they presented to the President on August 15. This memorandum, signed by Acheson, Forrestal, and Secretary of War Robert Patterson, warned: "If the Soviet Union succeeds in its objective of obtaining control over Turkey, it will be extremely difficult, if not impossible, to prevent the Soviet Union from obtaining control over Greece and over the whole Near and Middle East . . . [including] the territory lying between the Mediterranean and India. When the Soviet Union has once obtained full mastery of this territory . . . it will be in a much stronger position to obtain its objectives in India and China."[32] The three signers agreed that only the threat of force would preserve the peace of the Middle East against Soviet aggression. To them the Straits were a matter of international concern. The President captured the mood of the memorandum when he declared that the United States might as well fight in 1946 as later, if the Soviets were bent on world conquest, but he agreed to the recommended course of action. Acheson handed the Soviet Chargé d'Affaires in Washington a note which accepted three of the five Soviet requests, including a revision of the Montreaux Convention. But the note rejected the Soviet proposal for bilateral control of the Straits and affirmed Turkey's primary responsibility for their defense. On August 21 the British sent a similar note to the Soviet Union; one day later the Turkish government sent its rejection. In September the Soviets circulated another round of notes; again the Turks refused to compromise their favored position in the Straits. Some State Department officials advocated American security guarantees to stiffen Turkish resistance to Soviet pressures.

III

During the autumn of 1946 Washington turned to Greece, where a Communist-led revolution attempted to overthrow the British-backed government in Athens. During the recent war two guerrilla organizations, one Communist-led and one bitterly anti-Communist, had cooperated with British agents to conduct sabotage operations against the Germans. The Greek king in London was the third contender for power in postwar Greece. Churchill favored the return of the king; in August 1944 the Communist-dominated National Liberation Front agreed to support him. As the Germans left Greece in November, however, it was apparent that the Greek guerrillas would make a bid for power. On December 3 police clashed with demonstrating Communists to set off a civil war which raged on through 1945 and into 1946. The British supplied the Greek monarchy with their declining resources. During the autumn of 1946 United States officials planned an American rescue operation in Greece, convinced that the Greek guerrillas, supplied indeed from Yugoslavia and Albania, were actually agents of Soviet expansionism in Greece. For the United States the British request of February 21, 1947, that the U. S. accept responsibility for stopping the Communist advance in Greece, came as a salvation.[33]

In defending aid to Greece and Turkey, Secretary of State George C. Marshall warned congressional leaders on February 27: "It is not alarmist to say that we are faced with the first of a series which might extend Soviet domination to Europe, the Middle East and Asia." Acheson told the same group that "a highly possible Soviet breakthrough might open three continents to Soviet penetration. Like apples in a barrel infected by a rotten one, the corruption of Greece would infect Iran and all to the east . . . Africa . . . Asia Minor and Egypt . . . Italy and France. . . ."[34] State Department official Will Clayton submitted a memorandum on March 5: "If Greece and then Turkey succumb, the whole Middle East will be lost. France may then capitulate to the communists. As France goes, so Western Europe and North Africa will go." One week later President Truman repeated these warnings in his famed Truman Doctrine speech to Congress. In that speech he declared:

> It is necessary only to glance at a map to realize that the survival and integrity of the Greek nation are of grave importance in a much wider situation. If Greece should fall under the control of an armed minority, the effect upon its neighbor, Turkey, would be immediate and serious. Confusion and disorder might well spread throughout the entire Middle East. More-over, the disappearance of Greece as an independent state would have a profound effect upon those countries in Europe whose peoples are struggling against great difficulties to maintain their freedoms and their independence while they repair the damages of war.[35]

This widely repeated rationale for the defense of Greece established the Munich syndrome as the guiding principle for meeting the Soviet challenge. Greece and Turkey had become the symbols of resistance to Soviet expansion; their fall, like that of Austria and the Sudetenland to Nazi Germany in 1938, would merely invite further aggression. Congress and the administration dared not permit totalitarian regimes, through direct or indirect pressure, to "undermine the foundations of international peace and hence the security of the United States." To meet the immediate threat to Greece and Turkey the President emphasized economic aid, but he included the promise of military aid and military advisers as well. Republican Senator Vandenberg accepted the President's prescription uncritically. As he explained in a letter of May 12:

> Greece must be helped or Greece sinks permanently into the communist order. Turkey inevitably follows. Then comes the chain reaction which might sweep from the Dardanelles to the China sea. . . . I do not know whether our new American policy can succeed in arresting these subversive trends (which ultimately represent a threat to us). I can only say that I think the adventure is worth trying as an alternative to another "Munich" and perhaps to another war. . . .[36]

Acheson carried the administration's case before Congress during the hearings on the aid appropriations. After predicting that the fall of Turkey would expose Iran to Soviet encroachments, he continued: "Iran borders on Afghanistan and India. . . . India carries us on to Burma and Indonesia, and Malaya, areas in French Indochina . . . and that carries you to China. . . . And what we are trying to point out is that a failure in these key countries would echo throughout that vast territory." Senator Walter George of Georgia, after a briefing with the American ambassador to Turkey, declared that the aid bill was essential to stop Soviet expansion. "If unchecked," he said, "Russia will inevitably overrun Europe, extend herself into Asia and perhaps South America. . . . [T]his process may go on for a full century."[37] Such predictions of disaster had their effect. Congress voted the aid bill, 67 to 23 in the Senate, 287 to 107 in the House.

These fears rose less from objective assessments of Soviet intentions and capabilities than from Russia's well-known historic interests in the eastern Mediterranean and the Middle East. The administration detected no apparent significance in the evidences of Soviet demobilization; in the partial withdrawal of Soviet troops from Eastern Europe; in the Kremlin's moderate, even cooperative, policies in Finland, Hungary, and Czechoslovakia; in Yugoslavia's increasing independence from the Soviet Union; and in the termination of Soviet demands on Turkey.[38] But the Soviet pressures on Iran and Turkey awakened memories of the Western retreat from Manchuria to Munich. So pervading were the fears of the U.S.S.R., that one State Department report of 1947 warned that the very absence of any recent Soviet demands on Turkey rendered Soviet intentions ominous. Assuming the worst of the Soviet Union, the Truman administration would assure the Kremlin that it could not expand beyond the areas of Soviet occupation without facing armed resistance.

United States military aid and advisers assured the eventual triumph of the Greek monarchy. In July 1949, Marshal Tito of Yugoslavia announced that he would close the border, thus ending all outside assistance for the Greek guerrillas. Before the end of the year the Greek revolutionary movement collapsed. Meanwhile Secretary of State Marshall had formally announced the Marshall Plan at Harvard on June 5, 1947. American support for Iran, Turkey, and Greece—added to Europe's rapid recovery under the Marshall Plan—stabilized the regions along the Russian periphery from western Europe to the Middle East. These early Cold War policies, limited to precise geographical objectives, triumphed largely because they conformed to the country's historic interests. Washington gained its immediate objectives easily and quickly, simply because Europe's postwar challenges gave the economic and military supremacy of the United States a special relevance. The marvelous triumphs of American policy were measurable largely by what the nation's power could command at a time when that power was excessive: the economic rehabilitation of western Europe and Japan, the promotion of international trade and investment, and the maintenance of a massive defense structure which underwrote the containment effort and played an essential role in Europe's potwar political development. Even as American military power reinforced the division of Europe, its economic power, working through international agencies for trade and monetary stabilization, contributed to the world's unprecedented prosperity. Whether or not these policies were required to stop the advance of Russian Communism, they brought confidence, and eventually prosperity, to tens of millions of people who had emerged from the recent war amid chaos, hopelessness, and ruin.[39]

United States initiatives after 1945, especially those that secured measurable gains to Europe and the Middle East, placed the U.S.S.R. on the defensive. Greece had not been an area of direct Soviet concern, but in Turkey the Soviets, as a result of the Truman Doctrine, faced American efforts to build air bases and strategic highways for the effective deployment of American aircraft and heavy weapons. The Marshall Plan, designed especially to strengthen the West German economy, appeared also to threaten the Soviet control of Eastern Europe. The predictable success of the Marshall Plan prompted the Soviets to tighten their control of Eastern Europe and, in February 1948, to add Czechoslovakia to their satellite empire through a Communist coup. The American, British, and French decisions to integrate the economies of their three zones in Germany and to improve the prospect of German recovery through currency reform anticipated the creation of a West German republic. The Soviets responded by blocking the Western access routes into West Berlin. This Soviet action, in turn, led to the Berlin air lift, the Brussels Pact, and ultimately to the formation of the North Atlantic Treaty Organization.

IV

Despite the remarkable success of American efforts at Western rehabilitation and stabilization, the world was not conforming to the nation's postwar vision at all. The United States had not achieved peace on its own terms; nor would it in the future. Whether contained or not, the U.S.S.R. continued to loom as a mighty barrier to the fulfillment of the "American Century." Not only did it defy American principles of self-determination in Eastern Europe but it also proclaimed an ideology that challenged totally the creation of a liberal-democratic world order. In July 1947 the Kremlin announced the formation of the Communist Information Bureau (Cominform), consisting of spokesmen of the U.S.S.R. and of all the Eastern European satellites. Three weeks later Soviet ideologue Andrei Zhdanov announced the new Soviet outlook at a meeting of the Cominform in Warsaw. He accused the United States of transforming the capitalist states of western Europe into an anti-Communist bloc. To meet the threat, Russia and the "democracies" of Eastern Europe would form an opposing group. Zhdanov had divided the world into two competing ideological camps. For some American officials the struggle with the U.S.S.R. had now transcended the original purpose of keeping the Russians out of western Europe and the eastern Mediterranean; it had become a global confrontation between communism and freedom, a confrontation unlimited in scope and magnitude.

Essentially this broader, less precise, definition of the Soviet danger attributed the Kremlin's expansionary power less to Russian armies than to the Marxist-Leninist advocacy of world revolution. Thus, the immediate threat to Eurasia did not lie in Russia's military capabilities but in the chaotic economic and political conditions that prevailed through much of Europe and Asia. The political and social turmoil in India, China, Indochina, and the Dutch East Indies, the economic paralysis of Germany and Japan, the Communist movements in France and Italy, and the collapse of most traditional sources of international stability seemed to offer limitless opportunities for Soviet ideological exploitation. The doubtful viability of liberal ideas and capitalist institutions in a revolutionary world suggested that much of Eurasia and its resources might still escape the West and fall into the clutches of the Kremlin. President Truman furthered the tendency to view the Soviet challenge as one of ideology when he failed to distinguish between Soviet policy and the Communist-led assault on the Greek government. His central Cold War assumption attributed to Russia the unprecedented capacity to expand without direct armed aggression and advance its power and influence in regions far beyond the reach of Russian armies. It mattered little whether Soviet forces or even Soviet officials were present at all.

By 1948 some American officials could detect no visible limit to Soviet power and ambition. The National Security Council's study, NSC 7, dated March 30, 1948, emphasized the Soviet challenge's global dimensions. Declared NSC 7:

The ultimate objective of Soviet-directed world communism is the domination of the world. To this end, Soviet-directed world communism employs against its victims in opportunistic coordination the complementary instruments of Soviet aggressive pressure from without and militant revolutionary subversion from within. . . . The Soviet Union is the source of power from which international communism chiefly derives its capability to threaten the existence of free nations. The United States is he only source of power capable of mobilizing successful opposition to the communist goal of world conquest.

With its control of international communism, the U.S.S.R. had engaged the United States in a struggle for power "in which our national security is at stake and from which we cannot withdraw short of national suicide." Already, declared NSC 7, Soviet-directed world communism had turned Poland, Albania, Hungary, Bulgaria, Rumania, and Czechoslovakia into satellites; it posed a direct threat to Italy, Finland, and Korea; it had prevented peace treaties with Japan, Germany, and Austria; it had rejected an agreement on atomic energy in the UN. "The Soviet world," ran the document's survey of Soviet gains, "extends from the Elbe River and the Adriatic Sea on the west to Manchuria on the east, and embraces one-fifth of the land surface of the world."[40]

In August 1948, the Policy Planning Staff drafted a more precise statement of American strategy, embodied eventually in NSC 20/1. This document focused less on defense than on the sources of ultimate success in confronting Soviet expansionism. It advocated a program to contract Russian power and influence until the Kremlin could no longer endanger the interests of the Western World. NSC 20/1 distinguished between the Soviet Union, its power and ambitions, and the world Communist movement. Outside Russia the Kremlin wielded power directly in Eastern Europe and indirectly in the revolutionary parties beyond the satellite regions. The document assumed that the United States could separate the U.S.S.R. from Third World revolutionary movements by destroying the myth that global revolution was creating some new order of peace and economic progress. Discontented intellectuals who comprised the core of Communist leadership outside Russia, the document advised, listened to Soviet preachments for reasons that would cause them to listen to other notions equally extreme and erroneous. The United States, therefore, would succeed in destroying the ideological influence of Moscow in foreign countries only when it had removed "the sources of bitterness which drive people to irrational and utopian ideas of this sort. . . ."[41]

NSC 20/1 acknowledged the special difficulties in undermining Soviet control of Eastern Europe. Still, the Soviet satellite empire appeared so vulnerable to overextension and fragmentation that even the goal of liberating that region seemed well within the reach of a countering strategy. NSC 58 of September 1949 argued additionally that Western security required the elimination of Soviet influence from the countries of Eastern Europe because they, in varying degrees, were "political-military adjuncts of Soviet power."[42] Yugoslavia's defection from the Soviet camp in 1948 demonstrated that stresses in Soviet-satellite relations could lead to a disruption in Russian domination. By increasing these stresses the United States might enable other states to extricate themselves from Soviet control. This could be achieved, predicted NSC 20/1, "by skillful use of our economic power, by direct or indirect informational activity, by placing the greatest possible strain on the maintenance of the iron curtain, and by building the hope and vigor of Western Europe to a point where it comes to exercise the maximum attraction to the peoples of the east. . . ." The problem, of course, was that of breaking up the Soviet empire without inciting war. To this end NSC 20/1 cautioned the government to "do everything possible to keep the situation flexible and to make possible a liberation of the satellite countries in ways which do not create any unanswerable challenge to Soviet prestige."[43]

NSC 68, the National Security Council's noted policy recommendation of April 1950, comprised the final and most elaborate attempt of the Truman leadership to arrive at a definition of national security policy. This document, like its predecessors, described the danger of Soviet expansionism in global, limitless terms. It concluded that the U.S.S.R., "unlike previous aspirants to hegemony, is animated by a new fanatic faith, antithetical to our own, and seeks to impose its absolute authority over the rest of the world. Conflict has, therefore, become endemic and is waged, on the part of the Soviet Union, by violent and non-violent methods in accordance with the dictates of expediency."[44] Only by recognizing that threat could the United States frame an adequate response. "The issues that face us," NSC 68 warned, "are momentous, involving the fulfillment or destruction not only of this Republic but of civilization itself." The Kremlin design called for subversion of the non-Soviet world. "To that end," the document continued, "Soviet efforts are now directed toward the domination of the Eurasian land mass. The United States, as the principal center of power in the non-Soviet world and the bulwark of opposition to Soviet expansion, is the principal enemy. . . ."[45]

Defeat at the hands of the U.S.S.R. would be total defeat. "These risks," warned NSC 68, "crowd in on us, in a shrinking world of polarized power, so as to give us no choice, ultimately, between meeting them effectively or being overcome by them."[46] However grave the danger, NSC 68, like its predecessors, assumed that the United States, with "calculated and gradual coercion," could unleash the forces of destruction within the Soviet empire. Thus, the country had no reason, even in war, to curtail its overall objective of frustrating the Kremlin design. Rather than pursue unconditional surrender, however, the United States would seek Soviet acceptance of "the specific and limited conditions requisite to an international environment in which free institutions can flourish, and in which the Russian people will have a new chance of working out their own destiny." For this purpose of curtailing Soviet ambitions to the needs of Soviet citizens, the United States could anticipate support even within the U.S.S.R. "If we can make the Russian people our allies in this enterprise," NSC 68 predicted, "we will obviously have made our task easier and victory more certain."[47] In the process of inducing change the United States would avoid, as far as possible, any direct challenge to Soviet prestige and "keep open the possibility for the U.S.S.R. to retreat before pressure with a minimum loss of face. . . ."[48]

V

What eliminated the need for precision in strategic planning even against the haunting dangers of NSC 68 was the burgeoning reliance on atomic weapons. President Truman revealed the military potential of the bomb when he reported to the nation on September 2, 1945, that it was "too dangerous to be loose in a lawless world." He announced that the United States and Britain, therefore, would not reveal the secrets of the bomb's production until world leaders had created the means to control that power effectively and thereby remove the threat of total destruction. With war such a recent and devastating experience, the Truman administration in late 1945 was concerned far more with the control than with the use of atomic energy. Before the end of the year American, British, and Russian leaders had agreed to assign the task of managing the future of atomic power to the United Nations General Assembly. In January 1946 the General Assembly created the United Nations Atomic Energy Commission to design a satisfactory formula for atomic weapons control. Secretary of State Byrnes appointed Acheson and David E. Lilienthal, chairman of the Tennessee Valley Authority, to prepare the United States position. The Acheson-Lilienthal Report of March 28, 1946, proposed an International Atomic Development Authority to govern all phases of the development and use of atomic energy. Truman selected financier and long-time presidential advisor Bernard Baruch to present the American proposal to the UN Atomic Energy Commission. The Baruch Plan, unveiled in June, differed from the Acheson-Lilienthal Report by providing for sanctions, not subject to veto, as well as a program of inspection, without which the United States would not destroy its weapons or reveal its secrets. Andrei Gromyko, representing the U.S.S.R., rejected the American proposal and countered with a Soviet plan similar to that of Acheson and Lilienthal. Determined to have guarantees based on inspection, the administration rejected the Soviet proposal.[49]

Despite the profound disagreement over inspection, United States and Soviet leaders continued to seek some agreement on atomic energy. While members of the United Nations Atomic Energy Commission argued hopelessly over matters of inspection and control, Washington officials understood clearly that the Soviets were pushing their own atomic program. In August 1947 the Policy Planning Staff concluded that the United States could better protect its security by building its own atomic arsenal, whatever the absence of defense against such weapons, than by pursuing some elusive agreement on inspection. It recommended that the United States make clear to the Kremlin that it had an alternative to such an agreement and that it could recuperate from an atomic attack and impose severe retribution. Whereas the Joint Strategic Plans Committee of the JCS did not anticipate war in the immediate future, it agreed that the United States, supported by the British Commonwealth, required the power to confront the Soviet Union with superior force.[50] By mid-1948 the JCS predicted that the United States, in the event of war, would use atomic weapons in counterforce operations against the U.S.S.R. In September the National Security Council, in consultation with other Washington agencies concerned with national defense, concluded again that the country had no choice but to plan for the use of atomic weapons. In December the JCS insisted that atomic bombs would "be used to the extent determined to be practicable and desirable." In May 1949 a joint Army–Navy–Air Force committee, headed by General H.R. Harmon, recognized the self-imposed problems that would result from atomic bombing, but concluded that "the atomic bomb would be a major element of Allied military strength in any war with the U.S.S.R., and would constitute the only means of rapidly inflicting shock and serious damage to vital elements of the Soviet war-making capacity."[51]

American officials assumed that United States atomic power would underwrite European security, especially after the Soviet success in detonating an atomic device. Air Force Secretary W. Stuart Symington warned the administration in a memorandum of November 8, 1949: "Only the power of the United States is preserving the integrity of Western Europe. If the military power of the United States were destroyed or severely damaged, Western Europe would fall almost without struggle."[52] The need for a decisive deterrent to protect Europe encouraged the Truman administration, in January 1950, to embark on the program to produce the "super" or hydrogen bomb. Not to do so in a world where peace and security relied so completely on the military capability of the United States would suggest to the Soviets that the country had lost its resolve. The hydrogen bomb was, for most American officials and citizens alike, the logical projection of the American preparedness program.

If the United States purpose in Europe was that of stabilizing a divided continent—beyond which no policy would be effective anyway—the U.S., by 1950, had achieved its goal. Europe had, by then, reached a stalemate. The United States, alone or with its allies, would not change the status quo; and Russia had no power to do so. With both major antagonists compelled to accept existing conditions, whatever their ideological preferences, Winston Churchill, George Kennan, and others called for negotiations to adjust differences, relieve tensions, and perhaps stall an arms race. Delay would serve no purpose. Churchill declared before the House of Commons as early as January 1948: "I will only venture to say that there seems to me to be a very real danger in going on drifting too long. I believe that the best chance of preventing a war is to bring matters to a head and come to a settlement with the Soviet government before it is too late." Two years later Churchill put his case before the House of Commons with even greater urgency. The Western position, he warned, would become weaker. "Therefore," he concluded, "while I believe there is time for further effort for a lasting and peaceful settlement, I cannot feel that it is necessarily a long time, or that its passage will progressively improve our own security."

For Acheson and official Washington, Western power had eliminated the need for negotiation with the U.S.S.R. Confronted with inflexible will over West Berlin, the Soviets had retreated. Following the show of Western unity at the Paris Foreign Ministers Conference in May 1949, Acheson announced that the West had gained the initiative in Europe and could thereafter anticipate Russia's eventual capitulation. On June 23 he informed the press:

> [T]hese conferences from now on seem to me to be like the steam gauge on a boiler. . . . They indicate the pressure which has been built up. They indicate the various gains and losses in positions which have taken place between the meetings, and I think that the recording of this Conference is that the position of the West has grown greatly in strength, and that the position of the Soviet Union in regard to the struggle for the soil of Europe has changed from the offensive to the defensive.[53]

Settlements, when they came, would simply record the corroding effect of Western power on the ambitions and design of the Kremlin. For Acheson, negotiation recorded facts; it did not create them.

That minority of Americans and Europeans who doubted that NATO, whatever its military effort, would have its way in Europe without war pressed Acheson to explain the Western buildup of power. If the immediate goal of Western policy was security, the ultimate purpose could only be a negotiated settlement or war. Yet it was clear that Washington was determined to avoid both alternatives under the assumption that negotiation was both futile and unnecessary—futile because the Russians refused to offer any proof of sincerity, unnecessary because the Soviet Union would in time retreat anyway. In confronting his critics, Acheson rationalized his preoccupation with power as a temporary condition, preparatory to an eventual resolution of the Cold War largely on Western terms. To give the nation's defense policies a needed sense of direction, especially after the President's decision to proceed with the development of the hydrogen bomb, Acheson developed the promising concept of negotiation from strength. He first developed this theme in a press conference of February 8, 1950:

> What we have . . . observed over the last few years is that the Soviet Government is highly realistic, and we have seen time after time that it can adjust itself to facts when facts exist. We have seen also that agreements reached with the Soviet Government are useful when those agreements register facts. . . . So it has been our basic policy to build situations which will extend the area of possible agreement; that is, to create strength instead of the weakness which exists in many quarters. . . . Those are illustrations of the way in which, in various parts of the world, we are trying to extend the area of possible agreement with the Soviet Union by creating situations so strong they can be recognized and out of them can grow agreement.[54]

Acheson's concept of negotiation from strength meant, in practice, no negotiation at all. Strength adequate to alter Soviet purpose would render compromise unnecessary. NSC 68 assumed that the United States could create conditions which would force the Kremlin to accommodate itself to its declining world role and eventually alter its policies.[55] Until Western advantage was sufficient to produce precisely that result, Acheson preferred that the West avoid any settlements. The very notion of a global conflict in a fluid power relationship rendered all diplomatic settlements illusive, meaningless, and even dangerous. Any general settlement that reflected the existing spheres of influence, or reduced Germany and Japan to islands of neutrality in a divided world, would merely encourage the Soviets in their career of world domination.[56] It was easier to assume a world of unrelenting hostility in which diplomacy had no place. Power in itself would not produce change or assure the triumph of self-determination in Europe, but it could add an essential element of stability to a situation already established. Thus NATO, backed by American nuclear power, would sustain the military division of Europe with a vengeance; it would not do more.

VI

America's burgeoning defense structure would not guarantee the postwar status of Asia with the same success that it achieved in stabilizing a divided Europe. Not even the American occupations of Japan and South Korea, successful as they were in imposing governments friendly to the United States, assured the continuance of peace in the Far East. Japanese expansionism had not been the only threat to the West's historic hegemony in the Orient. Asian nationalism was another. Whereas the United States possessed the power to harness Japanese ambition and block the postwar extension of Soviet influence into Japan and South Korea, it could not—however complete its military dominance in the Pacific—return the Far East to its prewar passivity. Nor could it regulate the processes of change. Asian nationalism, evolving slowly throughout the century, was fundamentally a quest for political independence and economic progress. Most nationalists found their emotional and intellectual resources in Western notions of self-determination. A significant minority, characterized by such revolutionary leaders as China's Mao Tse-tung and Indochina's Ho Chi Minh, found their intellectual authority in the anti-colonial writings of Marx and Lenin.

Emerging from the Pacific war confident and armed, Asia's new leaders, exploiting the anti-colonial emotions generated by Japan's wartime successes, began their assault on the old order. The still-existing imperial structures began to disintegrate under the pressure. By 1947 Britain, exhausted by war and facing a determined nationalist movement in India, granted independence to India, Pakistan, Burma, and Ceylon. The Dutch, capitulating at last to nationalist and UN pressures, granted independence to Indonesia in 1948. Thus, Japan's defeat marked the beginning of the end for the Western colonial empires in Asia and the emergence of perceived dangers to Asian and American security scarcely predictable when the processes of imperial disintegration began.

France raised the issue of Western security in the Far East when it made the decision to recapture its lost empire in Southeast Asia. With British help, it reentered Indochina in the autumn of 1945, only to face an organized and determined independence movement. During the war Ho Chi Minh, a recognized Communist, had captured control of the League of Vietnam Independence, known as the Vietminh, forcing all non-Communist Indochinese nationalists either to support his cause or to accept French rule. Following Japan's surrender, Ho, in September 1945, proclaimed the independence of Indochina. Washington, convinced that it needed French support in Europe, officially approved the

French effort to regain control of its colony. This crucial decision had enormous consequences for United States policy in Asia. Secretary of State Marshall, by February 1947, concluded that Ho's Communist connections made him a tool of the Kremlin.[57] This notion quickly elevated the war in Indochina to one element in the global struggle against Communism.

Marshall's assumption defied the warning of the State Department's Division of Southeast Asian Affairs that Ho Chi Minh, as a native nationalist, did not endanger Asian or American security; moreover, the Far East experts predicted that Ho would win. The State Department's report on Indochina of September 27, 1948, analyzed the dilemma precisely:

> Our greatest difficulty in talking with the French and in stressing what should and what should not be done has been our inability to suggest any practicable solution of the Indochina problem, as we are all too well aware of the unpleasant fact that Communist Ho Chi Minh is the strongest and perhaps the ablest figure in Indochina and that any suggested solution which excluded him is an expedient of uncertain outcome.[58]

American writers and officials warned the French that they had no chance against Ho's forces unless they separated Ho from the main thrust of Indochinese nationalism, both by promising independence and by supporting a native leader capable of bidding against Ho for the support of the anti-colonial revolution. Finally in the Élysée Agreements of March 1949, the French government promised eventual independence to the Associated States of Cambodia, Laos, and Vietnam, and named Bao Dai, former king of Annam, as spokesman for the new state of Vietnam.[59] By converting the Indochinese civil war into a Cold War struggle, the United States gave up its freedom of diplomatic maneuver. The assumption that Ho Chi Minh was the advance agent of Soviet expansionism in Southeast Asia permitted Washington no choice but to adopt the French cause.

Mao Tse-tung's revolutionary assault on the Nationalist government of China reinforced the notion that the Cold War was moving into Asia. The failure of the Marshall mission of 1946 to fulfill American ambitions in China—the creation of a united country still under Nationalist control—followed by the renewal of the Chinese civil war, troubled those Americans who assumed Kremlin dominance of any Communist-led government in China. As Chiang Kai-shek's fortunes entered a predictable decline in 1947, the Joint Chiefs of Staff warned that a Communist victory in China would upset the world's balance of power. The

Chinese Communists, ran the report of June 1947, "are Moscow in-
spired and thus motivated by the same basic totalitarian and anti-dem-
ocratic policies as are the Communist parties in other countries of the
world. Accordingly, they should be regarded as tools of Soviet policy."[60]
General Albert C. Wdemeyer, in his special report of September, warned
that China under Communist control "would make available for hostile
use a number of warm water ports and air bases. Our own air and naval
bases in Japan, the Ryukyu islands and the Philippines would be subject
to relatively short range neutralizing air attacks." As late as August
1948 the Joint Chiefs argued that "United States security interests require that China be kept free from Soviet domination, otherwise all of
Asia will in all probability pass into the sphere of the U.S.S.R."[61]

As the Chinese Communists moved relentlessly toward victory in
1948, the fears of Soviet expansionism in Asia began to mount. State
Department officials warned the administration that Communist advances were bringing China under Kremlin control. "In the struggle
for world domination," declared the State Department's report of October 13, 1948, to the National Security Council (NSC 34),

> . . . the allegiance of China's millions is worth striving for . . . if only to
> deny it to the free world. In positive terms, China is worth having because
> capture of it would represent an impressive political victory and, more prac-
> tically, acquisition of a broad human glacis from which to mount a political
> offensive against the rest of east Asia.[62]

Except for Soviet imperialism in China, the report concluded, the Chinese
Communists would comprise no threat to Asia at all. Throughout 1949
the administration continued to search for a definition of the Asian
problem, with many officials questioning the sweeping assumptions of
Soviet influence in Chinese affairs. But, in November, Foreign Service
Officer Karl Lott Rankin warned from Hong Kong that Communist
China would, through subversion, attempt to extend its influence
throughout South and Southeast Asia. "Now that communist control
of China proper is all but assured," he wrote,

> it may be taken for granted that efforts will be redoubled to place communist
> regimes in power elsewhere in Asia. . . . China may be considered weak
> and backward by Western standards, but . . . in Eastern terms, communist
> China is a great power, economically, militarily, and politically. Supported
> by communist dynamism, China might well be able to dominate not only
> Indochina, Siam, and Burma, but eventually the Philippines, Indonesia,
> Pakistan, and India itself.[63]

Such warnings suggested that much of the Asian land mass was in danger of falling into the Soviet empire. Such fears soon began to dominate Washington's official outlook.

By the spring of 1950 American leaders had completed their conceptualization of a Soviet-based Communist monolith, extending the Kremlin's power across Asia. When revolutionary China appeared to be achieving true national independence, Acheson told the Commonwealth Club of California, its leaders were forcing it into the Soviet orbit. "We now face the prospect," he admitted, "that the Communists may attempt to apply another familiar tactic and use China as a base for probing for other weak spots which they can move into and exploit." He warned Asians that they "must face the fact that today the major threat to their freedom and to their social and economic progress is the attempted penetration of Asia by Soviet-Communist imperialism and by the colonialism which it contains."[64] United States officials in Asia took up the new theme. Ambassador Loy Henderson agreed before the Indian Council of World Affairs at New Delhi in late March that the United States, with its long tradition of involvement in the Atlantic world, understood better the culture of Europe than that of Asia. Recent events in the Far East, however, had given the American people a new and enlarging interest in that region. "It should be borne in mind, in considering various policies of the United States in respect to Asia," he said, "that the United States does not pursue one set of policies with regard to the Americas and Europe and another with regard to Asia. The foreign policies of the United States by force of circumstances have become global in character."[65]

Much of this expanding fear of Soviet aggression centered on Indochina where the French continued to fight their losing war for empire against the Communist-led revolution of Ho Chi Minh. Official Washington now viewed Ho as the mortal enemy of the independence of Indochina. In early February 1950 the United States recognized the Bao Dai regime of Vietnam; thereafter, the notion that this Paris-chosen native aristocrat had better claims to Vietnamese leadership than Ho and would eventually triumph became official American doctrine. Assistant Secretary of State Dean Rusk denied before the Senate Foreign Relations Committee that the struggle for Indochina was a civil war. "It is part of an international war," he declared, ". . . and because Ho Chi Minh is tied in with the [Moscow] Politburo our policy is to support Bao Dai and the French in Indochina until we have time to help them establish a going concern. . . ."[66] The French now carried the heavy burden of Communist containment in Southeast Asia. In March 1950, State Department officer Livingston T. Merchant reminded the adminsitration that another Communist triumph on the Asian mainland "could be expected adversely to affect our interests in India, Pakistan, and even the Philippines." In April the Joint Chiefs defined Indochina's importance in similar terms: "Southeast Asia is a vital segment in the line of containment of communism stretching from Japan southward and around the Indian Peninsula. The security of . . . Japan, India, and Australia . . . depends in large measure on the denial of Southeast Asia to the Communists."[67]

For United States officials the North Korean invasion of South Korea on June 25 was the final demonstration of the Kremlin's control of the Communist forces of Asia. The President explained his decision to order United States air and sea forces to Korea: "The attack upon Korea makes it plain beyond all doubt that Communism has passed beyond the use of subversion to conquer independent nations and will now use armed invasion and war."[68] United States officials, in attributing the Korean War to Soviet imperialism, placed enormous faith in China's refusal to become involved. To Washington observers, China's decision would be a measure of its independence from Kremlin domination. This explains why the Chinese advance across the Yalu in November 1950 produced a traumatic reaction in Washington. China's intervention seemed to demonstrate not only Peking's irrationality but also the absolute control that Moscow had gained over China and China's external policies. "Those who control the Soviet Union and the international Communist movement," Acheson warned the American people on November 29, "have made clear their fundamental design." Truman declared the next day: "We hope that the Chinese people will not continue to be forced or deceived into serving the ends of Russian colonial policy in Asia." The President repeated the charge of Chinese subservience in his State of the Union message of January 8, 1951: "Our men are fighting . . . because they know, as we do, that the aggression in Korea is part of the attempt of the Russian communist dictatorship to take over the world, step by step."[69] John Foster Dulles, in his capacity as State Department adviser, brought the notion of Chinese subjugation to its ultimate rationale in a New York address of May 1951: "By the test of conception, birth, nurture, and obedience, the Mao Tse-tung regime [of China] is a creature of the Moscow Politburo, and it is in behalf of Moscow, not of China, that it is destroying the friendship of the Chinese people toward the United States."[70] Soon the pattern of Soviet subversion seemed equally apparent throughout South and Southeast Asia as well as the western Pacific.[71]

For Washington the American interest in opposing Asian Communism had become a "given," rarely if ever explicated, rarely if ever questioned by those charged with the conduct of national policy. Early in 1952 the National Security Council issued a statement on "United States Objectives and Courses of Action with Respect to Southeast Asia." It presented the following proposition: "Communist domination, by whatever means, of all Southeast Asia would seriously endanger in the short term, and critically endanger in the longer run, United States security interests." What those security interests were neither that document nor any which followed defined. But the document went on to warn:

> In the absence of effective and timely counteraction, the loss of any single country would probably lead to relatively swift submission to or an alignment with communism by the remaining countries of [Southeast Asia]. Furthermore, an alignment with communism of the rest of Southeast Asia and India, and in the longer term, of the Middle East . . . would in all probability progressively follow: Such widespread alignment would endanger the stability and security of Europe.[72]

That language of despair, culminating in Truman's last years in the presidency, revealed how far the country had moved from its mood of euphoria as it entered the postwar era, possessing, in 1945, greater power and wealth than any nation in history. That minority of officials who had emerged from the war harboring a deep distrust and potential hatred of the Soviet Union had captured the American mind. Their successive formulations of the dangers which the country faced determined the minimum requirements of an adequate national strategy.

Notes

1. Christmas Eve Fireside Chat, December 24, 1943, Samuel I. Rosenman, ed., *The Public Papers and Addresses of Franklin D. Roosevelt, 1943* (New York: Harper & Bros., 1950), 558.

2. George F. Kennan, *Memoirs: 1925–1950* (Boston: Little, Brown, 1967), 210–11.

3. Harriman to Harry Hopkins, September 9, 10, 1944; Map Room, Box 13, Franklin D. Roosevelt Library, Hyde Park, New York.

4. John R. Deane, *The Strange Alliance* (New York: Viking, 1947), 84–86. See also Harriman to Secretary of State, April 6, 1945, *Foreign Relations of the United States: Diplomatic Papers, 1945, V* (Washington: Government Printing Office (GPO), 1967), 822–24.

5. Harriman to Secretary of State, April 4, 1945, *ibid.*, 819–20.

6. Quoted in Daniel Yergin, *Shattered Peace: The Origins of the Cold War and the National Security State* (Boston: Houghton Mifflin, 1977), 85.

7. Harry S. Truman, *Memoirs, I: Year of Decision* (Garden City, N.Y.: Doubleday, 1955–1956), 82.

8. Diary, April 24, 1945, in Arthur H. Vandenberg, Jr., and Joe Alex Morris, eds., *The Private Papers of Senator Vandenberg* (Boston: Houghton Mifflin, 1952), 176.

9. Forrestal to Homer Ferguson, May 14, 1945, Walter Millis, ed., *The Forrestal Diaries* (New York: Viking, 1951), 57.

10. Joseph Grew, *Turbulent Era: A Diplomatic Record of Forty Years, 1904–1945*, ed. Walter Johnson, 2 vols. (Boston: Houghton Mifflin, 1952), II, 1946.

11. See Ernest R. May, *"Lessons" of the Past: The Use and Misuse of History in American Foreign Policy* (New York: Oxford University Press, 1973), 24–26.

12. Harriman to Secretary of State (drafted by Kennan), October 23, 1945, *Foreign Relations*, 1945, V, 901.

13. Marquis Childs quoted in *Time*, December 15, 1941, 18; Vandenberg's speech, January 10, 1945, in Vandenberg and Morris, *Private Papers of Senator Vandenberg*, 135.

14. Marshall quoted in Michael S. Sherry, *Preparing for the Next War: American Plans for Postwar Defense, 1941-45* (New Haven: Yale University Press, 1977), 4.

15. Forrestal quoted in *ibid.*, 57.

16. Officer quoted in *ibid.*, 53.

17. Arnold quoted in *ibid.*, 112.

18. Thomas M. Campbell, *Masquerade Peace: America's UN Policy, 1944–1945* (Tallahassee: Florida State University Press, 1973), 139, 170. Thomas M. Campbell and George C. Herring, eds., *The Diaries of Edward R. Stettinius, Jr., 1943–1946* (New York: New Viewpoints, 1975), 210–11.

19. For this material on American bases policy, I am indebted to Melvin P. Leffler's written commentary prepared for the West Point symposium.

20. Michael Sherry discusses the views of American military planners toward the U.S.S.R. in *Preparing for the Next War*, 168.

21. Dorr quoted in *ibid.*, 185.

22. See *ibid.*, 182. The Joint Chiefs, arguing against any agreement which would extend Soviet power, warned on July 23, 1945: "This war has been fought to prevent an aggressor nation from dominating Europe, and ultimately threatening the Western Hemisphere." *Foreign Relations, 1945*, V, 97.

23. H. H. Arnold, *Global Mission* (New York: Harper & Bros., 1949), 586.

24. *Foreign Relations, 1946*, I (Washington: GPO, 1972), 1165, 1166.

25. Stimson quoted in Sherry, *Preparing for the Next War*, 200.

26. Harold J. Laski, "America—1947," *Nation, 165* (December 13, 1947), 641. Article dated at London, November 30, 1947.

27. Walter LaFeber focused on the issue of American unilateralism in his written commentary at the West Point symposium.

28. Churchill quoted in Kenneth W. Thompson, *Winston Churchill's World View: Statesmanship and Power* (Baton Rouge: Louisiana State University Press, 1983), 194.

29. For a brief survey of the Iranian question, see Joseph Marion Jones, *The Fifteen Weeks: An Inside Account of the Genesis of the Marshall Plan* (New York: Viking, 1955), 48–52. The views of the Iranian ambassador reported in Acheson to Harriman, December 21, 1945, *Foreign Relations, 1945*, VIII (Washington: GPO, 1969), 508.

30. See Jones, *The Fifteen Weeks*, 53–58.

31. Byrnes and Henderson quoted in Yergin, *Shattered Peace*, 143, 152.

32. *Foreign Relations, 1946*, VII (Washington: GPO, 1969), 840–41.

33. See Jones, *The Fifteen Weeks*, 67–76.

34. Dean Acheson, *Present at the Creation: My Years in the State Department* (New York: Norton, 1969), 219.

35. Truman's message to the Congress, March 12, 1947, *Department of State Bulletin, 16* (March 23, 1947), 536.

36. Vandenberg to R. F. Moffett, May 12, 1947, Vandenberg and Morris, *Private Papers of Senator Vandenberg*, 342.

37. Acheson quoted in May, *"Lessons" of the Past*, 44; George quoted in Richard J. Barnet, *Intervention and Revolution: The United States in the Third World* (New York: World, 1968), 123.

38. For these observations I am indebted to the written commentary of Melvin P. Leffler, presented at the West Point symposium.

39. Quite naturally those directly involved in the evolution of United States policy between 1946 and 1948 took great pride in the decisions. See, for example, Jones, *The Fifteen Weeks*, 259.

40. For NSC 7 see Thomas H. Etzold and John Lewis Gaddis, eds. *Containment: Documents on American Policy and Strategy, 1945–1950* (New York: Columbia University Press, 1978), 166–67.

41. NSC 20/1 in *ibid.*, 184–85.

42. NSC 58 in *ibid.*, 212.

43. For the promises of NSC 20/1 see *ibid.*, 183.

44. NSC 68 quoted in *ibid.*, 385-86.

45. *Ibid.*, 386, 387.

46. *Ibid.*, 413.

47. *Ibid.*, 391.

48. *ibid.*, 402.

49. For a survey of early United States atomic policy through the Baruch Plan, see Gregg Herken, *The Winning Weapon: The Atomic Bomb in the Cold War, 1945–1950* (New York: Knopf, 1980), 151–91.

50. PPS 7, August 21, 1947, Etzold and Gaddis, *Containment*, 284–85.

51. JSC 1844/13, July 21, 1948, *ibid.*, 315–23; NSC 30, September 10, 1948, *ibid.*, 339–43; JCS 1952/1, December 21, 1948, *ibid.*, 357; Report of the Army–Navy–Air Force committee, headed by General H. R. Harmon, May 11, 1949, *ibid.*, 361–63.

52. Symington's report to the Secretary of Defense, Louis Johnson, November 8, 1949, *ibid.*, 367.

53. Acheson quoted in David S. McLellan, *Dean Acheson: The State Department Years* (New York: Dodd, Mead, 1976), 163.

54. Acheson's press conference of February 8, 1950, *Department of State Bulletin*, 22 (February 20, 1950), 273. Coral Bell has analyzed the concept of negotiating from strength in her book, *Negotiation from Strength: A Study in the Politics of Power* (New York: Knopf, 1963).

55. NSC 68 in Etzold and Gaddis, *Containment*, 422–23.

56. *Ibid.*, 429.

57. Marshall to Caffrey, February 3, 1947, *Foreign Relations, 1947*, VI (Washington: GPO, 1972), 67–68.

58. O'Sullivan to Marshall, July 21, 1947, *ibid.*, 121–23; Department of State Policy Statement on Indochina, September 27, 1948, Gareth Porter, ed., *Vietnam: The Definitive Documentation of Human Decisions* (Stanfordville, N.Y.: E. M. Coleman Enterprises, 1979), I, 180.

59. The Elysée Agreements: President Vincent Auriol to Bao Dai, March 8, 1949, *ibid.*, 184–85.

60. Memorandum of the Joint Chiefs of Staff to the State-War-Navy Coordinating Committee, June 9, 1947, *Foreign Relations, 1947*, VII (Washington: GPO, 1972), 840.

61. Wedemeyer report, September 19, 1947, Department of State, *United States Relations with China* (Washington: GPO, 1949), 809.

62. NSC 34, October 13, 1948, Etzold and Gaddis, *Containment*, 241.

63. Rankin to the Department of State, November 16, 1949, Karl Lott Rankin, *China Assignment* (Seattle: University of Washington Press, 1964), 35.

64. *Department of State Bulletin*, 22 (March 27, 1950), 469–72.

65. Henderson's New Delhi address, March 27, 1950, *ibid.*, 22 (April 10, 1950), 562.

66. Rusk quoted in Porter, *Vietnam*, I, 266.

67. Merchant to Butterworth, March 7, 1950, *Foreign Relations, 1950*, VI (Washington: GPO, 1976), 750; Johnson to Acheson, April 14, 1950, *ibid.*, 781.

68. *Foreign Relations, 1950*, VII (Washington: GPO, 1976), 200, 202.

69. *Department of State Bulletin, 24* (January 22, 1951), 123.

70. "Sustaining Friendship with China," *ibid., 24* (May 28, 1951), 844.

71. *Ibid., 24* (March 26, 1951), 484.

72. Policy Statement on United States Goals in Southeast Asia, 1952, Neil Sheehan, ed., *The Pentagon Papers as Published by The New York Times* (New York: Quadrangle Books, 1971), 28.

THE COURSE OF THE NATIONAL SECURITY POLICY

1

The National Security Policy from Truman to Eisenhower

Did the "Hidden Hand" Leadership Make Any Difference?

RICHARD D. CHALLENER

The concept of national security was not institutionalized in the United States until 1947—not until Congress, as part of the complex and controversial process that "unified" the armed services under a single Department of Defense, passed the National Security Act. That legislation established the National Security Council, whose mission was to "integrate the domestic, foreign and military policies relating to the national security so as to enable the military services and the other departments and agencies to cooperate more effectively in matters involving the national security."[1] The National Security Act called for the creation of a formalized structure within which American military leaders would work directly with cabinet-level officials responsible for the political, diplomatic, economic, and financial affairs of the nation. The objective was to create a unified, coherent national security policy. The overall concept was a striking departure in the military and diplomatic experience of the United States. And its implications went far beyond those of the more familiar term "national defense."[2]

Americans, throughout most of their history, had conducted their civil-military relations in strict accordance with a long-standing Anglo-Saxon tradition that harked back to seventeenth-century England and Parliament's struggle with Oliver Cromwell. The underlying premise was that the spheres of the civil and the military were separate and distinct; that the former was superior to the latter; and that, above all, soldiers and sailors did not get involved in politics. Historians, admittedly, have all too often tended to exaggerate the tradition of civil supremacy and the separation of the two spheres. Recent scholarship—

for example, Andrew Bacevich's biography of General Frank McCoy—has suggested that at least a handful of exceptional officers managed to bridge the gulf.[3] Moreover, ever since the Spanish-American war and the establishment of an American "empire" in Asia and the Caribbean, there was at least informal if irregular consultation between civilian policymakers and military officers. The State, War, and Navy departments did exchange memoranda and reports, and, at the irreducible minimum, officers and civilians met in the corridors of the old State-War-Navy building in Washington. Occasional Presidents and secretaries of state listened, often with care, to the advice which army and navy officers had to offer about diplomatic as well as security affairs. President Theodore Roosevelt's policies toward Santo Domingo and Japan are a clear case in point, while General McCoy, a protégé of Henry Stimson, served the Department of State in diplomatic capacities in Nicaragua and Manchuria. But all attempts to formalize these relationships in the interest of coordinating diplomatic and military policy foundered on the charge that they would "Prussianize" the democratic American military system and lead to unwarranted military intrusions into civilian prerogatives. Thus, up until the very eve of World War II the United States possessed no formal mechanisms, no organizational structure, to bring civilians and military together to work out a coherent national policy. It was not until 1939, when President Franklin D. Roosevelt created the Standing Liaison Committee—a group intended to bring intermediate State Department officials into contact with their military counterparts—that the United States possessed, even in rudimentary form, any institutional apparatus to harmonize the hitherto separate strands of foreign and military policies.[4]

World War II was the catalyst for change. The attack on Pearl Harbor and the new technology of war, primarily airpower, made it obvious that the two oceans had ceased to be an effective military barrier. In his persuasive book, *Preparing for the Next War,* Michael Sherry has argued that the principal lesson which Americans, in all walks of life, learned from the tragic events of December 7, 1941, was that the United States must never again get into such a condition of military unpreparedness that would make another Pearl Harbor possible.[5] His book chronicles the development in the United States, between 1941 and 1945, of the "ideology of national preparedness"—simply stated, the belief that the permanent existence of powerful American ground, sea, and air forces was essential not only for the future security of the United States but also—an important corollary—for the maintenance of world order in the postwar years. As Assistant Secretary of War Robert Patterson phrased it, "the military position of the United States will determine the maintenance of world peace." This belief in the need for predominant military power to safeguard postwar America *and* to maintain world order had been, as Sherry properly emphasizes, firmly embedded in the American mind well before World War II ended. Thus it can be reasonably argued that it was not growing tensions with the Soviet Union after the spring of 1945 that created the desire for postwar military preparedness; rather that such a mind-set had been created during the war, had already established itself by 1945, and simply made it easier for Americans, after the breakdown of the Yalta accords, to make their passage into the cold war.

Other and equally important factors led to the National Security Act of 1947. There had been the sheer complexity of coordinating the scattered pieces of a war that had been both total and global. No less important was the perception of the sloppy, uncoordinated, and sometimes simply haphazard way in which Franklin D. Roosevelt had appeared to conduct military and diplomatic affairs from 1941 to 1945. FDR—who practiced what has been called "a competitive approach to administration"—not only had relied on personal advisers such as Harry Hopkins but also had frequently shut the State Department, and especially Cordell Hull, out of the decision-making process. Hull's successor as Secretary of State, Edward Stettinius, went off to Yalta with what at best—and with real charity—could be called incomplete knowledge of the extent to which the Army still believed that Russia must be brought into the war against Japan. "Competitive administration" was, to be sure, a device whereby FDR maximized his options, but it led to such policy disasters as Treasury Secretary Henry Morgenthau's plan of 1944 for turning Central Europe into a pasture, and, when that plan aborted, the United States was left—at a time when Allied armies were closing on the Rhine—with no effective policy for postwar Germany. Not surprisingly many of Roosevelt's critics compared his conduct of the war unfavorably with the far more orderly and structured way in which Churchill's War Cabinet had presumably functioned in Britain. Postwar American national security policy, therefore, had to be built upon a firmer foundation.

In the months after Roosevelt's death, and especially as the Russians began to consolidate their hold on Eastern Europe, criticism of the late President grew in intensity. There was the familiar lament that FDR had been "soft" on the Russians. But, more importantly, a new generation of critics—misguided critics, we now know—began to make the charge that Roosevelt, to the grave disadvantage of the national interest, had pursued a military strategy which had aimed solely and exclusively at victory—unconditional surrender at the earliest possible moment—and which had neglected the political consequences of military decisions. To Hanson Baldwin, the military analyst of the *New York Times,* Roosevelt's greatest wartime mistake had been to insist upon the cross-Channel attack because it promised an early victory and to reject Churchill's Balkan strategy which, presumably, would have gotten Allied armies into Eastern Europe ahead of the Russians.[6] Likewise, according to the postwar critique—because the President and the Joint Chiefs of Staff (held equally guilty, as victims of their nonpolitical education at West Point and Annapolis) could not think beyond the battlefield—the United States also spurned Churchill's advice to beat the Russians into Berlin.

These charges, to be sure, have long ceased to withstand serious historical scrutiny. Recent studies, based on newly declassified wartime records, have made it abundantly clear that neither FDR nor the Joint Chiefs dichotomized strategy and politics as the early postwar critics had claimed.[7] Nevertheless, in their day, in the immediate postwar years when cold war tensions were beginning to build, such criticisms were fashionable, widely circulated, and, more to the point, carried weight. Combined with other factors—among them emergent interservice rivalries for scarce postwar dollars and the perceived need to consolidate intelligence activities— they helped to fuel the drive to create an organizational structure within which military, diplomatic, economic, and political concerns could be fused into coherent national policy. The National Security Act of 1947— and the National Security Council which it established—was, in short, the consequence of a widespread postwar imperative to create an organization capable of developing an overarching, unified, coherent national security policy. The emerging cold war was the catalyst. But the underlying demand arose out of "the lessons of the past"—the wartime experience, perceptions of Roosevelt's shortcomings, and the development of the ideology of national preparedness.

Both the theory and practice of national security, however, would develop after 1947 in ways far different from those anticipated by the architects of the National Security Act. The main body of this chapter will focus on developments in the Truman era, about which there is by now an abundance of sound and recent scholarship, and, especially, on the Eisenhower era, about which scholarly evaluation is now rapidly changing.

I

There are nearly as many interpretations of the origin of the cold war and the development of the national security state as there are historians who have written on the subject. It is, to be sure, well beyond the purposes of this chapter to dwell upon the myriad issues raised by these historians. Nonetheless, while Daniel Yergin's "Yalta-Riga Axioms" model is only a rough measuring tool, it would be hard to improve upon his analysis of the way in which American leaders, between 1945 and 1947, moved from regarding Russia in "Yalta" terms as a traditional nation state with whom at least a modicum of agreement was possible, to accepting the "Riga" axiom that Russian expansion was a given and that Soviet policy was founded upon a messianic drive for world mastery. In a few short years the United States was well advanced on the road to becoming, to borrow again from Yergin's provocative terminology, a national security state—that is, a nation in which external and national security concerns become dominant, while domestic objectives (as evidenced by the fate of Harry Truman's Fair Deal) are subordinated to them. The process was unquestionably furthered by internal political pressures, above all by the irrational fears of domestic subversion, which soon took root after the war and which culminated in the ugly phenomenon of McCarthyism.[8]

Still, as more than a few analysts have noted, the process of creating the national security state was both complex and uneven. The foreign policy record of Truman, at least through his first year or so in office, was not so much that of the decisive "Give-'em-Hell" Harry legend, as of a man who was erratic, often indecisive. His first Secretary of State, James Byrnes, fluctuated between toughness and hopes for making the same kind of political deals with the Soviets that he had once made with United States Senators: "You build a post office in my state, and I'll build a post office in yours." Moreover, even after policy had hardened in 1947, perceptions of the nature of the Soviet danger changed markedly. At first it was believed to be something that could be thwarted largely by economic responses—the Marshall Plan, foreign aid, the regeneration of the European economy. Within a year, fueled by Berlin and Czechoslovakia, the threat was seen as something which required alliances—permanent, peacetime military alliances—and, in brief, the militarization of the cold war.

There was the same unevenness on the military and national security aspects of policy. The early plans which the military services attempted to develop for overseas air and naval bases suffered, as Eliot Converse has demonstrated, from a lack of realism, because they were not integrated with war planning until at least 1947.[9] Similarly, Gregg Herken's *The Winning Weapon* has shown that, for many and diverse reasons, the military were uncertain about the place of the atomic bomb in their early plans.[10] Even a cursory examination of the selected papers of Dwight Eisenhower when he was Chief of Staff in 1945–47 reveals a curious ambivalence: on the one hand, there are lengthy explanations to Army leaders about the reasons why they would have to survive on lowered appropriations; on the other, there are letters which highlight growing cold war tensions.[11] Indeed a cynic might be tempted to conclude that, in the early postwar years, not a few American military leaders were less concerned with developing an overarching concept of national security than they were in making certain that their particular branch or service received its proper slice of the diminishing appropriations pie.

When the National Security Council was created in 1947, many had hoped that it would soon develop a single, comprehensive Plan—Plan with a capital P—that would provide an overall strategy for conducting (and, hopefully, winning) the cold war. But not a few—for example, Ferdinand Eberstadt, one of the original architects of the unification plan for the armed services—were soon disappointed with what they interpreted as the inability of the new organization to develop such a master plan.[12] Recent analysts have reached comparable conclusions. Norman Graebner, for example, has noted an overall lack of precision in American strategic planning, a lack that arose, he feels, from the fact that the United States enjoyed an absolute monopoly of atomic power until 1949 and therefore long nurtured the comforting belief that the bomb was not only "the winning weapon" but also something that would permit reduced expenditures for the various military services.[13] John Gaddis has recently added the important corollary: "The Truman administration never worked out a clear strategy for deriving political benefits from its possession of nuclear weapons."[14]

These judgments are not surprising. As David Rosenberg has noted, Truman left an "ambiguous" legacy on the role of the atomic bomb in national security policy. His early emphasis was not upon strategic planning but upon civilian control, and he seems to have believed that the atomic bomb was a "terror weapon" to be employed not as a first but as a last resort to prevent a war from being lost.[15] It is no less clear that the newly minted National Security Council got off to a less than auspicious start. The Department of State, for example, looked suspiciously upon the Council as a mechanism whereby the military might undercut State's primacy and ferret its way into long sacred civilian preserves. James Forrestal, the first Secretary of Defense and the man most responsible for the inclusion of the military in the National Security Council, played badly his already weakening hand. He took literally—and unwisely—the language of the National Security Act, which said that the Secretary of Defense should be the President's "principal assistant" in all matters relating to national security. Believing that the NSC should function autonomously under his aegis, Forrestal even proposed to house it in the Pentagon. Truman, never a chief executive willing to tolerate any diminution of his prerogatives, resisted from the start. "Now, Jimmy," he said to Forrestal at the first NSC meeting, "this is going to be *my* Council." But even when the Secretary of Defense had been put down, the President remained suspicious. Truman, as one writer put it, "embraced the Council in order to smother it. He regarded it as a potential intruder, an annoying brake upon his powers and freedom of decision."[16] Indeed, of the first thirty-six meetings of the NSC, the President attended only six and sat through all of only three. It was not until the summer of 1950—at the time of the Korean war and of NSC 68—that Truman announced he would henceforth meet regularly with the Council. Not till then did the NSC begin to function as its architects had intended.

In recent years historians have focused increasing attention upon NSC 68, which was a policy document begun in the fall of 1949, completed early in 1950, but still under examination when the Korean war erupted.[17] The historians have been right to emphasize the significance of the document—and not simply because of its strident cold war language, which proclaimed that the "Soviet Union, unlike previous aspirants for hegemony, is animated by a new fanatic faith, antithetical to our own, and seeks to impose its absolute authority over the rest of the world."

NSC 68 was the first genuinely all-inclusive statement of American national security policy, the overarching declaration that men such as Eberstadt and Forrestal had first sought in 1947. It was designed to shock the bureaucracy—and through it, the American public—into greater resolution and firmer action.[18] More importantly, NSC 68 demonstrated just how far the concept of national security had evolved in the few years since the proclamation of containment and the Truman Doctrine and, it should be emphasized, *before* the Korean war had seemingly validated the reality of the Kremlin's expansionist goals. For, despite the universalist language of Truman's proclamation in 1947 with its rhetorical flourishes about defending free peoples everywhere, the administration had, in actual fact, sought, through 1948, to focus its containment policy on Europe, to concentrate on those areas (Europe) in which American power could be employed effectively, and to avoid those areas (Asia), in which it could not. There had been a realization of the limitation of American resources, of our inability, as Dean Acheson once put it, to scatter our shots everywhere. "We just haven't got the shots," he once told the Senate Foreign Relations Committee.[19] John Gaddis has underlined the notable changes that NSC 68 proclaimed: the new emphasis on Soviet capabilities rather than intentions (which led to predictions that Russia might actually dare to make war by 1954); the clear belief that both the Soviet threat and American interests were global (henceforth, no more attempts to distinguish between peripheral and central American interests or to limit containment to those areas of the world in which it was believed that American intervention would be cost-effective); and, above all, the imperative to be militarily prepared, via massive rearmament, for *any* type of aggression from localized to general war (no more concern about budgetary limits). All of this, the globalistic implications of the Truman Doctrine notwithstanding, represented a new departure in the concept of national security in the cold war.

But NSC 68 was by no means a "pure" strategic document, the result, simply, of rational political and military analysis or of new insights into the nature of the Soviet challenge. Rather, it underscored the extent to which American national security policy was—as it always has been, and always will be—influenced and shaped by domestic political and economic forces. NSC 68 clearly reflected American politics—above all, the increasingly militant criticism that the administration was receiving from Republicans. Ever since their unexpected defeat in the 1948 election, the Republicans had begun to seize upon Truman's alleged failures in foreign and national security policy, particularly in the Far East, as their avenue for capturing the White House. A classic example was the way in which the hitherto innocuously moderate New Jersey Republican Senator, H. Alexander Smith, began in 1949 to charge that the Truman administration was suppressing a report by the Joint Chiefs of Staff that Taiwan was central to the defense of American interests in Asia.[20] Indeed, the extent to which NSC 68 argued that American interests were global and could no longer withstand the loss of additional countries anywhere in the world was a direct reflection of the fact that Truman and his advisers, with political pressures mounting everywhere, realized that they could no longer afford to sit on the sidelines and wait for the Communist dust to settle in Asia. And NSC 68 also reflected the frustration of the loss of the atomic monopoly in 1949.

Most significant of all was the fact that the new statement of national security policy, which called for a nearly 300 percent increase in the defense budget, reflected a changed assessment of the ability of the United States to have both massive rearmament and a continued rise in the American standard of living—in the classic phrase, to have both guns and butter. The previous concentration on Europe had, in a very real sense, reflected not simply geopolitical considerations but also a belief that it was economically unfeasible for the United States to spread its security net around the globe. Acheson's lament that the United States could not afford to scatter its shots everywhere can, after all, be interpreted as implying that he would be willing to do so if he had more resources. But NSC 68, as John Gaddis has emphasized, reflected the growing influence of Keynesian economics on the Truman administration.[21] The new economics insisted that, via the route of deficit financing, an ever expanding economy could support vastly increased expenditures for national security and, at the same time, increase the shares of the pie for the domestic sector. The authors of NSC 68, indeed, argued that the American experience in World War II proved their point. It is not without importance that Leon Keyserling, the Keynesian economics adviser whose star was then rising in the Truman firmament, was not only consulted in the preparation of NSC 68 but also endorsed its economic argument.

But the significance of NSC 68 can be exaggerated. Its postulates had not yet been officially accepted at the moment when North Korean forces crossed the 38th parallel in June of 1950. Truman, the onetime small businessman from Missouri, was, like FDR, not a Keynesian, and he was still resisting the fiscal and budgetary implications of NSC 68. It cannot be said with absolute certainty that he would have approved its recommended 300 percent increase in the defense budget if Korea had not occurred. Moreover, after June, the general recommendations of NSC 68 were eventually so caught up in and intermingled with the actual American response to Korea that it is almost impossible to determine, as Douglas Kinnard has noted, whether the national security policies thereafter pursued were the consequence of NSC 68 or simply a reaction to the war in Korea.[22] Perhaps the safest conclusion is to argue that, for the Truman administration, the Korean war appeared to validate the assumptions on which NSC 68 was based and toward which the administration had been moving in early 1950, but which, just conceivably, it might not have fully embraced if the North Koreans had not attacked.

II

The declassification of NSC 68 in the mid-1970s, sparking revised assessments of the concept of national security in the Truman years, shifted the emphasis of historical scholarship from 1947 to 1950. But, more recently, historians and political scientists have been turning their attention to, and significantly revising their assessments of, the Eisenhower administration. It was, after all, under Eisenhower, much more than Truman, that the United States attempted to develop long-range, all-encompassing national security policies. The President, indeed, had a virtual fixation on planning, a fixation which led him to make numerous proposals for coordinating and consolidating cold war strategy and national security policy. (These included, for example, the idea of creating, to the discomfiture of John Foster Dulles, a kind of "super" secretary of state who would be free to focus on planning and coordination.)[23] Moreover, from the beginning of the Eisenhower presidency, and especially after the administration secured a truce in Korea, Ike and his advisers began drafting policies for the long haul. These were based on the assumption, contrary to NSC 68, that there was no specific year of maximum danger (in the Truman era, assumed to be 1954) when the possibility of war would be greatest and toward which the country's military preparations should be geared. His was a policy, Eisenhower told the National Security Council in April of 1953, that was "premised on the concept of a 'floating D-Day'—a maintenance of forces and materials that can be paid for without breaking our backs and that can be lived with over the years ahead." The Truman policy of building for a specific D-Day, he continued, "largely overlooked or totally ignored the length of time which this costly level of preparedness would have to be maintained."[24]

The new administration made far greater use of the formal NSC apparatus than its predecessor had. This, too, was in keeping with Eisenhower's predilections. As early as 1948, indeed, on his last day as Army Chief of Staff, he had sent James Forrestal a long, detailed memorandum on how best to coordinate the efforts of the individual service chiefs in developing a coherent national defense policy.[25] As a candidate in 1952 Eisenhower had somewhat scornfully described Truman's NSC as a mere "shadow agency" and pledged an overhaul of the nation's national security machinery—a task promptly and efficiently carried out by Robert Cutler, who became the first national security adviser. NSC meetings, presided over by the President, were an almost weekly occurrence, and, as many participants have since testified, the National Security Council became a much more vital decision-making apparatus than the cabinet. (Witness Dulles's complaint late in 1958 that "cabinet meetings have degenerated into a group of lectures on unimportant subjects.")[26] Indeed, on coming into office in 1961, John F. Kennedy, with no little ostentation, summarily proceeded to dismantle much of that machinery on the grounds that it limited the President's initiative and freedom of action.

Since 1975, moreover, a voluminous number of declassified documents has been flowing out of the Eisenhower Library in Abilene. In consequence, books and articles reinterpreting the Eisenhower presidency are an almost daily occurrence. For example, the spring 1982 issue of the *American Historical Review* featured Robert Griffith's article, which argued that the key to understanding the domestic history of the Eisenhower years lies in examining the President's well-formed ideas about "the corporate commonwealth."[27] The common thread that runs through all of this literature, one hardly needs to be reminded, is that Dwight Eisenhower, contrary to conventional wisdom, was not a passive but rather an "activist" chief executive who was thoroughly in command of the ship of state. It is simply a myth, we are told, that Ike was a President who reigned but did not govern. Fred Greenstein, one of the pioneers in the new Eisenhower scholarship, has maintained, in his glowing accounts of the presidency in the 1950s, that Ike was a skilled practitioner of "hidden hand" leadership and suggested that the Eisenhower style might be an appropriate model for the presidency in the 1980s.[28] John Gaddis has well summarized the new wisdom:

> One thing that is clear, though, is that historians of Eisenhower's presidency . . . have with unusual unanimity in recent years come around to praising Eisenhower's conduct of national security affairs as reflecting a degree of prudence, restraint and common sense not found in other postwar administrations.[29]

Even Blanche Cook, whose *Declassified Eisenhower* (1981) is often decidedly critical, has given her book the subtitle, "A Divided Legacy of Peace and Political Warfare."[30] And Gary Wills, in his slashing attack on the Kennedy legend and John Kennedy's relentless lust for power, which extended from the Oval Office to the Lincoln bedroom, stopped off for a few sentences to observe that what the Kennedys most objected to was that "the Eisenhower years represented a tacit acceptance of limits, at odds with [their] aspiration for universal control."[31]

But many of these new interpretations are, as Robert Griffith has properly noted, sometimes little more than a reworking of the old questions: Did Ike really do anything before and after his golf game at Burning Tree? Did he really let Sherman Adams run the White House? Did he delegate both authority and decision-making in foreign policy to John Foster Dulles? Much of the reassessment has also been a debate over styles of presidential leadership, an argument between political scientists over the best way to conduct the modern presidency. Professor Greenstein's pioneering article was, in many ways, an attempt to offer a counter-model to Richard Neustadt's familiar thesis about presidential power.

But, in assessing the theory and practice of national security in the 1950s, does it really make any difference to know, as we now do, that Eisenhower was an activist President, involved not only in the big decisions but often in the specific details of daily affairs? Or that his relationship with Dulles was a close association of shared assumptions with much give-and-take on both broad policies and daily details? Does it really change our assessment of the policies of the Eisenhower era to know that the number of actors on the policy stage was larger than once thought and that the President played a leading role instead of being, as we once believed, a "bit" actor? More is involved than just the role of the President. What is the relationship between presidential activism and domestic political and economic considerations? Specifically, in terms of this chapter, what does the new documentation suggest about the way in which national security policy was affected by internal considerations as well as by the influence of the Chief Executive?

It is abundantly clear that the Eisenhower administration, despite its gaudy rhetoric in the 1952 campaign about rollback and "liberation," continued more than it changed from the Truman era. Over time it even came to accept the underlying concept of containment—albeit a vastly expanded global interpretation of containment—which Republicans had once loudly rejected as sterile and negative. The new administration also clearly accepted the underlying postulate of NSC 68 that American interests were global and that national security—indeed, it was always argued, the security of the entire "free world"—rested upon the ability of the United States to prevent additional countries from being "lost" to Communism. Dulles, for example, publicly orated about the imperative to defend the "10,000 mile frontier of freedom" that stretched from Asia to Europe via the Formosa strait, Indochina, and the Middle East. Specifically he told the National Security Council at an early meeting in 1953: "We must hold the present outpost position. There is no place around the orbit of the Soviet world which we can now afford to lose, because further losses cannot now be insulated and will inevitably set up a chain reaction."[32] In the midst of the Dienbienphu crisis of 1954, he told Admiral Radford, "We must have a policy of our own, even if France falls down. We could lose Europe, Asia and Africa all at once if we don't watch out."[33] Eisenhower subscribed fully to the same outlook. During an NSC debate over whether or not to intervene to save the French in Indochina, Treasury Secretary George Humphrey complained that if the United States adopted "a policy of intervening every time that local Communist forces became strong enough to subvert free governments, would this not amount to a policy of policing all the governments of the world?" Moreover,

Humphrey continued, he "could see no terminal point in such a process." The President,

> again speaking with great warmth, asked Secretary Humphrey for a reasonable alternative. Indochina was the first in a row of dominoes. If it fell its neighbors would shortly thereafter fall with it, and where did the process end? If he was correct, the President said, it would end with the United States directly behind the 8-ball. "George," said the President, "you exaggerate the case." Nevertheless in certain areas at least we cannot afford to let Moscow gain another bit of territory. Dien Bien Phu may be just such a critical point.[34]

But the chosen means were far different from those of Truman. The basic policy, articulated forcefully and stridently by John Foster Dulles, was massive retaliation. And the concomitant defense posture, labeled the "New Look," was a national security program that rested upon American atomic power and which, to the discomfiture of the Army and the Navy, exalted air over land and sea power. In the words of NSC 162–2 (the policy statement that replaced Truman's NSC 68 in the fall of 1953), the security of the United States "requires the development and maintenance of a strong military posture, with emphasis upon the capability of inflicting massive retaliatory damage by offensive striking power."[35] Even casual perusal of declassified NSC and JCS documents for 1953 and 1954 demonstrate, for example, that in all planning for NATO, the Joint Chiefs of Staff counted upon the atomic weapon to make up for the discrepancy between Soviet and Western forces—even if the latter were augmented by a sizable German contribution.[36] The atomic bomb became so firmly embedded in the fabric of American military planning and defense posture that Eisenhower was only stating the obvious when, during the second Quemoy-Matsu crisis of 1958, he wrote—almost casually, it seems—to British Prime Minister Macmillan:

> There is also a question as to whether if we did intervene we could do so effectively without at least some use of atomic weapons; I hope no more than small air bursts without fallout. This is of course an unpleasant prospect but one I think we must face up to because our entire military establishment assumes more and more that the use of nuclear weapons will become normal in the event of hostilities. . . .[37]

David Rosenberg, who has examined the role of nuclear weapons in American strategy in the postwar years, has underscored the point: "Where Harry Truman viewed the atomic bomb as an instrument of terror and a weapon of last resort, Dwight Eisenhower viewed it as an integral part of American defense and, in effect, a weapon of first resort."[38]

Massive retaliation—with Dulles's grisly appendage, "at times and places of our own choosing"—and the "New Look,"—the reliance on air-atomic power— were designed to accomplish many and varied purposes. They would presumably reduce military expenditures; place more emphasis upon the role of indigenous forces instead of American troops to supply the basis of local defense; restore American initiative by presumably keeping potential enemies uncertain both about the area in which America might respond and the exact nature of that response; and, at least in Dulles's mind, deter war by solving the problem of war by miscalculation. (War by miscalculation, it should be noted, was always Dulles's greatest concern. When he first outlined his thinking to the National Security Council in 1953, he indicated that he did not think war with Russia was "inevitable." The greatest danger was, in his words, "miscalculation by our potential enemies as to our intentions if they aggress further.")[39]

Massive retaliation was and remained the basic deterrent strategy. That it had preserved national security was an article of faith. Dulles, for example, always insisted that North Korea had agreed to a truce only because that country recognized that the Eisenhower administration was prepared to expand the war in ways hitherto denied. As he said to Churchill at the Bermuda conference in late 1953, "the North Koreans were convinced by our willingness and our ability to wage a more intensive and vigorous war than had been the case up to the armistice."[40] Moreover, despite *Sputnik* and, also in the late 'fifties, increasing doubts about its credibility, massive retaliation lasted. When he was on his death bed in Walter Reed Hospital in the spring of 1959, Dulles telephoned his successor, Christian Herter, about the best way to handle the Berlin crisis: "There is basically a total failure to grasp or accept the whole concept of our deterrent strategy. Whenever there is a threat, we can't buy our way out by making concessions rather than standing firm and relying on our deterrent power to keep the peace."[41]

In a very real sense it was, from a technological point of view, not surprising that the Eisenhower administration would choose to emphasize nuclear weapons. When the Republicans came into office, the United States—to use the language of nuclear deterrence—was just moving out of the era of "nuclear scarcity" and into the age of "nuclear plenty." There were only nine atomic bombs available in 1946, and by the end of 1948 only fifty. Moreover, it required at least 48 hours of effort by a large crew to arm a bomb for action, and in the late 'forties there were fewer than three dozen B-29 aircraft in the entire air force equipped to carry an atomic bomb. But, especially after 1950, there were rapid technological advances. Greater sophistication and "mini-aturization" in weaponry meant that, by the time Eisenhower came into office, far more powerful weapons were available in all sizes and forms—for example, as tactical weapons in the form of 155 artillery shells.[42] Moreover, and symbolically, the first successful hydrogen bomb test was conducted in October of 1952. In his recent (1983) autobiography General Omar Bradley, then chairman of the Joint Chiefs of Staff, recalled that shortly after the election he briefed the President-elect on the new options available to him as a result "of our swelling nuclear arsenal."[43] Production facilities had also been expanded. While Truman may have been ambiguous about the actual use of the bomb, he had ordered vast increases in production facilities—so much so that since then, as Rosenberg has pointed out, no President has ever had to request funds for more nuclear building capacity.[44] Thus, by the time Truman left office the nuclear arsenal had expanded to at least 1000 weapons. The Eisenhower administration increased the pace. By the end of the decade, when Ike was about to leave office, the arsenal included some 19,000 atomic weapons of all sizes and forms.

Nevertheless, both massive retaliation and the New Look have most frequently been interpreted as national security policies that flowed directly from the fiscal conservatism of the Republicans, the conse-quence of the administration's never-ending search for that holiest of all conservative holy grails: the balanced budget. Most certainly, when the new administration came into office, most party leaders, notably those in the camp of Senator Robert A. Taft, believed that, the ar-guments of NSC 68 notwithstanding, Truman's policies, domestic as well as foreign, threatened national bankruptcy. John Foster Dulles, unable to attend an early March meeting of legislative leaders, later phoned Press Secretary Jim Hagerty to find out what had happened. "It went well," Hagerty reported, "until Senator Taft blew up, said the overall Eisenhower budget was the same as the Truman budget, and told Ike that neither he nor other Republicans in Congress could support it."[45] Secretary of the Treasury George Humphrey long enjoyed the reputation of being, within the administration, the most vocal advocate of budgetary restraints upon national security policy. Typical was his performance at a National Security Council meeting in 1956 when mu-tual aid expenditures of two billion dollars were under discussion. It was high time, Humphrey insisted, for the United States to become selective. As he saw it, the National Security Council "ought to focus its attention on what we could afford."[46] Dulles could echo the same themes. In 1958, when many Congressional as well as outside critics were pressing for additional expenditures to close the alleged "missile gap," Dulles complained to the NSC, asking if there wasn't any group in the government who thought about the right kind of ceiling for our military capabilities. Too many people, Dulles lamented, wanted the United States to have the best and the most of everything. If we didn't watch it, all our national production would be centered in the military establishment.[47]

Eisenhower felt no less strongly. In his April 30, 1953, presentation to the National Security Council, the new President emphasized that there were two basic threats to the United States—the external threat posed by the Soviet Union and, no less important, the internal threat "that the cost to the United States, as the leader of the free world, of strengthening free world opposition to this external threat may seriously weaken the economy of the United States and thus destroy the very freedom, values and institutions which we are seeking to maintain." He strongly criticized the national security policies of Truman for concentrating so much on the external threat that they had neglected the equally serious internal threat. Promising new policies to get "more security for less dollars," Ike concluded that his administration intended to take "conclusive account, not only of the *external* threat posed by the Soviets but also of the *internal* threat posed by the long continuance and magnitude of Federal spending."[48]

But what emerges most clearly and unequivocally from the available NSC minutes is the central role of the President in these matters. While always expressing his firm belief in the need to exercise budgetary restraints, the President sought to steer a middle course. Typical was his response to Humphrey's complaint that the NSC should concentrate "on what we could afford." First, Ike suggested the necessity of studying the extent to which the United States should reduce its foreign assistance programs, a need that was all the more pressing, the President added, because foreign governments had come to regard these expenditures as part of a solemn American commitment to help them. The President, agreeing at least in part with Humphrey, noted that "every one thought that our foreign aid program was excessive." However, he went on, the real problem was how to reduce such expenditures without causing political repercussions in the countries affected. Ike then directly addressed Humphrey. In the words of the minutes:

> . . . while the Secretary of the Tresury was right in a general business sense, the issue ought to be stated differently. How much would you rather spend than have a global war or an armed attack upon the United States. Every one knew that he didn't want to take the road that would lead to socialism

or totalitarian controls in this country. Nevertheless, you couldn't look at the problem the way Humphrey did. You have to start with the question as to what the security of the United States demanded. Once that question was answered, then you can proceed to break it down into the priority claims of our various national security programs on our resources. But you can't base a vital decision like this on purely budgetary considerations.[49]

Eisenhower responded in like fashion to Dulles's complaint two years later: "Too little would destroy our national defense, but, on the other hand, too much would reduce the United States to a garrison state or ruin our free economy."[50]

Amidst Eisenhower's constant search for a balance between the often conflicting demands of national security and fiscal restraints, there was always one constant: the President's recurrent emphasis upon the danger that excessive expenditures for national security would imperil the free economy and eventually produce the "garrison state." The words which appear with greatest frequency in his discourse are "adequacy" and "sufficiency"—words which clearly implied that the security of the United States did not require either weapons or forces in existence that exceeded those of the Soviet Union. Of Eisenhower's many statements, none is more characteristic than his response to a group of legislative leaders in 1959 at a time when many in Congress were insisting that the United States must be able to meet any contingency with a complete range of weapons and forces:

It is perfectly clear that you can't provide security with a checkbook. . . . If these people try to put another three billion into the budget every time Russia begins to push, then you might as well go all the way to a garrison state. . . . Once you spend a single dollar beyond adequacy, then you are weakening yourself. Those people who are advocating more spending think that it's money rather than brains that are needed now. Any one who has read a little bit on Communism . . . knows that the Communist objective is to make us spend ourselves into bankruptcy.[51]

Robert Griffith has argued that Eisenhower's search for a corporative commonwealth on the domestic front—his hope to "resolve what he saw as the contradictions of modern capitalism and to create a harmonious, corporative society without class conflict, unbridled acquisitiveness and contentious party politics"—can serve as an organizing principle for understanding his domestic policies.[52] The statements just cited would seem not only to parallel his domestic ideas but also to serve as a comparable organizing theme for assessing his national security policies. And these statements underscore the conclusion of John Gaddis that the national security pronouncements of the Eisenhower administration always stressed two objectives: "maintaining the security of the United States *and* the vitality of its fundamental values and institutions."[53] Also, given Eisenhower's recurrent nightmare of the "garrison state," it should have been no surprise that he turned his valedictory speech of January 1961 into an eloquent warning of the threat "the military-industrial complex" posed to the nation's free institutions.

III

In 1956 *Life* magazine published a famous article, "Three Times to the Brink," which forever tagged John Foster Dulles as the "brinkman" who reveled in nuclear confrontations with the Soviets and the Chinese on the edge of Armageddon. Dulles later complained that the journalists made him look like a tough guy who flew around the world drinking I. W. Harper whiskey and scaring people. But the new documentation tends to reinforce the hard-line image as well as to demonstrate Dulles's remarkable consistency. In his pre-inaugural voyage on the cruiser *Augusta*, Dulles advised the President-elect that the United States had to be prepared to use the same tactics as the Soviets. "We are like a boxer who abides by the Marquis of Queensbury rules," he said, "while our opponent strikes foul blows." The United States would have to be ready to beat the Soviets at their own game. The Soviets and Chinese were vulnerable, he continued, to initiatives which we could mount by civil war or revolutionary tactics—for example, from Formosa. "If you don't develop such approaches, then our enemies will be convinced that we are permanently supine, and they will press their tactics against us." Moreover, said Dulles, the Communists expect a Republican administration to be tougher than a Democratic one. "If it is not tougher, they will enlarge their estimate of what they can get away with. Our future will be worse than our past."[54] He believed in massive retaliation; during the Dienbienphu crisis, his brother Allen phoned to express his hope that Foster wasn't "hooked" on using ground troops. In no way, the Secretary replied. "This is the place to apply my theory."[55] Prior to the Lebanese landings in 1958, Dulles complained to his staff that UN Ambassador Henry Cabot Lodge was far too interested in effecting a compromise. Lodge's solution, he complained, was the "Munich solution." Later, when he talked on the phone to Lodge about their disagreement, the former Massachusetts Senator insisted that he always followed the Secretary's instructions— to which Dulles retorted that it was one thing to follow them, "another to understand them."[56] In the second Quemoy-Matsu crisis Dulles tried to persuade Eisenhower that the islands were so thoroughly integrated into Chiang's defense plans for Taiwan that the United States had no choice but to defend them, or the consequences "would be fatal."[57] From his hospital bed in 1959 he advised Christian Herter to remain firm on Berlin. "It must be realized that if the Soviets by threatening to do things by force do destroy our rights and force us to retreat and make concessions, it is just the beginning. . . . If we are perfectly firm in our position . . . there is not one chance in a thousand that the Soviets will push it to the point of war."[58] And with a summit conference now in the offing, the ailing Secretary made it clear that he saw no point in going at all. He had "been successfully avoiding this [a summit] for a year and a half on valid grounds . . . . How do you justify going to another Summit when all the former pledges have been violated?"[59]

Dwight D. Eisenhower was also a cold warrior. As he bluntly stated in an early meeting of the National Security Council, "It is the rooted conviction of the present administration that the Kremlin intends to dominate and control the entire free world. The 'peace feelers' put forth by the new Soviet leadership, since Stalin's death, have not altered a full appreciation of the continuous, terrible threat posed to the free world by the USSR."[60] Yet at the same time Eisenhower always seemed to be particularly aware of the political and public constraints that affected the formulation of American national security policy, and his perceptions quite frequently seem broader than those of his Secretary of State. In the fall of 1953, for example, Dulles sent the President some extensive suggestions for changes in national security policy. Ike, though on vacation in Colorado, responded with a five-page, single-spaced letter, which focused not on the details of the recommendations but rather on the need "for programs informing the American public, as well as other populations . . . if we are to do anything except to drift aimlessly, probably to our own destruction." The following paragraph from his letter captures his understanding of the problem:

> There is currently much misunderstanding among us. Our own people want tax relief; but they are not well informed as to what drastic tax reduction would mean to the security of the country. They have hoped, and possibly believed, that the Armistice achieved on the Korean battlefield is a prelude to an era of better relations between ourselves and Russia. The individual feels helpless to do anything about the foreign threat that hangs over his head and so he turns his attention to matters of individual interest—farm supports, Taft-Hartley Act, taxes, drought relief, and partisan politics. Abroad we and our intentions are suspect because we are known to be big and wealthy, and believed to be impulsive and truculent.

Ike's conclusion was blunt:

> Even the adoption on a unanimous basis of revised policies by the President,
> the Cabinet and the bi-partisan leaders of the Congress would not, in them-
> selves, be sufficient to assure the accomplishment of the resulting objective.
> *We must have the enlightened support of Americans* and the informed un-
> derstanding of our friends in the world."[61]

One page of the letter was a critique of the draft of a speech that
Dulles intended to deliver at the UN later in the month. Eisenhower
gently chided his Secretary for writing "an indictment of the Bolshevik
Party. . . . Now I have no quarrel with indicting and condemning them,
but I wonder whether or not, in front of the General Assembly, this
would be the proper approach. . . . I rather feel," the President went
on, "that it would be well to state flatly in the beginning that you have
no intention of producing a Phillipic—that your purpose is to advance
the cause of conciliation and understanding. . . ."

The same consciousness informed Eisenhower's approach to the actual implementation of national security policies and the handling of
day-by-day realities. The President's role in the two crises of 1955 and
1958 over the "offshore islands" of Quemoy and Matsu illustrates the
point. From the beginning, out of his own military expertise, Eisenhower had grave doubts about the defensibility of the islands and questioned Chiang Kai-shek's military judgment for placing so many
Nationalist troops on these islands so close to the mainland and so
vulnerable. Moreover, as he told Dulles during the 1955 crisis, "he felt
that the Quemoy-Matsu situation was a liability for the United States."[62]
He also made it clear that one of the first priorities should be "to develop
the thinking of the Chinese Nationalists along different lines."[63] But at
the same time (and he never wavered on this point) the President firmly
believed that the defense of Taiwan—as distinguished from the offshore
islands—was vital to American security. He understood, though he did
not necessarily always sympathize with, the symbolical importance that
Quemoy and Matsu had for the Nationalist regime. He always felt that
too much American pressure on Chiang—direct pressure to force or
compel him to abandon the islands—would be counterproductive, might
undermine Nationalist morale, conceivably lead to the collapse of the
Taiwan regime, and ultimately produce a disaster for American policy
in the Far East. As the President once put it, the only military reason
for holding the islands "is the estimated effect of their loss upon morale
in Formosa."[64] Yet at the same time Eisenhower was always frustrated

by his inability to get Chiang to change his mind or decrease his commitment to Quemoy and Matsu.

In both crises the President did, it is true, frequently support the Dulles position about defending the islands, especially if an attack on Quemoy and Matsu seemed a prelude to an assault on Formosa. But, clearly, he was also always looking for alternatives. Indeed, by late March of 1955 even members of Dulles's staff were wondering if the President wasn't about to change his thinking about the defense of the offshore islands. Dulles was at great pains to reassure his colleagues that, "while their discussion shouldn't be interpreted to mean that the President had necessarily changed his mind, . . . the President is intensely disturbed by the entire situation, and wants every possible avenue of action leading to a possible peaceful and successful conclusion explored thoroughly."[65] And Ike felt strongly enough that, a week later, he composed and sent his Secretary a lengthy memorandum outlining his own thoughts on the Quemoy-Matsu impasse. In it the President emphasized that

> our active participation would forfeit the good opinion of much of the Western world, with consequent damage to our interests in Europe and elsewhere. There is much opposition in our own country to becoming involved militarily in the defense of the offshore islands, and in the event of such involvement our people would be seriously divided at the very time when the increased risk of global war would underline the need for unity.[66]

Eisenhower's own solution (which Chiang could not be persuaded to accept) was that the Nationalists should focus their defense efforts on Taiwan and treat the offshore islands as "outposts" and not "garrisons"; and, "without actually abandoning them, make it clear that neither the Nationalists nor the Americans were committed to full-out defense . . . so that no matter what the outcome of an attack upon them, there would be no danger of a collapse of the free world position in the area." In return the President was prepared to offer extended help—an American air wing, possibly a regiment of marines—to strengthen the Nationalist position on Taiwan itself.

In both the crises of 1955 and 1958 the President received many letters from American citizens who, in effect, described themselves as loyal supporters of the administration but who went on to indicate that, while they could accept the commitment to defend Taiwan, they simply could not comprehend the apparent support for Chiang's position on Quemoy and Matsu. Eisenhower, sensitive to these communications, often passed them on to Dulles with a covering note that they were worth looking at. ("It reflects an honest man's adverse reaction," read one such note.)[67] One letter in the late summer of 1958 that gave the negative findings of a public opinion poll on Quemoy-Matsu "shook the President."[68] Moreover, the frequent Eisenhower-Dulles telephone conversations during the 1958 crisis bear increasing witness to Ike's mounting frustration with Chiang's stubborn commitment to the off-shore islands. "All I am looking for," Ike said on one occasion, "is for a way to get out of that damned place where we are caught."[69] In another conversation, just as he had done in 1955, Ike offered his own solution. Wouldn't it be possible, he suggested to Dulles, for the United States to give Chiang additional naval equipment—for example, some reconditioned destroyers, amphibious craft? This would give the Nationalists additional mobility and, the thought, help them to keep alive the illusion that they might some day return to the mainland. All of this, of course, would be in return for Chiang's agreement to cut back his commitment to the offshore islands.[69]

The offshore islands crises, then, do furnish evidence of Eisenhower's "hidden hand leadership" as well as the President's close involvement in the minutiae of national security policy. The correspondence, phone calls, and memoranda reflect not only his continuous frustration over Nationalist policy but also his equally continuous effort to find some sort of middle-of-the-road policy that would accomplish the seemingly impossible: to get Chiang to reduce his commitment to Quemoy and Matsu while at the same time providing support for his regime and not undercutting it. And his overall policy was marked by a desire to avoid a conflict with Communist China over the offshore islands, a war which, Ike understood, the American public would never understand.[70]

Both public and political constraints—and the President's awareness of them—were also clearly in evidence in the decisions on Indochina at the time of the French agony at Dienbienphu in 1954. Again, as in the case of underlying support for Chiang, there is no question about the fact that the entire administration regarded maintenance of the French position in Southeast Asia as crucial for American security. Containment had long since been extended beyond the Taiwan straits. One of the critical decisions in early 1954—hailed in some accounts as "the day we didn't go to war"[71]—occurred at a meeting with legislative leaders on April 3. Dulles and Admiral Radford, chairman of the Joint Chiefs, came armed with a proposal to ask Congress for the authority to permit the President to use air and naval forces to rescue the French garrison at Dienbienphu. Radford, followed by Dulles, put the case strictly on the grounds of national security. But the legislators objected.

There would be no Congressional approval, they made it clear, until and unless the administration had firm commitments from America's allies, the British and the French. But of greatest significance was the point stressed by the Senators and Congressmen present: "The feeling was unanimous that we want no more Koreas with the United States furnishing 90 percent of the manpower." Dulles and Radford naturally denied any intention of sending ground troops. But the legislators persisted: "Once the flag was committed, the use of land forces would inevitably follow."[72]

The meeting of April 3 did not, in fact, end the idea of some form of direct intervention. It was not "the day we didn't go to war." What emerged, rather, was an understanding that, if the Secretary of State could get British and French concurrence to intervene with the United States, then the Congressional leaders did believe that the necessary legislative approval would be forthcoming. What followed was a complex, indeed, a dual policy. Dulles embarked (with, it should be emphasized, Eisenhower's full approval) on his ill-fated plan for "united action," an attempt to put together an ad hoc coalition before the opening of the Geneva Conference. His scheme soon ran afoul of Anthony Eden's reluctance to consider intervention before Geneva and, no less important, the French unwillingness to accept the American demand of complete independence for Indochina. But, on the other hand, the "military option"—air and sea intervention, whether the French held Dienbienphu or not—lasted even after the French fortress had surrendered.

But certainly the April 3 meeting demonstrates how domestic and popular constraints—the Congressional sentiments produced by the bitter memories of Korea—circumscribed options. The Korean war, after all, had been, up to that time, the most unpopular war in American history, and much of Eisenhower's popularity rested on the truce that he had achieved in ending what many Republicans had long labeled "Harry Truman's war."

The ups and downs, the convolutions, the many variants in the thinking of both Eisenhower and Dulles about the Indochina crisis in the spring of 1954 are beyond the scope of this chapter. But it should be emphasized that Eisenhower, aware of Congressional opinion, was always firm that there could and would be no unilateral American intervention. At the NSC meeting of April 29, Harold Stassen, Director of Mutual Security, took the hard line, insisting that the danger was so grave, the United States should be prepared to intervene alone. The transcript reads:

Difficult as this decision was, Governor Stassen expressed confidence that the Congress and the people of the United States would support direct intervention in Indochina by the United States if the Commander-in-Chief made it clear to them that such a move was necessary to save Southeast Asia from Communism.

The President expressed considerable doubt as to whether Governor Stassen's diagnosis of the attitude of the Congress and the people in this contingency was correct. He further accused Governor Stassen of making assumptions that leaped over situations of the gravest difficulty. . . .

Stassen did not give up easily and tried to continue the argument but

The President remained skeptical in the face of Governor Stassen's argument, and pointed out our belief that a collective policy with our allies was the only posture that was consistent with U.S. national security policy as a whole. To go in unilaterally in Indochina or in other areas of the world which were endangered, amounted to an attempt to police the entire world. If we attempted such a course of action, using our armed forces and going into areas whether we were wanted or not, we would soon lose all our significant support in the free world. We should everywhere be accused of imperialist ambitions.[73]

An additional and significant aspect of the Indochina episode that emerges from the new documentation is Eisenhower's deep and abiding suspicion of the French and French policy. He was highly critical of their military planning and of the strategy that had led them to Dienbienphu; he suspected that the "French want us to come in as the junior partners, and provide materials, while they themselves retain the authority in that region."[74] At times, he could be contemptuous. "The French go up and down every day—they are very voluble," he told Jim Hagerty. "They think they are a great power one day and they feel sorry for themselves the next."[75] He was always hostile to what he flatly called "French colonialism," insisted always (more so than Dulles, who, on occasion, wavered on the point) that the price of American support was full independence for Indochina.

Characteristic was his statement to legislative leaders that "the United States would tar itself with the charge of imperialism and colonialism if we permitted anything less than full independence."[76] In his criticism of Stassen, he made much of the argument that unilateral American action would "in the eyes of many Asiatic peoples merely replace French colonialism with American colonialism."[77] And he also recognized the growing power of Asian nationalism. As he wrote his lifelong friend, General Alfred Gruenther, "No Western power can go to Asia militarily, except as one of a concert of powers, which concert must include local Asiatic peoples. To contemplate anything else is to lay ourselves open to the charge of imperialism or colonialism, or—at the very least—of objectionable paternalism."[78] In the language of the minutes of an NSC meeting: "The President strongly reaffirmed his anxiety over any arrangement which was confined to five white nations and left out the Asian states."[79] And while he agreed with the "united action" concept of Dulles, he was not without occasional doubts. He concluded his long letter to Gruenther, "If we could by some sudden stroke assure the saving of the Dien Bien Phu garrison, I think that under the conditions proposed by the French, the free world would lose more than it would gain."[80]

The shooting down of the South Korean air liner in September 1983, followed by predictable Soviet charges that it was a "spy plane" on mission for the CIA, raises an old issue—reconnaissance flights over Soviet territory for intelligence purposes—that, at least toward the middle of his second term, had already begun to worry Eisenhower. At a January 1958 meeting in the White House he told General Nathan Twining, then chairman of the Joint Chiefs, that he was worried about "overflights for intelligence purposes." These overflights, the President maintained, might well "lead to a Soviet reaction which, superficially at least, would seem justified." The reaction, Ike went on, might take place in Berlin. Foster Dulles, who was present (and who knew considerably more than he was willing to admit), waffled. "I said that I had gone along with the program in general terms without knowing the details because I understood that this would probably be our last chance and that very valuable intelligence might be procured." Twining tried to reassure the President. Overflights, he said, had been a rather regular pratice for the previous ten years, and he doubted that there would be any serious reaction.[81]

But then, in early March, an American military—and clearly espionage—plane was shot down over Korea. Foster Dulles discussed it at length with his brother Allen. The head of the CIA thought it might be reprisal, to which the Secretary of State, true to his "brinkman" image, candidly responded that "they did what we would have done and did under similar circumstances." He also noted that the Soviets "had made the suggestion that this kind of thing could lead to mistakes which would set off nuclear war." But what worried both men was that, as Foster Dulles put it, the incident "would reinforce the President's prejudice against the whole thing." Both hoped to persuade Ike not to make a sudden decision to call off such flights in the future.[82]

Two days later the President did bring up the matter. He read to Dulles the note that the Soviets had delivered "protesting an alleged invasion of Soviet air space in the Far East." As the transcript of the meeting indicates, Ike expressed "a strong view that such infractions should be discontinued. He thought we should reply to the Soviets by saying that we were not aware of the matter referred to but that strong measures were being taken to prevent any recurrence." What was on the President's mind (and here, of course, he was throwing back into Dulles's face one of the Secretary's own strong beliefs) was the fear that "any such operations carried a danger of starting a nuclear war by miscalculation." He said, Dulles later reported, "that his military advisers had pressed upon him the necessity of retaliation if there seemed to be a movement of Soviet planes toward the United States. The President felt that the Soviets might have the same attitude and might misinterpret an overflight as being designed to start a nuclear war against which they would react."[83] General Goodpaster was instructed to communicate the sense of Ike's remarks to appropriate officials. Clearly, Eisenhower was becoming aware of Russian sensitivities as well as the danger that intelligence-gathering by overflights might conceivably trigger infinitely more serious consequences.

A few months later Ike also cracked down on Project Moby Dick, a bizarre caper that involved floating high-altitude balloons, loaded with cameras, across the Soviet Union. Moby Dick was, if not a white whale, certainly a white elephant. The erratic drifting patterns of the balloons, which couldn't be tracked, made it more than a little difficult to figure out just what had been captured on film by the cameras. Then, to every one's discomfiture, it turned out that Soviet radar had picked up a balloon at 116,000 feet, when American radar had failed to detect it at half that altitude—which suggested the unpalatable conclusion that Soviet radar might be superior. To make matters worse, the balloons had a regrettable habit of coming down behind the Iron Curtain. In late July, when General Goodpaster "reported that some of the balloons were coming down in Poland . . . the President expressed his deep concern at this failure and indicated that he would not again permit measures of this sort to be taken." The story given out to cover the incident was that the balloon operation "was designed to gather scientific data."[84]

Massive retaliation, presumably at times and places of our own choosing, was and remained the basic deterrent strategy. Yet from the outset there were challenges to the New Look and its air-atomic strategy. JCS papers, for example, abundantly indicate the extent to which military leaders initially resisted the proposed budget cuts that attended the new policies. Any reduction in the levels that Harry Truman had proposed would, in the words of the Joint Chiefs, "increase the risk to the United

States so as to pose a grave threat to the security of our allies and the security of the nation."[85] Once Radford had succeeded Omar Bradley as chairman, the potential mutiny subsided. But in the fall of 1953 both the Navy and the Marine Corps, possibly for parochial reasons, argued that the age of nuclear plenty would soon emerge in Russia as in the United States, in which case, they contended, each side might be reluctant to unleash its nuclear weapons out of fear of counterstrikes. It therefore followed that "there would be need for more rather than less conventional weapons."[86] Nor was it long, either, before both General Ridgway and General Taylor began to argue, often forcibly, that the Army had been shortchanged by the New Look and that the United States must develop a greater capacity to wage limited and/or conventional war.[87] (Indeed, even Dulles, the arch-spokesman for massive retaliation, sometimes worried about this. In 1954 he asked the President to make certain that America had sufficient conventional weapons in its arsenal, while in 1958 he worried lest budget cuts reduce the conventional forces, which, as he put it, "we need in our everyday business.[88]) Eventually, after the Russians launched *Sputnik*, an increasing group of influential critics began to charge that America was lagging in technology, and, more importantly, that, with the Soviets now presumably able to launch their own atomic reprisals, the doctrine of massive retaliation was fast losing its credibility. And others insisted that so much emphasis had been placed on nuclear weapons that the United States simply did not have the capacity to wage limited war.

Doubts were raised not only by Army officers like Ridgway and Taylor but also by foreign critics, such as Charles de Gaulle, and especially by Democrats who, by the late 'fifties, were positioning themselves to exploit the political possibilities of the much proclaimed "missile gap." Even Dulles, while remaining true to his overall stragegy of deterrence, began to develop concerns, indeed, increasing concerns. By 1958 his memoranda and telephone calls were marked by statements to the effect that the nuclear deterrent was beginning to run its course. "The fact is," he confessed, "that our present policies are running into a dead end."[89] He was cognizant also of the fact that America's allies were beginning to question the willingness of the United States to invoke in nuclear sanction. On several occasions it was the Secretary of State who was in the forefront of those who called for a reexamination of the basic strategic concepts of national security policy.

These issues came to a head at a May 1958 meeting of the National Security Council. Robert Cutler, the President's national security adviser, opened the session with a proposal that NSC 5810, the document then before the Council, should be emended to read that "in an era of relative nuclear plenty, it might not be in the American interest to meet every limited war aggression by applying whatever force was necessary to suppress it." What *was* needed, Cutler argued, was a flexible capacity so that the United States could determine the application of force *best* suited to the particular circumstances of the aggression. Air Force General Twining, speaking as chairman of the Joint Chiefs, objected that Cutler wasn't presenting anything new. He was, Twining insisted, merely raising an old and familiar question: Should we emphasize our deterrent forces and, at the same time, increase our capacity to wage limited war?

Each one of the Joint Chiefs then spoke for himself and the service he represented. Maxwell Taylor, not surprisingly, placed the Army's apostolic blessing on the Cutler amendment, while General Thomas White, speaking for the Air Force, predictably claimed that there was, in reality, no issue to debate—nothing about which to argue. The United States, White maintained, already possessed the capacity to fight both limited and unlimited conflicts. More importantly, White went on, it was psychologically important to reject the amendment and retain the original language of the NSC document. To adopt the amendment would make it appear as if the United States did not possess the capacity to wage limited war.

Twining summed up. His principal argument was that the issue before the National Security Council was a political and not a military issue. In both Indochina and Korea, he claimed, the United States had possessed military capability that it had not employed. The decision to employ or not to employ that capacity had been a political decision and not a question of whether or not the United States actually had the capability. Then Twining, like White, fell back on the psychological argument. NSC decisions, he pointed out, invariably "leaked." Any change in the basic policy statement about national security policy would eventually become public knowledge. And more importantly, he continued, it would have an adverse political impact—at home, on America's allies, on the Soviets. His concluding comment was the flat statement that the Joint Chiefs could not accept any solution which expanded tactical capacity at the expense of the general strategic deterrent.

John Foster Dulles, contrary to his usual conduct, was the first civilian into the fray (Secretary Anderson had primed him to speak). He argued forcefully that the United States could not permit any gap or any doubt to emerge about its willingness to resort to nuclear retaliation. Above all, he went on, we could not afford it until we had something to take its place. It was true, Dulles admitted, that the nuclear deterrent was running its course as the principal weapon in the American arsenal. In the next few years, "we must indeed place emphasis upon the elements that could replace it." Moreover, the Secretary went on, the United States must be prepared to fight different kinds of wars—conflicts that did not involve the total defeat of the enemy. As for himself, he concluded, he didn't care how the language of the NSC document was actually phrased. All that really counted was the ability to develop a supplemental strategy.

President Eisenhower responded that the Council had two choices before it. If NSC decided to increase the tactical, limited war capacity of the United States, then it faced the further decision of either decreasing the strategic nuclear deterrent or accepting a massive increase in the resources allocated to national security. And if the Council accepted the latter, then it needed to study further the means by which such an increased allocation could be accomplished; because these means, Ike emphasized, "implied what is euphemistically called a controlled economy but in effect amounts to a garrison state."[90] Eisenhower had come full circle. Here again was his recurrent emphasis upon the need to preserve a free economy; and here, too, the recurrent dilemma of trying to strike an appropriate balance between the needs of national security and the imperative to avoid the "garrison state." Ultimately, Eisenhower, as David Rosenberg has pointed out, "overruled any significant modification of current policy."[91]

IV

What, to begin summarizing, do these fragments from the documents newly released from the Eisenhower Library suggest about the national security policies of the Republican administration from 1953 to 1961? How do they help us to assess the new Eisenhower "revisionism," and the relationship between presidential activism and domestic economic and political factors?

It is clearly evident that national security policy *was* shaped by budgetary considerations, most notably by the President's insistence that enough was enough, that dollars spent beyond adequacy and sufficiency were counterproductive. But there is reason to question both Douglas Kinnard's emphasis upon financial management and John Gaddis's assertion that the "asymmetrical" national security policy of the Eisenhower administration rested primarily upon calculations of what the national economy could bear.[92] There was, as previously noted, the reaction to Korea, the political constraint imposed by the prevalent belief that the United States could not afford another land war in which America's limited manpower would have to confront the endless millions of Chinese or Soviet soldiers. Hence, America—a nation which, once before in World War II, had sought to exploit its technological and industrial supremacy rather than its manpower—should, it was argued, develop a strategy which rested upon the one area, nuclear power, in which it possessed overwhelming superiority. There was also the desire of many Republicans, long critical of Truman's allegedly reactive strategy, to invent a policy—"at times and places of our own choosing"—that would presumably restore the strategic initiative to America. Also furthering the adoption of a nuclear strategy was not only the great increase in the nuclear arsenal but also the realization that European force levels, even with German troops fully integrated into NATO, would never be able to halt the Russians without the nuclear component. Indeed, with or without the New Look, the use of nuclear weapons was a "given" in JCS planning for NATO.

The new documentation—minutes of meetings with legislative leaders and of the NSC, telephone transcripts, White House memoranda—all portray the President as a man sensitive to popular and political constraints. When, during the Dienbienphu crisis, South Korean President Syngman Rhee offered to send troops to help the French,

> the President said, with great emphasis, that he thought that public opinion in the United States would never support the removal of a ROK division for adventures in other parts of the world while the United States itself was still obliged to maintain forces in Korea. He would certainly hate to have to explain such a situation to the mothers of American soldiers.[93]

Ike was also often forceful. Irritated by Senator William Knowland's perpetually fervid support of the Chinese Nationalist cause, he wrote Gruenther, "Knowland has no foreign policy except to develop high blood pressure whenever he mentions the words Red China."[94] Told that Dulles might have discussed the use of nuclear weapons at Dienbienphu, he exploded, "How can Foster promise the French nuclear weapons? Why I wouldn't trust Foster with enough dynamite to blow up a dam!"[95] Informed, during the Suez crisis, that the government of Panama was talking with Nasser, presumably to get tips on how to nationalize the Panama Canal, Ike erupted, "If we left the Panama Canal, we would take the locks with us."[96]

Eisenhower was, above all, unflappable, confident of his own ability, as the Supreme Commander in World War II, to assess the national security needs of the United States. His own military experience led him to question the French strategies that led to Dienbienphu as well as the military wisdom of Chiang's commitment to Quemoy and Matsu.

As an army officer he could sympathize with Matthew Ridgway's constant assertions in 1954 that the French could not be rescued simply by air and sea operations. Indeed, there is considerable evidence—much of it summed up in John Prados's recent (and misleadingly titled) *The Sky Would Fall*—that the longer the Indochina crisis lasted, the more Eisenhower came to accept Ridgway's view that it would require the sending of American ground forces, an operation which the Army opposed for a multitude of reasons.[97] But Eisenhower was equally prepared, out of his own military expertise, to stand up to and oppose the ideas of his Joint Chiefs, as both Ridgway and Taylor found out when they urged him to increase the nation's limited war capability. The point about the importance of his military background and his confidence in his own national security judgments scarcely needs further embellishment. It fully emerges from his exasperated reply to Representative Charles Halleck at a time when many legislators, even in his own party, wanted to push expenditures for national security beyond what Ike considered prudent. "Look, Charlie," he said, "I think I know a little more about the military than some so-called experts who are sounding off on it. I'll ask you one question. If you had a bigger army today, where in hell would you put it?"[98]

The case of Dulles also proves the point. Historians have often been tempted to exaggerate the influence of the dour Presbyterian who lashed out at godless Communism, coined catch phrases like "agonizing reappraisal," and, more importantly, often sought to draw the spotlight upon himself. (As Christian Herter wryly remarked some years later, "I think Foster liked it [national policy] being known as a Dulles policy.")[99] Many of Dulles's colleagues prodded him to get involved in the strictly military aspects of the NSC debates over national security policy, arguing that, as Secretary of State, he had a real stake in the question of whether or not the United States actually possessed the military capability to carry out the operations that his foreign policies required.[100] But the Secretary rarely did so. Partially it was for reasons of turf, since Dulles, who jealousy guarded his own authority, realized that, if he got into disputes with the military over their area of expertise, then he could scarcely expect them to keep out of his foreign policy territory. But the reason for his refusal, except at infrequent intervals, to get involved in the purely military dimensions of these debates was that he, too, trusted Eisenhower and believed him the man whose judgment, in the last analysis, was to be respected. (Dulles did, on occasion, get angry with military leaders. "When you put them to the issue of limited war," he complained to Vice President Nixon, "it is a shocking thing. . . . They do not want to do this. All they think about is dropping nuclear bombs, and they don't like it when we get off that."[101]

This chapter is not intended to be a paean for either Eisenhower or his national security policies. Clearly it *does* make a difference that the President felt so strongly about "holding the line" on military expenditures. Throughout his eight years in office the overall defense budget remained remarkably stable; indeed, expressed as a percentage of the gross national product, it showed a slight decline.[102] But there were aspects of the Eisenhower national security policies—some of which there has not been opportunity to explore here—other than massive retaliation, the New Look, a budgetary restraints. There was, for example, the unfortunate dimension of psychological warfare with its abortive "liberation" strategy and also the way in which an expanded if not unleashed CIA launched into full-scale covert activities which, to say the least, reflected little moral credit on the administration. (Telephone calls: Allen Dulles to John Foster Dulles on Guatemala: "I don't think we can pull it off next month . . . unless a large part of the Guatemalan army is with us." John Foster Dulles to Christian Herter on the effort to unseat Sukarno: "I would like to see things get to a point where we could plausibly withdraw our recognition of the Sukarno regime and give it to the dissident elements of Sumatra and land forces to protect the life and liberty of Americans—use this as an excuse to bring about a major shift there. . . . There will never be a better time."[103]) Indeed, the very successes of the CIA in Iran and Guatemala fed the dangerous belief that similar methods would work in Cuba, thus paving the way for the first great disaster of Eisenhower's successor.

But there were real limitations to Eisenhower's "hidden hand" style. His personal concept of national security included a deep personal conviction that general war must be avoided. He believed that no nation could "win" a nuclear war. He also believed that, as President, he had an obligation to attempt at least a modest resolution of cold war tensions. Far more than Dulles, he was prepared to negotiate with the Soviets. But all too often there was a gap between what the President believed and what Dulles proclaimed in his hardline speeches, a gap that frequently created confusion about the administration's purposes and may well have left an impression different from what the President intended. Similarly, as John Gaddis has noted, Eisenhower was not notably successful in translating his hopes for significant negotiations into reality—not only during the time that the nay-saying Dulles was in office but also in the year and a half after Dulles's death when, with Secretary Herter's active encouragement, Eisenhower was making his own special initiatives.[104] The President, as we have noted, clamped down on espionage flights in 1958; thereafter they required his personal approval. It is doubly ironic that, on one of the flights that he did approve, Gary Powers was shot down—and shot down with him was the summit meeting that was to have brought Eisenhower's hopes to fruition.

There were other limitations. The President was, as has been emphasized, hostile to French colonialism and aware of the force and potential of nationalism in former colonial areas. But, aside from the insistence that Indochina be given full independence and some willingness to accept Tito, this too rarely got translated into action. The danger of Communism in the Third World always seemed more pressing than the potential of nationalism. Or consider Eisenhower's frustration with respect to the offshore islands of Quemoy and Matsu. American policy, under the New Look, rested upon atomic power and the ability of the air force to deliver it. But, as Norman Graebner has noted regarding atomic weapons, the power to destroy is not the same as the power to control.[105] The President's frustration over Quemoy and Matsu seems a classic example of that dilemma. Moreover, at Dienbienphu, as John Prados has pointed out, in the last analysis "the awesome striking power of the Strategic Air Command and the carrier task forces was not convertible into leverage in the actual situation."[106] It was John Foster Dulles who, in a rare and never repeated moment of introspection and doubt late in 1955, put his finger on the central dilemma of a national security policy that rested on the bomb:

> I told the President that I had come to the conclusion that our whole international security structure was in jeopardy. The basic thesis was local defensive strength with the backing up of United States atomic power. However, that striking power was likely to be immobilized by moral repugnance. If this happened, the whole structure could readily collapse.[107]

Ironies abound. Eisenhower's belief in sufficiency, his insistence that the United States did have the capacity for both limited and unlimited war, his refusal in the late 'fifties to panic in the face of the Gaither report, *Sputnik*, and the alleged missile gap only succeeded in stirring up a nasty political debate in the waning years of his second term. John Kennedy picked up the argument about the missile gap and ran with it. His contention that it was time to get America moving again was, as Robert Griffith has demonstrated, directed against Eisenhower's moderate, middle-of-the-road "corporative commonwealth" on the domestic scene, but it was equally directed against Ike's national security policy.[108] Eisenhower was charged with permitting America to fall behind in space age technology and also of leaving his country no options but massive retaliation.

Ike's warning about the military-industrial complex was embedded in his final State of the Union message, briefly noted (with some surprise) by the media, and quickly forgotten amidst the attention that the press and TV were already beginning to focus on the young Lochinvar riding in to move America from dead center to Camelot. It perhaps says something about the nature of Eisenhower's "hidden hand" leadership in national security that it took at least a decade and a half for historians to realize that, next to George Washington, Dwight Eisenhower had produced the most significant farewell address in American history.

Notes

1. Norman Graebner, "National Security in the Age of Global Power," paper presented at the United States Military Academy, West Point, October 1981, p. 2.

2. It is incorrect to employ the term "national security policy" before the Second World War. Till then the vast majority of historians, social scientists and military writers used the older, long-established term "national defense." Even in General Otto Nelson's pioneering study, *National Security and the General Staff* (Washington: Infantry Journal Press, 1945), the words "national security" are confined to the title and occasional subheadings; throughout the next, Nelson employed the still-standard phrase "national defense."

3. Andrew J. Bacevich, Jr., "Frank McCoy" (Ph.D. dissertation, Princeton University, 1982).

4. This paragraph is based on Chapter 1 of my book, *Admirals, Generals and American Foreign Policy* (Princeton: Princeton University Press, 1973).

5. This paragraph is drawn heavily from Michael Sherry, *Preparing for the Next War* (New Haven: Yale University Press, 1977).

6. See Hanson Baldwin, *Great Mistakes of the War* (New York: Harper, 1950); and Chester Wilmot, *The Struggle for Europe* (New York: Harper, 1952).

7. This is the thesis of Mark Stoler, *The Politics of the Second Front* (Westport, Conn.: Greenwood Press, 1977).

8. This paragraph is drawn from Daniel Yergin, *The Shattered Peace* (Boston: Houghton Mifflin, 1977), parts I & II.

9. Eliot Converse, "Overseas Bases and the Disposition of the Pacific Islands, 1943–1947" (Ph.D. dissertation in progress, Princeton University).

10. Gregg Herken, *The Winning Weapon* (New York: Knopf, 1980).

11. See Louis Galambos, ed., *Papers of Dwight D. Eisenhower*, Vol. 8: *The Chief of Staff* (Baltimore, Johns Hopkins University Press, 1978).

12. Papers of Ferdinand Eberstadt, Mudd Library, Princeton University. Diary entry, 15 May 1948.

13. Graebner, "National Security," 5–6.

14. John Lewis Gaddis, *Strategies of Containment* (New York: Oxford University Press, 1982), 148.

15. David Rosenberg, "The Origins of Overkill: Nuclear Weapons and American Strategy,

1945–1960," paper read at the USMA symposium on the Theory and Practice of American National Security, 1945–60, April 1982, pp. 8–9, 25–26.

16. John Osborne, "James Forrestal," unpublished manuscript in the possession of the author.

17. For the full text of NSC–68, see "NSC–68: A Report to the National Security Council," *Naval War College Review, 28* (May-June 1975), 51–108.

18. For an extended and thorough discussion, see Gaddis, *Strategies*, 107.

19. U.S. Congress, Senate, Committee on Foreign Relations, Hearing Held in Executive Session, *Reviews of the World Situation, 1949–1950* (New York: Garland, 1979), vi.

20. *Ibid.*, viii–ix.

21. Gaddis, *Strategies*, 92–95.

22. Douglas Kinnard, *President Eisenhower and Strategy Management* (Lexington: University Press of Kentucky, 1977), 7.

23. Papers of John Foster Dulles, Mudd Library, Princeton University, "Memorandum of Conversation with C. D. Jackson, 11 January 1958. See also Dulles's subsequent memoranda of conversations with Vice President Nixon on the same date and with his brother Allen on January 14.

24. JFD Papers, White House Memoranda Series, Box 8, General Foreign Policy Matters, April 30, 1953, Text of President's presentation to the NSC.

25. Fred Greenstein, *The Hidden Hand Presidency: Eisenhower as Leader* (New York: Basic Books, 1982), 118–19.

26. JFD Papers, Telephone Conversation Series, Dulles to Secretary Arthur Flemming, 7 November 1958.

27. Robert Griffith, "Dwight D. Eisenhower and the Corporate Commonwealth," *American Historical Review, 87* (February 1982), 87–122.

28. Fred Greenstein, "Eisenhower as an Activist President," *Political Science Quarterly, 94* (Winter 1979–80), 598. This, of course, is the theme of his book *Hidden Hand Presidency*.

29. Gaddis, *Strategies*, 165.

30. Blanche Cook, *The Declassified Eisenhower* (New York: Longmans, 1981).

31. Gary Willis, *The Kennedy Imprisonment* (Boston: Little, Brown, 1982), 287.

32. JFD Papers, WH Memoranda Series, Box 8, General Foreign Policy Matters, Notes on Remarks at NSC meeting, 31 March 1953.

33. JFD Papers, Tel[ephone] Con[versation] Series, JFD to Admiral Arthur Radford, 24 March 1954.

34. *Foreign Relations of the United States (FLUS)*, Vol, XIII, *Indochina*, Part I (Washington: GPO, 1982), 1260–61.

35. Papers of the Joint Chiefs of Staff, JCS memorandum 922, 10 February 1954, Note by the Secretaries.

36. See, for example JCS Papers, JCS 2101/107 Report by Joint Strategic Survey Committee on NSC 1641, 23 October 1953.

37. JFD Papers, WH Memoranda Series, Box 7, Meetings with the President, Eisenhower to Macmillan, 4 September 1958.

38. Rosenberg, "Origins of Overkill," 27.

39. NSC meeting, 31 March 1953 (see note 32).

40. JFD Papers, Subject Series, Alphabetical Subseries, Memorandum of Conversation, Bermuda Meeting of Heads of Government and Foreign Ministers, 4 December 1953.

41. JFD Papers, Tel Con Series, JFD to Christian Herter, 10 April 1959.

42. This paragraph draws heavily on the statistical information in Rosenberg, "Origins of Overkill," 12.

43. Omar Bradley and Clay Blair, *A General's Life* (New York: Simon & Schuster, 1983), 657–58.

44. Rosenberg, "Origins of Overkill," 22.

45. JFD Papers, Tel Con Series, JFD to Hagerty, 30 April 1953.

46. Eisenhower Papers, Whitman file, Minutes of 301st Meeting of the National Security Council, 26 October 1956.

47. *Ibid.*, Minutes of 363rd NSC Meeting, 25 April 1958.

48. JFD Papers, WH Memoranda Series, Box 8, General Foreign Policy Matters, 30 April 1953.

49. NSC Meeting of 26 October 1956 (see note 44).

50. NSC Meeting of 25 April 1958 (see note 45).

51. Eisenhower Papers, Whitman file, Minutes of meeting with legislative leaders, 10 March 1959.

52. Griffith, "Corporate Commonwealth," 58.

53. Gaddis, *Strategies*, 136.

54. JFD Papers, Subject Series, Alphabetical Subseries, Box 8 Pre-Inaugural Materials "Helena" notes, 11 December 1952.

55. JFD Papers, Tel Con Series, JFD to Allen Dulles, 19 April 1954.

56. JFD Papers, Tel Con Series, JFD to Allen Dulles, 19 June 1958, to Henry Cabot Lodge, 20 June 1958.

57. JFD Papers, WH Memoranda Series, Memorandum of conversation with the President, 4 September 1968.

58. JFD Papers, Tel Con Series, JFD to Herter, 6 March 1959.

59. *Ibid.*, to Greene, 24 March 1959.

60. NSC Meeting, 30 April 1953 (see note 24).

61. JFD Papers, WH Memoranda Series, 8 September 1953, Eisenhower letter to Dulles.

62. *Ibid.*, Box 8, Meetings with the President, Memorandum of conversation, 11 March 1955.

63. *Ibid.*, Conversation of 14 February 1955.

64. JFD Papers, WH Memoranda, Box 2, Position Paper on Offshore Islands, 5 April 1955, Eisenhower to Dulles.

65. *Ibid.*, Memorandum of Meeting held in the Secretary's office, 28 March 1955.

66. *Ibid.*, Eisenhower to Dulles, 5 April 1955 (see note 64).

67. JFD Papers, Tel Con Series, Dulles to Eisenhower, 10 September 1958. Typical was the memorandum from Dulles's personal secretary, Phyllis Bernau, to the Secretary (Tel Con Series, 15 September 1958: "Ann [Whitman, Eisenhower's secretary] called and read the following paragraph to me. It is from a letter the President received from someone he respects very much." The paragraph in question included the following sentence, " . . . I must say though that one thing troubles me. I wish our policy of opposing aggression coincided better with the legal and historic distinction between Formosa and the Pescadores on the one hand and Quemoy and Matsu on the other. Militarily this would be a happier solution, I assure, and our moral position would be more persuasive."

68. *Ibid.*, Tel Con of 10 September 1958, cited in preceding footnote.

69. *Ibid.*, Tel Con of 8 September 1958, Eisenhower to Dulles.

70. *Ibid.*, Tel Con of 22 September 1958, Eisenhower to Dulles. In the fall of 1958 Eisenhower was quick to pick up the rumor, which was unfounded, that the Joint Chiefs no longer thought the islands crucial to Chiang's defense of Formosa. Indeed, when Dulles said that "he doubted whether there would be an amputation without fatal consequences," Ike was quick to reply that this was not necessarily so from a military point of view. WH Memoranda Series, Box 7, Meetings with the President, 12 August 1958.

71. Chalmers Roberts, "The Day We Didn't Go to War," *Reporter 11* (September 14, 1954), 31–35.

72. JFD Papers, WH Memoranda Series, Memorandum for Secretary's File (Conference with Congressional Leaders concerning the Crisis in Southeast Asia), 5 April 1954.

73. *FRUS*, Vol. XIII, Part 2, pp. 1439–40 (Minutes of 194th NSC meeting, 29 April 1954.

74. *Ibid.*, Part 1, 1382.

75. *Ibid.*, Part 2, 1411.

76. JFD, WH Memoranda Series, minutes of meeting with legislative leaders, April 15, 1954.

77. *FRUS*, Vol. XIII, Part 2, 1440.

78. *Ibid.*, 1419.

79. *Ibid.*, 1489 (minutes of 195th NSC meeting, 6 May 1954).

80. *Ibid.*, 1419.

81. JFD Papers, WH Memoranda Series, Box 6, Meetings with the President, 22 January 1958.

82. JFD Papers, Tel Con series, JFD to Allen Dulles, 7 March 1958.

83. JFD Papers, WH Memoranda Series, Box 6, Meetings with the President, 7 March 1958.

84. *Ibid.*, Box 7, 29 July 1958 and 30 July 1958.

85. JCS Papers, Memorandum from Chairman Omar Bradley to Secretary of Defense, 19 March 1953.

86. *Ibid.*, See memo, Commandant, Marine Corps, to JCS, 7 Deceomber 1953, and Chief of Naval Operations to JCS, same date. All filed with JCS 2011/111.

87. The case was most forcibly stated in Maxwell Taylor, *An Uncertain Trumpet* (New York: Harper, 1960).

88. JFD Papers, WH Memoranda series, Meetings with the President, Box 1, 22 December 1954.

89. JFD Papers, Tel Con series, JFD to Robert Anderson, 30 April 1958.

90. Eisenhower Papers, Whitman File, Memorandum of meeting of 364th NSC meeting, 2 May 1958.

91. Rosenberg, "Origins of Overkill," 54.

92. Kinnard, *Strategy Management*, 95; Gaddis, *Strategies*, 132–35.

93. *FRUS*, Vol. XIII, Part 1, 1054.

94. Eisenhower Papers, Whitman file, Eisenhower to Gruenther, 2 July 1954.

95. Interview with Murray Kempton (courtesy Michael Mayer).

96. JFD Papers, WH Memoranda series, Memorandum of Conversation with the President, 8 August 1956.

97. John Prados, *The Sky Would Fall: Operation Vulture: The Secret U.S. Bombing Mission to Vietnam, 1954* (New York: Dial, 1983). Prados's book is actually a history, told from both the American and the French points of view, of the entire Dienbienphu crisis. The title has obviously been chosen to play up the comparison to the scandal of the "secret bombing" of Cambodia. There are, however, vast differences between the two incidents, the most significant of which is that Vulture never took place.

98. Eisenhower Papers, Hagerty Diary, 29 March 1955.

99. JFD Papers, Oral History Project, Transcript of Interview with Christian Herter.

100. *Ibid.*, Transcript of Interview with Robert Bowie.

101. JFD Papers, Tel Con Series, JFD to Richard Nixon, 15 July 1958.

102. Gaddis, *Strategies*, 171.

103. JFD Papers, Tel Con Series, 15 May 1954, to Allen Dulles; 8 May 1958, to Christian Herter.

104. Gaddis, *Strategies*, 189–97.

105. Graebner, "National Security," 27.

106. Prados, *Sky Would Fall*, 199.

107. JFD Papers, WH Memoranda series, Box 3, Meetings with the President, 26 December 1955. That Eisenhower recognized the same dilemma is implied in a memorandum of September 10, 1958: "Mrs. Whitman read the gist of a very private message from Abbott Washburn to the President: 'If we use nuclear weapons against the Chinese Mainland to hold Quemoy and Matsu, the United States would lose the respect of mankind for all time.' " (WH Memoranda series, Box 8, Correspondence with the President, Memo Phyllis Bernau to JFD 9 September 1958.)

108. Griffith, "Corporate Commonwealth," 121–22.

2
Economic Foreign Policy and the Quest for Security

LLOYD C. GARDNER

Reflecting on the situation at the war's end ten years after the fact, Dean Acheson observed:

> Hitler did what Napoleon was unable to do. He took an area which had to import from the rest of the world, he took that and made it self-supporting. That disrupted every kind of business connection in Europe. Factories didn't make the same things. Politically most of the governments were discredited; their countries were occupied. . . . There was a deep division between the workers and the owning classes who had either collaborated or left, escaped the country. We had underestimated all this. We thought UNRRA [United Nations Relief and Rehabilitation Administration] would do it, but it didn't.[1]

Economic planning for the peace was more complicated than the one-time Secretary of State acknowledged, but he pointed unerringly to the central assumptions shared by policymakers during the preceding years. At Yalta, in February 1945, President Franklin D. Roosevelt had promised that American troops would be out of Europe within two years. By that time, presumably, Europe would be ready to stand on its own feet again. Also, by that time the United Nations would be in operation, providing the political framework for a restored and self-adjusting world economy.

Whatever problems existed at the end of the war UNRRA would handle on an emergency basis. The more persistent economic challenges of the peace the International Monetary Fund (IMF) and the International Bank for Reconstruction and Development (IBRD) would resolve. After long and arduous pre-conference negotiating sessions, in which the details were hammered out, British and American experts had presented the IMF and the IBRD as a package to the conference of anti-Axis nations held at Bretton Woods, New Hampshire, in July 1944. Less than three months later, however, Prime Minister Winston Churchill and Marshal Joseph Stalin, in Moscow, divided Europe into spheres of influence. Western leaders had designed the Bretton Woods system, as it would be known ever after, to accommodate "state trading" nations such as the Soviet Union. But the system could not operate if "blocs" clogged all the avenues of world trade.[2] For that reason the Churchill-Stalin arrangement presaged a return to prewar conditions and their inherent dangers, even before the Allies had disposed of the Axis menace. Throughout the war American economic planners had concentrated on the prevention of the British backsliding into an imperial preference fortress, championed by Tory backbenchers and, more recently, by Labour theorists. Now it appeared that the Prime Minister had gone off to Moscow with the intent to undo all the achievements of Bretton Woods—not deliberately, of course, but that was the predictable result.

Russia's share of world trade before World War II had been small. From that perspective, and given the assumption that the Soviets would require outside aid to recover, the presence of a single "state trading" nation posed no great threat to the international economic system that Washington envisioned. It would be a different matter, however, if Stalin used his pact with Churchill as a precedent for dealing with all postwar questions of territorial and economic reconstruction. In that case Stalin would outdo both Napoleon and Hitler in disrupting, in Acheson's words, "every kind of business connection in Europe."[3]

I

Even if Marshal Stalin was a man of his word, that he meant what he said about the desirability of postwar East-West cooperation, the political division of Europe emerging from the war posed great difficulties for American policymakers. In May 1945 Elbridge Durbrow of the State Department's Division of Eastern European Affairs warned that Soviet agreements with the East European regimes might "create an almost airtight blackout in the entire area east of the Stettin-Trieste line." Despite their New Deal background, Roosevelt's advisers and indeed the President himself subscribed to a form of Hoover thesis on the causes of depression and war. The trouble, they recalled, had started with the breakdown of the international economic system in the late 1920s. During the war the priorities for national planning were reversed, placing greater emphasis on new sets of initials. Where such domestic programs as the WPA and the NRA had once held high positions in the hearts and minds of New Dealers, ITO and GATT had replaced them, to say nothing of IMF and IBRD as embodied in the Bretton Woods system. Along with initials came slogans, a sure sign of fundamental change in a highly developed bureaucratic government. Enemies in the marketplace can scarcely be friends around the conference table. Stalin's predilection for surrounding Russia with friendly states boded ill for postwar economic cooperation. The construction of rival economic and political systems on the European continent, especially at a time when the potential for psychological damage to recuperating national societies was at its greatest, threatened the health of liberal capitalism as an international system.

Aside from the general considerations of ideology and theory there was the practical and immediate question of postwar Germany. Where would that colossus of Central Europe fit into a divided continent? When policymakers spoke of the recovery of western Europe, they often had Germany in mind. Absorbed in their own arguments about the so-called "Morgenthau Plan," designed to reduce Germany to an agricultural state, Roosevelt's advisers defended alternative methods for dealing with Germany without considering that their decisions might have no relevance to postwar realities. That Roosevelt himself inclined toward some version of the Morgenthau approach seemed clear from his remarks to General Lucius D. Clay on March 31, 1945. "He believed," Clay recalled, "that a huge hydroelectric power development serving several of the European countries—a sort of international TVA—was essential to economic rehabilitation and would lead to better cooperation among the participating countries."[4]

There could hardly be a better example of the application of New Deal planning from national to international projects than Roosevelt's final prescription for solving the German problem. Morgenthau's colleagues in the departments of State, War, and Navy held a different view of a German solution, but one also premised on a "One World" approach to international security. Denationalization of the Ruhr, warned Secretary of War Henry L. Stimson, would go against a century and a half of economic evolution in Europe and would, therefore, be fraught with danger. Navy Secretary James V. Forrestal found support for this view in a surprising place. "One must remember," French leader Charles de Gaulle once told him,

that while there is a centrifugal law which makes things fly apart, there is also in the economic, political as well as the physical world, a centripetal force which makes things fly together. What you pull apart in defiance of this law cannot be prevented from ultimately coming together again.[5]

De Gaulle often forgot his own advice, but the point had special significance for Americans. Neither a plan for the internationalization of the Ruhr, nor a national German economy offered a safe solution if Europe's new political boundaries excluded the possibility of a general security arrangement. Europeans and Americans alike could feel nothing but horror at the thought of a revived Germany lurching backward and forward between East and West. In this context Stalin's persistent demand for $10 billion in reparations took on an especially ominous meaning at the Moscow Foreign Ministers Conference in early 1947. To pay that sum, reparations would need to come out of current German production. It took no great leap of the imagination to see that a rebuilt Germany oriented to production for Eastern requirements would lead to "special ties" with Hitler's old satellites, now under Russian domination. By 1947 concern about *Ostpolitik* emerged as a cold war theme.

At the Potsdam Conference of July-August 1945, Roosevelt's successor, Harry S. Truman, produced his own version of an international TVA in hopes of forestalling a permanent division of Europe. Truman proposed that the major international waterways of Central and Eastern Europe be put under multinational authority. To his great dismay, the President found himself in the middle of an old dispute in Anglo-Russian relations. Before he could extricate himself from the scuffle, he had heard all he'd wanted to hear about Suez and the Turkish straits, and he had resolved that summit meetings were largely a waste of time. If the world was going to be saved, it would require some other method.[7]

In his *Memoirs* Truman wrote that Stalin's negative reaction convinced him that the Russians were bent on world conquest. He also recalled that he had included the Panama Canal in his proposal. His contemporary account, a private diary he kept at the conference, was more accurate about the details:

> I have offered a waterway program and a suggestion for free intercourse between Central European nations which will help future peace. Our only hope for good from the European War is restored prosperity to Europe and future trade with them. It is a sick situation at best.[8]

Over the years the episode impressed itself more and more on Truman's mind as a turning point, the first clear indication that the "One World" assumptions held by Americans would require revision, perhaps abandonment. This was a painful prospect. And it was not surprising that, when the former President finally sat down to prepare his *Memoirs*, he exaggerated both the scope of his Potsdam proposal and the meaning of Russia's rejection.[9]

On March 23, 1946, Truman delivered an address at the annual Jackson Day celebration, a Democratic party tradition. In the past Roosevelt used the occasion to scourge economic royalists. Truman had other issues before him. "No phase of economic life," he said, "has been so completely disrupted as our international economic relations. During the war, the bulk of foreign trade was done by or for governments. Here, too, there must be reconversion. World trade must be restored—and it must be returned to private enterprise. We need a world in which all countries can do business with each other, and with us."[10]

Washington had not abandoned completely the rollback of Russian power from Eastern Europe, but the world of which Truman spoke, where trade needed to be restored to private enterprise, was in the West, a good portion of it in and with the sterling bloc. Congress had recently approved a plan for a $3.75 billion credit to London, a plan, the administration assured the lawmakers, that would go far toward reestablishing a genuine international economy. Within a year, officials promised, the British would begin the process of dismantling the sterling bloc by making the pound again convertible into francs, marks, and dollars. Initially that would free the more than $13.5 billion that had accumulated within the British Empire, because its holders could use it only for purchases in Britain. Over the long run the new British policy would mean that the great resources of the Empire the Victorians had built would again be put at the service of "liberalism" worldwide. Without the loan, administration witnesses had warned, London would have no option but to maintain rigid trade controls, withhold sterling from international circulation, and seek special arrangements with other countries.

Not everyone even inside the administration was convinced that the American loan would bring the desired result. Forrestal distrusted the British Labour government; he was watchful that Labour not socialize its zone of occupied Germany. He resented the attacks of Labour theorists on capitalism and, most of all, did not believe that American "help should be utilized to accelerate the drift toward socialism which, in the long run, in my opinion, will wind up as communism because it can't do the job."[11] Banker Thomas Lamont, who had more first-hand experience with revolutionary governments than perhaps any other individual in America, did not think that Forrestal exaggerated the danger of creeping socialism as much as he underestimated the immediate threat of communism. He believed also that Forrestal neglected entirely the need to put Great Britain on a sound financial basis for the sake of western European stability. What good would it do to crack down on socialism in Britain if that created profound disturbances elsewhere? The United States could not tell sovereign nations what form of government or economic system they should have. " 'One World,' " Lamont reminded Forrestal in June 1947, "may be out of the window for the present, but one 'Western Civilization' also will be out the window and the world will tend to greater fragmentation and more nationalism—with the U.S. isolated—if our relations with other countries are to be helpful only when their type of government or national economy is what you and I would wish it to be."[12]

What stands out much clearer in retrospect than it did to contemporaries was the ease whereby American policymakers worked with the British Labour government. In many important respects Labour was more congenial to American goals than the Conservative governments of Churchill and Anthony Eden. American diplomats were content to be seen in the company of British socialists, and not only for the sake of appearance. This harmony reached a high point when Secretary of State Dean Acheson and Foreign Minister Ernest Bevin strode arm-in-arm into a meeting with Andrei Vishinsky singing "The Red Flag" together. It no doubt helped to overcome the Yaleman's queasiness at this prospect when Bevin, a former dockworker, informed Acheson that the tune was "Maryland, My Maryland."[13] But Acheson never sang any songs with Anthony Eden. Their relationship was marked by a proper arm's length coolness, punctuated at times by sharp disagreements. Acheson's personal preference for the avuncular "Ernie" may have resulted not only from Bevin's ability to fill a void in Acheson's circle of friends but also from Acheson's affinity for Labour policies, especially Labour's traditional internationalism. Whether they sprang from Marxist or Fabian roots, were educated at Oxford, Cambridge, or the London School of Economics, Labour ministers were traditionally internationalist.

This could not be said of their Conservative counterparts. For all the differences between Neville Chamberlain and Winston Churchill, the Empire came first for both. Both men had dealt with totalitarian despots to protect its lifelines. Who was to say when this tendency for "appeasement" would emerge again if the Conservatives returned to power? If Labour required watching for fear of its overt drive to socialize Germany, the Tories needed equally close observation because of their suppressed desire to sustain the Empire and to come to terms with the enemy. After the return of the Conservatives to power in 1951, their ties to the Empire presented Acheson with a profound dilemma in Iran, and John Foster Dulles, with a nightmare at Suez.

II

This is not to say that American policymakers were uncritical of Labour's policies at home. What troubled Washington more than the British threat to socialize their zone in Germany was the diversion of creative energy into the socialist experiment in Britain itself, much to the detriment of European restoration. To be sure, the Truman administration welcomed the challenge of picking up the burden in Greece and Turkey. The "February" crisis of 1947 offered an opportunity both to demonstrate to the world that the Republican victory in the November 1946 Congressional elections did not signify a return to isolationism and to shock European leaders into a greater awareness of the dangers of drift in the face of the common danger from Russia. One passage deleted from the final draft of the Truman Doctrine speech, and Acheson's rationale for the deletion, made this point in a different manner. The excised words warned that the worldwide trend away from free enterprise toward state-controlled economies, as well as the disappearance of free enterprise in other nations, threatened the American economy and the country's democratic institutions. Acheson was not trying to hide anything. Truman's speech at Baylor University a week earlier had said the same thing. In the Truman Doctrine speech, however, such words would merely give unwanted attention to British socialism.[14] The administration wanted to encourage Europeans to think about external concerns, not their sovereign right to have whatever economic organization they preferred. Any rousing defense of free enterprise would cloud the real differences between Communists and Socialists and the perceptions of them in the United States. The timing of the speech was important also. A conference of foreign ministers was about to open in Moscow; at that meeting Germany would be the central topic of discussion.

For Under Secretary of State Acheson it seemed imperative that the President deliver an "all-out" speech before the Moscow Conference opened. Others demurred, wondering if it might not be preferable to await the Russian reaction to a final settlement of the German question. White House staffer George Elsey offered Truman's closest political adviser, Clark M. Clifford, a dissenting view:

The "All-Out" speech delivered on the opening of the Moscow Conference would, in my opinion, destroy that conference which gives promise of producing an acceptable Treaty of Peace for Austria, if not for Germany. The President must not be charged, as was Roosevelt, with torpedoing a major World Conference before it has had a chance.[15]

Roosevelt had torpedoed the London Economic Conference in 1933, at least in part, he said later, to correct the impression at home that Europeans always outsmarted Americans as well as to launch nationalist economic policies. Truman's advisers had a similar procedure in mind: shock Europeans out of their postwar doldrums, galvanize Congress into action, and then launch a recovery plan.

On March 12, 1947, Truman asked Congress for $400 million to save Greece and Turkey from a Communist fate. "I believe," he told Congress, "that it must be the policy of the United States to support free peoples who are resisting attempted subjugation by armed minorities or by outside pressures." By lumping together the situations in Greece, where a civil war had raged since liberation in 1944, and Turkey, then under pressure from Moscow to negotiate disputed territorial questions and a new regime for the Straits, Truman's advisers achieved one final purpose: they reduced a complex situation across southeast Europe to manageable proportions. In Moscow, meanwhile, Secretary of State George C. Marshall fended off Russian proposals for reparations out of current German production. If Truman could accept the necessity to "scare hell" out of the country, Marshall needed to worry about specific conditions. Consequently, he wanted to remain on speaking terms with the Russians. In fact, Marshall was annoyed when Bevin permitted himself to be drawn into arguments by the Russian foreign minister's provocative statements.[16]

Throughout the cold war, American policymakers would continue to confront apparently contradictory needs, requiring them to reconcile confrontation with coexistence, deterrence with détente. At Moscow, for example, Marshall was especially troubled by the French involvement in a united Western policy for Germany. He did not want to antagonize Stalin or cause him to threaten the French with some form of Communist retaliation. The French, Marshall informed American newsmen privately, were "terrified of the communists. They were even hesitant to speak above a whisper."[17]

France and Russia shared a common bond that surpassed ideological differences. Both had been invaded twice by the Germans within one generation. If western Europe was to survive with its economic and political institutions intact, France would require a considerable measure of security against Germany. For this Russia held the key. Moscow could remind the French of their mutual interest in preventing a German resurgence; at the same time it could threaten to disrupt internal French politics. For this reason, when it came time for Marshall to announce American willingness to provide massive aid for European recovery through the Marshall Plan, it was essential that the onus for dividing the Continent, should that trend continue, fall upon Russia. Thus Moscow received an invitation to participate in the Marshall Plan. There was poetic justice as well as political advantage in this strategy, recalled policy-planner George F. Kennan. It forced the Russians to come to terms with what they had created instead of waiting for the internal contradictions in Western capitalism or national rivalries to do their work for them:

> [A] price of Russian participation would have been cooperation in overcoming real barriers to East-West trade. Such a move toward a real merging of trade would have meant a reversal in Russian policy so, in a sense, we put Russia over the barrel. Either it must decline or else enter into an arrangement that would mean an ending of the Iron Curtain.[18]

But would this purpose triumph? In retrospect Kennan explained how the Russians had been put on the defensive; at the time he was much less confident. On May 9, 1947, he wrote Acheson that before Washington made any commitments to a program, it required "some reasonable assurance that the British [were] willing to move in the same general direction." Specifically, he asked, "How far are they planning to go in the dismantling of Empire and defense commitments or in further restriction of living standards and increase in labor discipline?"[19]

Ambassador Lewis Douglas conveyed this concern in his conversations with British Foreign Office spokesmen. The administration could improve its support in Congress, he told them, if they "made clear there would be no further nationalization of great industries in this country. This as a hint from a friend," he added, "and was in no way intended as an interference in [Britain's] internal affairs."[20] As Douglas's disclaimers suggest, the State Department was not determined to obtain a signed oath, but to convince Europeans that the Marshall Plan was a substitute, a viable alternative, to nationalist preoccupations—whether these be Britain's new enthusiasm for socialist experimentation or France's burdensome obsession with Germany. In that regard, the Marshall Plan was indeed a success as British and French leaders took upon themselves the obligation to respond on behalf of Europe to the American offer of aid.

Still the long-term outlook was clouded by a variety of unresolved problems. There was, for example, the "dollar gap." Since World War I the United States had found ways of supplying Europeans with dollars to buy the nation's surplus production. First there had been the bankers' credits and loans, then the Liberty Loans of the war years. After the war the United States had provided the government-sponsored Dawes Plan and Young Plan. Before and during World War II it offered Lend-Lease; now, after 1947, Marshall aid. Unlike Britain after the Napoleonic wars, the United States government adopted these expedients for the very simple reason that free trade was politically unacceptable. Europeans criticized the United States after World War I because it refused to behave like a creditor nation. It maintained its high tariff structure. Trade flourished despite the tariffs because Europe managed to earn dollars through sales of colonial products from Asia and Africa. "The important background fact, from the economic and trade standpoint," Assistant Secretary of Commerce Thomas C. Blaisdell would tell the Business Advisory Council in 1950, "is that the Marshall Plan, which made dollars available to Western Europe, was in part a substitute for the dollars which were formerly earned in the Far East by exports to the United States."[21] The breakdown of the colonial empires after the war raised the possibility that the Western trading nations would never close the dollar gap short of radical readjustments in American thinking. Again compared with Great Britain after the Napoleonic wars, the United States was far less dependent on foreign trade and investment to sustain its prosperity. That fact, and the overrepresentation of certain interest groups in Congress, made it unlikely that such adjustments could be made at all, let alone in time to save Europe.

Such were the challenges that faced American policy-planners. Closely related to the dollar gap issue was the run on sterling when the British, in accordance with the terms of the Anglo-American loan agreement, attempted to make sterling convertible in the summer of 1947. The run forced a hasty British retreat and raised the prospect that many more years would pass before the British Commonwealth would be fully open to world trade. So long as sterling remained a blocked currency, the rest of Europe would follow the British lead and limit trade to narrow bilateral channels, and living standards to political decisions. Such behavior would deny capitalism an opportunity to demonstrate what it could achieve in competition with the planned economies of Eastern Europe.

Additional private investment in Europe offered one remedy for

Europe's economic malaise. But American capitalists had little reason to risk their money in an area where political unrest threatened to erupt at any moment and from which they might be unable to send reconverted dollar earnings home. By mid-1948, as Acheson recalled in conversations with the writers then preparing Truman's *Memoirs* for publication, there was a crisis of confidence:

> You want to have capital brought back from out of the country and people who own factories to build anew. In 1948 two things happened which scared them to death—Czechoslovakia and Poland. The whole Marshall Plan business just stopped. The airlift's going on at Berlin. What's going to happen? No one will build factories in Paris as long as that's going on. George Kennan had a group meet in the State Department to hash this whole thing over. It seemed clear to them that some kind of important political step had to be taken to offer them economic help and make businessmen believe there was security there, that they would not be rolled over by a Russian tank division. . . . NATO was conceived of first as a political act.[22]

Actually the original stimulus for NATO appears to have had other origins. Reflecting on the failed attempt to resolve the German problem at the foreign ministers' level, Ernest Bevin suggested to Marshall that the issue was no longer the quarrel between Russia and the Western powers; it was part of a struggle to see where power would ultimately rest. To meet the challenge, Bevin suggested "a sort of spiritual federation of the west." A few weeks later he observed that the countries of western Europe would need to look to Washington and London "for political and moral guidance and for assistance in building up a counter attraction to the baleful tenets of communism within their borders and in recreating a healthy society. . . ."[23]

In both of these appeals Bevin avoided the word "patriotism," a Tory concept that went straight to the heart of the matter and the reason for having national military establishments beyond the literal requirements of defense and internal security. The established arrangements with the European countries, observed a top-level State Department official, could handle the purely military aspects of European security. Thus the purpose of an alliance would be psychological, to promote public confidence within the Western community.[24] Acheson elaborated on this notion in executive hearings before the Senate Foreign Relations Committee. Peaceful and constructive relations with the Soviet Union would not be possible, he said, until there was "a much more settled situation in the West. The Soviet Union was drawn into the troubled situation in the West, and that made quiet relations within the rest of the world impossible."[25]

III

Within six months Stalin had lifted the Berlin blockade, thus ending a crisis that had begun almost a year earlier. He ended the crisis, moreover, without winning a single concession from the West. The key issue had been the creation of a West German government out of the three Western occupation zones. Through the Marshall Plan, moreover, Western leaders had responded to the challenge of putting the German productive machine back into operation. For the first time economic diplomacy had apparently brought results in dealing with the Russians. Ever since Truman had warned V. M. Molotov in 1945 not to expect American economic aid unless Russia accepted the Western position on Poland, the administration had searched for an effective economic lever. The counter-blockade against East Berlin and East Germany had concerned the Russians deeply. The Kremlin had imposed restrictions on travel and traffic between West Germany and Berlin in the hope of checking what they feared was an effort to subvert the Russian zone through various economic means, especially currency revaluation. Soviet leaders discovered at the Paris Foreign Ministers Conference in June 1949 that the American delegation was prepared to ease restrictions on East-West trade within Germany. After the conference ended, Acheson made a great show of explaining to news reporters that the Western powers had rejected all Russian overtures, that the conference had achieved nothing except the lifting of the Russian blockade. Yet on the way to Paris, Acheson's adviser Paul Nitze recalled, the American delegation had decided that an increase in East-West trade would be advantageous. Indeed, trade had become a matter of major concern.[26]

Nitze opened the discussion on trade within the American delegation by observing that any United States attempt to raise the question of a "natural German trade," would risk an overly eager response from Andrei Vishinsky, who might counter by proposing a series of pacts between West Germany and the countries of Eastern Europe. Then he might argue, Nitze hypothesized, that the Marshall Plan was unnecessary for German economic recovery. Acheson believed that the United States could avoid that danger by simply proposing more trade without going into details. At one point another adviser, John Foster Dulles, raised the issue of cold war sentiment at home. How would Congress react to an expansion of East-West trade? The obligation to deal with practicalities without arousing cold war emotions required great skill indeed. Acheson never fell below the necessary standard. For one thing, he noted, Congress would not agree to any policy that continued to pour money into Germany.

Other members of the delegation agreed. They predicted that Germany would soon again be a powerful competitor to other West European nations and the United Kingdom. Where was German production to go if not to foreign markets, some of which would of necessity be in the East? Dulles, meanwhile, heard the views of Robert Schuman, France's foreign minister, in a private conversation that made a deep impression on him:

> We then discussed the importance of developing outlets for German trade in the East. Mr. Schuman expressed himself very strongly on the importance of this. He was fearful that there would soon be a period of surpluses and excess capacity. France, he said, was greatly increasing its industrial capacity and the same thing was going on in England. And he did not think either France or England could stand violent German competition.

During a final discussion yet another adviser, Robert Murphy, pointed out that while the Social Democrats in West Germany desired as little trade as possible, the Christian Democrats would be willing to accept a large volume of East-West trade. Acheson summed up the issue: "[W]e are in a postion where we have to be proponents of increased East-West trade."[27]

To protect both sides from undue embarrassment, the final communiqué of the Paris conference simply listed increased East-West trade as a point of agreement without assigning authorship to the proposal. Over the next several months France's Jean Monnet, honored later as the principal architect of the European common market and community, faced the problem of excess German energy and production. Monnet's starting point was the same as Robert Schuman's, except that Monnet harbored deep forebodings about stimulating Germany to look eastward. Momentarily that might ease competition, but ultimately it would mean an end to hopes for trade liberalization and, more threateningly, "the re-establishment of prewar cartels; perhaps, Eastward outlets for German expansion, a prelude to political agreements; and France back in the old rut of limited, protected production."[28]

From this gloomy assessment Monnet arrived at a breathtaking conclusion. The West could avoid disaster if France would take the lead in establishing an international authority to regulate coal and steel production. Acheson greeted this proposal with absolute astonishment. It was a plan for the most grandiose cartel in industrial history. Almost at once, however, astonishment turned to ardor. Here was the kind of imaginative thinking that might overcome the dollar gap as well as the continuing pariah status of Germany. "I think the inherent, deep-seated weakness of the whole alliance of the West is France," Acheson would tell colleagues, "but at the same time there is the greatest inventiveness and ingenuity coming out of France, and this was a brilliant idea."[29] Monnet's brilliant scheme inaugurated a brisk debate inside France. Schuman accepted authorship because Monnet expected him to carry the political burden of convincing the National Assembly. The final drafting session added a sentence as follows: "Europe will be able, with increased resources, to pursue the realization of one of her essential tasks, the development of the African continent." Gaullists in the Assembly seized upon this sentence to accuse the "Schuman Plan" sponsors of being willing to open up Africa to a German invasion. Actually what Monnet and his colleagues had in mind was de Gaulle's own future goal, a Europe able to establish its independence from the two cold war superpowers.[30]

With the "old colonialism" in its death throes, France, ironically, would fight in Algeria and Indochina the last two great imperial wars. If Europe was to meet American competition in the post-imperial era, it would require a domestic market comparable to that of America. For Americans the significance of the move toward Franco-German cooperation in 1950 was not the menacing prospect of an economic challenge, but relief that Europeans could begin to address their own problems in a sensible fashion. The British were less happy at the prospect. They saw correctly that one thing would lead to another and soon they would face a very unpleasant choice: the Commonwealth or Europe. In Washington, tolerance of British "peculiarities" had reached a low point. Marshall Plan Administrator Paul G. Hoffman complained that dealing with the British Treasury had become a frustrating business. If Sir Stafford Cripps had his way, Hoffman observed, nothing would ever be done to bring about a European Payments Union, or anything else needed for economic unity. About every other minute, he told the Senate Foreign Relations Committee, "I would like to say, 'To hell with them.' "[31]

Steel was a good example. Ambassador to London Lewis Douglas informed a meeting of American diplomats in Europe that the West's decision to nationalize steel weakened British impetus toward cooperation with the Continent. Too intimate a connection with the Schuman Plan would reduce the sovereign power of British socialists to exercise control over their own affairs. "This," said Douglas, "is the fundamental contradiction of Socialism with the conception of economic and political integration of Western Europe."[32] Clearly Forrestal and

Kennan had not been far wrong in viewing British socialism as perhaps the greatest obstacle to European economic security. Yet Bevin was still Acheson's most reliable colleague whenever the American Secretary assumed the obligation to turn back the Russian bear lest he ramble too far west for Europe's good—and the good of the United States.

War in Korea shifted Europe's attention from its stymied momentum toward economic unity, although the war soon brought complications of its own. Acheson employed the heightened concern about Soviet military aggression to secure agreement in principle for German rearmament. In time increased military production in Europe and America eased Europe's dollar crisis. Western leaders had scheduled the end of Marshall Plan aid in 1952. Expenditures for military items immediately took up much of the slack as the United States balance of payments rose from $576 million in 1949 to $2.6 billion in 1953.[33] The benefits fell unequally, with Germany the major beneficiary, Britain the loser. The "military Keynesianism" of the Korean war left Britain in a reduced competitive position, perhaps permanently, vis-à-vis Germany. Germany was not Britain's only powerful competitor. Americans were pushing everywhere for Japan's reacceptance into the world marketplace. If German production was good for Europe, Japanese prosperity would be good for Asia. The Korean war, moreover, provided an opportunity for Washington to accomplish the difficult business of a Japanese peace treaty. The treaty, signed in September 1951, raised the issue not only of Japan's internal economic growth but also of Japan's future expansionism.

Japan's alternatives were obvious. That country could move north, toward Communist China, or reach out to the south in the direction of Indonesia, the Philippines, and Southeast Asia. The United States had gone to war to prevent the creation of this latter "Co-Prosperity Sphere," or, more accurately, had created conditions that convinced Japanese leaders that Pearl Harbor was necessary to protect Japan's economic and security interests in the Pacific. However that may be, once China was "lost" to Mao Tse-tung in late 1949, American leaders saw the need of ensuring Japan an economic outlet in the non-Communist Far East lest its vast productive capabilities be placed at the service of "world communism." Having had very unpleasant experiences in the prewar decade with Japanese exports to the British Empire, London had little difficulty in suppressing its enthusiasm for Washington's proposed solution. Japanese treaty negotiator John Foster Dulles created considerable consternation when he obtained from Japanese Prime Minister Yoshida a letter promising that his government would not open up a strategic trade with Communist China once the nations ratified the peace treaty.

British officials feared that they had become the victims of a Yankee confidence game. Many of the provisions which Dulles had written into the Japanese treaty, largely to placate the United States Senate, appeared as harmful to British interests as another American venture into Asian diplomacy, the Washington Naval Conference of 1922. That time United States diplomats had insisted on wrecking the Anglo-Japanese alliance as a prerequisite to a solution of Anglo-American difficulties; now, it appeared, Washington was prepared to pit Britain and Japan against one another in competition for the markets of the non-Communist world.

IV

During the Eisenhower years Dulles gained a reputation as a hardliner on European colonialism. If his assault on the old imperial structure began with the Japanese treaty, then a straight line runs from San Francisco, the site of the Japanese treaty conference, to Suez, the site of the most confused debacle of the cold war. Actually the road had many twists and turns. Like other American policymakers, Dulles had given considerable thought to finding a substitute for East-West trade that would keep Europe happy and prosperous. Like other policymakers, the Republican leader did not believe that the United States could absorb the output of a revived Europe. Hence the dollar gap was a fact of life, perhaps never to be eliminated. Testifying before the Senate Foreign Relations Committee on the Marshall Plan in 1948, Dulles had suggested that Europeans pay more attention to Africa. "Africa is a continent of the future so far as Europe is concerned," he said, "and the resources of Africa are incalculable. It is just a mine of all sorts of wealth, mineral and agricultural, and the surface has barely been scratched."[34]

In his notes made "for purposes of mental clarification" before he accompanied Acheson to Paris for the Foreign Ministers Conference of June 1949, Dulles wrote of the "natural affinity" of dynamic regimes for one another, an affinity that made it natural for the new government of West Germany to be drawn toward the Soviet Union. The way to overcome this affinity was to supply positive alternatives: "Find outlets to minimize claustrophobia, e.g., technical participation in European projects such as Danube Basin development; Point IV project in Africa; encourage north German fishing and shipping, etc."[35] Dulles's Point IV reference was to a section of President Truman's inaugural speech of January 1949 calling for technical aid to underdeveloped countries. If American officials had assumed that European recovery was merely a question of providing United Nations aid setting the Bretton Woods system into operation, they had also assumed that decolonization and Third World development was an additional remedy. Acheson explained that Point IV was a recognition not only that the administration should pay more attention to the problems outside Europe but also that Asia and Africa offered untold opportunities for Western economic expansion:

> [I]n so far as [the Point IV] program is successful, and in so far as peoples in less developed areas acquire skills, they may also create the conditions under which capital may flow into those countries. He did not say this was to be governmental capital and indeed, if the proper conditions are created, the reservoirs of private capital are very great indeed. He pointed out that these must be two-way operations. . . . There is also in many places a failure to understand that unless the conditions are created by which investors may fairly put their money into that country, then there is a great impediment to development.[36]

Pressed by newsmen to specify countries and conditions for United Sttates aid under Point IV, Acheson responded: "I [have] tried to make it clear that it isn't for the purpose of installing modern plumbing all over the world. That isn't what we are trying to do." The President, Acheson added, was prepared to work with anyone who wanted to cooperate in the program that he had proposed.[37]

Acheson may have satisfied himself with such statements, but Dulles inherited a very tangled economic policy toward the underdeveloped areas. In the first place, American policy statements, both public and private, had convinced Europeans that they could assume Washington's support in the Third World. What troubled the British even more than the Japanese peace treaty was the oil crisis in Iran. Returned to power late in 1951, Conservative leaders Churchill and Eden hurried off to Washington in an attempt to strike a new bargain in which the British would offer support for American policy in the Far East in exchange for the same favor in the Middle East. The record of the conversations contained the following summary of the British argument:

> [I]f [the United States] would put only a brigade of troops into Suez, the British could withdraw a whole division or more. This one step would indicate such solidarity between us that the Egytians would stop their unlawful conduct and get on with . . . discussions [over British rights]. Similarly, in Iran, if we undertook to give financial support to the Iranians, the problem

would never be solved. Whereas, if we would stand solidly with the British, the Iranians would come to terms in short order.[38]

Acheson hated these encounters over non-European questions. His sympathies were with the Europeans always. "I was always a conservative," he would say. "I sought to meet the Soviet menace and help create some order out of the chaos of the world. I was seeking stability and never had much use for revolution."[39] His dislike for revolution and revolutionaries was remarkably egalitarian. Iran's Mohammed Mossadegh or Vietnam's Ho Chi Minh, it was all the same. Still, the problems they created required clear distinctions in policy. When Asian and African struggles challenged imperial structures, they inevitably brought three-way conflicts, with the United States trapped in the middle. In Iran, Acheson would not permit the British to push Mossadegh over the cliff into the waiting Communist net below. Thus Acheson simply could not accept the Churchill-Eden offer, smacking as it did of an Anglo-American "spheres of influence" deal.

Dulles may not have felt much differently about Third World revolutionaries, although that conclusion is open to question. Changing conditions, however, compelled him more and more to take outright stands against the European metropolitan powers. In regard to French Indochina, Dulles agreed that a certain displacement of European influence was inevitable, perhaps necessary. Individual French firms would be hurt, but by and large, he concluded, "the impact on the French economy will not be serious."[40] Dulles recognized Japan's need for economic outlets in the Far East, but his concern for China transcended his search for Japanese markets on the Asian mainland. He believed the Chinese Revolution a crucial turning point in Asian history. Unlike Russian expansion into Eastern Europe, the unhappy result of the war, the Chinese revolution—for all Washington's efforts to play down the nationalist elements in that situation—offered Asian and African countries an alternate route to modernization. For him liberation of the mainland was necessary, not simply because passive containment turned so many hundred million souls over to atheistic communism, but because the new status of China was an unacceptable danger to the newly independent areas in the Orient.

In time the liberation Dulles advocated took the form of liberation from European allies, not the rollback of Communist power in East Germany, Hungary, or China. Dulles's first official trip after becoming Secretary of State in 1953 was to the Middle East. His conclusions were simple and straightforward. European influence in the area had so deteriorated that it was beyond repair, and thus a factor in the region's instability. Dulles regarded Washington's association with European policies as millstones around the American neck. His conclusions on almost every trip he took thereafter were the same: The United States must free itself from European policies in the Third World or lose the cold war.[41]

Eisenhower's instructions to Dulles concerning the 1952 Republican platform set forth the objectives of their diplomacy, political and economic, for the next eight years. All United States policies had to be measured, said Eisenhower, by "the yardstick of our own enlightened self-interest." Eisenhower continued:

> The minimum requirement of these programs is that we are able to trade freely, in spite of anything Russia may do, with those areas from which we obtain the raw materials that are vital to our country. . . . America's position of strength enhances her natural capabilities for leadership in this necessary task. We must state that no foreign power will be allowed to cut us off from those areas of the world that are necessary to the health, strength and development of our economy.[42]

One of the first opportunities Dulles had to put these instructions into operation after Eisenhower's election came in a conversation with Eden in mid-November, 1952. His report to the President-elect accurately pinpointed the major concerns in both Washington and London:

> I expressed my personal feeling that when the Western nations had to face such non-Western problems as those of Colonial Africa, Iran, China, etc., it was of the utmost importance that the U.S., UnK [*sic*], and France should first, if at all possible, create a united position because our policies, when contradictory, are almost sure to fail, and only our enemies profit. He expressed concurrence and satisfaction with this point.

> Eden felt that the most urgent Western European problem was that of securing French and German ratification of the German Peace Contract, with consequent creation of a German military force which in turn would divert a part of German's economic activity from competition with the United Kingdom into rearmament.[43]

The Eisenhower administration attempted to comply with Eden's request, although in ways that often forced British diplomats to choose between Europe and the Empire. The movement for greater European unity included, eventually, the European Defense Community (EDC) and the Common Market. The goal of these efforts was twofold: to reduce the dollar gap and to ease the burden on American finances at a time when the cold war required global policies.

Republicans were committed to fiscal conservatism, but that should not mask the fact that the problems they inherited, as much as their own ideology, determined the nature of the Eisenhower-Dulles policies. Dulles's famous warnings to Europe and the world on matters of massive retaliation and agonizing reappraisal reflected his view of the world as much as his desire to limit the nation's expenditures. At a meeting of President-elect Eisenhower's closest economic and military advisers in late 1952, Dulles described the global challenges facing the United States. The Soviet program, he said, was designed to exhaust American resources and patience and produce divisions in the Western alliance. Many trouble spots around the world, both inside and outside Europe, Dulles added, presented Moscow unlimited opportunities for creating problems. The United States could cope with these ubiquitous challenges only at heavy cost. The answer, the only answer, said Dulles, was "to be ready & able to beat [the Communist] at his own game."[44] The enemy was sufficiently vulnerable, Dulles concluded, that the United States could weaken Russia and the Soviet bloc through a variety of revolutionary tactics. Acheson would have said many of the same things, albeit in high-church phrases rather than Presbyterian bluntness. After all, the Truman administration had produced such a blueprint of cold war initiatives three years earlier in NSC 68.

Dulles did not lack subtlety. His answer to Senator Hubert Humphrey, who had questioned the propriety of publishing the Yalta Papers in 1955, is a case in point. What the Secretary had in mind, he acknowledged, was the need to teach Europeans an object lesson in summitry. Dulles was most anxious about the effect of the publication on Paris and Bonn especially where leaders were debating the decision on German rearmament. "I concluded," said Dulles, "that the impact would, if anything, be favorable. It showed, to Germans, the awful abyss from which they had been rescued by enlightened post-war policies. It showed to the French, the danger of the 'empty chair,' for France was not represented at Yalta."[45]

V

Publication of the Yalta Papers was a minor piece of diplomatic handiwork in the final construction of the Western bloc, both economically and militarily. For Dulles the real challenge to Western unity came not when France rejected the European Defense Community (EDC) in the summer of 1954, but in Indochina and at Suez. Dulles wanted a unified policy for the Third World as well as for Europe. A unified policy meant, of course, one that followed Washington's lead. If the Secretary had complained in 1953 that European policy in the Middle East was an unwelcome burden for the United States, Europeans regarded America's obsession with Communist China and Dulles's condemnation of neutralism as manifestations of Wilsonian perfectionism mated to material riches. With these fundamental disagreements harassing Western diplomacy, the real wonder is that American-European approaches to the Third World were as well coordinated as they were. Of course, as Eisenhower's chief delegate to the United Nations, Henry Cabot Lodge, phrased it in a letter to the President, "The colonial powers have really nowhere else to go."[46]

Eventually that assumption would be tested to the fullest. Meanwhile, Dulles needed to convince other members of the Eisenhower administration, especially Treasury Secretary George Humphrey, that not only was nineteenth-century colonialism outmoded, but also that the techniques of "informal empire" in the Third World required modification. Humphrey was solidly against "soft loans" and, indeed, against most loans that did not stimulate trade. Dulles explained carefully that the financial rules of the game had changed. The United States stood to lose much more than the money it granted in "soft loans," say to Latin America. "It might be good banking to put South America through the wringer," he said, "but it will come out red."[47] At length Humphrey agreed that private capital could not do the job alone. At this confrontation Harold Stassen, Director of Mutual Security, suggested "that what was needed was some kind of counterpart to the East India Company." The allusion was a useful one, because Dulles faced the task of persuading budget-conscious Republicans and anxious Europeans that the United States was ready and able to take up the development functions once performed by the East India Company

Dulles's belief in regional security pacts suggested that the joint stock company (or companies) he had in mind would include partnerships with Third World countries as well. Unfortunately, the prospects for the proposed Southeast Asia Treaty Organization (SEATO) were dim from the outset. The French resented Dulles's efforts to pull them down the aisle to a shotgun wedding where they would be expected to exchange vows with all the guests Dulles invited to the ceremony. The British, fearful of what would happen to the remnants of their economic position in Asia, did not want to antagonize China. Nevertheless, America's allies finally agreed to a plan for collective action in Southeast Asia after the Geneva Conference.

Eisenhower's famous press conference of April 7, 1954, at which he compared Asian countries to a long row of dominoes, was not an example of his idiosyncratic tendency to make a short story long. Instead, it was an accurate representation of the conviction of the Washington policy-making machine, under both Democrats and Republicans, that the consequences of another defeat anywhere would be disastrous. Despite the effort to portray America's role in Vietnam as that of a disinterested friend of freedom, the President recognized explicitly a body of United States security interests in that region. After listing the possible loss of additional millions of people to Communism and of vital raw material sources in Southeast Asia as well, the President returned to one starting point of America's post-1949 Asian policy. Another defeat there would take away "that region that Japan must have as a trading area or Japan, in turn, will have only one place in the would to go—that is, toward the Communist areas in order to live."[48]

At the Geneva Conference, which opened in late April 1954, Western and Communist leaders negotiated a peace. Behind the scenes Eden deliberately adopted a stance of close cooperation with Russia's Molotov. The basis for this cooperation was their presumed mutual interest in checking the extremist tendencies represented by Dulles and China's Communist leaders. "[Eden] cheerfully told Moltov," recorded his private secretary, "his joke about Russia and UK being 'inside left and inside right,' and says he enjoyed it very much."[49] The division of Vietnam, whether temporary or permanent, was not the only separation worthy of comment after Geneva. Britain and France eventually joined SEATO and, much to everyone's surprise, South Vietnam began its existence suspiciously under Washington's hand-picked leader, Ngo Dinh Diem. But the Eden-Molotov collaboration at Geneva suggested considerable resentment that the allies were being victimized by the ongoing process whereby the United States substituted American influence and Japanese goods for European notions of empire. Waiters in Saigon might continue to speak French, but soon they would be serving *coq au vin* to American officers rather than to French *légionnaires*.

In part, or course, this resentment was a healthy sign, an indication that Europeans were feeling stronger and that American medicine was having an effect. But on the darker side Washington's behavior appeared threatening. The high-handed manner, to Europeans at least, by which the United States established Diem in power raised suspicions that Washington had in mind a similar role for Egypt's Gamal Abdel Nasser. There Dulles seemed to be gambling for much higher stakes. If he lost, the whole Western position in the Middle East would be put in jeopardy. That Western position comprised a jumbled collection of issues, historical and future, psychological as well as substantive, that Europeans thought would determine their fate. Dulles had courted Nasser from the beginning, putting him at the top of a list of Third World leaders with whom the United States could work. If Dulles could convince Nasser that Washington's friendship was more valuable than close association with self-styled neutralists, the uphill road American policymakers had been traveling in the Third World might flatten out. Europeans feared, on the other hand, that the route ahead was downhill, for them a descent into oblivion. Once inflated by American encouragement, Nasser's Pan-Arabist ambitions might swell until they eliminated every remaining evidence of European influence.

Dulles hoped to build America's special relationship with Nasser's Egypt, at least in part, by financing the Aswan Dam. If the United States could divert Egyptian energies into harnessing the Nile, the issue of American unwillingness to sell Cairo large supplies of arms would gradually fade from view. Still, Eisenhower and Dulles felt uncertain about the ultimate outcome of their great gamble. On November 29, 1955, the two discussed the situation at some length, with the President asking if there was any reason "not to go all out for the Dam in Egypt." Dulles answered with diminishing confidence that he wondered if Nasser was "playing an honest game or is in the Communist pocket." In any event, he concluded, the United States needed to take the risk. It was not only that Washington had to find some way of balancing its military support to Isreal, but also that it had to assuage the British for not having joined the Baghdad Pact in 1955.[50]

Aswan was a multipurpose solution, but a highly problematical one at best. It was proposed initially by the British whose friendship for Nasser was questionable. American officials may well have wondered if the whole plan was simply designed to drag them into a dubious allied relationship. None of this contradicts the popular impression that the Eisenhower administration ultimately made Aswan its project. Still, when things began to go sour, American officials remembered how it all started. Even Eisenhower seemed puzzled by the sequence of events surrounding the American withdrawal of support for Aswan and Nasser's decision to nationalize the Suez Canal. At some point a reverse bandwagon effect took over; soon everyone was eager not to be the last one to desert the Aswan project. Dulles had several premonitions of impending disaster. In an effort to arrest the adverse trend in the spring of 1956, he asked Senator Mike Mansfield to make himself an expert on the Middle East, hoping that Mansfield would play a role similar to the one he had once played in explaining Far Eastern and Southeast Asian realities to his Senate colleagues. The United States faced a dual problem, Dulles informed the Senator, in wanting to support Israel yet protect Western access to Middle Eastern oil—vital to "Europe's industry and military establishment and the UK balance of payments."[51]

The Suez crisis brought this discussion almost full circle. In proposing the Aswan Dam the British presented two paradoxical suppositions to

Washington. They argued that unless the West came up with a plan for financing the project, the Rusians would take on the assignment and thus gain a strategic foothold in the area. They argued additionally that unless Washington cooperated, they would no longer accept a long-standing list of banned items in East-West trade.[52] For Americans the Anglo-French-Israeli invasion of Egypt was a tragic conclusion to the imperial era and a terrible setback to cold war strategy in the Third World. Eisenhower thought it might have one blessing in disguise. It might impel British leaders to seek membership in the Common Market. Suez would not have happened, the President implied, if European ambitions had not dominated good sense.[53]

VI

In the decade, 1947–57, American policymakers had attempted to rear-range the world and bring order to it by using the threat of a monolithic peril to civilization—Soviet Communism—and thereby create a state of permanent emergency. They no doubt believed in the reality of the peril, even while they dismissed the likelihood of a Russian invasion of the West. Of far more immediate concern to American officials was what they called "subversion," essentially the ability of the Communists to exploit both the basic weaknesses of Western capitalism and the possibilities afforded by Asian nationalism. Initially American eco-nomic policy reflected a need, not to secure markets in Eastern Europe per se but to establish a capitalist order immunized against the dread diseases of depression and war. Once the shock wore off, the loss of a viable East-West trade connection had decided advantages, at least for waging successful economic policy in a cold war. It was the cold war that compelled the industrial powers of Western Europe to cooperate with the United States. Acheson's handling of the German trade ques-tion was perhaps the best illustration of the intricate subtleties of eco-nomic policy in the cold war. At best, however, the Marshall Plan and the "military Keynesianism" of the Korean war were only short-range solutions to such persistent problems as the dollar gap and unequal trade competition.

European unification was a much-desired goal of American planners, but it embodied a variety of disadvantages. The creation of an internal market in Europe, as envisioned by the Schuman Plan, did not ter-minate Europe's interests in the Third World and its clash with Amer-ican purposes in Asia and the Middle East. For Dulles the Chinese Revolution was a more far-reaching challenge than the Russian occu-pation of Eastern Europe. Europe, on the other hand, adopted a more relaxed view of the meaning of Mao's victory. Official perceptions of the Chinese Revolution, as one element in a monolithic Communist assault on the world, helped to shape the American image of what the Europeans were failing to do in Indochina and the Middle East. Americans saw the pathetic effort of Europeans to hold onto the remote past. To Europeans the situation was quite different, involving the effort to overcome the more recent past and to plan for the future. What the French fought for in Indochina, and what led Eden toward the Suez debacle, was not nostalgia, but an effort to protect historic interests against revolutionary change. Americans not only saw danger in revolution and thus sought to limit it, but also assumed that the United States, lacking a colonial background, was uniquely prepared to deal with revolutionary situations.

It is beyond the scope of this chapter to consider the frustrations that faced President John F. Kennedy and his successors in their attempts to demonstrate their power to control Third World developments. One irony of the Kennedy years, however, was central to the nation's economic foreign policy. By the end of the 1950s the balance of payments problem was shifting dramatically against the United States. Having assumed the leading role in the defense of Europe as well as in countering revolutionary pressures in Southeast Asia, Latin America, and the Middle East, the United States stretched its resources too thin and created for itself a dilemma of major proportions. If it withdrew its troops from Germany and Japan to help with the balance of payments or to improve its capabilities in the Third World, what would happen to the notion of a single, monolithic threat to civilization? What would happen to Washington's assurances that Germany, Japan, Russia, and China would not again menace the peace? Little wonder, then, that American policymakers became obsessed with the word "credibility," whether applied to Cuba, to Vietnam, or, ultimately, to themselves.

Notes

1. Transcript of Interview, "Morning," February 18, 1955, Papers of Harry S. Truman, Harry S. Truman Library, Independence, Missouri.

2. For differing interpretations, see Alfred E. Eckes, Jr., *A Search for Solvency: Bretton Woods and the International Monetary System, 1941–1971* (Austin: University of Texas Press, 1975); and Lloyd C. Gardner, *Economic Aspects of New Deal Diplomacy* (Madison: University of Wisconsin Press, 1964), 261–91.

3. As late as 1952, American policymakers were still concerned that Churchill harbored ambitions to end the cold war through a "spheres of influence" deal. See, for example, "Negotiating Paper: U.S. and U.K. Appreciation of Probable Soviet Action in the Near Future," January 3, 1952, prepared by the Steering Group on Preparation for Talks by the President and Prime Minister Churchill, Truman Papers. Recently, historians have stressed the British initiative in awakening American policymakers to the Soviet threat in Europe at the outset of the Cold War. See, for example, Terry Anderson, *The United States, Great*

Britain, and the Cold War, 1944–1947 (Columbia: University of Missiouri Press, 1981). The fact remains, Washington never fully trusted the British commitment to its approach to dealing with the Soviets, as this paper demonstrates.

4. See Lucius D. Clay, *Decision in Germany* (Garden City, N.Y.: Doubleday, 1950), 5.

5. Diary Entry, July 17, 1945, Papers of Henry L. Stimson, Yale University, New Haven, Conn,; James V. Forrestal to Homer Ferguson, May 14, 1945, Papers of James V. Forrestal, Princeton University Library.

6. In this regard it is useful to remember that John Foster Dulles was an early opponent of building a security system in Europe based upon Germany, whether bizonal or reunited. See, for example, "Memorandum" for Secretary George C. Marshall, March 7, 1947, Dulles Papers, Princeton University Library.

7. See the discussion in Lloyd C. Gardner, *Architects of Illusion: Men and Ideas in American Foreign Policy, 1941–1949* (Chicago: Quadrangle Books, 1970), 55–83.

8. Quoted in Robert Ferrell, *Off the Record: The Private Papers of Harry S. Truman* (New York: Harper and Row, 1980), 57–58.

9. *Ibid.*, 218–19; and Gardner, *Architects*, 55–83.

10. *Public Papers of the Presidents of the United States: Harry S. Truman, 1946* (Washington: GPO, 1962), 165–69.

11. Forrestal to Thomas Lamont, June 10, 1947, Forrestal Papers.

12. Thomas Lamont to Forrestal, June 6, 1947, Forrestal Papers.

13. See Gaddis Smith, *Dean Acheson* (New York: Cooper Square Publishers, 1972), 101–2.

14. See Joseph M. Jones, *The Fifteen Weeks* (New York: Viking, 1955), 156–57.

15. George M. Elsey to Clark Clifford, March 8, 1947, Papers of George Elsey, Truman Library.

16. James Reston to Arthur Krock, encl. notes of off-the-record session, undated, 1947, Papers of Arthur Krock, Black Books, Princeton University Library.

17. *Ibid.*

18. Interview with George F. Kennan, Truman Oral History Project, Truman Library.

19. Kennan to Dean Acheson, May 9, 1947, Papers of the Policy Planning Staff, National Archives, Washington, D.C.

20. Minutes by Robert Hall-Patch, July 8, 1947, on FO 371 [UE 6096/168/63], Public Record Office, London, England.

21. Summary of Remarks, May 6, 1950, Papers of Thomas C. Blaisdell, Jr., Truman Library.

22. Transcript of Interview, "Afternoon," February 18, 1955, Truman Papers.

23. See British Memorandum of Conversation, undated [ca. December 19, 1947), *Foreign Relations of the United States: Diplomatic Papers, 1947*, II (Washington: GPO, 1972), 815–22; and British Ambassador (Inverchapel) to Secretary of State, January 13, 1948, *ibid.*, *1948*, III (Washington: GPO, 1974), 3–6.

24. Theodore Achilles, "Thoughts on Western European Security," January 20, 1948, Department of State Records, 840.00/ 1–2048, National Archives, Washington, D.C.

25. United States Senate, Committee on Foreign Relations, *Hearings: The Vandenberg Resolution and the North Atlantic Treaty*, 80th Cong., 2nd Sess. (Historical Series) (Washington: GPO 1973), 86.

26. Transcript, "Princeton Seminar," July 22, 1953, Papers of Dean Acheson, Truman Library.

27. United States Delegation Minutes, May 24, May 30, June 1, and June 9, 1949, Dulles Papers. For some reason, the Department of State did not publish these very enlightening minutes in the Foreign Relations series. For Dulles's discussion with Schuman, see "Memorandum of Conversation," June 2, 1949, *ibid.*

28. Jean Monnet, *Memoirs*, trans. by Richard Mayne (Garden City, N.Y.: Doubleday, 1978), 292.

29. Transcript, "Princeton Seminar," October 10, 1953, Acheson Papers.

30. Monnet, *Memoirs*, 300. DeGaulle's objections still allowed him to envision a similar prospect for Franco-German unity. "If one were not constrained to look at matters coolly, one would be dazzled by the prospect of what could be achieved by a combination of German and French strength, the latter embracing also Africa. . . . Altogether, it would mean giving modern economic, social, strategic, and cultural shape to the work of the Emperor Charlemagne." *Ibid.*, 287.

31. United States Senate, Committee on Foreign Relations, *Executive Sessions of the Senate Foreign Relations Committee* (Historical Series), II, 81st Cong., 1st and 2nd Sess., 1949–50 (Washington: GPO, 1976), 192. See also Interview with Paul Hoffman, Truman Oral History Project, Truman Library.

32. Summary Record of a Meeting of United States Ambassadors at Paris, October 21–22, 1949, *Foreign Relations, 1949*, IV (Washington: GPO, 1975), 472–94. Dean Acheson put the situation in a somewhat different context by referring to the contradictions of empire and democracy. The British were practicing socialism at home, yet relying on control of the Empire, capitalist-style, to keep themselves afloat. Transcript, "Princeton Seminar," October 10, 1953, Acheson Papers.

33. See the interesting discussion in Fred L. Block, *The Origins of International Economic Disorder: A Study of United States International Monetary Policy from World War II to the Present* (Berkeley: University of california Press, 1977), 114–15.

34. United States Senate, Committee on Foreign Relations, *Hearings: European Recovery Plan*, 80th Cong., 2nd Sess. (Washington: GPO, 1948), 624–25.

35. "Memorandum," May 19, 1949, Dulles Papers.

36. Copy of Acheson's remarks and press conference, in Francis Russell to Clark M. Clifford, January 26, 1949, Papers of Clark M. Clifford, Truman Library.

37. *Ibid.*

38. "Memorandum of Dinner Meeting . . .," January 5, 1952, Acheson Papers.

39. *Time*, October 25, 1971, 19.

40. Background Press Conference, May 7, 1955, Dulles Papers.

41. "Conclusions on Trip," May 1953, *ibid.*

42. Eisenhower to Dulles, June 20, 1952, *ibid.*

43. Dulles to Eisenhower, November 14, 1952, *ibid.*

44. "Summary of JFD Remarks . . .," December 11, 1952, *ibid.*

45. Dulles to Hubert Humphrey, March 25, 1955, *ibid.*

46. Lodge to Eisenhower, June 26, 1956, copy to Dulles, *ibid.*

47. "Memorandum Re NAC Meeting," September 30, 1953, *ibid.*

48. On SEATO as a freamework for economic cooperation, see Eisenhower to Dulles, December 5, 1955: "I think that the promotion of economic associations, somewhat as we have done in the military area, would be helpful. . . . Long term planning would give every individual nation a stake in *cooperation* with the United States." *Ibid.* Portions of the news conference reprinted in, Mike Gravel, *The Pentagon Papers, The Senator Gravel Edition*: 4 vols. (Boston: Beacon Press, 1971–72), I, 597.

49. On this issue, and on Eden generally in this context, see David Carlton's thought-provoking, *Anthony Eden: A Biography* (London: A. Lane, 1981), 349. Carlton has had access to an invaluable source in the private diaries of Sir Evelyn Shuckburgh, Eden's personal secretary.

50. Memorandum of a Telephone Conversation, Dulles Papers.

51. Memorandum of Conversation, April 2, 1956, *ibid.*

52. Carlton, *Eden*, 390–91.

53. "Memorandum of Conference with the President," November 21, 1956, Dulles Papers.

THE EVOLUTION OF
NUCLEAR PLANNING

3
Scientists, Arms Control, and National Security

MARTIN J. SHERWIN

On July 16, 1945, dawn broke twice over the Alamagordo desert in New Mexico. At 5:30 a.m., 30 minutes before the sun rose, science preempted nature with "a lightning effect . . . equal to several suns at midday."[1] Just five and one-half years after the discovery of nuclear fission, Manhattan Project scientists had constructed and successfully tested an atomic bomb.[2] As a result of this accomplishment, science was linked to military strategy, and scientists became involved in the planning and politics of national security. By increasing the stakes of war the atomic bomb altered the life of science and the life of the world. "Suddenly the day of judgment was the next day and has been ever since," physicist I. I. Rabi has observed.[3]

From the early days of the Manhattan Project to the hydrogen bomb decision in 1950, the scientists who built the bomb were involved in a great debate over its relationship to the theory and practice of American national security.[4] On one side were a majority of the Project's most prominent alumni, who believed that America's atomic monopoly was a temporary advantage, that United States security would be served best by neutralizing it through international agreement, if possible, and, if that proved impossible, by minimizing the country's reliance upon it.[5] On the other side were a minority of their colleagues, who looked upon the American atomic monopoly as a guarantor of national security, a weapon that should be fully exploited as an instrument of diplomatic and military power.[6]

The outcome of that debate established the basic nuclear weapons policies of the United States government, policies supporting the principle of the nuclear containment of the Soviet Union. And because national leaders never discarded the assumptions that brought that principle and those policies into existence, they remain with us today. But all of the ideas associated with atomic weapons, from the extremist notions of nuclear warriors to the beneficent proposals of disarmament advocates, are based on assumptions and attitudes formulated during the war: Deterrence and the "warning shot" mentality, if not the terms themselves, were implicit in the decisions that led to the destruction of Hiroshima and Nagasaki.[7] The Strategic Arms Limitation Talks were presaged by suggestions from Niels Bohr and James Conant in 1944 and then proposed officially in 1946 in the State Department's Acheson-Lilienthal Report, the earliest official proposal for nuclear arms control through international agreement.[8] Nuclear intimidation, the psychological premise of the Eisenhower administration's massive retaliation doctrine, the *sine qua non* of the principle of nuclear containment, was anticipated in 1944 at the atomic bomb targeting committee meetings. And the idea of limited nuclear war, popularized in 1958 by Henry Kissinger's *Nuclear Weapons and American Foreign Policy*, entered the wartime discussion as an integral part of international control planning.[9]

"No one can think intelligently on the many complicated problems of American foreign policy," Senator Robert A. Taft wrote in 1951, "unless he decides first what he considers the real purpose and object of that policy."[10] A similar point must be made with respect to nuclear weapons. What is their purpose and object? This essay attempts to understand how the scientists of the Manhattan Project answered this question during the war, and how their answers affected nuclear weapons policies afterwards. There are several ancillary queries that must be addressed as well: (1) What influence did scientific traditions have on the formulations of scientists' policy recommendations? (2) What were their expectations about their own responsibilities in the formulation of weapons policies in the nuclear age? and (3) How did the ideas of scientists influence the formulations of policymakers?

I

Wars produce their own objectives and values, which cling like barnacles to a society's conscience, leaving traditional concerns intact, but not necessarily in control. World War II was no exception, as Allied strategic bombing strategies make clear. The Manhattan Project was an integral part of that wartime experience.[11] The physicists who worked on the atomic bomb had no choice but to substitute an ethics of survival for the traditional values of science and, even before their creation destroyed Hiroshima and Nagasaki, to recognize, as several of the more prominent atomic scientists did, that their invention might destroy the peace as well as win the war. The international control of atomic energy was an outgrowth of this concern, but it was linked to another as well—the need to remove the encrustations of war that threatened to smother the freedom of science. After the war scientists did not succeed in restoring the old values of science because the world in which those values had flourished no longer existed, and because the emerging cold war produced yet another set of objectives and values. In this new environment the atomic bomb appeared to be a "winning weapon," one that, according to Presidential adviser Bernard M. Baruch, guaranteed American security.[12] If we cannot be sure that the world will remain safe, insisted Major General Thomas Farrell, "we must arm to the teeth with the winning weapon."[13]

The concept of the "winning weapon" (as distinct from the phrase) did not originate with Baruch in 1946; it was implicit in the discovery of nuclear fission in 1938. Leo Szilard, Albert Einstein, Edward Teller, Robert Oppenheimer, and numerous others in America who were familiar with the physics of this discovery recognized that in *theory* a weapon of extraordinary power might be fashioned if the technical requirements could be mastered. To this end scientists enlisted the President's support; they formed committees to study the possibility of an atomic bomb, they lobbied the military, and they conducted experiments. But it was not until the summer of 1941, two-and-a-half years after fission was discovered in Germany, that scientists in England thought of a way to harness the theory in practical technology. In the fall of 1941 President Franklin D. Roosevelt established the Manhattan Project. Its goal was to beat the Germans in a race for the atomic bomb.[14]

The delay literally terrified the scientists associated with the bomb project. Aware of the weapon's potential, and of their own desultory start, they reasoned that the Anglo-American effort lagged behind the Germans', perhaps by as much as two-and-a-half years. In their minds the atomic bomb *was* a winning weapon; if the Germans developed it first, the Allied cause was lost. Arthur Compton, the director of the atomic energy project at the University of Chicago, was so distressed at the slow rate of progress that, in June 1942, he urged a program for researching and developing "counter measures" against a German atomic bomb.[15] In July, Oppenheimer wrote despairingly that the war could be lost before an answer to the immediate problems under consideration could be found.[16] "What Is Wrong with Us?" was the heading Leo

Szilard chose for a memorandum in September, criticizing the rate of progress.[17]

Despite the concern for speed which dominated a high level meeting at the White House in October 1941, the actual development of the bomb had not yet started by the beginning of 1943; and only limited progress had been made in constructing the many facilities necessary for the construction of atomic bombs. General Leslie Groves did not assume the headship of the project until September 17, 1942. The government acquired the site for the uranium separation plant at Oak Ridge, Tennessee, only two days later. It did not even purchase the land on which it would construct the bomb laboratory outside of Los Alamos, New Mexico, until November; and it was December 1942 before Oppenheimer became director. Thus, four years after the discovery of fission, scientists were not confident that the United States was closing the lead the Germans were assumed to have. A feeling of desperate urgency grew with each passing month, and with it the sense of the bomb's potential as a decisive factor in the war moved sharply through the entire chain of command.[18] Vannevar Bush and James Conant, the science administrators who oversaw the Manhattan Project, kept President Roosevelt informed of both their colleagues' progress and their fears. In effect, Manhattan Project scientists had a direct line to the White House to express their collective concerns and assessments.[19]

The implications of this line of communication can hardly be exaggerated. Through it both Roosevelt and Prime Minister Winston Churchill came to accept the scientists' view that the Allies were involved in a two-front war; on the one hand, there were the enemies on the fields of battle; and on the other, there were the enemies in German laboratories, scientists who might be first to develop the bomb. This view of the bomb as a winning weapon, combined with the apocalyptic vision of it in German hands, assured that its importance would not be underestimated by policymakers. Indeed, it assured the exaggeration of its value and that those responsible for the military security of the United States after the war would view it, as Secretary of War Henry L. Stimson did at the Potsdam Conference, as a "badly needed equalizer," as a panacea for the deficiencies of American power.[20]

Policymakers easily transposed the atomic scientists' view that the bomb could win the war for Germany to the notion that it could win the war for the United States. By the spring of 1944 the bomb's development appeared likely, but the timing of its completion remained uncertain. January 1945 became a possibility, but a later date, perhaps the summer of that year, appeared more probable. The target was Japan, and General Groves initiated preparations for the raid.[21]

While this is not the place for a full discussion of Japan's selection, there is an ironic element in the decision that is relevant—the fear that an atomic attack on Germany might under certain conditions increase the possibility of a retaliatory attack in kind. This embryonic form of a nuclear deterrence policy appeared early. The minutes of a Military Policy Committee meeting on May 5, 1943, note that "the point of use of the first bomb was discussed and the general view appeared to be that its best point of use would be on a Japanese fleet concentration in the Harbor of Truk. General Styer suggested Tokio [*sic*], but it was pointed out that the bomb should be used where, if it failed to go off, it would land in water of sufficient depth to prevent easy salvage. *The Japanese were selected as they would not be so apt to secure knowledge from it as would the Germans.* [italics author's]"[22]

Two years later, in the spring of 1945, with the Germans on the verge of defeat, confidence replaced caution and urban centers replaced military targets. While this shift in atomic bomb targets paralleled an earlier shift in conventional bombing strategy, it also marked a new appreciation of the atomic bomb as a psychological weapon of intimidation. American leaders did not expect that the destruction and havoc that two atomic bombs might wreak would suddenly break the back of Japan's war machine; but they hoped that such attacks would shock the Japanese government into discontinuing its hopeless struggle. The selection of targets reflected this intention.

Guided by instructions from Groves, a Target Committee composed of Manhattan Project scientists and ordnance specialists studied the available options and developed criteria for their selection. The report of the Committee's second and third meetings, held in Oppenheimer's office at Los Alamos in May 1945, reveals a major concern with the weapon's psychological impact. The minutes record the Committee's view that any small, strictly military target should be located in a much larger area subject to blast damage "to avoid undue risks of the weapon being lost due to bad placing of the bomb." The members of the Committee agreed, too, that the psychological impression the bomb made was not merely a matter of wartime interest. "Two aspects of this," the report states, "are (1) obtaining the greatest psychological effect against Japan and (2) making the initial use sufficiently spectacular *for the importance of the weapon to be internationally recognized* when publicity on it is released."[23]

II

The Target Committee's concern that the full implications of the bomb be recognized *internationally* reflected a pervasive anxiety among those atomic scientists who had begun to worry about the role of the bomb in the postwar world. As an instrument of peace based on the international control of atomic energy, or as an instrument of diplomacy to be used in postwar negotiations, the influence of the weapon depended upon a general recognition that pre-atomic age calculations had to give way to new realities. If the Japanese did not accept this view, the war would continue; if the Soviets ignored it, the peace would be lost. In this sense the bomb became its own message, and within the context of the war the atomic scientists who participated in the decision to bomb Japan were consumed by a single objective—to transmit in the most dramatic fashion possible the message that the new age required new forms of international organizations.[24]

Leo Szilard, who had written Einstein's famous letter to Roosevelt warning of the military implications of the discovery of fission, was the first to suggest a resolution to the problem of the bomb in the postwar world. Writing to Bush in January 1944, he referred to the potential development of bombs of even greater power (probably an oblique reference to the hydrogen bomb) and commented that "this weapon will be so powerful that there can be no peace if it is simultaneously in the possession of any two powers unless these two powers are bound by an indissoluble political union." The world would need to create some type of international control, "if necessary by force," he argued, to prevent a war that would recreate the dark ages, or worse.[25]

This was not the last time that a scientist would suggest that military force be enlisted to achieve security against nuclear uncertainty. The overwhelming sense of hopelessness before an unprecedented power in-the-process-of-becoming, created an urge to seek assurance against that power being turned upon its inventors. Bound to their task by their fear of German progress, and terrified by the consequences of their own success, men of sensibility, culture, and peace were driven in desperation to recommend policies that under normal circumstances would be judged irrational at best, and perhaps even barbaric. The discovery of fission at the dawn of war created a quandary without an apparent solution. Some of the best minds were driven to pursue the worst ideas. Like Kurt Vonnegut's Trafalmadorians in *Slaughterhouse Five*, the scientists could see into the future: a postwar nuclear arms race leading to circumstances that literally could bring about the end of the world.[26] But no one with the power to prevent such a catastrophe seemed to recognize that this problem existed. As they worked desperately to build the bomb, scientists who were alert to these issues grasped at schemes that might keep its potential destructive force under control.

The renowned Danish physicist Niels Bohr, who escaped to England from Nazi-occupied Denmark in September 1943, offered the first serious attempt to meet this challenge. "Officially and secretly he came to help the technical enterprise," Oppenheimer noted, but "most secretly of all . . . he came to advance his case and his cause."[27] In the broadest sense, Bohr's cause was to ensure that atomic energy "is used to the benefit of all humanity and does not become a menace to civilization."[28] More specifically, he warned that "quite apart from the question of how soon the weapon will be ready for use and what role it may play in the present war," the United States government needed to reach some agreement with the Soviet Union about the future control of atomic energy before the bomb was developed.[29]

Bohr's ideas on the international control of atomic energy remain significant today beyond any actual effect they might have had on Anglo-American policy. He eschewed force and opted for diplomacy, arguing that the time to prepare for security in the nuclear age was before the bomb's development overwhelmed the possibility of international cooperation. Whether or not other scientists ultimately agreed with his political proposals, most of them shared the basic view of science and its role in the world from which his political ideas developed. His proposals therefore reveal more than the insights and oversights of an individual scientist; they represent the transfer of the scientific ideal into the realm of international politics.

Bohr believed that the intellectual traditions of science preserved the fundamental values of Western civilization: individual freedom, rationality, and the brotherhood of man. Science and progress, science and rationality, science and peace, all went hand in hand. With reference to the discovery of nuclear fission and its consequences he wrote, "Knowledge is itself the basis of civilization, [but] any widening of the borders of our knowledge imposes an increased responsibility on individuals and nations through the possibilities it gives for shaping the conditions of human life."[30]

In 1944 Bohr's concerns and his understanding of the new discoveries that he had done so much to introduce into the world led him to reject traditional approaches to international relations for the postwar years. In his view, economic, ideological, territorial, and military questions all had to be reconsidered within the new framework of limitations imposed by the threat of a postwar nuclear arms race. In formulating his proposals, he did not ignore the role of traditional considerations in international affairs; he sought only to reassess these in the light of this totally unprecedented situation. His proposals were based on his perception of the frightful insecurity of a nuclear-armed world—the consequence of the atomic arms race that he considered inevitable if leaders were unsuccessful in their attempts to institute effective international control of atomic energy.

At the heart of Bohr's plan for the international control of atomic energy was a scientist's natural distrust of secrecy, together with a Wilsonian desire to alter radically the means and methods by which nation states had historically conducted their relations with each other. International control of atomic energy was only possible in an open world, a world in which each nation could be confident that no potential enemy was engaged in stockpiling atomic weapons. He urged Roosevelt to consider "any arrangement which can offer safety against secret preparations."[31] International inspectors must receive full access to all military and industrial complexes and full information about new scientific discoveries. In essence, he based his argument on the proposition that the values of science—the very same values that had contributed to the discovery of fission—had to govern international relations after the war, if the accomplishments of scientists were not to destroy the world.

Behind Bohr's faith in the possibility of arranging such international controls was his estimate of the potential influence of statesmen over the course of international relations. He assumed that relations between states were guided by calculated decisions. The judgments of statesmen were often in error, and their perception of their own and the world's best interest often dangerously myopic; nonetheless, in Bohr's view, it was governments composed of people, not immutable laws of history or of international politics, that controlled the cycle of war and peace. He was convinced, therefore, that if statesmen could be made to understand the political and military implications of atomic energy, they would respond positively to the new international conditions. There were no historical precedents to encourage him, but the lack of precedent seemed irrelevant; the threat of atomic warfare was also unprecedented. Referring to the quantum theory, he once remarked to Oppenheimer in jest that what the world required was "another experimental arrangement."[32]

In a deeper sense Bohr was not jesting, for his proposals called for a political quantum leap into the era of the atomic bomb. In 1944 such a leap did not seem impossible; on the contrary, if the world was to survive, he considered it a necessity. Applying the ideals of science to the conduct of human affairs, he took, as the components of his model, idealized versions of international relations and of the international scientific community, with scientists responsible for educating statesmen to the necessity for a new international order.

That Churchill and Roosevelt rejected Bohr's proposals out-of-hand may amount some day to a tragedy for Western civilization. But there is no use in belaboring this point. Roosevelt and Churchill shared neither his assumptions nor his vision, and perhaps it is too much to expect that they could. Harnessed to the yoke of war, without a scientist's intuitive understanding of the long-range implications of a weapon that did not even exist, they accepted the bomb as it had been presented, as a winning weapon. "The suggestion that the world [the Soviet Union] should be informed regarding [the atomic bomb], with a view to an international agreement regarding its control and use, is not accepted," ran their response in September 1944. "The matter should continue to be regarded as of the utmost secrecy."[33]

It was not only idealists such as Bohr who tried to lighten the dark shadow which the bomb cast across the future. Scientists of a more conventional turn of mind, once alerted to the problem, turned to unconventional ideas. James Conant certainly had "no roseate view of human nature." His modus operandi was "the calculated risk," and to achieve a fair chance of success he was inclined "to talk in terms of concrete and limited objectives."[34] Yet in May 1944, several months earlier than previously suspected, Conant confronted the problem of the atomic bomb in the postwar world and came to the conclusion that limited objectives were dangerously inadequate. In the long run, he wrote to Bush, "the only hope for humanity is an international commission on atomic energy with free access to all information and right of inspection."[35]

In a memorandum entitled, "Some Thoughts on International Control of Atomic Energy," Conant peered into the future and discerned only two alternatives: an atomic arms race and "in the next war destruction of civilization," or "a scheme to remove atomic energy from the field of conflict."[36] The second alternative clearly was a necessity, not a choice, and to achieve it Conant proposed 14 points (he did not refer to them as such and appears to have been unaware of this subtle Wilsonian touch). He argued for the formation of an association of nations specifically committed to control atomic energy, as well as an international commission on atomic energy that included Britain, the United States, Russia, and perhaps six other nations to govern all atomic energy work. The commission would license, finance, and control all research and development work, and publish all results. Agents of the commission would police the system by frequent inspections of all laboratories, factories, or other relevant facilities, and irrespective of whether two countries were at war, the inspectors would have the right of entry. The commission was to have its own international air force and an army of 10,000 men to prevent the seizure of supplies. If any nation refused to permit inspections, or interfered with the commission in any other important way, its actions would be "considered an act of war."

But, Conant asked, "what happends if a nation refuses entry of agents to factories etc. or disobeys [the] edicts of [the] commission?" His answer was "war," declared by the other members of the international organization who might, if the Commission approved, *use atomic bombs* to bring the renegade nation to heel. This idea of a limited nuclear war to prevent a general conflagration he even extended to the "use of bombs by arsenal guards," if the United States, Canada, or Britain tried to seize the Commission's atomic arsenal, which Conant had located in Canada. By recommending the use of atomic bombs to prevent a nuclear war, Conant succumbed to the temptation that lay across the path of all nuclear arms control efforts. If the desire to rid the world of the potential danger of nuclear weapons stems from a fear of their destructive potential, then why not use that threat in the service of international security?

III

Conant believed not only that the bomb was an ideal weapon to *shock* Japan's leaders into surrender, but that its use was necessary to impress upon the world (in general, but on the Soviet government in particular) his vision of the terror and annihilation that it could inflict. Assuming "that in another war atomic bombs will be used,"[37] he recommended to Stimson that in the present war "the bomb *must be used*," for that remained "the only way to awaken the world to the necessity of abolishing war altogether. No technical demonstration . . . could take the place of the actual use with its horrible results. . . ."[38] Nor was Conant the only scientist to hold this view. "If the bomb were not used in the present war," Arthur Compton, the director of the Manhattan Project's University of Chicago laboratory, wrote to Stimson in June 1945, "the world would have no adequate warning as to what was to be expected if war should break out again."[39] Later Winston Churchill described the essential nature of this policy: "Then it may well be that we shall, by a process of sublime irony, have reached a stage in this story where safety will be the sturdy child of terror, and survival the twin brother of annihilation."[40] Conant's policy was a quest for absolute security that led him toward terror and annihilation, toward a prescription for nuclear deterrence in the service of nuclear disarmament, and toward a recommendation to use the atomic bomb in a surprise attack against an urban center in Japan. Nuclear war and arms control were wrapped in the same package.

One group of Project scientists at the University of Chicago reasoned quite differently, their analysis flowing from alternative assumptions formulated during the closing months of the war. Far removed from political pressures, and from the clutter of extraneous considerations associated with the policymaking process, they broadcast a prescient warning to a deaf audience: the indiscriminate military use of the atomic bomb would undermine the possibility of achieving the international control of atomic energy.[41]

Early in June 1945 they assembled as a Committee on the Social and Political Implications of the Atomic Bomb under the chairmanship of the distinguished émigré physicist James Franck. Their central concern was "the conditions under which international control is most probable," and their basic assumption was that the "manner in which this new weapon is introduced to the world will determine in large part the future course of events." They too saw the path from atomic bombs to superbombs with limitless destructive power. They too described the uncertain security that an attempt at monopoly would bring. And they too outlined methods of international control that might be feasible. Their primary purpose, however, was less to enumerate the dangers of the atomic age than to recommend policies that might circumvent those dangers. The central argument of the report was that a surprise atomic attack against Japan was inadvisable—whether one was optimistic or pessimistic about the possibility of international control. "If we consider international agreement on total prevention of nuclear warfare as the paramount objective, and believe that it can be achieved," they argued, "this kind of introduction [surprise attack] of atomic weapons to the world may easily destroy all our chances of success. Russia, and even allied countries which bear less mistrust of our ways and intentions, as well as neutral countries may be deeply shocked."

Their view of the influence of a demonstration of the bomb's capacity for terror and annihilation was diametrically opposed to the assessments of Conant and Compton. "It may be very difficult," these scientists agreed, "to persuade the world that a nation which was capable of secretly preparing and suddenly releasing a weapon as indiscriminate as the [German] rocket bomb and a million times more destructive, is to be trusted in its proclaimed desire to having such weapons abolished by international agreement."

The Franck group of Chicago scientists made the converse case for not using the atomic bomb even "if one takes the pessimistic point of view and discounts the possibility of an effective international control over nuclear weapons at the present time. . . ." In this case, the scientists concluded, "the advisability of an early use of nuclear bombs against Japan becomes even more doubtful—quite independently of any humanitarian considerations. If an international agreement is not concluded immediately after the first demonstration," they reasoned, exhibiting Bohr's sense of timing that was lacking elsewhere, "this will mean a flying start toward an unlimited armaments race. If this race is inevitable, we have every reason to delay its beginning as long as possible in order to increase our head start still further.

It is noteworthy that the members of the Franck Committee shared a basic assumption with those who had a sanguine view of the results that would flow from using the bomb: an atomic attack against Japan would "shock" the *Russians* as well as the Japanese. But their reasoning about the effect of such a shock was very different. Neither Conant nor Compton, nor Truman, Stimson, or Byrnes, considered a weapon untested in combat a very useful *bargaining counter*, a concept that is all too familiar today.[42] They believed that an actual combat demonstration would make a far greater impression on those who needed to be convinced to bring the war to a conclusion, and upon those who needed to be persuaded that the postwar international control of the atomic bomb was in their long-range interest. It was the quest to make an *impression*—the psychological impact of a single bomb dropped from a lone aircraft causing damage equal to that caused by thousands of bombs dropped from hundreds of aircraft—upon which national leaders founded the decisions that led to Hiroshima and Nagasaki.

But the members of the Franck Committee drew the diametrically opposite conclusion: the more awesome the bomb's demonstrated power, the more likely an arms race. The most important demonstration needed was some means of conveying to the Soviets an American commitment *not to use* the bomb, a commitment that might install in the Russians a measure of confidence that the Anglo-American monopoly would not be turned against them, a commitment that might persuade them that the objective of American policy was the neutralization of the atomic bomb. Szilard made this point to Oppenheimer when they saw each other in Washington in June 1945. "Don't you think," Oppenheimer rejoined, "if we tell the Russians what we intend to do and then use the bomb in Japan, the Russians will understand it?" "They'll understand it only too well," was Szilard's reply.[43]

In a sense more moderate and perhaps more complex than first stated, physicist P. M. S. Blackett's charge "that the dropping of the atomic bomb was not so much the last military act of the second World War, as the first major operation of the cold *diplomatic* war with Russia," contains an essential truth.[44] The scientists and policymakers who promoted the international control of atomic energy and supported the use of the bomb against Japan never expected that good relations with Russia would be possible if diplomatic efforts to achieve a nuclear arms control pact were not successful. They never thought that achieving such an agreement would be easy, nor that the government should avoid tough negotiations and a measure of intimidation. Hiroshima and Nagasaki were part of that diplomatic strategy, and so were the atomic tests at Bikini, held in the summer of 1946, at the same time that Bernard Baruch was presenting the United States plan for the international control of atomic energy to the United Nations.[45]

Following a line of reasoning that President Truman stated in January—that "unless Russia is faced with an iron fist and strong language another war is in the making"[46]—Conant believed that atomic diplomacy would serve a useful purpose in bringing about security from atomic war. Speaking before an off-the-record dinner sponsored by the Council of Foreign Relations in New York on April 12, in response to a question about the relationship between the Bikini tests and the upcoming UN international control conference, he stated that "the Russians are more rather than less likely to come to an effective agreement for the control of atomic energy if we keep our strength and continue to produce bombs."[47]

Atomic testing was not the only arrow in the quiver of this atomic diplomacy. History also had a role to play. The atomic bombings of Japan received the approval of the majority of Americans, but in the aftermath of the war Conant discerned a spreading accusation that it had been entirely unnecessary to use the atomic bomb—particularly from those, whom he described to Stimson, as "verbal minded citizens not so generally influential as they were influential among the coming generations of whom they might be teachers or educators."[48] To combat that view he urged Stimson to write an article on the decision to drop the bomb. This appeared under that title in the February 1947 issue of *Harper's* magazine. If "the propaganda against the use of the atomic bomb had been allowed to grow unchecked," Conant wrote to Stimson after reading a pre-publication version of the article in January, "the strength of our military position by virtue of having the bomb would have been correspondingly weakened," and the chances for international control undermined.[49] "Humanitarian considerations" that led citizens to oppose the strengthening of America's atomic arsenal, in

Conant's opinion, were likely to subvert the common effort to acheive an international atomic energy agreement. "I am firmly convinced," he told Stimson, "that the Russians will eventually agree to the American proposals for the establishment of an atomic energy authority of world-wide scope, *provided* they are convinded that we would have the bomb in quantity and would use it without hesitation in another war."[50]

That Conant and those who supported this view were wrong is less a criticism of their logic than of their fundamental assumptions about the nature of the forces underlying the atomic arms race. If the Americans viewed the bomb as an effective instrument of diplomacy and as a winning weapon to be used "without hesitation in another war," the Soviets could hardly be expected to take a more lofty view. America's atomic monopoly heightened their fears and threatened to thwart their most fundamental security needs. No play for international control, presented under a canopy of an American nuclear arsenal, and guaranteeing the perpetuation of the American monopoly through a series of "stages" conditioned upon Soviet good behavior—which was the fundamental premise of the Baruch Plan—would be accepted by the Soviets. If atomic bombs were a threat to human existence, they had to be controlled by a concern for universal rather than national security. U.S. diplomatic objectives in Europe and elsewhere had to be *uncoupled* from efforts to achieve the international control of atomic energy. The early forms of linkage, of tying American atomic initiatives to Soviet political concessions, simply assured that the Soviets would pursue a parallel line of logic that led inexorably to atomic competition.

Notes

1. Major General L. R. Groves, Memorandum to the Secretary of War, Subject: The Test, July 18, 1945. Manhattan Engineer District Records, Top Secret of Special Interest to General Groves files, folder no. 4, Trinity Test, National Archives, Washington, D.C. Reprinted in Martin J. Sherwin, *A World Destroyed: The Atomic Bomb and the Grand Alliance* (New York: Vintage Books, 1977), 308–14.

2. The most complete study of the bomb's development can be found in volume one of the official history of the United States Atomic Energy Commission. Richard G. Hewlett and Oscar E. Anderson, Jr. *The New World, 1939–1946: A History of the United States Atomic Energy Commission, I* (University Park: Pennsylvania State University Press, 1962).

3. Quoted in Alice Kimball Smith, *A Peril and a Hope: The Scientists' Movement in America: 1945–1947* (Chicago: University of Chicago Press, 1965), ii. This is the most complete and useful account of the scientists' efforts to exercise control over the U.S. government's domestic and international policies related to nuclear weapons.

4. That debate is part of the story in Hewlett and Anderson, *The New World*. It continues in Richard G. Hewlett and Francis Duncan, *Atomic Shield, 1947–1952*: Volume II of a *History of the United States Atomic Energy Commission* (University Park: Pennsylvania State Uni-

versity Press, 1969). The most sharply drawn picture of this debate is found in Herbert York, *The Advisors: Oppenheimer, Teller, and the Superbomb* (San Francisco: W. H. Freeman, 1976). See also Herbert York, *Race to Oblivion: A Participant's View of the Arms Race* (New York: Simon & Schuster, 1970); Robert Gilpin, *American Scientists and Nuclear Weapons Policy* (Princeton: Princeton University Press, 1962); and Smith, *A Peril and a Hope*.

5. The classic statement of this position may be found in a letter Oppenheimer wrote to James Conant during the hydrogen bomb debate: "What concerns me is really not the technical problem. I am not sure the miserable thing will work, nor that it can be gotten to a target except by oxcart. It seems likely to me even further to worsen the unbalance of our war plans. What does worry me is that this thing appears to have caught the imagination, both of the Congressional and military people, as the answer to the problem posed by the Russians' advance. It would be folly to oppose the exploration of this weapon. We have always known it had to be done; and it does have to be done, though it appears to be singularly proof against any form of experimental approach. But that we become committed to it as the way to save the country and the peacy appears to me full of dangers." October 12, 1949, United States Department of Energy Archives, Energy History Collection.

6. Speaking for Edward Teller, Ernest Lawrence, and others who took this position, Lewis L. Strauss, a member of the Atomic Energy Commission, made this case precisely to President Truman on November 25, 1949: "I believe that the United States must be as completely armed as any possible enemy. From this, it follows that I believe it unwise to renounce, unilaterally, any weapon which an enemy can reasonably be expected to possess." United States Department of Energy Archives, Energy History Collection.

7. Appearing before the Senate Foreign Relations Committee on November 4, 1981, Secretary of State Alexander Haig talked about the contingency plans that existed for exploding a nuclear warhead as a demonstration to "warn the Russians that if they went any farther they would run the risk of a nuclear exchange." Senator Charles Percy told Haig that he "was reassured" after listening to him. Quite aside from the debate that arose soon after Haig's testimony about whether there was such a plan currently in existence, the former Commander of NATO revealed how easy it is to slip into a "warning shot mentality," a mindless reliance upon nuclear weapons as a panacea for problems they are not likely to solve. Would the Soviets really launch a major attack assuming that the U.S. was not going to use nuclear weapons? *New York Times*, November 5, 1981, p. 1.

8. See Hewlett and Anderson, *The New World*, 534–54, for the most complete account of the development of the report under the guidance of Robert Oppenheimer.

9. Henry A. Kissinger, *Nuclear Weapons and Foreign Policy* (Garden City, N.Y.: Doubleday, Anchor Books edition, 1958). Kissinger concluded that "limited nuclear war represents our most effective strategy against nuclear powers or against a major power which is capable of substituting manpower for technology," (p. 166). Substituting technology for manpower had been the major role in America's nuclear arsenal from the beginning. The limited nuclear war strategy was originally formulated after the hydrogen bombing decision by scientists who opposed the obliteration bombing strategy of the Strategic Air Command. Oppenheimer was one of these scientists and throughout the 1950s he continued to believe that a limited nuclear war strategy was the lesser evil. As a member of the Council on Foreign Relations, which sponsored Kissinger's study, Oppenheimer offered Kissenger encouragement and positive criticism; see the Kissinger folder, Box 43, Papers of J. Robert Oppenheimer, Library of Congress, Washington, D.C.

10. Robert A. Taft, *A Foreign Policy for Americans* (Garden City, N.Y.: Doubleday, 1951), 11.

11. For the development of strategy bombing strategy, see Bernard Brodie, *Strategy in the Missile Age* (Princeton: Princeton University Press, 1959). For the application of strategic bombing during World War II, see A. Russell Buchanan, *The United States and World War II*, Vol. I (New York: Harper, Torchbooks edition, 1964), chap. 9, "Strategic Air Warfare." For a scientist's view of strategic air warfare during World War II, see Freeman Dyson, *Disturbing the Universe*, which propounds a humanistic view from a scientist who was there.

See also Dyson's Compton Memorial Lecture, "Fighting for Freedom with the Technologies of Death," given at MIT, February 22, 1982.

12. Quoted in Gregg Herken, *The Winning Weapon: The Atomic Bomb in the Cold War, 1945–1950* (New York: Knopf, 1980), vii.

13. *Ibid.*

14. Sherwin, *World Destroyed*, chaps. 1 and 2; Hewlett and Anderson, *New World*, chaps. 5, 6, and 9; Margaret Gowing, *Britain and Atomic Energy, 1939–1945* (New York: St. Martin's, 1964), chaps. 1–4.

15. Compton to Henry Wallace, June 23, 1942, F. D. Roosevelt, President's Secretary's File, Vannevar Bush folder, Roosevelt Library, Hyde Park, N.Y. In the same place see Bush's comment to Roosevelt on Compton's letter, June 24, 1942. Sherwin, *World Destroyed*, 47.

16. Oppenheimer to John Manley, July 14, 1942; for expressions of similar concern, see also Oppenheimer to M. McKibben, June 10, 1942, and to Emilio Segre, June 10, 1942, Oppenheimer Papers, Boxes 49 and 50, Library of Congress. Sherwin, *World Destroyed*, 47.

17. Hewlett and Anderson, *New World*, 179; Sherwin, *World Destroyed*, 47.

18. The critical role played by Conant and Bush is described in detail in Sherwin, *World Destroyed*, chaps. 1–4 especially. Bush's constant effort to keep Roosevelt aware of Manhattan Project matters is illustrated by his reaction to Arthur Compton's anxious letter to Vice President Henry A. Wallace. When Bush was shown a copy of the June 23 letter, he immediately forwarded it to Roosevelt with a cover letter. See Bush to Roosevelt, June 24, 1942, President's Secretary's file, Bush folder, Roosevelt Library.

19. Sherwin, *World Destroyed*, chapters two and three.

20. Henry L. Stimson and McGeorge Bundy, *On Active Service in Peace and War* (New York: Harper, 1947), 617. Throughout the Stimson diaries there are frequent references to the atomic bomb as a "mastercard" for American diplomacy. Gar Alperovitz's study, *Atomic Diplomacy: Hiroshima and Potsdam* (New York: Vintage Books, 1967), is based largely on Stimson's obvious tendency to construct postwar U.S. diplomatic initiatives vis-á-vis the Soviet Union on the advantages that would come to the United States as a result of having a monopoly of the atomic bomb. The Stimson diaries are at the Sterling Memorial Library, Yale University, but they are also available on microfilm. See also Sherwin, *World Destroyed*, chaps. 3–9.

21. Hewlett and Anderson, chap. 11. See also Leslie Groves, *Now It Can Be Told: The Story of the Manhattan Project* (New York: Harper and Bros., 1962).

22. Quoted in the Vintage edition of Sherwin, *World Destroyed*, 209. This document was declassified after the hardback version was published.

23. Derry and Ramsey to Groves, May 12, 1945, Manhattan Engineers District—Top Secret Records, Box 3, Target Committee Meetings, folder 5D.2. The target selection process may be traced through documents in MED-TS, Box 3, Proposed Targets, folders 5D.1 and 5D.2. In their quest to impress the world with the bomb's power, the Targeting Committee selected Kyoto, explaining in terms that defy logic: "Kyoto has the advantage of the people being more highly intelligent and hence better able to appreciate the significance of the weapon." See Sherwin, *World Destroyed*, 229–30.

24. *Ibid.*

25. Szilard to Bush, January 14, 1944, in Gertrude Weiss Szilard and Spencer R. Weart, eds., *Leo Szilard: His Version of the Facts* (Cambridge, Mass.: MIT Press, 1978).

26. Kurt Vonnegut, *Slaughterhouse Five*. " 'How does the universe end?' " Billy Pilgrim asks his omniscient Trafalmadorian captors, who have shuttled him to their planet through a time warp. " 'We blow it up, experimenting with new fuels for our flying saucers. A Trafalmadorian test pilot pressed a starter button, and the whole Universe disappears.'

'If you know this,' said Billy, 'isn't there some way you can prevent it? Can't you keep the pilot from pressing the button?'

'He has *always* pressed it, and he always *will*. We *always* let him and we always *will* let him. The moment is *structured* that way.' "

27. J. Robert Oppenheimer, "Niels Bohr and Atomic Weapons, *New York Review of Books, 3* (December 17, 1966), 7. The details of Niels Bohr's efforts to convince Roosevelt and Churchill to initiate diplomatic contacts with the Russians during the war for the postwar international control of atomic energy may be found in the Frankfurter-Bohr folder, Box 34, Oppenheimer Papers, LC. See also the Felix Frankfurter Papers, Bohr Folder, Box 35, LC. Frankfurter had the complete file of Bohr's correspondence with Roosevelt during the war. Margaret Gowing, *Britain and Atomic Energy*, was the first historian to publish the details of Bohr's personal diplomacy; see chap. 13. See also Sherwin, *World Destroyed*, chap. 4. Since the manuscript material is so detailed, both accounts are similar, following the details of Bohr's efforts as he recorded them.

28. Bohr memorandum, May 8, 1945. Oppenheimer Papers, Box 34.

29. Bohr to Roosevelt, July 3, 1944, Oppenheimer Papers, Box 34.

30. Bohr, *Open Letter to the United Nations* (Copenhagen, 1950), 13.

31. Bohr to Roosevelt, March 24, 1945; Bohr to Roosevelt, July 3, 1944, Oppenheimer Papers, Box 34.

32. Oppenheimer, "Neils Bohr and Atomic Weapons," 8.

33. Hyde Park Aide-Memoire, September 18, 1944, President's Map Room Papers, Naval Aide's File, Box 172—General folder, Roosevelt Library, Hyde Park, N.Y. The document is reprinted in Sherwin, *World Destroyed*, 284.

34. "The Tough-Minded Idealist," September 23, 1946, *Harvard Alumni Bulletin, 49* (October 12, 1946), 2. Quoted in James Gordon Hershberg, *Ends Versus Means: James B. Conant and American Atomic Policy, 1939–47* (unpublished Senior Thesis, Harvard College, 1982), 208–9. Hershberg's thesis is a lucid and insightful study of the evolution of Conant's views on atomic energy.

35. This is a marginal comment by Conant on a memorandum, Bush to Conant, April 17, 1944, entitled: "Shurcliff's Memo on Post-War Policies." AEC Historical Document no. 180, DOE Archives, Energy Research Collection.

36. Conant, "Some Thoughts on the International Control of Atomic Energy," handwritten memorandum dated May 4, 1944, Bush-Conant files, Box 9, folder 97, Office of Scientific Research and Development, S–1 Section files, National Archives, Washington D.C. Reprinted in Hershberg, *Ends Versus Means*, 189–90.

37. Conant to Grenville Clark, November 8, 1945, Bush Papers, Box 27, Conant folder.

38. Stimson to Raymond Swing, quoting Conant, February 4, 1947, Stimson Papers, Swing folder, Sterling Memorial Library, Yale University.

39. Arthur Holly Compton, *Atomic Quest: A Personal Narrative* (New York: Oxford University Press, 1956), 239–40.

40. Winston Churchill to the House of Commons in 1955. Quoted in Ralph Lapp, *The Weapons Culture* (Baltimore: Penguin Books, 1969), 61.

41. The Franck Report is reproduced in Smith, *A Peril and a Hope*, Appendix.

42. The Stimson diary has numerous references that make this point including May 15, 1945, when Stimson referred to the bomb as a "mastercard in diplomacy," and June 6, 1945, when he told Truman that after the war the bomb could be used as a *quid pro quo* for the "Settlement of the Polish, Rumanian, Yugoslavian, and Manchurian problems" with the Soviets. See Alperovitz, *Atomic Diplomacy*, passim.

43. Quoted in Sherwin, *World Destroyed*, 212.

44. P. M. S. Blackett, *Fear, War and the Bomb: Military and Political Consequences of Atomic Energy* (New York: Whittlesey House, 1949), 139.

45. Hewlett and Anderson, *The New World*.

46. Harry S. Truman, *Memoirs: Year of Decisions* (Garden City N.Y.: Doubleday, 1955), 551–52.

47. Conant, "International Controls of Atomic Energy," April 12, 1946. *Records of Meetings*, Vol. XII, July 1945–June 3, 1947, Council on Foreign Relations Archives, New York City. Quoted in Hershberg, *Ends Versus Means*, 157.

48. Stimson to Frankfurter, quoting Conant, December 12, 1946, Stimson Papers, Box 154, folder 14, Sterling Memorial Library, Yale University.

49. Conant to McGeorge Bundy, November 30, 1946, Stimson Papers, Box 154, folder 11, SML, Yale University.

50. Conant to Stimson, January 22, 1947, Stimson Papers, Box 154, folder 18, SML, Yale University.

4
The Origins of Overkill: Nuclear Weapons and American Strategy

DAVID ALAN ROSENBERG

On the morning of August 11, 1960, Secretary of Defense Thomas Gates met at the White House with President Dwight D. Eisenhower and top Defense officials to present his proposal for the coordinated employment of strategic nuclear forces in the massive, simultaneous strike against the Sino-Soviet bloc planned for the first twenty-four hours of a war. Gates advised that the commander of the Strategic Air Command (SAC) now become Director of Strategic Target Planning with the authority to develop, on behalf of the Joint Chiefs of Staff (JCS), a National Strategic Target List (NSTL) and a Single Integrated Operational Plan (SIOP). The Defense Secretary stopped short of endorsing the Air Force position that SAC should be given operational command of all United States nuclear forces. He argued, however, that the advent of operational ballistic missile forces, particularly Polaris missile submarines, created an urgent need for an integrated target-and-attack plan to replace the current system of joint-target guidance, separate command operational plans, and periodic coordinating conferences. His proposal would also eliminate duplication of effort, estimated at 200 to 300 targets, and thereby reduce weapons requirements.[1]

A heated two-hour discussion ensued. Admiral Arleigh Burke, the Chief of Naval Operations, told the President: "This is not a compromise. . . . This proposal is a radical departure from previous practice. I am fearful that if the responsibility and authority for making a single operation plan is delegated to a single commander [then] the JCS will have lost control over operations at the beginning of a general war."

Burke argued that the JCS should retain not only basic responsibility for directing the national effort in a general war, but the means for generating the basic plans and controlling the development of these plans.[2] Putting the NSTL and SIOP under the Strategic Air Command would undermine JCS authority, restrict the military options available to unified theater commanders, alarm NATO allies, and give SAC excessive influence in determining atomic weapons requirements and allocations, force levels and deployments, and military budgets. Coordination should be achieved, thought Burke, by assigning retaliatory tasks to the unified commanders, including SAC, with the JCS directing implementation. Burke recommended that no final decision be made until the procedure had been tested and the Joint Chiefs had thoroughly evaluated the product. Air Force General Nathan Twining, the chairman of the JCS, bristled at Burke's presentation. For ten years, he stated, the JCS had tried and failed to improve coordination in nuclear planning. The major stumbling block was always the Navy, whose leaders adamantly refused to adapt their carrier task forces or attack plans to a unified command. Now Burke wanted the first NSTL and SIOP developed on an experimental basis only, in hopes that the Navy could sabotage the process.

The President rebuked Twining for this accusation, somewhat gently, Burke thought, and noted that the service commanders were displaying too much emotion over the question. This was not, Eisenhower said, "a good way to respond to serious military problems, nor did it speak too well of the ability of good men to get together and work out solutions in the nation's interest." There must be agreement, he said, that it would not be "sufficient to assign retaliatory missions from the JCS to the different commanders." "This whole thing," he stressed, "has to be on a completely integrated basis. It must be firmly laid on. The initial strike must be simultaneous," and must utilize both Navy and Air Force nuclear capability. "If we put large forces outside of the plan," he said, "we defeat the whole concept of retaliatory effort, which takes priority over everything else." The President was inclined to agree with Gates that SAC was the logical choice to develop the plan. He approved preparation of the proposed NSTL and SIOP, but agreed with Burke that the JCS should review the completed plans and recommend whether the government should continue the procedure. Eisenhower wanted the final decision by December 1960 so that he would not "leave his successor with the monstrosity" of the uncoordinated, unintegrated forces now in prospect.[3]

Within two weeks, the new Joint Strategic Target Planning Staff (JSTPS) headed by General Thomas S. Power, the SAC commander, was at work in Omaha, manned by 219 SAC personnel (who also retained their SAC staff jobs), 29 Navy, 10 Army, 8 Air Force, and 3 Marine officers. What guided efforts was a National Strategic Targeting and Attack Policy (NSTAP) previously prepared by the JCS and approved by Gates.[4] Still classified, it appears to have called for a plan which would provide for the optimum integration of committed forces for attack on a minimum list of targets. Soviet strategic nuclear capability received first priority, followed by "primary military and government control centers of major importance." The NSTAP also called for a 90 percent probability of severe damage to at least 50 percent of industrial floor space in urban-industrial targets. The assurance of delivery factor in each case was to be at least 75 percent.[5]

By November, the JSTPS had produced the first NSTL and SIOP. Navy papers declassified since 1980 outline their grim parameters.[6] The JSTPS selected 2600 separate installations for attack, out of a target data base of 4100. This translated into an NSTL of approximately 1050 Desired Ground Zeros (DGZs) for nuclear weapons, including 151 urban-industrial targets. Given sufficient warning, the United States would launch its entire strategic force carrying 3500 nuclear weapons against the Soviet Union, Communist China, and the satellite nations. At the very least, an "alert force" composed of 880 bombers and missiles would attack some 650 DGZs (including 170 defense suppression targets) with over 1400 weapons having a total yield of 2100 megatons.[7] The SIOP aimed for a delivery factor of 97 percent for the first 200 DGZs, and 93 percent for the next 400.[8] To achieve such levels of destruction, multiple strikes with high yield weapons were laid on many individual targets. Planners made little effort to determine what targets the United States would need to destroy to achieve its war aims. Instead, the SIOP was a capabilities plan, aimed at utilizing all available forces to achieve maximum destruction.[9] Although it eliminated duplication in targeting, it did not reduce the size of the target list. The plan made no distinction among different target systems, but called for simultaneous attacks on nuclear delivery forces, governmental control centers, and the urban-industrial base.

Navy leaders were quick to criticize the complete SIOP. They pointed out that the JSTPS had failed to determine the minimum force necessary to achieve military objectives, and had failed to leave an adequate reserve for follow-up strikes. They strongly objected to the excessively high damage and assurance criteria, and to SAC's failure to consider the secondary effects of blast, fire, and radiation in projecting damage. One Navy estimate noted that according to SAC's criteria, the damage caused by a 13-kiloton bomb on Hiroshima would now require 300 to 500 kilotons of weapons.[10] Such inefficient, redundant targeting would cause unmanageable levels of radioactive fallout. Admiral Harry Felt charged that if SAC executed the whole SIOP, his Pacific Command might have to be "more concerned about residual radiation damage resulting from our own weapons than from those of the enemy." Another Navy message noted that the execution of only the alert force portion of the SIOP, with one weapon delivered to each DGZ, would produce a fallout exceeding JCS limits for points such as Helsinki, Berlin, Budapest, Northern Japan, and Seoul.[11] Even more important, the SIOP was not tailored to retaliation or preemption. As Admiral Burke observed: "Counterforce receives higher precedence than is warranted for a retaliatory plan, and less precedence than is warranted for an initiative plan."[12] Nor did it seem to discriminate among Russian, satellite, and Chinese targets.

Burke communicated the Navy's concern to Eisenhower, who in early November dispatched his science adviser, Harvard professor George B. Kistiakowsky, to Omaha. Kistiakowsky came away convinced that the SAC/JSTPS "damage criteria and the directives to the planners are such as to lead to unnecessary and undesirable overkill."[13] He found that many judgments made in preparing the plans were arbitrary, and that SAC's vaunted computer procedures were in some cases "sheer bull." The SIOP itself, made up from a "background of plenty" in weapons and delivery systems, made a virtue of excess: "I believe that the alert force is probably all right, but not the follow-on forces which carry megatons to kill 4 and 5 times over somebody who is already dead."[14] Kistiakowsky presented his evaluation to the President on the morning of November 25, 1960. The presentation, Eisenhower confided to his naval aide, Captain E. P. Aurand, "frighten[ed] the devil out of me." The sheer numbers of targets, the redundant targeting, and the enormous overkill surprised and horrified him. Kistiakowsky, a scientist who represented no parochial service interest, had informed the President that the SIOP was not a rational instrument for control of nuclear planning, but rather an engine generating force requirements. Eisenhower pondered a strategy to use Polaris forces as a back-up, and to allow SAC "to have just one whack—not ten whacks" at each target, relying on Polaris "to clean up what isn't done." For the President the essential challenge lay in limiting the expansion of the nuclear arsenal while still maintaining an adequate deterrence.[15]

I

This chapter describes the events and decisions within the United States government that led from the advent of the atomic age in 1945 through the first SIOP of 1960. It addresses nuclear strategy not as an exercise in conceptualization, but rather as a complex endeavor, partly intellectual and partly bureaucratic. It focuses specifically on the strategic and operational planning process for nuclear war—the most rudimentary level of nuclear strategy—and how that process related to dynamics such as high policy guidance, strategic theory, and technological development which should have served to control and regulate it. It is essentially a study in the failure of regulation.

During the 1945–60 period, American nuclear strategy progressed at three separate levels of government. At the highest level, the National Security Council (NSC), with the approval of the President, defined national security objectives and promulgated policy guidance concerning nuclear weapons in foreign affairs and military strategy. The Secretary of Defense, the Secretary of State, and the Chairman of the Atomic Energy Commission (AEC) were the most important actors in NSC decisions on such matters as the expansion of nuclear production, the deployment of nuclear weapons in the United States and abroad, and the sharing of nuclear weapons information with allies. Although the Secretary of Defense was the primary link between the military and the President, most Defense secretaries during this period, with the notable exceptions of James Forrestal and Thomas Gates, did not take the initiative in advising the President on fundamental questions of nuclear strategy.[16] It was the President himself, by virtue of his constitutional authority as Commander in Chief of the Armed Forces, and his statutory responsibility under the Atomic Energy Acts of 1946 and 1954, who possessed the ultimate authority on nuclear weapons. Because of the compartmentalized secrecy surrounding these weapons, any analysis of high policy in the Truman and Eisenhower years often comes down to the question: how well did the President understand the information that he received?

At the second level of nuclear strategy were the military planners who attempted to translate high policy guidance into strategic plans and concepts. From 1948 on, the Joint Chiefs of Staff produced a series of strategic plans, usually on an annual basis. The two most directly concerned with nuclear conflict were the Joint Outline Emergency War Plan, changed in 1952 to the Joint Strategic Capabilities Plan (JSCP), and the Joint Mid-Range War Plan, which in 1952 became the Joint Strategic Objectives Plan (JSOP). The JSCP covered global war planning for the immediate future, while the JSOP had a four- to six-year time horizon. Through the mid-1950s, the Air Intelligence Production Division (later Air Targets Division) of the Air Force Directorate of Intelligence prepared the target lists. The Strategic Air Command had primary responsibility for operational planning. At this level, nuclear strategy was a pragmatic exercise in problem-solving. The challenge confronting SAC was how best to employ available nuclear resources to achieve the objectives contained in the JSCP.[17]

SAC occupied a unique position in operational planning. It was both a separate major Air Force command and a specified command within the JCS national unified command structure. As a specified command, SAC prepared its own annual war-plans, and submitted them directly to the JCS for review and approval. The Army and the Navy did not prepare their own nuclear war plans because their nuclear forces fell under the operational control of the unified commanders in Europe, the Atlantic, and the Pacific. Nevertheless, both services had a strong interest in SAC's nuclear targeting and attack plans, and sought to influence the content and direction of those plans through the JCS review process.

Three external dynamics influenced the development of nuclear strategy. The first was technological change, which created new strategic challenges and options, while setting real, though expanding, limits on how nuclear weapons could be employed. The second was the work of strategic theorists, both inside and outside the government, who engaged in critical and speculative inquiry into the possibilities and dangers of nuclear power.[18] The third and most significant variable was intelligence estimates. The Central Intelligence Agency (CIA) controlled most intelligence resources, but it had to share intelligence-gathering with the Air Force, which had control of air intelligence, as well as the U-2 high-altitude reconnaissance aircraft. The Air Force inaugurated its over-flights in 1956 and launched the first reconnaissance satellites in 1960. None of these sources provided completely accurate and timely information. The intelligence estimates often produced bureaucratic disputes. Targeting estimates, prepared by Air Force analysts in Washington and Omaha, were less controversial. The JCS and the services had neither the time nor the staff to challenge such estimates in detail, and the lists grew unchecked as additional intelligence suggested new strategic possibilities.[19]

II

Harry S. Truman laid the groundwork for postwar nuclear planning, but his legacy was one of ambiguity. Through the Atomic Energy Act of 1946 Truman established a system that made atomic weapons a separate part of the nation's arsenal over which the President had sole authority. Truman presided over the rapid expansion of the nuclear stockpile, approved steps which led to the production of both tactical nuclear weapons and the thermonuclear "super bomb," and accepted a pattern of strategic planning which made a first strike on the Soviet Union's nuclear capability the highest priority in the event of war.

Until 1947 President Truman remained isolated from the entire issue of nuclear strategy. So obsessive was the secrecy surrounding all atomic information that even the highest policymakers had no access to information about American nuclear capability. From the fall of 1945 to the spring of 1947, President Truman was not informed officially of the size of the American nuclear stockpile, although General Dwight Eisenhower, who as Army Chief of Staff received reports from Manhattan District head General Leslie Groves, apparently briefed the President informally in September 1946. As late as February 1947 the Secretary of the Navy and the Chief of Naval Operations each thought the other knew the size of the nuclear stockpile when in fact neither had been told.[20]

Truman's conception of the atomic bomb as an apocalyptic terror weapon of last resort compounded the secrecy. His official policy initiatives through 1948 focused exclusively on the goals of establishing civilian control over American nuclear resources and seeking international control of atomic energy in the United Nations. In favoring the Atomic Energy Commission (AEC) he sought to fend off the efforts of the military to gain control of the stockpile. His quest for international control, however, faced strong opposition among scientists and policymakers who believed the United States could use the atomic bomb to mould the postwar world, as well as among those who understood the inherent difficulty of defining a reasonable diplomatic framework for controlling a powerful but still immature technology. Ultimately Truman's effort could not overcome the imperious posturing of the United Nations delegation, headed by Bernard Baruch, and the intransigence of the Soviet Union. Nevertheless, through the summer of 1948 international control of atomic weapons remained the administration's official purpose.[21]

Lack of high level policy guidance, aggravated by extreme secrecy, retarded coordinated planning for nuclear war. For two years after Hiroshima, the JCS did not collectively or formally review or approve any plan which contemplated the use of atomic bombs, although joint and service war planners (who did not receive specific clearance for nuclear weapons information until early 1947) generally agreed that the nation would have to employ its atomic arsenal in any major confrontation with the Soviet Union.[22]

War planners prepared the first realistic atomic target list in the summer of 1947 and incorporated it into emergency war plan BROILER that fall. JCS war plans FROLIC and HALFMOON, which followed BROILER, placed heavy emphasis on an atomic air offensive. In May 1948, however, President Truman, still believing that nuclear weapons might be outlawed, and convinced that the American people would not tolerate their use for aggressive purposes, ordered the preparation of an alternate conventional plan. The Joint Chiefs began work on such a plan, but abandoned the effort when, on July 28, 1948, in the midst of the worsening Berlin crisis, Secretary of Defense James Forrestal ordered them, on his own authority, to reinstitute planning for the atomic offensive.[23]

Beginning in the spring of 1948, Forrestal, Secretary of the Army Kenneth Royall, and Air Force leaders sought some definition of the circumstances that might justify an atomic war. In early July the Air Force placed a paper before the NSC staff which discussed the possible repercussions of any policy statement on the use of atomic weapons, and the inherent tension between the presidential prerogative to control those weapons and the need to make advance plans and preparations for their use. This open-ended statement won the concurrence of the State Department, including Policy Planning Staff head George F. Kennan, Undersecretary Robert Lovett, and Secretary George Marshall. The NSC received it in September with two additions. The first recognized that the military "must be ready to utilized promptly and effectively all appropriate means available, including atomic weapons" in the event of hostilities. The second assigned the decision to employ atomic weapons solely to the President.[24] Truman approved these additions in NSC 30 on September 16, 1948. That document remained the sole specific statement on American policy for atomic welfare approved by the NSC until 1960. NSC 30 did not address what conditions might justify the use of the atomic bomb, what objectives it was to achieve, or against what targets it might be used. As early as November 1947, Air Force General Hoyt Vandenberg posed two questions: "In a war with the USSR is our purpose to destroy the Russian people, industry, the Communist party, the Communist hierarchy, or a combination of these? Will there be a requirement to occupy, possibly reconstruct, Russia after victory, or can we seal off the country, letting it work out its own salvation?"[25]

On November 23, 1948, the NSC addressed these questions in part in NSC 20/4, a State Department paper which Defense Secretary Forrestal had requested.[26] NSC 20/4 declared that in a general war the United States would seek to reduce or eliminate Soviet or "bolshevik" control inside and outside the Soviet Union. The document did not establish a "predetermined requirement for unconditional surrender," nor did it foresee the need to occupy the Soviet Union.[27] This general guidance, aimed at total victory in a Russian-American conflict, was the last that the military received under the Truman administration; it prefaced all war plans through 1954. NSC 30 and NSC 20/4 embodied the ambiguous if not schizophrenic character of Truman's strategic policy. Unwilling to predetermine a scenario for the destruction of Soviet society, the NSC sidestepped the issue by leaving the decision to use the bomb, and the burden of moral responsibility, with the President alone. What Truman and the NSC apparently did not foresee was that the increasing number of prospective Soviet targets, the growing complexity of atomic weapons and their delivery systems, improvements in Soviet air defenses, and Soviet acquisition of atomic bombs would require increasingly rigid operational planning, a trend which would steadily reduce the choices available to the President in a nuclear confrontation.

In the absence of specific policy guidance, the most critical determinant in strategic and operational planning was capability. From 1945 through 1948, the vaunted era of American nuclear monopoly, the nation's stockpile and delivery capability remained limited. There were only two weapons in the stockpile at the end of 1945, nine in July 1946, thirteen in July 1947, and fifty in July 1948. None of these weapons was assembled. They were all Mark 3 "Fat Man" implosion bombs, which weighed 10,000 pounds each, were relatively inefficient in their use of fissionable material, and took thirty-nine men over two days to assemble. Because the bombs were so large and heavy, they could be loaded on their bombers only by installing a special hoist in a deep pit, trundling the bomb into the pit, rolling the aircraft over it, and then lifting the weapon into the specially modified bomb bay. Through 1948 there were only some thirty B-29s in the Strategic Air Command modified to drop atomic bombs, all in the 509th Bomb Group based in Roswell, New Mexico. There were other limitations, equally profound. The enemy's territory was vast and unknown. Target planners had to rely on pre-World War II and even Tsarist era maps, or at best German aerial photos from 1942–43. Because of limited capability and inadequate intelligence, American bomber crews could only hope to reach their targets under cover of darkness and bad weather; they also lacked the necessary radar data to locate precise aim points.[28]

World War II experience had shown that attacks on specific target systems such as transportation, petroleum, and electric power were more effective in crippling an enemy's war-making capacity than the indiscriminate bombing of urban areas. Air Force conventional war plans of 1946 and 1947 identified the Russian transportations system as "the most vital cog in the war machine of the U.S.S.R.," but concluded that at least one million tons of bombs would be required to destroy even a small portion of the rail network of Eastern Europe alone. Since disruption of the entire Soviet bloc transportation system was clearly impossible, planners identified the petroleum industry, located primarily in cities, as the most critical target system vulnerable to bombing attack. By the fall of 1947 they had identified 100 urban centers for atomic attack. Some Air Force officials spoke of "bonus effects and industrial capital." "What was a city," they asked, "besides a collection of industry?" From 1947 through 1949 governmental control centers and "urban industrial concentrations" became primary objectives. In 1948, when SAC prepared its first operational plan, it could not maintain even this level of distinction. Ultimately SAC selected its aim points "with the primary objective of the annihilation of population, with industrial targets incidental."[29]

The contemplated air offensive against Russian targets expanded with the nuclear stockpile. The target list in war plan BROILER called for 34 bombs on 24 cities. The Air Force HARROW war plan, which served to support JCS war plans FROLIC and HALFMOON, contemplated 50 bombs on 20 Soviet cities. Joint war plan TROJAN, approved in December 1948, called for attacks on 70 Soviet cities with 133 atomic bombs. The expansion of the stockpile did not resolve the planners' strategic problems. In May 1949 an ad hoc committee headed by Air Force Lieutenant General H. R. Harmon reported to the JCS that even if all 133 bombs detonated precisely on their aim points this would not in itself "bring about capitulation, destroy the roots of Communism, or critically weaken the power of Soviet leadership to dominate the people." Soviet military capability to seize selected areas of Western Europe, the Middle East, and the Far East would continue although fuel and lubricant shortages would decrease troop mobility. A 30 or 40 percent reduction in industrial capacity would slow the Soviet war effort but only follow-up attacks could prevent recovery. The Harmon Committee recognized that the air offensive would produce "reactions detrimental to the achievement of Allied war objectives," but concluded that since an air attack would be "the only means of inflicting shock and serious damage to vital elements of the Soviet war making capacity . . . the advantages of its early use would be transcending."[30] The Harmon Report produced three significant reactions. First, it reinforced the argument of critics in the Navy and elswhere who questioned the efficacy of relying on mass destruction of urban areas. Second, its reassessment of the requirements of effective nuclear attack required a substantial expansion of nuclear production. Third, in conjunction with the NATO treaty, which committed the United States for the first time to the defense of Western Europe, it led the JCS to assign the Strategic Air Command the task of retarding Soviet advances into Western Europe.[31]

Through 1950, the nuclear stockpile was still too small, the weapons too large and unwieldy, to be employed against true tactical targets, such as troops and transportaton bottlenecks. The October 1949 target annex for Joint Outline Emergency War Plan OFFTACKLE called for attacks on 104 urban targets with 220 atomic bombs, plus a re-attack reserve of 72 weapons. The prime objective was still the disruption of the enemy's urban-industrial system and the elimination of central control. The only retardation targets were petroleum refineries, electric power plants, submarine yards, and synthetic ammonia plants, some in Eastern Europe.[32] The third targeting category soon appeared. On August 15, 1950, amid mounting anxiety over the ongoing conflict in Korea, the JCS formally assigned "first priority" to "the destruction of known targets affecting the Soviet capability to deliver atomic bombs." The retardation mission received second priority. Third priority went to attacks on the Soviet liquid fuel, electric power, and atomic energy industries. Planners subsequently code-named these categories BRAVO, ROMEO, and DELTA, for blunting (destroying Soviet atomic installations), retardation, and disruption/destruction of war-making capacity, respectively. With some changes, particularly a broadening of the industrial targets category, they formed a basic framework for United States nuclear targeting for nearly a decade.[33] Despite the new targeting priorities, strategists did not incorporate blunting targets into operational plans and target lists. The target annex submitted for JCS consideration in November 1950 included neither BRAVO nor ROMEO targets. The new target lists emphasized specific industries. An aim point which had been directly over the Kremlin, for example, now appeared halfway between the Kremlin and an electric power station located one mile to the south.

Since September 1945 military planners had been worried about defense against an enemy armed with atomic weapons and long-range aircraft. The first JCS postwar strategic concept had noted that the United States must be ready "to strike the first blow if necessary . . . when it becomes evident that the forces of aggression are being arrayed against us." The 1947 final report of the JCS Evaluation Board on the Bikini tests recommemded that Congress redefine "acts of aggression" to include "the readying of atomic weapons against us," and authorize the President, after consultation with the Cabinet, to order atomic bomb retaliation to prevent an attack on the United States. This proposal remained active until August 7, 1950, when the JCS dropped it at the recommendation of Admiral Forrest Sherman, the Chief of Naval Operations, because its constitutionality seemed hightly questionable.[34] By then, war plans provided for advance allocations of nuclear weapons to be used in a counteroffensive against possible Soviet atomic forces.[35]

III

In December 1950 Yale University professor Bernard Brodie, author of several seminal studies on the impact of the atomic bomb on international politics and military strategy, accepted Air Force Chief of Staff Vandenberg's request to review and comment on this target list. Brodie prepared two reports, now lost, which he considered the best and most important documents he ever wrote. Brodie was strongly critical of the air target planners' failure to calculate the impact of the proposed air offensive. The planners did not know where all the Soviet electrical power facilities were located, did not calculate how much damage they could expect from planned attacks, and had not estimated how much power the Soviet Union could afford to lose. There was no calculated strategy for destroying the Soviet capacity to make war. The strategists, Brodie recalled, "simply expected the Soviet Union 'to collapse' as a result of the bombing campaign. . . . People kept talking about the 'Sunday punch.' " Brodie urged planners to identify the targets more selectively and stressed the need for "city-avoidance" strategies to enhance deterrence.[36]

The new target list received strong criticism from another quarter as well. On January 22, 1951, General Curtis LeMay, the SAC commander, met in Washington with a high level Air Staff target panel to explain the unreasonable operational demands the targets would place on his command. He pointed out that SAC would require visual prestrike reconnaissance for a disproportionately large number of targets, that air crews could not locate isolated target complexes visually or with radar in unfamiliar and hostile terrain, and that isolated targets reduced opportunities for "bonus damage." LeMay was convinced that the United States should concentrate on industry located in urban areas so that even if a bomb missed its target, "a bonus will be derived from the use of the bomb." Such careful selection of target systems would conserve the stockpile of atomic weapons while it ensured that SAC would cause maximum damage to Soviet war-making capacity.[37] This meeting proved to be a turning point. The target panel accepted SAC's concerns about isolated targets, reconnaissance requirements, and bonus damage as major considerations in target selection. It agreed to submit future lists to SAC for comment before sending them to the JCS for approval. Too late to revise the list pending before the Joint Chiefs, the group agreed that SAC should base its planning on the more general OFFTACKLE target list.

Three months later Brodie presented his reports to General Vandenberg during a hurried meeting. Brodie never learned the impact of their reception, but he received some encouragement when, in July 1951, the JCS returned the new target list to the planners for revision. He did not discover until later that this decision came in response to the concerns that General LeMay formally presented to the Chiefs in May. Looking back many years later, Brodie wrote that the experience was "certainly a shocking one with respect to what I observed as sheer frivolousness and stupidity with respect to the treatment of the No. 1 strategic problem confronting the U.S. at the time."[38]

Shifts in the structure of target planning compounded SAC's apparent veto power over target selection. The Air Force Air Intelligence Production Division (AIPD), which prepared target lists for Air Force and joint war plans, had been staffed equally by Air Force and Navy personnel through January 1949. In the spring of 1950, Army Chief of Staff J. Lawton Collins, who wanted the Army to have a voice in retardation target planning, pushed the JCS to include Army representatives in the AIPD and provide review of AIPD target studies by the Joint Strategic Plans and Joint Intelligence Committees before they reached the JCS. After LeMay's rejection of the first target list prepared under this system, AIPD approved no substitute list until 1952. In that year the Air Force moved unilaterally to abolish the AIPD and incorporate its functions into the Directorate of Intelligence, to better meet Air Force needs. Many Army and Navy officers in the AIPD simply lost their jobs. Both services protested the change, and proposed the establishment of a target planning group under the JCS. Instead, in May 1953 a new "joint" arrangement permitted the other two services to assign representatives to the Estimates and Targets Divisions of the Air Intelligence Directorate. Although joint committee review of the completed target lists continued, this new system minimized the effectiveness of the Navy and Army planners, who were now working within Air Force organizations even larger than the AIPD.[39] The emergence of the Strategic Air Command as the dominant force in operational planning for nuclear war was a crucial step in the evolution of American strategic planning.

When General LeMay assumed command of SAC in October 1948 he was appalled at the lack of operational readiness in his new command

and quickly initiated a crash program to build up a mobile operational force capable by January 1, 1949, of delivering at least 80 percent of the atomic stockpile simultaneously.[40] At the Dualism Conference at the Air University in December 1948, the Air Force high command rallied behind LeMay's position that the service's highest priority mission was to deliver the SAC atomic offensive "in one fell swoop telescoping mass and time." From then on, LeMay's budgetary and programming requirements for building SAC into a "cocked weapon" received top priority. Although matériel and personnel deficiencies continued to plague SAC into the mid-1950s, its nuclear capable aircraft increased from 60 in December 1948 to over 250 by June 1950. By October 1951, SAC was composed of 28 bomber and 7 fighter wings, with fifteen considered combat ready.[41] SAC emergence reflected Air Force experience. The air strategists were all veterans of the bombing campaigns against Germany and Japan. They were convinced of the efficacy of strategic bombing and believed that the Air Force must serve as the nation's new first line of defense.[42] They were reacting as well to the fear, largely unfounded, that the Navy and its aviators were attempting to take over the strategic bombing mission.

LeMay instilled a spirit in his command that made SAC the nation's most elite military unit. He sponsored the development of innovative technology to increase SAC readiness, such as the specially etched lucite plate radar screen overlays which simulated radar images of Russian target areas. These projections he used to train air crews to recognize fixed geographic features as guides in locating assigned aim points. SAC developed special ultrasonic maps and radar intensity charts, adopted special radar reconnaissance procedures, made improvements in bombing and navigational equipment, and built mock Soviet warning radars.[43] By 1952, SAC was training in earnest for the blunting mission, using its radar prediction and offset bombing techniques to simulate strikes against airfields whose precise coordinates were unknown.[44]

Improvements in intelligence gathering complemented SAC's training techniques. Beginning in the late 1940s, Air Force bombers and transports and Navy patrol planes flew Special Electronic Airborne Search Operations to ferret out Soviet radar capabilities for the purpose of developing electronic countermeasures and locating Soviet air defenses. By 1950, SAC RB-36 and RB-50 aircraft were flying electronic and photo reconnaissance missions, although few if any of these spy flights actually crossed Soviet borders.[45] On rare occasions, Central Intelligence Agency operatives checked out specific targets. The most bizarre intelligence operation of this period was the CIA sponsored "Moby Dick" program, which sent large Skyhook balloons equipped with Air Force cameras drifting across the Soviet Union from Western Europe to Japan. Unfortunately, since no one could track the balloons in flight, analysts could not identify what the Air Force had photographed.[46] The bulk of Air Force basic intelligence on the U.S.S.R. between 1949 and 1953—well over 50 percent in 1951—came from Project WRINGER. WRINGER employed 1300 military and civilian personnel in Germany, Austria, and Japan to interrogate thousands of repatriated prisoners of war from the Soviet Union and to correlate the reports for use in target and other planning.[47]

The concurrent build-up of United States nuclear capability required a shift in presidential thinking. On July 14, 1949, Truman told his top policy advisers: "I am of the opinion we'll never obtain international control. Since we can't obtain international control we must be strongest in atomic weapons." The budgeting and programming decisions of the next several years reflected, in part, Truman's reluctant acceptance of nuclear weapons as the centerpiece of American defense policy. In the fall of 1949, Truman approved the substantial increase in nuclear production which the JCS had requested in response to the Harmon Report. In October 1950, following the outbreak of the Korean war, he approved a second increase.[48]

In December 1950, NSC 68/4 established objectives for a phased and balanced build-up of American armed forces through June 1952. During budget deliberations the following summer and fall, however, Air Force Secretary Thomas K. Finletter and Chief of Staff Vandenberg argued forcefully that only the Air Force could deliver the nation's expanding nuclear arsenal, and that failure to provide adequate delivery capability would nullify the effect of the nuclear production increases. As Vandenberg explained:

> In the event of war, there will be concurrent requirements for the destruction of Soviet atomic delivery capability, direct atomic attack on Soviet ground and tactical air forces, and destruction of the critical components of the enemy's war sustaining resources. It must be pointed out that if we do not provide an air force tactically strong enough to deliver atomic weapons on target with a high degree of reliability (and we thereby run out of delivery capability while appropriate targets and unexpended bombs remain) we will have committed a military blunder which will defy logical explanation to the American people. We will have failed to make provision to exploit our one major military advantage over the USSR.

The JCS subsequently assigned primacy to the build-up of the Air Force and SAC. The Fiscal Year 1953 defense budget embodied the Air Force objective for June 1954, of 143 wings, 48 more than proposed in NSC

68/4, with no corresponding increases in Army and Navy force objectives. President Truman cut this goal to 133 wings at the end of Fiscal 1954, but the Air Force retained its priority position, receiving over 40 percent of the military budget.[49]

Escalating target estimates influenced this growth of the nuclear stockpile just as the stockpile itself encouraged the expansion of SAC. In January 1952 President Truman approved a third increase in fissionable material production, amounting to a 50 percent increase in plutonium production and 150 percent increase in uranium 235. General Vandenberg, who had originated the request within the JCS, justified it in terms of prospective Soviet targets. Even allowing for incomplete intelligence, he told the President, there appeared to be "perhaps five or six thousand Soviet targets which would have to be destroyed in the event of war."[50] This would require a major expansion in weapons production. Critics in the other services labeled this line of argument "bootstrapping." Air Force–generated target lists justified the weapons production, which in turn justified increased appropriations to provide matching delivery capability. The new blunting mission greatly facilitated the bootstrapping dynamic. As intelligence improved, Air Force target lists steadily outpaced the growth of the stockpile.[51] By January 1953 a construction program was under way which would add eight plutonium production reactors and ten gaseous diffusion U-235 production plants to the five reactors and two gaseous diffusion plants then operating. These plants and reactors could support an enormous expansion of the nuclear weapons stockpile. According to authoritative unclassified estimates, the stockpile grew from approximately 1000 weapons in the summer of 1953 to nearly 18,000 by the end of the decade.[52] No subsequent administration found it necessary to authorize any further expansion of nuclear production facilities to meet weapons requirements.

These weapons grew increasingly sophisticated and powerful. Innovations perfected between 1948 and 1952 multiplied the nominal 20-kiloton yield of the Mark 3 bomb more than 25 times. These innovations included advances in the design, composition, stability, and power of the high explosives used to detonate a fission core, and improvements in the mechanics, structure, and composition of the fissile "pit" itself. The pit improvements included development of composite U-235 and plutonium cores, and the employment of the levitation design concept, which utilized an air space to allow the detonation shock wave generated by the high explosive assembly to gather momentum before imploding the core. This resulted in higher yields and increased efficiency in the use of fissionable material. These developments permitted the November 1952 test of the Mark 18 Super Oralloy (U-235) bomb, which yielded 500 kilotons.[53]

Mass-produced atomic weapons already possessed a variety of interchangeable fission cores. The new "boosted" weapons, which employed a small amount of fusion fuel within a "hollow implosion" core to further increase efficiency and yield, received the first test in April 1951. These weapons appeared capable of producing yields approaching one megaton. In October 1952 the United States fired the first true thermonuclear weapon—a 21-ton, cryogenically cooled, liquid-fueled monster that yielded 10.4 megatons but was far too cumbersome for delivery against Soviet bloc targets. The development of "dry" lithium deuteride-fueled fusion bombs weighing between 4000 and 40,000 pounds was already under way. By 1953 the necessary delivery capability in SAC B-36s was ready for the new bombs.[54] Air Force planners had demanded such powerful weapons because the Soviet Union had constructed industries behind the Urals with improved blast resistance. The demand for the new weapons flowed as well from General LeMay's emphasis on bonus damage and the 1951 "Buster" tests, which revealed that measurements of earlier nuclear explosions had vastly exaggerated blast effects, indicating that officials had underestimated weapons requirements in all previous war plans.[55]

By the time Truman left office in January 1953 the framework for nuclear strategy had emerged. The United States had launched an era of nuclear plenty, had approved a series of targeting categories that emphasized preemption of Soviet nuclear capability, and had assigned the Strategic Air Command a major voice in target selection and in the establishment of damage criteria. In addition, American war planning was conducted routinely with an intensity unprecedented in peacetime. Through the Korean war, the JCS stressed emergency war planning, although it made efforts to institutionalize mid- and long-range planning as well. In the summer of 1952 the Joint Chiefs authorized the creation of a new "family" of war plans: the Joint Strategic Capabilities Plan (JSCP), designed to deal with military situations in the current fiscal year; the Joint Strategic Objectives Plan (JSOP), which established force and mobilization requirements for the next three to five years; and the Joint Long Range Strategic Estimate, which looked ahead five years or longer to guide research and development. These plans were to be completed annually, but interservice debates often delayed the latter two and forced them to appear somewhat more irregularly. In the 1950s the JSOP became increasingly a "wish list" rather than a realistic estimate of requirements. Nevertheless these three efforts provided a permanent structure for organizing strategic planning into the

1970s.[56] The JSCP and the operational plans it guided, including the SAC Emergency War Plan, appeared consistently each year. They fostered a process of debate and analysis which, in the absence of real global conflict, served as a form of "surrogate war" for generating and testing forces and concepts. Each new planning effort built on the experience gained in the preceding "war," thereby creating a dynamic which tended to discourage radical changes.

The NSC made little effort to guide nuclear war planning beyond the summary guidance it provided in NSC 30. NSC 68 of April 1950 explicitly rejected preventive war, but left the door open for preemption with the parenthetical notation: "The military advantages of landing the first blow . . . require us to be on the alert in order to strike with our full weight as soon as we are attacked, and, if possible, before the Soviet blow is actually delivered." NSC 114/3 of June 1953 described the highest priority Air Force mission in equally ambiguous terms: "To defend by both offensive and defensive air operations critical areas in the Western Hemisphere, with particular emphasis on defense against atomic attack."[57] The NSC did little to clarify how the President would determine where and when the country would use atomic bombs. An eighteen-month staff study, begun in the spring of 1951 but never formally approved, outlined the procedures by which the President could obtain needed advice. It recognized that the JCS, as the President's chief military advisers, would play a key role. "Unless," the report advised, "there is an initial determination by the Joint Chiefs of Staff that the use of atomic weapons in a given situation is militarily desirable, it is difficult to see how the question of such use can arise in any realistic way."[58] If the JCS recommended use of nuclear weapons, then the President would seek, at a minimum, the views of the Secretaries of Defense and State, and the Chairman of the Atomic Energy Commission. If time permitted, he would consult congressional leaders, and give some thought to the need of informing the American people and other governments. This study once again stressed presidential prerogative, and, although hinting at the problem, did little to close the gap between policy and planning, which had been codified by NSC 30.

It is not clear whether Truman grasped fully the fundamental dilemma posed by the Soviet possession of nuclear weapons. How could the United States plan to defend itself against a potential Soviet strike while ruling out the option of striking first? Truman believed that preventive war was contrary to American values and thus not a policy option. "Starting an atomic war is totally unthinkable for rational men," he told the nation in his farewell address. But whether he had resolved the issue of preemption to his own satisfaction is not known. When

AEC commissioner Thomas Murray asked the President whether he had really meant to rule out the option of preempting Soviet nuclear capability under the threat of imminent Soviet attack, Truman sidestepped the question. "I rather think you have put a wrong construction on my approach to the use of the Atomic bomb," he wrote. "It is far worse than gas and biological warfare because it affects the civilian population and murders them by wholesale."[59] Whether Truman deliberately avoided Murray's question, or simply had not understood it, remains a mystery.

IV

Dwight D. Eisenhower entered the presidency in January 1953 with a more thorough knowledge of nuclear weapons than any President before or since. As Army Chief of Staff in 1946, he had jurisdiction over the Manhattan Engineer District and was the sole channel to high civilian policymakers for nuclear stockpile information. He was the chief advocate of the first JCS nuclear war plan in 1947, and in 1949, while temporary chairman of the JCS, championed increased nuclear production. As the first NATO Supreme Allied Commander from 1950 to 1952, he became familiar with JCS targeting categories and priorities, and encouraged planning for the tactical nuclear defense of Europe.[60]

Eisenhower was not awed by nuclear weapons, neither was he sanguine about them. In March 1953 he admonished his Cabinet against thinking of the bomb as "a cheap way to solve things." "It is cold comfort," he noted, "for any citizen of Western Europe to be assured that—after his country is overrun and he is pushing up daisies—someone still alive will drop a bomb on the Kremlin." Nevertheless, the President knew that nuclear weapons could not be "disinvented," and that they had permanently altered the character of warfare.[61] Shortly after taking office, he reversed Truman's long-standing policy of maintaining almost complete civilian control of the atomic stockpile and took steps to make the bombs immediately available to the military. On June 20, 1953, responding to a Defense Department request for custody of the entire national war stockpile, he transferred a sizable number of complete atomic weapons to the military for deployment to specified bases afloat and ashore.[62] Such transfers would continue throughout his administration, both to decrease the vulnerability of the stockpile through dispersal and to increase operational readiness. In 1961 less than 10 percent of the stockpile remained under civilian control.[63] Where Harry Truman viewed the atomic bomb as an instrument of terror and a weapon of last resort, Dwight Eisenhower viewed it as an integral part of American defense, and, in effect, a weapon of first resort.

President Eisenhower was not happy with the crisis-oriented defense program and record peacetime defense budgets he had inherited from the Truman administration. He was convinced that budgeting to meet a projected "year of maximum danger" would result in runaway expenditures and undermine the American economy. Believing that the United States must approach military preparedness "only on a defensive, which means a long-term basis," he sought to develop a balanced, integrated defense posture for the indefinite future. It took the Eisenhower administration almost a year to thrash out its national security policy and defense program. This multilevel process included NSC studies on security policy, economic defense, and protection of the continental United States; a high level review of the policy options of containment, spheres of influence, and rollback code-named Operation SOLARIUM; and JCS analysis of defense strategies and priorities.[64]

On October 30, 1953, Eisenhower approved NSC 162/2 as his administration's Basic National Security Policy. This document explored the nature of the Soviet threat, the implications of American alliances and foreign commitments, and the economic ramifications of defense. It concluded that national security required:

1. A strong military posture, with emphasis on the capability of inflicting massive retaliatory damage by offensive striking power;
2. U.S. and allied forces in readiness to move rapidly, initially to counter aggression by Soviet bloc forces, and then to hold vital areas and lines of communication; and
3. A mobilization base, and its protection against crippling damage, adequate to insure victory in the event of general war.[65]

In December 1953 a new three-year defense program reflected these priorities.

Eisenhower's emphasis on massive retaliatory striking power meant that the Air Force would continue to play a central role in national defense. Although the Navy's attack aircraft carriers were an integral part of the nation's offensive striking power, the vast bulk of the nation's air power resided in the Strategic Air Command. By the end of 1953, SAC contained 10 heavy and 25 medium bomb and reconnaissance wings, nearly 23 of which were considered combat-ready, along with 28 refueling squadrons, totaling, in all, over 1500 aircraft, including 1000 nuclear-capable bombers. The propeller-driven medium bomb and reconnaissance force, then converting to the all-jet, 600-mile-per-hour B-47, greatly enhanced SAC striking power.[66] Although the Air Force had borne the brunt of Eisenhower's cuts of five billion dollars in the defense budget during the spring of 1953, the object, the President explained, was not to downgrade SAC, but to get "as much effectual strength as we can immediately" by assuring that all operational wings would be manned and equipped. The Fiscal Years 1954 to 1957 defense program, approved in December 1953, had an ultimate objective of 137 wings. During these three years, the Air Force received an average share of 47 percent of total defense appropriations, compared to 29 percent for the Navy and 22 percent for the Army.[67]

Another element in Eisenhower's nuclear strategy was defense against local aggression, especially in Western Europe. The new strategy would require a manifest willingness to use not only massive retaliatory striking power but also tactical nuclear weapons. By the fall of 1953 the preparation of the tactical nuclear defense of Europe had been under way for nearly two years. In January 1952 the JCS authorized General Eisenhower to plan for the use of a specific number of atomic bombs by Navy and soon to be deployed Air Force tactical air units.[68] One month later, Project VISTA, a scientific and technical study completed by the California Institute of Technology, concluded that "the tactical employment of our atomic weapons resources holds outstanding promise" for defending Western Europe. A draft chapter had even proposed that nuclear weapons be employed initially only in a tactical role, and that the strategic offensive be withheld for humanitarian as well as political and military reasons. General Lauris Norstad, Air Force Commander in Europe, subsequently convinced most of the scientists responsible for the draft (although not the prominent J. Robert Oppenheimer) that tactical nuclear air forces would not be available for several years, and that SAC would be critical in deterring any attack in the interim. The final VISTA report made no mention of SAC's offensive, but emphasized small weapons with yields of one to fifty kilotons, and urged the creation of a Tactical Atomic Air Force that would rival SAC in both professionalism and appropriations.[69]

By 1953, technological advances were rapidly expanding the possibilities for the tactical use of nuclear weapons. The 10,000-pound implosion fission bombs of 1945–1949 were giving way to the 3000-pound Mark 5 and the 2700-pound Mark 7. By 1954 the 1000-pound Mark 12 would be available. Each of these weapons could detonate cores with yields as high as their larger predecessors, and could fit into most existing and planned Air Force fighter bombers and Navy attack planes. In addition, they could become warheads for the Regulus and Honest John surface-to-surface guided missiles, shells for long-range artillery, depth charges for anti-submarine warfare, atomic demolition land mines, and, eventually, warheads for surface-to-air and air-to-air missiles.[70]

Despite the increasing feasibility of tactical nuclear weapons, planners had not fully integrated such weapons into operational plans at the time Eisenhower took office. The reluctance of civilian policymakers to use nuclear weapons in Korea had created doubts in the minds of many military planners as to when, if ever, the government would authorize such use.[71]

NCS 162/2 was the first statement of national policy to address this issue of tactical weapons directly. The first draft, dated September 30, contained only an ambiguous reference to the use of "special weapons" in the interests of national security. The NSC, at its meeting on October 7, strengthened that sentence to read: "In the event of hostilities, the United States will consider nuclear weapons to be as available for use as other munitions." This statement, approved as national policy on October 30, was for the JCS an assurance that they could confidently plan for the use of nuclear weapons in both limited and general conflicts. The December 1953 defense program identified, for the first time, the provision of tactical atomic support for United States or allied military forces in general war or in a local aggression.[72] Over the next few years tactical nuclear weapons increasingly entered into calculations of force requirements and effectiveness. By the late 1950s all unified and specified commanders routinely submitted their requirements for tactical nuclear weapons for inclusion in the overall JCS request for atomic production.[73]

A third element in Eisenhower's nuclear strategy, spelled out in NSC 162/2, sought the defense of the nation's striking force, its mobilization base, and its people. From the beginning of the nuclear age, the problem of direct defense against nuclear attack had appeared all but insurmountable. It was estimated in 1950 that sixteen atomic weapons, if properly targeted, could seriously disrupt the United States government.[74] The Air Force began its initial search for an answer in 1947 with scientific studies of the problems of air and civil defense. It was not until December 1952, however, that President Truman authorized the construction of an early warning radar system, which would provide three to six hours' notice of approaching bombers. One month later he created a special subcommittee of the NSC to "evaluate the net capabilities of the Soviet Union to inflict direct injury on the United States. . . ."[75] The Net Evaluation Subcommittee reported to the NSC on May 18, 1953. Its still-classified findings were reflected in a June 1953 study which stated that the continental defense programs then under way were not now adequate either to prevent, neutralize, or seriously deter the military or covert attacks which the USSR is capable of launching, nor are they adequate to ensure the continuity of government, the continuity of production, or the protection of the industrial mobilization base and millions of citizens in our great and exposed metropolitan centers.

This, the NSC concluded, "constitutes an unacceptable risk to our nation's survival." No defense structure could achieve complete invulnerability, but, the NSC added, "a reasonably effective defense system can and must be obtained." It recommended the expansion of the country's nuclear delivery capability to match the growing Soviet air force, and the development of a defense and early warning system adequate to "prevent disaster, and to make secure the mobilization base necessary to achieve United States victory in the event of general war."[76]

This move to develop a reasonably effective system of continental defense accelerated two months later when the Soviet Union tested a 300- to 400-kiloton fission weapon and announced that it had achieved thermonuclear capability. NSC 162/2 warned that the Soviet Union might soon have the ability to strike a crippling blow against the American industrial base in a surprise attack. Thereafter the Net Evaluation Subcommittee reappeared annually to assess the balance between Soviet and American nuclear capabilities.[77] During the next seven years the Eisenhower administration gave high priority to the completion of radar early-warning networks extending above the Arctic Circle; the development and deployment of conventional and, beginning in 1957, nuclear-armed jet interceptor squadrons and surface-to-air missile batteries throughout the United States; completion of a low frequency analysis and recording sound surveillance system (SOSUS) for the distant detection of submarines; construction of alternate joint and national command posts for the relocation of governmental and military leadership in the event of attack; in which even the President and the Cabinet took part, to test the ability of the government to relocate and continue functioning in an emergency.[78]

Possible nuclear threats to the United States suggested that the nation's defense might force it to initiate war. Although seldom explicitly argued in writing, preventive war was implicit in some major policy deliberations. In the spring of 1953, Eisenhower's top foreign policy advisers rejected a proposal from the SOLARIUM Steering Committee, headed by retired Air Force Reserve General James Doolittle, that they study a fourth policy alternative: giving the Soviet Union two years to agree to terms, with the warning that failure to cooperate might lead to general war. In August 1953 an Air Force study "The Coming National Crisis" raised a similar argument—that soon the United States would find itself in a "militarily unmanageable" position. Before that time arrived, the nation would need to choose whether to trust its future to "the whims of a small group of proven barbarians" in the USSR, or "be militarily prepared to support such decisions as might involve general war."[79]

President Eisenhower and Secretary of State John Foster Dulles discussed preventive war seriously in August 1953. When the Soviet Union acquired thermonuclear weapons, Eisenhower wrote, the United States might find itself vulnerable to a crippling strike. Its only security would then lie in the deterrent effect of its ability "to inflict greater loss against the enemy than he could reasonably hope to inflict upon us." But, added the President,

> if the contest to maintain this relative position should have to continue indefinitely, the cost would either drive us to war—or into some form of dictatorial government. In such circumstances, we would be forced to consider whether or not our duty to future generations did not require us to initiate war at the most propitious moment we could designate.[80]

In March 1954 the NSC approved a new statement of American objectives for general war to replace that in NSC 20/4. The first objective enunciated in the new document, NSC 5410/1, was to "achieve a victory which will insure the survival of the United States." Formal recognition that the nation's survival might be in doubt generated renewed pressures for consideration of preventive war. In May 1954 Eisenhower received a briefing on the JCS's Advance Study Group proposal that the United States consider "deliberately precipitating war with the USSR in the near future," before Soviet thermonuclear capability became a real menace. Army Chief of Staff Matthew Ridgway denounced this course as "contrary to every principle upon which our Nation had been founded" and "abhorrent to the great mass of American people."[81] At this briefing the President did not commit himself, but subsequently in the fall of 1954 approved an updated Basic National Security Policy paper which stated unequivocally that "the United States and its allies must reject the concept of preventive war or acts intended to provoke war."[82]

If preventive war ceased to be a strategic option, preemption appeared both militarily and constitutionally feasible. Warning of a Soviet attack—even a surprise attack—the CIA still calculated in terms of days or even weeks because of the time required to prepare Soviet forces and bases for strikes against the United States. The CIA estimated that, even after the first Soviet strikes, the United States had time to blunt a full attack simply because the Soviets would need up to thirty days to deliver all of their nuclear weapons. Response to an impending or actual strike, Eisenhower told a group of Congressmen in January 1954, would occur as quickly as Congress could meet. In fact, he added, "if you were away and I waited on you (before taking retaliatory action) you'd start impeachment proceedings against me." If war broke out in Western Europe, he told the JCS later that year, the United States would employ tactical nuclear weapons to hold the line, while giving first priority to SAC to blunting the enemy's initial threat. After "averting disaster" in this initial phase, the United States would proceed to mobilize to win the war over an extended period.[83] This scenario required no change in JCS policy. The blunting mission remained the highest targeting priority, followed by retardation of Soviet troop advances and the destruction of the urban industrial base and government control centers. General LeMay, the man who would determine the precise manner in which SAC would fight a war, remained committed to the preemption of the Soviet nuclear delivery capability, believing that if the United States was pushed into a corner it should not hesitate to strike first. By 1953, SAC had identified 409 airfields from which the Soviets could launch nuclear strikes. The next year LeMay proposed the development of a "comprehensive plan for the defeat of Communist air power."[84]

In March 1954, SAC's Basic War Plan called for up to 735 bombers to hit Soviet early-warning screens from all directions simultaneously, using chaff and other electronic countermeasures to overwhelm the Soviet defenses. This single massive blow would strike all designated targets. It would minimize the time American bombers would remain in hostile air space, maximize destruction, and reduce the need for costly follow-up strikes. Given adequate warning time, SAC would execute the basic "optimum" strike plan in full, recognizing the need for options to allow for such variables as aborts, malfunctions, and losses of bases and aircraft to a surprise Soviet attack. Such a combined SAC offensive against military and urban-industrial targets was not necessarily what the President and his top policy advisers had envisaged. In October 1953, JCS Chairman Admiral Arthur Radford unsuccessfully urged the NSC to establish a clear policy for the graduated use of nuclear weapons that gave top priority to the destruction of military forces operating against the United States or its allies, and of the facilities that supported those forces, before launching unrestricted retaliatory operations.[85] In June 1954 Eisenhower expressed his own preference for concentrating on military targets. "If we batter Soviet cities to pieces by bombing," he asked his JCS in June 1954, "what solution do we have to take control of the situation and handle it so as to achieve the objectives for which we went to war?" Eisenhower urged the war planners "to use more imagination in contemplating the best way to fight the next war with the least dislocation to the world."[86]

Eventually the Air Force itself had its critics of the SAC approach to strategic bombing. In 1952 Bernard Brodie had helped prepare a RAND Corporation study which warned that American cities were more vulnerable to thermonuclear attack than those in the Soviet Union and recommended that the nation use the soon-to-be-tested H-bomb strictly in a tactical role to reduce the dangers of escalation. The study received a wide briefing in the Air Staff and the Defense Department, but had little effect. The Air Force, Brodie noted, remained hostile to the notion that it might need to eliminate strategic bombing in the interest of limiting war.[87] But in 1954 other RAND strategists led by James Digby; a number of Air Staff planners including the future head of ballistic missile development, Brigadier General Bernard A. Schriever; and the Evaluation Staff at the Air War College were quietly promoting a "no-cities" strategy, which would focus United States nuclear strikes on Soviet nuclear capability and military forces. Former Air Force Secretary Thomas K. Finletter also advocated this strategy.[88]

Still the Air Force high command continued to favor the combined offensive. In the fall of 1953, the Weapons Systems Evaluation Group completed a year-long assessment of the possible impact of the planned SAC offensive. Countering the arguments put forward by the VISTA report and RAND, WSEG-10 concluded that unless the United States launched strikes against industrial and government control centers, the Soviet Union "could support *immense* armed forces for at least two years of intensive warfare." Even with the successful completion of these strikes, the United States might still require four to six months to stop the flow of fuel and lubricants to Soviet forces in the field. For Air Force planners the possibility that SAC could deliver a single war-winning blow remained the ultimate temptation. Within two years, that capability appeared to be nearly within reach. In the spring of 1954 the United States began testing thermonuclear weapons with yields as high as 15 megatons, a level which both the AEC and the military believed large enough for the foreseeable future.[89] With one of these weapons, which would begin entering the stockpile within the year, SAC could destroy a city, a hardened command center, or an airfield. Such weapons enhanced the possibilities for bonus damage and destruction of multiple targets, factors which were still believed important "in view of the many targets requiring destruction and the limited size of the Strategic Air Command." In June 1955, SAC received the first of its eight-jet B-52 heavy bombers. The B-52, which could carry up to four-megaton-yield bombs over an unrefueled combat radius of 3000 miles at more than 550 miles per hour, would by 1959 replace the lumbering B-36.[90]

SAC's growing independence enhanced its expanded capability. After 1951 General LeMay did not submit his annually updated Basic War Plans, as required, for JCS review, believing that SAC should guard the details of operational planning. In June 1955 Air Force Chief of Staff Nathan Twining sent LeMay a formal request for information on SAC missions, priorities, and concept of operations to facilitate inter-service coordination. That October, LeMay provided a briefing to the JCS and a limited number of summaries of the current plan.

By late 1955 SAC had achieved virtual control over target selection. In October 1954 Army Chief of Staff Ridgway, noting that SAC's target list was not fully consistent with the JSCP list approved by the JCS, urged tighter control over SAC planning. He wrote:

> I consider it imperative that the Joint Chiefs of Staff insure that the great striking power of the Strategic Air Command be employed in accordance with the sound military principle of economy of force and in accordance with a national policy which seeks to attain national objectives without indiscriminate mass destruction of human life.[91]

In April 1955 Ridgway proposed the establishment of a Joint Target Selection and Evaluation Group to achieve this objective. The Joint Staff committees assigned to study his proposal, however, reported back after Ridgway's retirement that joint, Pentagon-based planning had ceased to be feasible because nuclear targets could not be pre-identified. They recommended that two joint committees prepare the damage criteria to guide target selection, but that the acutal selection process belong to the unified and specified commands, including SAC. This recommendation the JCS approved on November 18. Although SAC's target list was still subject to JCS approval, the Joint Staff had neither the time nor the resources to evaluate the finished product thoroughly, especially since SAC had acquired its own IBM 704 computer to analyze and prioritize the increasingly complex target data base. Since none of the other services could duplicate this capability, they found it even more difficult to intervene in target planning and thus interrupt the ongoing bootstrapping process.[92]

V

Expansion of the Soviet nuclear arsenal forced the Eisenhower administration to reevaluate its defense strategy. In March 1954 the President urged the Science Advisory Committee of the Office of Defense Mobilization (ODM) to undertake a study of the problem of a surprise nuclear attack. Modern weapons, he noted, "had made it easier for a hostile nation with a closed society to plan an attack in secrecy and thus gain an advantage denied to the nation with an open society." The Technological Capabilities Panel (TCP), chaired by James R. Killian, Jr., president of the Massachusetts Institute of Technology, undertook a study of this new challenge. The February 1955 report of the TCP, "Meeting the Threat of Surprise Attack," provided an important benchmark in the evolution of Eisenhower's thinking about nuclear strategy. The report focused on the technical aspects of defense and attempted to project a sense of urgency without despair. The Soviet Union already had enough mid-range bombers and bombs of up to one-megaton yield, it concluded, to damage the United States seriously. This threat, it predicted, would expand geometrically as the Soviets acquired true thermonuclear weapons and long-range delivery aircraft. The United States could expect to maintain its strategic superiority for three to five years, but even then it would be vulnerable to a devastating and possibly decisive surprise attack. The report gave highest priority to improved intelligence and tactical warning capabilities and the preparation for instantaneous response, including the use of nuclear-armed air defense missiles. It urged the President to proceed with the dispersion of nuclear weapons to offensive and defensive forces, and to grant "advance authority for the instant use of the atomic warheads wherever needed over the land areas of the United States and Canada."[93]

The TCP report reaffirmed the BRAVO, ROMEO, and DELTA targeting priorities, while stressing the interrelationship between offensive and defensive forces: "Our striking forces must blunt the attack at its source: defense must protect our retaliatory power as well as our people and our cities. Together they provide overall strength and a substantial deterrent to war."[94] Dispersing the bomber force would provide interim protection against surprise attack; but sure survival of the bombers, the TCP concluded, required that they be enroute to their targets before any attack arrived. It warned that the United States must prepare for a period of transition and instability after 1958 or 1960, during which the advantage would rest with whichever side acquired and deployed ballistic missiles in threatening numbers. It urged, therefore, a continued commitment to ballistic missile development. Eisenhower, much impressed by the TCP report, relied increasingly thereafter on the advice of scientists, whom he viewed as honest brokers with regard to the complex and often politicized issues of nuclear strategy.

Another report of February 1955 provided a more detailed analysis of American thermonuclear capability, and raised a disturbing question not addressed by the TCP. What if the United States no longer had the capability to blunt an impending Soviet attack at its source? WSEG-12, a study by the Weapons System Evaluation Group, predicted that the atomic offensive outlined in the JSCP for Fiscal Year 1956 could achieve the ultimate goal of ending a general war in a single blow. It would destroy virtually all Soviet atomic production capability, obliterate 118 out of 134 major cities, cause 60 million deaths, eliminate the Soviet bloc industrial capabilities, and preclude any significant recuperation for at least one year. But WSEG-12 also pointed out that even if SAC destroyed the 645 targeted airfields, there would still be at least 240 remaining where Soviet bombers could survive attack. "To achieve a high degree of assurance of destroying all known Soviet operational and staging bases," the report concluded, "would require an allocation of approximately twice that evaluated." Even these additional bombs and bombers, it added, "cannot prevent the Soviets launching a strike unless we hit first."[95]

This projection that the United States might no longer be able to substantially disarm the Soviet Union assumed a potential, not actual, dispersion of the Soviet bomber force. The problem would emerge inescapably as the size and range of the Soviet force expanded. In May 1955 a National Intelligence Estimate (NIE) set current Soviet medium bomber strength at more than 1300. Some 1100 of these were obsolete TU-4 "Bull" propeller-driven imitations of the B-29, and the rest were "Badger" jet bombers equivalent to the B-47. Planners assumed that all were capable of striking the American targets on one-way missions. The NIE also estimated that the Soviet Union had some 20 "Bear" turbo-prop and 20 "Bison" jet heavy long-range bombers. Much more disturbing was the forecast that the Soviets would have approximately 700 heavy bombers by mid-1959, as well as 700 "Badgers." Advances in weapons technology merely complemented the expanding Soviet delivery capability. In November 1955 a 1.6-megaton test confirmed Soviet achievement of a true two-stage thermonuclear capability.[96] With such weapons the U.S.S.R. could seriously damage the United States even if only a few bombers managed to escape destruction and penetrate American defenses. The "bomber gap" comprised a technological or numerical challenge, but for Eisenhower and the JCS it also represented a serious threat to the country's ability to disarm an impending Soviet strike.

In mid-January 1956 Eisenhower sought to impress on the NSC the appalling "chaos and destruction" the United States would suffer in a thermonuclear war. He urged the NSC to continue to maintain a five-year strategic materials stockpile, believing it was "crazy" to think that any war could be "won or lost in a period of thirty days." Nevertheless, he asked his advisers to consider seriously what would happen when "we reach a point where we will have passed the limits of what human beings can endure." The President's concerns received affirmation in the Net Evaluation Subcommittee report of January 23, 1956, which projected that by mid-1958, even with advance warning, the nation would be virtually defenseless against a devastating Soviet attack. The United States could probably inflict three times as much damage in retaliation, Eisenhower wrote in his diary, but

> there was little we could do during the month of warning in the way of dispersal of population, of industries, or of perfecting defenses that would cut down losses. The only possible way of reducing losses would be for us to take the initiative sometime during the assumed month in which we had the warning of an attack and launch a surprise attack against the Soviets.

Because this would not only violate national tradition but also require rapid, totally secret Congressional action and immediate implementation, he added, the strategy appeared unacceptable.[97]

That the United States might be confronting an enemy which it could virtually destroy, but could not effectively disarm, raised serious questions about massive retaliation as national defense strategy. Eisenhower, despite his increasing pessimism regarding the outcome of a general war, responded to the challenge by strengthening rather than revising his scenario for nuclear exchange. During the winter and spring of 1956 he took steps to bring United States force structures more clearly into line with a policy of instant nuclear response, and sought more explicit NSC endorsement of such a strategy. In April he proposed a $500-million supplemental defense appropriation to expand B-52 production from 17 to 20 a month. Although there might be no winners in a thermonuclear war, the President told his JCS, "we don't want to lose any worse than we have to."[98]

From the beginning the JCS had divided over the concept of massive retaliation and, in particular, what force structure could effectively implement it. The four-day marathon of August 1953 aboard the yacht *Sequoia*, during which the Chiefs hammered out the New Look in defense policy, succeeded more as a result of exhaustion than real consensus. To what degree, the JCS debated, should the United States rely on strategic air power to achieve its national security objectives? From 1953 until his retirement in 1955, Army Chief of Staff Ridgway argued repeatedly that the country should place greater emphasis on the problems of limited conflicts and the need for conventional forces. General Maxwell Taylor, his successor, took up this argument even more forcefully.[99]

By January 1956, primarily as a result of Army dissents, the JCS again disagreed over strategy. In late January, determined to unify the Chiefs behind the President's policy, Secretary of Defense Charles Wilson requested a new three-year statement of force requirements and strategy to replace the 1953 New Look. This statement was to reflect the assumptions, approved by Eisenhower, that "if general war should be forced upon us, the United States will employ atomic weapons from the outset of hostilities." The country would employ them in lesser conflicts if it appeared militarily advantageous to do so.[100] Taylor argued that these assumptions were inconsistent with both national interest and national policy despite Eisenhower's admonishments that the JCS must achieve consensus on such critical issues.

On March 15, 1956, the NSC adopted a revised statement of basic national security policy which called for flexibility and emphasized the importance of containing limited conflicts, but ultimately deferred to presidential prerogative in establishing nuclear strategy. NSC 5602/1 declared that nuclear weapons "will be used in general war and in military operations short of general war as authorized by the President." It again rejected preventive war but affirmed the national determination to prevail in a general war. Most significant, it anticipated the need for pre-authorization for the use of nuclear weapons. "Such authorization as may be given in advance," it stated simply, "will be determined by the President." On March 30, Eisenhower met with the JCS to explain his interpretation of this policy statement. He ruled that any war which involved Russian troops directly against United States forces or the United States would be a general war, to be met by launching SAC and by requesting Congress to declare war.[101]

Taylor met, on May 24, 1956, with Eisenhower to argue for modification of this strategy. By 1960, he argued, both the United States and the U.S.S.R. would have such large thermonuclear stockpiles that the greatest danger then would lie in the possible escalation of an initially small conflict into a massive struggle. By focusing on the "worst case" scenario of a full-scale nuclear exchange, the United States seemed to be preparing for the least likely eventuality and freezing out conventional forces needed to contain limited conflicts. Taylor urged the President to reconsider the use of nuclear weapons in local conflicts, given the dangers of escalation. Eisenhower remained unconvinced. The use of tactical nuclear weapons would not provoke escalation any more than "twenty-ton block-busters," and he was determined not to let American forces become bogged down in small conventional wars. Taylor's arguments, Eisenhower stated, depended "on an assumption that we are opposed by people who would think as we do with regard to the value of human life." If the Soviets decided to risk a "life and death struggle," they would certainly use atomic weapons at once, "and in full force." The only prudent course would be "to get our striking force into the air immediately upon notice of hostile action by the Soviets." Massive retaliation was the "key to survival."[102]

Recognizing defeat, Taylor abandoned his protest. The President's strategic concepts requiring nuclear response in any general war were incorporated into both the JSCP and JSOP. The Army resigned itself to consequent force reductions, and by September had begun to reorganize some of its combat forces into a "Pentomic" Division to maximize their effectiveness on a nuclear battlefield.[103] To strengthen the American position further, Eisenhower approved a JCS request for increased production of both high-yield thermonuclear weapons and small warheads suitable for air defense. In February 1956, when informed that air defense requirements might absorb a considerable portion of United States nuclear production, the President responded that "nuclear production is now so vast that it may be possible to have everything that is needed." In early 1957 the United States deployed the first MB-1 "Genie" two-kiloton-yield atomic air-to-air missiles; in 1958 it added the nuclear-armed "Nike Hercules" surface-to-air missiles.[104] In April, Eisenhower, it seems, authorized the Air Defense Command to use these missiles immediately in case of surprise attack. The TCP report in 1955 had proposed this type of advance authorization.

In endorsing the JCS production goals for high-yield weapons, Eisenhower overrode strong objections within the JCS to the Air Force weapons requirements. The President justified increased production through 1959 and a leveling off thereafter. He saw merit, however, in the objections to the use of such weapons, and urged the JCS to review their targeting plans to reduce application of thermonuclear weapons "inappropriately against industrial targets of too little overall importance," and to avoid overlapping "of large numbers of large yield weapons on specific targets." Bombs with yields greater than two megatons should be reserved for very special targets, he warned, and targeting should avoid unnecessarily high population-losses.[105] This directive, which reaffirmed Eisenhower's preference for targeting military capability rather than the urban-industrial base, marked the beginning of a serious effort to contain escalating force and weapons requirements during the difficult years ahead.

VI

Intercontinental ballistic missiles (ICBMs) and their projected deployment by the Soviet Union forced President Eisenhower to reevaluate yet another time his scenario for general war. The Soviet missile threat posed a twofold strategic challenge. Because tactical warning of a surprise attack would now be measured in minutes, SAC could scarcely launch its bombers before the attack arrived. Ballistic missiles, moreover, would be very difficult to locate and destroy. In coming to grips with these challenges, the Eisenhower administration faced a series of crucial decisions between 1957 and 1961. How should the United States deal with bomber force vulnerability? What types and numbers of ballistic missile systems should it authorize? How should it base and target these missiles for preemptive or retaliatory attacks? During these four years, planners repeatedly proposed alternatives to the planned SAC offensive. Eisenhower often agreed in principle to the recommended limitations, but ultimately rejected them.

All three services had worked on missile development after World War II, although progress through 1950 faced the Truman administration's budget ceilings. Many doubted, futhermore, that the United States could develop missiles capable of delivering the large and heavy weapons then in production, or that such missiles would have the accuracy necessary to destroy specific targets. The Korean war rearmament program, with its two- to four-year time frame, facilitated development of Army and Navy air defense missiles and atomic armed tactical ballistic and cruise missiles, but gave little impetus to the ICBM. The successful test of a true thermonuclear weapon in October 1952, portending yields high enough to compensate for poor accuracy and assuring the warhead weight reductions predicted by the AEC, now improved prospects for the ICBM. In December an Air Force ad hoc committee, to facilitate missile development, recommended the reduction of accuracy requirements from 1500 feet to one mile, and the lowering of warhead weight from 10,000 to 3000 pounds. Eisenhower's cuts in the Air Force budget prevented an immediate follow-up on these recommendations.[106]

In November 1953, during the adoption of New Look, Trevor Gardner, special assistant for research and development to Secretary of the

Air Force, established the Strategic Missiles Evaluation Committee. Its report of February 1954 and a concurrent RAND Corporation study projected that the country could deploy an ICBM by 1960 or soon after if the government broadened yield, payload, and accuracy requirements; allocated additional funds; and gave the entire program high priority. The report of the Technological Capabilities Panel, the result of a Gardner briefing, gave crucial support to ballistic missile programs. The TCP emphasized the importance of maintaining the United States technological lead over the Soviet Union and recommended accelerated development of both land-based ICBMs and land- and sea-based Intermediate Range Ballistic Missiles (IRBMs), all armed with megaton warheads. By the end of 1955, the Army, Navy, and Air Force had each organized an IRBM development program, and these, along with the Air Force ICBM effort, received highest national priority.[107]

Eisenhower supported these programs, but he retained serious reservations. In December 1956 the President informed the JCS that he did not value ballistic missiles as military weapons and had only approved the acceleration recommended by the TCP because of the "psychological importance" of the new technology. He did not foresee the need for a large missile force once the nation proved it could master the technology; bombers would be the mainstay of SAC for ten years or more, especially since the United States already possessed large bomber forces. Secretary of Defense Charles E. Wilson proposed, and Eisenhower apparently concurred, that 150 well-targeted missiles might be sufficient.[108]

In 1956 the Air Force began to address the problem of bomber force vulnerability and the need to recognize the drastically reduced tactical warning time. As early as 1951 the RAND Corporation had inaugurated a series of studies for the Air Staff on "the effectiveness of our strike force under surprise attack." The first reports focused on the problem of protecting overseas bases and produced the Air Force's decision to use such bases only for pre- and post-strike refueling.[109] In 1956, echoing the findings of the TCP report, RAND analysts warned that bombers based in the United States might also be in danger of air or even missile attack, and recommended improvements in early warning systems and SAC response time, dispersal of the bomber force, and more effective airfield defenses. In response, SAC moved to construct or acquire additional bases in the United States and Canada. It conducted a series of tests from November 1956 through September 1957 to evaluate the human and material requirements of holding one-third of the bomber force on fifteen-minute "ground alert."[110]

Responding to growing concern about national vulnerability, the Federal Civil Defense Administration in the spring of 1957 proposed an ambitious $32- to $50-billion civil defense program. At the request of the NSC, the ODM Science Advisory Committee formed the Security Resources Panel to analyze the merits of the proposal. The chairman of the panel, H. Rowan Gaither, a long-time RAND trustee and adviser, subsequently requested and received permission to expand the scope of the study to include the entire question of national defense in the ballistic missile era.[111] The President received the final report of the Gaither Committee, "Deterrence and Survival in the Nuclear Age," in November, and the NSC, three days later. It expressed only moderate support for fallout shelters, and, instead, assigned highest priority to the improvement of SAC's survivability. To protect the American people, the report concluded, the country required an effective deterrent in the form of a secure and effective retaliatory striking force. It warned that "by 1959 the U.S.S.R. may be able to launch an attack with ICBMs carrying megaton warheads against which SAC will be almost completely vulnerable under present programs." It urged the reduction of SAC reaction time, improved tactical warning, increased bomber dispersion, and improved active and passive airfield defenses. It also recommended further acceleration of the ballistic missile programs, with particular emphasis on the Polaris-submarine-launched IRBM because of its advantages of mobility and reduced vulnerability. Three committee members, the President was informed privately, had advocated reconsideration of the option of preventive war as a means of avoiding a situation of extreme jeopardy. [112]

Eisenhower responded to the Gaither Committee briefing cautiously. It was his belief, he stated, that many were overestimating the threat, and that Soviet ballistic missile technology was not progressing as fast as planners had projected. For at least the next five years, he said, "aircraft would still be the primary means of carrying out destruction, and during this period we have the capability of delivering the greater blow." He agreed that ballistic missile development programs were essential and that SAC response-time required some reduction to sustain the possibility of retaliation. "We must not allow the enemy," he said after the briefing, "to strike the first blow." R. C. Sprague, the chairman of the Gaither steering committee, who had conducted his own highly secret investigation of SAC readiness, briefed Eisenhower on the following day. Sprague reported that SAC had not yet implemented a ground alert, and on a particular, randomly selected day "not a single plane could have left the ground within six hours except for a few that were by chance in the air on a test at the time." In an actual surprise attack, the United States could probably count on launching only 50 to 150 large weapons, and these would be totally inadequate to achieve a substantial retaliatory attack.[113]

Despite its political volatility, the Gaither report was more a symptom than a cause of change. Eisenhower believed that the United States was facing a gradual deterioration of strategic advantage, as forecast by the TCP report, but not an immediate crisis. "Until an enemy [has] enough operational capability to destroy most of our bases simultaneously and thus prevent retaliation by us," he stated in February 1958, "our deterrent remains effective." Recalling the illusory "bomber gap" dissipated by U-2 reconnaissance, the President was skeptical of the 1958 National Intelligence Estimates, which projected 100 Soviet ICBMs by mid-1959 or 1960, and 500 by 1963; subsequent estimates suggested that his doubts were justified. Unfortunately, the "missile gap," despite Eisenhower's efforts to dispel it, would become an exploitable political issue for Democratic presidential hopefuls, and would not prove to be an illusion until the first Discoverer and SAMOS satellites documented the minuscule size of Soviet missile capability in 1960–61.[114]

Eisenhower's approach to protecting United States bombers in the missile age was not to increase their survivability on the ground, but to ensure that they would be in the air at the time of any surprise attack. The government did not implement the program of bomber blast-shelters recommended by the Gaither Committee, and from 1957 on it reduced airfield defense programs such as air defense missiles, interceptors, and survivable command and control systems. On the other hand, it made a concerted effort to increase tactical warning time and rapid response. In January 1958 Defense Secretary Neil McElroy approved the development of the Ballistic Missile Early Warning System (BMEWS) to complement the Distant Early Warning Line activated in August 1957. Construction began on BMEWS stations in England, Greenland, and Canada. In 1958, development work commenced as well on the Midas early warning satellite.[115] To reduce reaction time further, Eisenhower, on May 22, 1957, issued an authorization, still classified, for the employment of nuclear weapons. This apparently went beyond the air defense authorization of the previous year, and gave permission for an immediate nuclear response under a variety of emergency conditions. So complex were the instructions needed to implement this authorization that the departments of Defense and State did not approve it until February 17, 1959. At about the same time other Emergency Action Documents, including possibly a secret executive order covering the transfer of nuclear weapons from the AFC to the military and their subsequent utilization, began to appear. Finally, in late 1960, each of the unified and specified commanders received a series of still classified directives regarding the immediate use of nuclear weapons.[116]

Some personnel and technological changes also reduced SAC response time. In 1959, SAC achieved its goal of holding one-third of the bomber force on ground alert. It added more bomber crews, restructured maintenance schedules, and redesigned runway approach ramps.[117] On March 1, 1958, the Chief of Staff of the Air Force authorized SAC to implement the "fail safe" or "positive control" system, which would permit rapid response without the risk of initiating war through miscalculation. Bombers would take off at the first sign of a Soviet strike and proceed along Emergency War Plan routes toward their targets, but their missions would be aborted at a pre-specified point unless they received the "go" code to continue. SAC pushed ahead with its plans to establish an airborne alert consisting of one-fourth of the B-52 force. In 1959, the JCS approved the airborne alert in principle, but because of the considerable cost of continuous operations, recommended that it be put into operation only when the President considered such special precautions necessary.[118]

Advance in weapons design greatly facilitated the development of SAC alert plans. Through the mid-1950s, crews could not insert the fission cores used to fuel atomic weapons and to initiate the fusion reaction in two-stage thermonuclear bombs until immediately before take-off or in flight. The new "sealed pit" advanced bomb design, which contained smaller amounts of high explosives and fissionable material, solved this problem. The sealed-pit weapons were efficient, lightweight, high-yield thermonuclear bombs, equipped with safety devices which reduced the risk of inadvertent detonation to almost zero. They could be stored fully assembled in alert bombers, or atop ballistic missiles, for long periods without substantial maintenance, permitting almost instantaneous response. By 1959 the majority of weapons assigned to SAC were of sealed-pit design.[119]

SAC delivery capability continued to expand. At its peak in 1959, SAC had nearly 500 B-52s, more than 2500 B-47s, and over 1000 propeller and jet-driven tanker aircraft. Development was under way on the supersonic B-58, which would enter service in August 1960, and on the proposed follow-on to the B-52, the Mach 3 B-70 "Valkyrie." As recommended by the TCP report, the Air Force was pressing for the development of a nuclear powered bomber with unlimited range. This growth of the bomber force remained linked to expanding target lists. The SAC target list totaled 2,997 in 1956, and 3,261 in early 1957. By the end of the decade, SAC had analyzed over 20,000 potential Soviet-bloc targets, grouping the most important of these into Desired

Ground Zeros consistent with the blast radii of large-yield thermonuclear weapons. Expansion of the list resulted largely from the identification of additional "counterforce" targets, especially airfields and suspected missile sites, and to the poor quality of target intelligence that encouraged creative guesswork. The most sophisticated intelligence-gathering system, the U-2 program initiated in 1956 in response to the TCP recommendations, apparently involved only 20 or 30 deep-penetration overflights of the Soviet Union, mostly between 1956 and 1958. Because the program was under CIA control, the Air Force could not dictate the timing or routing of these flights to maximize their usefulness for target identification or verification.[120]

VII

SAC's command of the proposed strategic offensive, added to the vulnerability of land-based bombers, led eventually to a concerted JCS effort to break the bootstrapping dynamic. In the spring of 1957, possibly responding to the President's 1956 directive, Army Chief of Staff Taylor and Chief of Naval Operations Arleigh Burke instructed their staffs to prepare a joint analysis of high-yield weapons requirements, focusing on the radiation and fallout that would follow any implementation of the SAC war plan. On August 28, 1957, the hastily prepared but devastating critique, code-named Project BUDAPEST, reached the JCS. It demonstrated that far more weapons were being assigned to targets than were needed to achieve the damage required by the JSCP, and that the resulting radiation and fallout would be dangerously and unnecessarily high. Blast radii were huge, and there were as many as seventeen overlaps on a single location. Additional and duplicate weapons had been assigned in profusion, even when the supplemental damage they would achieve was minimal. Air Force leaders—including Nathan Twining, who had recently become JCS Chairman; his successor as Air Force Chief of Staff, Thomas White; and the new Air Force Vice Chief, Curtis LeMay—were incensed by this indictment. White ridiculed the Army and Navy for proposing that SAC should seek to do any less than the maximum damage. Every additional gallon of fuel oil destroyed, he declared, could otherwise help carry another Russian bomber toward the United States.[121]

Navy's participation in Project BUDAPEST marked a significant shift in interservice alignment that was to have far-reaching implications. Through 1957, Navy spokesmen had generally acquiesced in the Eisenhower administration's emphasis on the strategic air offensive as the keystone of national defense. Although many continued to doubt the feasibility, effectiveness, and even morality of attacking urban-industrial targets as the opening move in a general war, their efforts to change this strategy were relatively muted. Unlike the Army, the Navy could meet most of its priority budgeting needs within the context of massive retaliation, since the Eisenhower administration counted carrier task forces as part of the nation's offensive striking power. Unhappy with the SAC war plan, but unable to propose any real alternative, Navy leaders directed the expanding, carrier-based, nuclear delivery forces against targets directly or indirectly of naval interest, such as ports, shipbuilding facilities, submarine pens, and naval airfields. Despite counterproposals, they left the bulk of the national retaliatory mission to SAC.[122]

The Polaris sea-based IRBM provided the Navy a major weapon for strategic innovation. In 1955 a joint Army-Navy effort to develop a liquid-fueled missile that could be based on land or on surface ships followed the recommendations of the TCP report. By the fall of 1956, Navy leaders, especially Arleigh Burke, were convinced that a submarine-launched IRBM was possible because of promising experiments with solid-fuel propulsion and the prospective development of a new generation of lightweight thermonuclear warheads weighing as little as 600 pounds, with yields approaching one megaton. In December 1956 the Navy withdrew from the joint Army-Navy effort, and initiated the Polaris program. The following month the objective of deploying, by 1965, a nuclear-powered submarine armed with 1500-mile IRBMs received approval.[123]

Some Navy planners believed that the service should stake out a claim in the area of strategic bombing in response to "unremitting attempts by the Air Force to exercise absolute control over all air operations." The submarine-based IRBM—a January 1957 study noted—was more invulnerable to surprise attack than any other system under consideration and thus could make a major contribution to the national deterrent mission.[124] The Gaither report's concern over SAC vulnerability accelerated Navy efforts to present Polaris as an alternative to land-based bombers or missiles. By November 1957, Navy planners were actively promoting the idea that Polaris might provide an "interim emergency capability for all-out deterrence" to "fill the gap between the Soviet ICBM and our own counterpart" and become the ultimate national deterrent. In November 1957 the government accelerated the development schedule to produce a deployed Polaris system with 1200-mile missiles by 1961.[125]

Building on the findings of Project BUDAPEST and taking advantage of revelations regarding SAC vulnerability, Army and Navy leaders in the fall of 1957 mounted a major assault on established patterns of nuclear war planning. If a substantial portion of the American bomber force were destroyed in a surprise attack, they argued, a massive retaliatory strike against all targets in the Soviet Union would be impossible. The existing JSCP guidance regarding nuclear targeting was thus only applicable to situations in which general war began gradually or with enough strategic warning to permit SAC to launch its strike before the Soviet attack arrived. The United States needed alternative guidance to provide for the possibility of general war initiated under disadvantageous conditions. The alternative planning would require that each unified and specified commander "select from his target list those high priority targets which would be attacked if only 25 percent of his atomic delivery forces would be available for employment." Strategists would assign the minimum number of weapons necessary to achieve at least moderate damage to each target to ensure the most efficient use of depleted resources. SAC would target nuclear delivery capability only to the "extent profitable" on the assumption that much of that capability would already have been expended.[126]

This "alternative undertaking" would supplement rather than replace existing guidance and target lists. The government would implement the plan only if the JCS determined that American forces had been sufficiently depleted to make execution of the "primary undertaking" impossible. Nevertheless, the change had far-reaching implications. It introduced into JCS guidance for the first time the concept of a strictly retaliatory nuclear strategy which would necessitate the preparation of a list of high-priority targets. Although Air Force leaders could not deny the need to prepare for the possibility of a devastating Soviet surprise attack, they were justifiably concerned that the Army and Navy might eventually substitute the "alternative undertaking" for existing guidance, and break the lucrative link between expanding Soviet nuclear delivery capability and SAC force requirements. After a heated paper debate, the JCS approved criteria for the alternative undertaking in early 1958. Preparation of the new target lists, however, proceeded slowly.[127]

Army and Navy efforts to place limits on the proposed strategic nuclear offensive reflected, in large measure, a shared concern that United States security required greatly improved capabilities for limited conflict. In the spring of 1958, during the annual review of the NSC statement of Basic National Security Policy, Army Chief of Staff Taylor renewed his 1956 argument that the nation should redirect its resources toward the problem of limited war. This time Taylor's position received the backing of both the Navy and the Marine Corps and went forward to the NSC as the JCS majority view. Secretary of State John Foster Dulles by this time also supported revision of national policy to place greater emphasis on preparation for local conflicts. Massive retaliation, he argued, had all but outlived its usefulness as an instrument of national policy; expanded naval and conventional forces alone could meet situations such as the recent Suez crisis. President Eisenhower, however, overruled any significant modification of current policy. An increase in conventional forces, he told the NSC on May 1, 1958, would mean either increased defense spending, or reduced strategic forces. He was unwilling to consider the first alternative, since larger military budgets would eventually lead to "what is euphemistically called a controlled economy, but which in effect would be a garrison state."[128] He would cut strategic forces only after a careful analysis of what would constitute a minimum adequate deterrent and retaliatory capability. The President urged the NSC to give further attention to this extremely critical question.

Eisenhower's interest in identifying minimum force requirements emerged as policy the following fall. Some time during the spring of 1958 the President apparently approved a proposal to have the NESC supplement its current evaluation of net capabilities with a study of what level of force applied against urban-industrial targets would destroy the Soviet capability to make war.[129] In November 1958 Eisenhower's new special assistant for national security affairs, Gordon Gray, reported that the NESC analysis had shown that targeting an urban industrial/military mix, with the emphasis on the urban-industrial component, would result "in effective paralysis with fewer weapons and less kilotonnage" than would be required to blunt Soviet nuclear delivery capability. Gray proposed that the NESC follow up this analysis with a more detailed study of the relative effectiveness and cost of alternative targeting systems. This would support the then current top-secret NSC Planning Board review of United States war objectives and would prove invaluable in estimating future force requirements, since the United States could not separate the question of effective deterrence from the question of war objectives and military targets. The President, Gray reported, expressed doubt that the United States could plan effectively against the possibility of mutual devastation but approved the idea. On November 20 he formally asked the NSC to provide an appraisal of the relative merits of alternative retaliatory efforts directed toward primarily military targets or an optimum mix of a combined military-urban industrial targets. The study was to consider the requirements of a counterforce capacity and how it would relate to the alternative target lists.[130]

Eisenhower accepted the conclusion that the United States could, if it chose, deliver a decisive war-winning blow against Soviet cities and had begun to question the necessity of trying to maintain a complete counterforce capability. In December 1958 he challenged the need for further U-2 target indentification flights, saying that the country had already located adequate targets. In January 1959, when planners asked his approval for the construction of a replacement plutonium production reactor at Hanford, Washington, the President observed that military estimates of weapons requirements were grossly inflated. "They are trying," he said, "to get themselves into an incredible position of having enough to destroy every conceivable target all over the world, plus a three-fold reserve." In the early 1950s, he recalled, the JCS had believed that destroying only 70 targets would be enough to defeat the Soviet Union. Lacking a clear definition of what would constitute an adequate minimum striking force, however, he could see no basis for denying the request.[131]

In February 1959 Gray reported that the instructions to the NESC were ready. Disagreement with the JCS on the structure of the study had delayed the report. JSC Chairman Twining had worked out a compromise in consultation with Gray and Defense Secretary McElroy. The new approach considered three alternative target systems instead of two: primarily military, primarily urban-industrial (proposed by the Army and Navy), and an optimum mix of the two. It would analyze each system in terms of the effort that the country would require not simply to deter war, but to achieve the objective of prevailing in a general war. This modification, made over Air Force objections, embodied the assumption that there was no logical link between target selection and deterrence, since deterrence depended on Soviet perceptions and the Soviet Union was not privy to American target lists. One of the three lists would serve as the pattern for future planning. Eisenhower considered the analysis so sensitive that he approved the assignment of the study, not to the NESC itself, but to the NESC staff under the direction of Army Lieutenant General Thomas Hickey.[132]

The JCS debates that surrounded the operation of the Hickey committee demonstrated a significant maturation of opposing strategic doctrines. After 1957, Navy leaders evolved a sophisticated strategy to exploit the flexibility and invulnerability of Polaris. In July 1958 Admiral Burke laid out the basic elements of this concept, which came to be known as "finite deterrence." All-out war, he wrote, "is obsolete as an instrument of national policy." As long as the United States had been able to disarm the Soviet Union, it had made sense to maintain a striking force capable of achieving this objective. But a deployed

Soviet ICBM force, sited in unknown locations, would render the American blunting or disarming mission impossible and hence meaningless. Simultaneously, it would make United States land-based forces vulnerable, thus inviting surprise attack and encouraging open-ended expansion of these forces to compensate for their lack of survivability. To harden and defend land-based forces would involve considerable expense and would motivate the Soviet Union to increase its nuclear fire-power until it could engage in "fortress busting." A better alternative, Burke argued, would be a mobile and concealed striking force. This would discourage an arms race because, he said, "numbers of missiles will avail the enemy nothing, if he does not know the location of his target." Most important, a secure striking force would provide United States strategists the necessary time to think by eliminating the pressure to strike first in order to avoid being disarmed. The United States could choose to respond gradually and selectively to an attack and "apply political coercion, if we like, to gain national objectives more advantageous than simple revenge." This strategy would require a small force adequate for deterrence alone (i.e., for an ability to destroy major urban areas). Once this force was in place, the United States could achieve a stable thermonuclear stalemate. This would eliminate the pressure to expand the nuclear arsenals and channel the competition into more limited and manageable arenas.[133]

Navy strategists, by the summer of 1959, had further refined finite deterrence. In September, Burke submitted a formal statement of Navy thinking to the JCS. The age of missiles, he argued, was in some ways comparable to the age of artillery, except that with land-based systems "the artillery battleground will be expanded to include the homeland of the belligerents." Sea-basing would remove the primary targets in the continental United States. It would be injudicious, after suffering a surprise attack, Burke argued, "to launch the remainder of our greatly depleted forces against a primary target system of empty bases and missile sites, even though we should know their location, which we probably won't." The most appropriate retaliatory targeting system would be political and military command and control centers, as well as critical industries.[134] The Navy projected a fleet of 45 submarines, with 29 deployed at all times, capable of destroying 232 Soviet targets or all of Russia. The total cost of such a program would be $7 to $8 billion with an annual operating cost of $350 million. This proposal, Budget Director Maurice Stans remarked, raised the obvious question as to why the United States needed "other IRBMs or ICBMs, SAC aircraft, and overseas bases." Navy leaders agreed, but were in no position to propose the virtual elimination of SAC. That, they told Stans, "was somebody else's problem."[135]

Finite deterrence and the implicit corollary that Polaris should eventually replace SAC posed a serious challenge to the Air Force. In response to an Air Staff request for a "factual and unbiased assessment," the RAND Corporation, in October 1958, produced its own analysis of the usefulness of the Polaris system. The report pointed out that the Navy would need to correct certain technical problems, particularly in the areas of communications and missile accuracy, but that Polaris promised to have both the longest useful wartime life because of its low vulnerability and the shortest response time from command to weapon-impact of any system currently under development.[136] Unable to fault Polaris technically, Air Force leaders challenged the Navy on strategic grounds by preparing a systematic defense of counterforce targeting. An adequate deterrent, General White argued in early 1959 during JCS discussions of the planned NESC study, would require American capability to neutralize Russia's military strength whenever strategic warning of an impending attack permitted such a response. If there were no warning, he said, the United States must be prepared to destroy any remaining Soviet offensive strength. Without that capability the country could not preserve its own security or maintain a credibile deterrent to attacks on its allies. Finite deterrence would not discourage limited Soviet aggression, protect the nation adequately in the event of a surprise attack, or keep the option of preemption open in cases of gradual escalation. The United States, White concluded, required forces adequate to maintain the initiative under all circumstances of war.[137] In May 1959, General White approved an estimate of future force objectives necessary to implement the Air Force strategy. It predicted that, by 1963, some 8400 Soviet targets would require destruction; by 1970, over 10,000. Since multiple weapons would of necessity be assigned to each Desired Ground Zero (DGZ) in order to achieve the 90 percent destruction specified in Air Force war plans, the United States would require by 1968 a force of 3000 Minutemen, 150 Atlas, and 110 Titan ICBMs, as well as a combined total of nearly 900 B-52, B-58, B-70 and nuclear-powered bombers.[138]

VIII

RAND analysts Herbert Goldhamer and Andrew Marshall produced, in April 1959, a sophisticated model for evaluating the comparative utility of alternative retaliatory strategies. This study focused on methods whereby the United States, for the next two years, could limit damage to itself. The conception of nuclear war as "mutual and sudden suicide," they argued, worked against a careful analysis of the "intrawar process," which would probably involve a complex series of strikes and counterstrikes.

> It is certainly not true, as certain publicistic and man-in-the-street reactions seem to imply, that once war comes "it makes no difference" what one does (which in effect is perilously close to saying it makes no difference whether ten, twenty, forty, eighty or more million Americans die or whether the United States retains or does not retain its political independence). There are few things so bad that not thinking about them won't make them worse.

To limit damage to the United States and exclude the possibility of an American first strike, Goldhamer and Marshall concluded that targeting Soviet population centers would be the least effective strategy, while the most effective would be to focus on counterforce targets, using high-yield weapons with ground bursts to produce high civilian casualties. Since population attacks would take precedence only if SAC had been damaged so seriously as to make counterforce attacks impossible, Goldhamer and Marshall cautioned, any exclusive attacks on population centers might be interpreted, not unjustly, as a confession of weakness. They also proposed serious consideration of a strategy of "partial withholding," launching only a portion of surviving SAC forces against selected targets, while threatening the destruction of Soviet cities unless the Soviet Union agreed to American terms. This would have the advantage of extending the pre-war deterrent threat into the intrawar period and might terminate the nuclear exchange.[139]

Beginning with the work of Bernard Brodie in the early 1950s, RAND analysts had periodically produced arguments for a "no cities" strategy with few positive responses from Air Force leaders. The damage-limiting counterforce concept, however, generated considerable interest. Brigadier General Noel F. Parrish and Lieutenant Colonel Donald F. Martin of the office of the Deputy Chief of Staff became convinced, on the basis of their own analysis, that the Air Force should be studying "no cities"/counterforce options. Early in 1960, persuaded by their arguments, Chief of Staff White authorized Parrish to direct a computerized war game of alternative targeting strategies, based on projected United States and Soviet bomber, ballistic missile, and defensive capabilities into the mid-1960s. Over the following year, aided by RAND strategist William W. Kaufmann and others, Parrish was able to demonstrate that a strategy in which the United States concentrated all available resources on the counterforce mission was likely to minimize damage to both the United States and the Soviet Union, and might leave the United States in a position to negotiate a successful conclusion to the war, provided that it could still hold Soviet cities hostage. The Soviet Union was likely to strike United States cities during a surprise attack, Parrish argued, since its immediate objective would be to destroy retaliatory capability. Soviet strikes against cities, however, would inevitably follow any American destruction of Soviet population centers during either a first or second strike. If this occurred, United States losses would be so heavy that the nation would be totally destroyed, even though it might technically have "won" the war. Impressed by these arguments, White encouraged discussion of the "no cities" concept within the Air Staff, and in August 1960 Vice Chief LeMay convened a special New Approach Group to explore this and other alternatives to established strategic approaches. SAC commander Thomas Power, however, who had succeeded LeMay in 1957, was unaffected by the paper analyses flowing from Santa Monica and Washington and continued to prepare for the combined attack on Soviet military and urban industrial targets for which his command had been planning and training since 1950.[140]

In March 1960 the Air Force Intelligence Directorate completed a detailed analysis of targeting requirements to support the 1960–70 force objectives approved by White the previous May. The target planners estimated that there would be a total of 3,560 targets in 1960, 6300 in 1965, and 6,955 in 1970, reflecting the projected increase in Soviet missile sites. The three largest groups of targets focused on Soviet air defenses and the prevention of nuclear attacks on the United States and its allies. A fourth group, apparently earmarked for the tactical air forces, proposed to halt Soviet land and sea operations, while the fifth and smallest group aimed at the disruption of war support and recuperation capability of Soviet industry. This targeting system justified explicitly the emphasis on counterforce targets. The Air Force rejected the Army and Navy argument that "deterrence is the sole objective," and that counterforce had become too costly in the missile age. The Air Force position is "based on the fact that it [counterforce] is national policy and on the contention that there is no satisfactory alternative."[141]

To contain the Navy's strategic challenge, Air Force leaders had no choice but to integrate Polaris into the nation's other strategic forces. In November 1958, SAC Chief Power proposed, in the interests of coordination, that SAC should receive control of the Polaris force. The Air Force formally submitted such a proposal to the JCS in April 1959. "It is essential," White wrote, "that all weapon systems directed toward accomplishment of the strategic mission be planned for and controlled in a manner which will permit our over-all strategic effort to achieve the necessary effect in the minimum time." To accomplish this required a United States Strategic Command under the commander of SAC. Once the Strategic Command was in place, SAC would transfer its functions and staff to the new Command. When asked about this proposal, a high ranking naval officer remarked: "Polaris is perhaps the most attractive missile system under development. . . . Of course they want control of Polaris. But they will have to walk over a prostrate Arleigh Burke to get it."[142] The disestablishment of SAC was an appealing idea, Burke wrote in his formal response to the JCS, but the concept of placing Polaris under a centralized command was "militarily unsound, and unsupportable by analysis and logic." Polaris operations required integration with those of other naval forces and could not be entrusted to commanders unfamiliar with operations at sea. There was, furthermore, no need for a new structure to coordinate Polaris and SAC operations, since the Navy would use its missiles selectively against "a relatively stable target system which readily lends itself to preplanning."[143]

To complicate matters further, on June 1, 1959, Army Chief of Staff Taylor, shortly before his retirement, proposed that target intelligence and planning be "withdrawn from the jurisdiction and organization framework of the USAF and vested in a Joint Target Support Agency" under direct JCS control. The 1955 arrangement, he argued, had not succeeded. Nor would it succeed, he warned, as long as a single service controlled and managed it. The JCS and the Air Force countered with proposals that operational and planning functions go to joint agencies, while target intelligence remain in the Air Force. In October the JCS deferred action on this issue.[144] By then the sheer number of forces involved in atomic operations had created serious command, control, and communication problems, even without the added complications of a Polaris fleet. JCS Chairman Twining observed that the "atomic coordination machinery" needed a major overhaul, but that the JCS were too divided to support any workable proposals. What was required was a "command decision." In August 1959 Twining sent Secretary of Defense McElroy his assessment of "Target Coordination and Associated Problems," and his proposed solutions. Although this memo did not produce immediate action, it laid the groundwork for the establishment of the Joint Strategic Target Planning Staff the following year.

As early as 1952 the United States had established Joint Coordination Centers in Great Britain and Hawaii to coordinate the operations of atomic-capable forces in war. After 1955 the unified and specified commanders met annually at the Pentagon for "Worldwide Coordination Conferences" to review target lists and war plans for inconsistencies and duplication before submitting them to the JCS for approval. Recent war games had indicated that in some 2400 current targets there were still 300 duplications. These could result in "fratricidal" kills of friendly aircraft under chaotic wartime conditions. It was apparent, Twining wrote, that atomic operations must be pre-planned for automatic execution. The solution, Twining believed, lay in a clear national targeting policy, presumably based on the forthcoming recommendations of the Hickey committee study. Since SAC had the most experience in nuclear war planning, the best computer resources, and the bulk of the nuclear delivery forces, SAC would be responsible for preparing the target list and operational plan. To integrate Polaris into this arrangement, an appropriate nucleus of naval officers would join the SAC staff. This approach, Twining believed, would establish a clear framework, subject to objective analysis, to resolve the conflict over targeting and coordination.[145]

Twining preferred the "optimum mix" targeting strategy, which combined counterforce targets with control centers, war-sustaining resources, and population centers. The Hickey committee endorsed this concept. Their February 1960 report recommended a target list for Fiscal Year 1962 consisting of 2,021 targets, including 121 ICBM sites, 140 air defense bases, 200 bomber bases, 218 military and govenmental control centers, and 124 other military targets, such as naval bases and nuclear weapons facilities, with the remaining targets located primarily within 131 urban centers. The list had emerged from SAC methods of analysis and clearly endorsed SAC's basic strategy. The committee had implicitly rejected both no-cities counterforce and finite deterrence and had opted for combining a decisive blow against Soviet will and capability with a blunting attack on Soviet nuclear delivery capability. The Hickey target list was similar in composition to the Air Intelligence Directorate's list for 1960. With Twining's enthusiastic support, Eisenhower approved the Hickey committee recommendation as the basis for all future JCS planning.[146]

By late 1959 Eisenhower's concept of massive retaliation had been reduced to a strategy of desperate resolve. Appalled by the unimaginable destruction the United States might inflict or suffer in general war, Eisenhower could no longer see beyond the first disastrous nuclear exchange. "All we really have that is meaningful is a deterrent," he repeatedly told his advisers. "The central question is whether or not we have the ability to destroy anyone who attacks us, because the biggest thing today is to provide a deterrent to war."[147] Eisenhower could not conceive of second-strike counterforce as a feasible option and turned aside the Air Force plea for the B-70 on these grounds. It was "crazy" to think that a manned bomber could search out and destroy mobile ICBMs on railroads after a Soviet strike. "We are not going to be searching out mobile bases for ICBMs," he said, "we are going to be hitting the big industrial and control complexes." He similarly dismissed Navy arguments for using Polaris to provide a controlled, deliberate, and selective response to surprise attack. Polaris, he declared in 1960, would be useful primarily "to disrupt and knock out organized defenses" in order to clear the way for SAC bombers.[148] He ruled against making a full commitment to the Polaris program until it received further testing.[149]

Although Eisenhower had largely abandoned hope of disarming the Soviet Union, and increasingly favored targeting Soviet cities, he continued to emphasize the importance of rapid response. In May 1960 the President received a briefing on the programming requirements for the solid-fueled, silo-based Minuteman ICBM, scheduled to be deployed in three squadrons of 50 missiles each in 1963. Current guidance, he learned, would permit only "volley" or "ripple" firing of an entire squadron and did not provide for alternative target tapes to permit retargeting. He discovered, furthermore, that the necessity of keeping the gyros in the inertial guidance system in constant operation to meet the requirement of firing within 30 seconds posed certain technical difficulties. Eisenhower favored efforts to make the Minuteman system more flexible, especially since the 30-second rule would allow no margin for error and would raise the chances of starting a war no one wanted. It might be better, he agreed, "to take a few extra minutes, to give someone high up in authority the decision." But a longer delay, even with hardened silos, might spell disaster.[150]

The Eisenhower administration's top-secret review of "U.S. Policy in the Event of War," approved by the NSC in March 1959, appeared to retain the option of preemptive response to an impending Soviet strike, without specifically endorsing it. NSC 5904/1 was so sensitive that even its title was classified. In December 1959, reflecting ambiguity in high policy as well as reflecting increasing doubts as to the feasibility of preemption, the JCS split over whether JSCP guidance should provide a strategic warning of sufficient precision "to impel the President to direct the initiation of operations by United States forces."[151] The following month Twining raised with the President questions relating to preemptive attack under conditions of conclusive advanced warning.[152] Although Eisenhower may have been less secure in his determination to launch SAC immediately in response to Soviet aggression, there is no indication that his basic position on preemptive strikes had shifted.

On July 6, 1960, Secretary of Defense Gates reported to the President that in fifteen meetings with the JCS since taking office in January he had been unable to resolve the basic disagreements over targeting and coordination. Gates did not believe that SAC and Polaris should enter a single operational command, but, like JCS Chairman Twining, he believed strongly that the nuclear striking force required an integrated target list and operational plan. Since the Joint Staff did not have the necessary computer capability, SAC should prepare these plans as an agent of the JCS. The Army and Navy, Gates reported, viewed this proposal as a power play by the Air Force and firmly resisted it. Eisenhower expressed disgust at the inability of the services, especially the Navy, to cooperate. "[The] original mistake in this whole business," he remarked, "was our failure to create one single Service in 1947." Perhaps he should order the JCS to work together and tell them that "if they fail to come up with an integrated plan within six months they will all be replaced." He agreed that the country required a single plan; he agreed to assign the task to SAC as an agent of the JCS as long as SAC planners were augmented with personnel from the other services. Gates agreed to formulate a solution that involved all the services. "If SAC takes over the functions of the Joint Chiefs," he assured the President, "it is the fault of the Chiefs themselves."[153]

IX

On August 11, 1960, President Eisenhower formally approved Gates's proposal for the creation of the Joint Strategic Target Planning Staff (JSTPS), under SAC domination, to prepare the National Strategic Target List and Single Integrated Operational Plan. Accepting the finality of the President's ruling, Arleigh Burke left the meeting prepared to put his weight behind an effort to produce the best possible strategy.[154] He sent a strong group of officers to SAC headquarters in Omaha, and urged Army Chief of Staff George Decker to do the same. Decker, however, considered the SIOP less relevant to Army concerns than the problem of limited war; he did not believe, moreover, that his planners could influence its development in the limited time allowed. Lacking effective Army support and greatly outnumbered within the JSTPS, the Navy planners could do little to curb what they perceived to be excesses in the plan. In late November, Burke prepared an analysis of potential problems in the SIOP for General Lyman Lemnitzer, who had replaced Twining as Chairman of the JCS in September. Although the plan was basically acceptable, Burke wrote, some problem areas needed attention, including matters of delivery, damage, and anticipated fallout.[155]

Eisenhower received Burke's memorandum on November 27, two days after Kistiakowsky's briefing. Shocked and angered by the level of overkill envisioned in the Single Integrated Operational Plan, the President realized that his attempt to set limits had failed. The National Strategic Target List was 29 percent longer than the approved Hickey committee list, and whatever restraints it had imposed on target selection by the increased overlapping of weapons to achieve the high assurance criteria had been negated. By this time, however, it was too late for reconsideration. Even Burke, despite his reservations about the SIOP, did not consider withholding approval, although he hoped the JCS might express qualified endorsement and subject the completed plan to rigorous war gaming.[156] On December 2, 1960, the JCS approved SIOP-62, apparently without reservations, and Eisenhower passed it on to his successor as the nation's operational nuclear war plan for Fiscal Year 1962.[157]

Although SAC's commitment to maximizing the impact of available forces accounted for the level of overkill embodied in the SIOP, it was the assumption of plenty in nuclear weapons and delivery vehicles that made it possible. Both the Truman and Eisenhower administrations had consciously promoted expansion of the strategic striking force. The overlapping and duplication that accompanied the shift from bombers to missiles toward the end of the Eisenhower years exacerbated the tendency toward excess. When Eisenhower left office, SAC had 538 B-52, 1,292 B-47, and 19 B-58 bombers, plus 1,094 tankers. The country had deployed 12 Atlas ICBMs in the United States and 60 Thor IRBMs in Britain. It was deploying 30 Jupiter IRBMs to Italy, and it had signed agreements to deploy them to Turkey as well. Over 650 additional Atlas, Titan, and Minuteman missiles were under contract, as were 14 Polaris submarines, each of which carried 16 missiles. The first Polaris submarine, the *U.S.S George Washington*, departed on deterrent patrol in November 1960.[158]

Expansion of the nuclear weapons stockpile was even more rapid. Despite his growing conviction that the nation already had more than adequate striking power, Eisenhower never took action to cut back the production of weapons designated for the strategic air offensive. He remained committed to tactical nuclear weapons in limited-conflict situations whenever militarily appropriate. He did not want to curtail their possible contributions to military success despite his increasing doubts about limiting a war if such weapons were employed. As a result, the government stockpiled large numbers of tactical nuclear weapons, as well as air defense warheads, against a time of need. Between 1958 and 1960 the stockpile tripled in size, apparently growing from 6000 to 18,000 weapons in only two years.[159] This growth of America's nuclear capability received its justification from the perceived need to counter a growing Soviet nuclear threat. The commitment to counterforce, established under Truman and reinforced by Eisenhower, was clearly a response to the unprecedented perils of the 1950s as the nation suddenly found itself facing the possibility of physical annihilation. The President and his military advisers, particularly the Air Force high command, understandably perceived that their most urgent duty was to defend the country against that threat. By the time Eisenhower left office, the Strategic Air Command had prepared and trained for nearly a decade not only for massive retaliation but also for massive preemption. United States forces were routinely expanded for the objective of neutralizing Soviet nuclear forces, which were often grossly overestimated because of inadequate intelligence.

Despite the growth of the planned nuclear offensive from a few dozen targets in 1948 to more than 2500 in 1960, the ability to disarm the Soviet Union still seemed beyond reach. In the late 1950s, WSEG and the Air Force both produced pessimistic assessments of present and future United States capability to locate, target, and destroy Soviet nuclear delivery forces, including mobile and concealed missiles.[160] Because planners considered counterforce critical, if possibly infeasible, the Air Force held to the concept of striking Soviet war-making capacity as a crucial back-up strategy. The nuclear offensive against the urban-industrial base was initially a means of maximizing the impact of scarce nuclear resources, but, with the advent of thermonuclear weapons, American power offered the possibility of carrying out a single war-winning strike, thus avoiding a costly protracted struggle. General Thomas Power, conscious of SAC's limitations in both target intelligence and capability for repeated, sustained high- and low-level bomber operations in hostile Soviet air space, was particularly adamant in his commitment to the "optimum mix" strategy. When RAND strategist William Kaufmann visited SAC headquarters in the winter of 1961 to present a briefing on his ongoing study of counterforce, Power reacted with an angry cable to Chief of Staff White. The SAC commander insisted that Kaufmann's arguments did not reflect the current or future thrust of Air Force thinking.[161]

RAND strategists found a receptive audience in the incoming Kennedy administration, and especially in Secretary of Defense Robert McNamara. When McNamara learned the details of SIOP-62 on February 4, 1961, he was disturbed by the rigidity of the plan, the "fantastic" fallout and destruction it would produce, and the absence of a clear strategic rationale for the counterforce/urban-industrial target mix. During the following month he initiated an intensive reevaluation of the American strategic posture, including a review of basic national security policy with regard to nuclear weapons, assumptions relating to counterforce strikes, and a JCS assessment of the feasibility of planning for "controlled response and negotiating pauses" in the midst of a thermonuclear war. He also reconvened the Hickey committee to study quantitative requirements for deterrence through 1967, utilizing new intelligence data. This report, which contained updates of the target list developed in 1959–60, appeared in June 1961.[162]

By September, McNamara's definition of the United States strategic posture was in place, incorporating second-strike counterforce and the kind of "partial withholding" stragegy which RAND analysts had long advocated. The nation must be able to respond to a surprise attack, McNamara stated, first by striking

> Soviet bomber bases, missile sites, and other installations associated with long-range nuclear forces, in order to reduce Soviet power and limit the damage that can be done to us by vulnerable Soviet follow-on forces, while, second, holding in protected reserve forces capable of destroying urban society, if necessary, in a controlled and deliberate way.

McNamara rejected finite deterrence on the grounds that it did not provide for essential damage-limiting and would not adequately deter Soviet attacks on the nation's allies. He likewise rejected the goal of a full first-strike capability. This goal, McNamara believed, would not only cost more than the nation could afford, given the urgency of other defense requirements, but would, he said, "put the Soviets in a position which they would be likely to consider intolerable," thus risking an arms race. Most important, acquiring such a capability would be "almost certainly infeasible" because the Soviet Union could, at low cost, defeat such a strategy by hardening and dispersing its ICBMs, scattering its bombers, and deploying increasing numbers of missile submarines.[163]

To adapt the SIOP to the new strategic posture, new directives of 1961 for SIOP-63 mandated the separation of the optimum mix target system into its major components. The new targeting categories were updated versions of the BRAVO, ROMEO, and DELTA priorities established in 1950: Soviet strategic nuclear capability; other military capability (including air defense and non-nuclear command installations); and the urban-industrial base. The new administration adopted arrangements to withold attacks against one or more of these categories, depending on the circumstances, as well as against the People's Republic of China and the satellite nations. These targeting options followed a series of preemptive and retaliatory options designed to permit flexibility in response to a variety of political and military conditions and opportunities.[164]

Despite the Kennedy administration's efforts to take control of the SIOP, the basic patterns of nuclear strategy it embodied proved resistant to change. From the beginning the SIOP became the highest priority mission of all its assigned forces, seriously limiting their availability for other military uses.[165] Despite McNamara's efforts to impose restraints, the continued commitment to damage-limiting perpetuated the upward pressure on force requirements. The Air Force especially remained convinced that the nation should strive for a first-strike capability, in order "to limit damage to the United States and our Allies to levels acceptable in light of the circumstances and the alternatives available." Finally, despite its targeting and attack options, the SIOP continued to emphasize capabilities rather than objectives, invariably mandating that larger forces than necessary be applied to those targeting categories identified for attack, and never including fewer than "thousands" of weapons.[166] For more than two decades the SIOP thus provided a floor beneath strategic force requirements and dominated United States thinking about nuclear war.

Eisenhower's defense decision responded primarily to organizational rather than strategic concerns. He was irritated and frustrated by the private and public disagreements among his service chiefs. Perhaps he never fully understood the gravity of the disputes over nuclear strategy and targeting that raged in the JCS during his final three years in office. He recognized a real need to improve coordination and control in order to integrate bombers and missiles into a single striking force without endangering the bombers and their crews. He did not anticipate the long-term consequences of placing the coordination machinery under SAC domination. This decision reflected the continuing belief that, as long as the President of the United States retained final authority over nuclear weapons, operational planning, no matter how firmly institutionalized, would remain a subordinate function.

Even if Eisenhower had fully understood the alternative strategies which his military advisers and others proposed, this would not, as McNamara was to discover, necessarily make them available. Not only is presidential power limited by political considerations, but the President must deal with current capabilities in maintaining the national defense. On this crucial point high policy and operational planning have much in common. Eisenhower never had a real opportunity to rule on the concept of finite deterrence because the technology was still nonexistent. The first Polaris missile was not test-fired from a submerged submarine until July 1960. In November, when Eisenhower began to wonder, as the Navy had argued, whether the Polaris system might provide an alternative to SAC and a means of limiting force requirements, the Polaris fleet, which could substantially supplement or substitute for other forces, was still years in the future.

Second-strike strategies which RAND analysts and a portion of the Air Staff advocated posed similar problems in terms of technology and current capabilities. To locate and destroy Soviet missiles after a surprise attack would be difficult; to carry out military operations, perhaps impossible. When McNamara asked the JCS for an evaluation of the doctrine of controlled response and negotiating pauses in the intrawar period, the Chiefs responded in April 1961 that the United States did not currently have the capability to implement such a strategy because it lacked adequate survivable warning, defense, and command and control systems, as well as a retaliatory force capable of enduring an indefinite period of attack.[167] All the effort had provided the country no assured defense against massive destruction in war.

The Joint Chiefs of Staff, operating at the middle level of nuclear strategy-making, carried major responsibility for taking a long view of United States capabilities and strategy, but often they were unable to agree. For example, the Joint Chiefs approved only one Joint Long Range Strategic Estimate from 1952, when it was mandated as an annual follow-on study beyond the JSOP, through 1957.[168] Such planning for nuclear forces faced even fiercer interservice disagreements than those which disrupted preparation of the JSCP and JSOP, and was also plagued with the difficulty of projecting accurately the outcomes of technological promise and political change. In fact, long-range concepts rarely entered the JCS arena. Only within the services that originated them, as well as outside the Pentagon and before Congress, did they receive any attention.

The creation of the Single Integrated Operational Plan, which elevated operational planning to the level of national policy, represented the victory of short-term concerns over long-term planning. In particular, it effectively killed a major effort within the JCS to redirect United States nuclear strategy away from capabilities planning. The alternative retaliatory target lists that the JCS received were designed to require only a fraction of the striking force and to seek the minimum damage necessary to accomplish specific military objectives. Army and Navy sponsors of the project made no secret of the fact that they hoped these alternative lists might eventually supplant the proposed massive SAC offensive. The lists were still uncompleted when Eisenhower left office.

Behind the "Alternative Undertaking" in 1957 was the assumption that the nation had passed the point where additional destructive power had any utility. Army and Navy leaders responsible for the effort believed that the nation could make reductions, without weakening its strategic posture, by developing a minimum deterrent/retaliatory strategy and channeling remaining resources into preparations for conflicts other than general war with the Soviet Union. Although Secretary McNamara's eventual endorsement of Assured Destruction as the nation's basic military posture in 1964–65 included elements of this argument, it came after the SIOP and missile programs based on the twin pillars of damage-limiting and assured destruction had operationally established force levels far above what critics of the SAC offensive, including Eisenhower toward the close of his administration, considered necessary. Although the proposed solutions of the early 1960s may be out-of-date as a result of the subsequent Soviet strategic force buildup, the basic question of whether the country could have reduced overkill without sacrificing security remains timely. As Arleigh Burke told Henry Kissinger's seminar at Harvard in the spring of 1960: "You very seldom see a cowboy, even in the movies, wearing three guns. Two is enough."[169]

Notes

The author gratefully acknowledges the assistance of Berend D. Bruins, Fred Kaplan, Thomas Cochran, Dr. Dean Allard and his staff at the Operational Archives of the Naval Historical Center, Mr. William A. Barbee of the Declassification Branch of the Secretariat of the Joint Chiefs of Staff, and Mrs. Sybil Taylor of the Directorate of Freedom of Information and Security Review of the Office of the Secretary of Defense in tracking down significant source material.

1. This meeting is described in two documents: Andrew Goodpaster, Memorandum of Conference with the President (herafter cited as MCP), August 11, 1960, dated August 13, 1960, in Staff Notes, August 1960—3 Folder, Box 51, DDE Diary, Ann C. Whitman File, Dwight D. Eisenhower Papers as President (hereafter ACWF, EPP), Dwight D. Eisenhower Library, Abilene, Kansas (hereafter DDEL); and Admiral Arleigh Burke, rough draft Memorandum for the Record, Subject: Meeting with the President on SecDef's Proposal to turn Targetting [*sic*] and the Preparation of Single Integrated Operational Plan over to SAC, 11 August 1960, in NSTL/SIOP Briefing Folder, Papers of Admiral Arleigh A. Burke (hereafter cited as AAB), Operational Archives, Naval Historical Center, Washington, D.C. (hereafter NHC).

2. Untitled memorandum, dated August 11, 1960, appended to MCP, August 13, 1960. This was a typed, unsigned version of Admiral Burke's arguments. The original handwritten and first typed draft of this memo are contained in NSTL/SIOP Briefing Folder, AAB, NHC.

3. MCP, August 13, 1960.

4. History and Research Division, Headquarters, Strategic Air Command, *History of the Joint Strategic Target Planning Staff, Background and Preparation of SIOP-62* (partially declassified history released by the declassification branch, Joint Secretariat, Joint Chiefs of

Staff, in April 1980), 14. There were 79 airmen and civilians among the 219 SAC personnel assigned to JSTPS.

5. Portions of the NSTAP are quoted or described in Message, CNO to CINCLANTFLT, CINCPACFLT, CINCUSNAVEUR, R201933Z November 1960, NSTL/SIOP Messages, Exclusives and Personals, AAB, NHC; Memo, Op-06C to Op-00, Subject: CNO Discussions regarding NSTL/SIOP with Generals Lemnitzer, Decker, and Spivy on 9 November, with Enclosure, Précis re Army participation in the NSTL/SIOP dated 1 November 1960, BM00211–60, 8 November 1960; Special Edition, Flag Officers Dope, 4 December 1960; amd Memo for the Record, by Rear Admiral Paul Blackburn, Subject: "Comments on the Questions," no serial, 12 October 1960—all in Memos and Letters (NSTL) Folder, AAB, NHC; and letter, Thomas Gates to Brigadier General A. J. Goodpaster, 10 August 1960, with draft memo to the JCS and TABS B and C, in Department of Defense Vol. IV–7, August 1960 Folder, Box 2, Department of Defense Subseries, Subject Series, White House Office, Staff Secretary (hereafter WHO-SS), DDEL.

6. In the summer of 1981 the Department of the Navy Declassification Team conducted two separate declassification reviews of five folders in the Arleigh Burke papers, NHC: the NSTL-SIOP Briefing Folder, the Memos & Letters (NSTL) Folder, the NSTL/SIOP Messages Folder, the Transcripts & Phone Cons (NSTL) Folder, and the NSTL/SIOP Messages Folder, the Transcripts & Phone Cons (NSTL) Folder, and the NSTL/SIOP Messages—Exclusives & Personals Folder. A substantial portion of each of these folders was declassified. The information and statistics on the NSTAP, NSTL, and SIOP in this paper are based on information contained in those folders. Since JCS papers remain classified, it is not possible to confirm the accuracy and completeness of this information.

7. This information is derived from material contained in Special Edition, Flag Officers Dope, 4 December 1960; Memo, Rear Admiral C. V. Ricketts (Op-60) to Op-00, Op-60 BM-0001028-60, Subject: JCS 2056/189, The Initial NSTL & SIOP, 22 November 1960; Memo, Arleigh Burke for General Lemnitzer, Op-00 Memo 000683-60, Subject: NSTL/SIOP, 22 November 1960; Memo, Rear Admiral Paul Blackburn, Op-60C, to Op-00, BM-000222-60, Subject: Message Traffic Between CINCs and CNO, comments concerning, with Enclosures 1 and 2 summarizing messages; Resume of NSTL-SIOP Briefing, Offutt AFB, 28 September 1960, Attached to Op-06C to Op-00, BM-000167-60, 29 September; and Joint Strategic Target Planning Agency, Memo for the Record, Subject: Minutes of 1st Meeting of the Policy Committee, B-76824, 14 September 1960, all in Memos and Letters (NSTL) Folder, AAB, NHC; and Message, to RBEP with JCS, Report of Preliminary Review of SIOP-62, 182250Z January 1961; Message, CNO to CINCPAC, CINCPACFLT, CINCLANTFLT, CINCUS-NAVEUR, 241843Z November 1960; Cable, Bridadier General J. A. Spivy, USA, JCS Liaison Group Offutt, to JCS for Director, Joint Staff, Subject: 11th Weekly Activity Report—14th Meeting of Policy Committee, November 15-16, 19 November 1960; Message, CNO to CINCPACFLT, CINCLANTFLT, CINCUSNAVEUR, 0051/06 November 1960; and Message, CINCLANT to CNO, From Vice Admiral Fitzhugh Lee for Rear Admiral Blackburn, Subject: JSTPS Progress, 2031Z/22 October 1960; all in NSTL/SIOP Messages Folder, AAB, NCH. 599 DGZs covered nuclear delivery capability and government and military control centers; 151 covered the urban industrial base. This comprised the "Minimum NSTL." There were also 227 defensive DGZs, and 65 "other" DGZs, for a total NSTL of 1042. Cable, Spivy to JCS, 19 November 1960.

8. Memo, Burke to Lemnitzer, 22 November 1960; Message, CINCLANT to CNO, Subject: JSTPS Progress, 2031Z/22 October 1960.

9. Message, CNO to CINCPACFLT, CINCLANTFLT, CINCUSNAVEUR, 0051/06 November 1960; and Special Edition, Flag Officers Dope, 4 December 1960.

10. Précis appended to Memo, Op-06C to Op-00, BM-00211-60, 8 November 1960.

11. Message, CINCPAC to RBEP with JCS, Report of Preliminary Review of SIOP-62, 182250Z January 1961; Message, CINCLANT to CNO, Subject: JSTPS Progress, 2031Z/22 October 1960.

12. Message, CNO to CINCLANTFLT, CINCPACFLT, CINCUSNAVEUR, R 2019337Z November 1960.

13. George B. Kistiakowsky, *A Scientist at the White House* (Cambridge: Harvard University Press, 1976), 396, 399–400, 405–7, 413–16; Transcript, Tel Con, Admiral Burke and Dr. Kistiakowsky, October 24, 1960, Transcripts & Phone Cons (NSTL) Folder, AAB, NHC.

14. Kistiakowsky, quoted in Transcript, Admiral Burke's Conversation with Admiral [James] Russell, November 11, 1960, in Transcipts & Phone Cons (NSTL) Folder, AAB, NHC.

15. Transcript, Admiral Burke's Conversation with Captain Aurand, 25 November 1960, in Transcripts & Phone Cons (NSTL) Folder, AAB, NHC.

16. This command structure is discussed in greater detail in Frank G. Klotz, *The U.S. President and the Control of Strategic Nuclear Weapons* (unpublished doctoral dissertation, Oxford University, 1980). Earlier, more general accounts include Ernest R. May (ed.), *The Ultimate Decision: The President as Commander in Chief* (New York: George Braziller, 1960); Richard F. Haynes, *The Awesome Power: Harry S. Truman as Commander in Chief* (Baton Rouge: Louisiana State University Press, 1973); and Douglas Kinnard, *President Eisenhower and Strategy Management: A Study in Defense Politics* (Lexington: University Press of Kentucky, 1977). On the role of the Secretary of Defense, the best recent study is Douglas Kinnard, *The Secretary of Defense* (Lexington: University Press of Kentucky, 1980).

17. The basic structure of United States war planning is described in Robert D. Lille, *Organizing for Strategic Planning: The National System and the Air Force* (Washington, D.C.: USAF Historical Division Liaison Office, 1964, declassified with deletions 1975); George F. Lemmer, *The Air Force and the Concept of Deterrence, 1945–1950* (Washington, D.C.: USAF Historical Division Liaison Office, 1963, declassified with deletions, 1975); George F. Lemmer, *The Air Force and Strategic Deterrence, 1951–1960* (Washington, D.C.: Office of Air Force History, 1967, declassified with deletions, 1980); and James F. Schnabel, Kenneth W. Condit, and Walter S. Poole, *The History of the Joint Chiefs of Staff, The Joint Chiefs of Staff and National Policy, Vol. 1: 1945–1947; Vol. 2: 1947–1949; Vol. 4: 1950–1952* (Wilmington, Del.: Michael Glazier, 1979, 1980). The JSCP/JSOP structure is mandated in JCS Policy Memo 84, Joint Program for Planning, July 14, 1952, and its revisions of 27 July 1955 and 8 April 1960, in CCS 381 (11–29–49) Sec. 3 and 24, and CCS 3100, Plans (13 April 1959), respectively, all in Record Group 218, Papers of the United States Joint Chiefs of Staff, Modern Military Branch, U.S. National Archives (hereafter cited as JCS).

18. The work of strategic theorists is best described in Bernard Brodie, *The American Scientific Strategists* (Santa Monica: Rand Corporation Paper P 2979, October 1964); Bernard Brodie, *War and Politics* (New York: Macmillan, 1973), especially chapter 10; Colin Gray, *Strategic Studies and Public Policy: The American Experience* (Lexington: University Press of Kentucky, 1982); and Bruce L. R. Smith, *The RAND Corporation, Case Study of a Non Profit Advisory Corporation* (Cambridge: Harvard University Press, 1966).

19. The best studies of this process are Lawrence Freedman, *U.S. Intelligence and the Soviet Strategic Threat* (Boulder, Colo.: Westview Press, 1977) and John Prados, *The Soviet Estimate: U.S. Intelligence Analysis and Russian Military Strength* (New York: Dial Press, 1982).

20. David Alan Rosenberg, "U.S. Nuclear Stockpile, 1945 to 1950," *The Bulletin of the Atomic Scientists, 38* (May 1982), 25–30.

21. The most reliable overviews of U.S. policy on domestic and international control of atomic energy are Barton J. Bernstein, "The Quest for Security: American Foreign Policy and International Control of the Atomic Bomb, 1942–1946," *The Journal of American History, 60* (March 1974) 1003–44; and Richard G. Hewlett and Oscar E. Anderson, *A History of the United States Atomic Energy Commission, Vol. I, The New World, 1939–1946* (University Park: Pennsylvania State University Press, 1962).

22. Rosenberg, "U.S. Nuclear Stockpile," 27–28. See also David Alan Rosenberg, "Planning for a PINCHER War: Policy Objectives and Military Strategy in American Planning for War with the Soviet Union, 1945–1948," unpublished paper presented at Annual Meeting of the Society for Historians of American Foreign Relations, July 1978. An example of the

paralysis imposed in U.S. war planning by Truman's continuing adherence to a policy of international control may be seen in JCS 1725/1, 13 February 1947, CCS 004.04 (11–4–46) Sec. 3, JCS, which is the United States' first strategic concept war plan in support of industrial mobilization planning, and which anticipated that the United States would not employ nuclear weapons in a conflict with the U.S.S.R. The first JCS discussions of what actions should be taken if international control efforts failed are contained in JCS 1764 to JCS 1764/1, 14 July to 13 August 1974, CCS 471.6 (8–15–45) Sec. 5, JCS.

23. JWPC 486/7, 29 July 1947, CCS 004.04 (11–4–46) Bulky Package 1–A, and JSPG 496/1, 8 November 1947, CCS 381, USSR (3–2–46) Sec. 8, both JCS; William D. Leahy Diary, 5–6 May 1948, William D. Leahy Papers, Manuscript Division, Library of Congress (hereafter cited as LC); David Alan Rosenberg, "American Atomic Strategy and the Hydrogen Bomb Decision," *The Journal of American History, 66* (June 1979), 79; Diary entry, 28 July 1948, James V. Forrestal Diary, NHC; William G. Lalor, Memo for the Record, DM–51, 28 July 1948, CCS 004.04 (11–4–46) Sec. 9, JCS.

24. NSC–30, United States Policy on Atomic Warfare, U.S. Department of State, *Foreign Relations of the United States* (hereafter cited as *FRUS*) *1948, Vol. I, General: The United Nations* (Washington, D.C.: Government Printing Office (GPO), 1976), 624–28.

25. Memorandum, Vandenberg to the Secretary of the Air Force, 8 November 1947, OPD 341 (5 November 1947) Record Group 341, Papers of the Chief of Staff of the United States Air Force, Modern Military Branch, National Archives (hereafter cited as CSAF).

26. The background of the NSC–20 series is most readily documented in *FRUS, 1948, Vol. I*, 589–669. See also Forrestal's argument that the JCS needed "to know what we propose to do with Russia after we may have defeated her," in Memorandum for the President, summarizing the 17th Meeting of the National Security Council, August 6, 1948, Memo for the President—Meeting Discussions (1948) Folder, Box 220, Subject File, President's Secretary's File, Harry S. Truman Papers (hereafter cited as PSF) Harry S. Truman Library, Independence, Missouri (hereafter cited as HSTL).

27. NSC 20/4, U.S. Objectives with Respect to the USSR to Counter Soviet Threats to U.S. Security, 23 November 1948, which was made available to the JCS as NSC 20/3 in JCS 1903/3, 5 November 1948, with Note by the Secretaries, 29 November 1948, appended, CCS 381 (5–13–45) Sec. 4, JCS.

28. Rosenberg, "U.S. Nuclear Stockpile, 1945 to 1950," 26–29; *ibid.*, 29. See also JIC 439/11, 19 July 1949, and JCS 1952/8, 25 August 1949, in CCS 373 (10–23–48) Secs. 3 and 5 respectively, JCS.

29. Air Plan for MAKEFAST, 10 October 1946, PO 381 (10 September 1946) CSAF; Robert Frank Futrell, *Ideas, Concepts, Doctrine: A History of Basic Thinking in the U.S. Air Force, 1907–1964*, 2 vols., (Maxwell Air Force Base, Ala.: Aerospace Studies Institute, 1971), I, 218; Robert D. Little, *The History of Air Force Participation in the Atomic Energy Program, 1943–1953, Vol. II, Foundations of an Atomic Air Force and Operation SANDSTONE, 1946–1948* (Washington, D.C.: Air University Historical Liaison Office, 1955, declassified with deletions, 1981), 264–65.

30. JWPC 486/7, July 1947; Rosenberg, "American Atomic Strategy and the Hydrogen Bomb Decision," 68–71: JCS 1953/1, 12 May 1949, CCS–373 (10–23–48) Bulky Package, JCS.

31. Rosenberg, "American Atomic Strategy and the Hydrogen Bomb Decision," 73–75.

32. *Ibid.*, 75–76; Rosenberg, "U.S. Nuclear Stockpile, 1945 to 1950," 26, 29–30; JCS 2056, 31 August 1949 (Enclosure B, declassified with deletions, October 1978), and JCS 2056/3, 23 November 1949, CCS 373.11 (12–14–48) Sec. 1, JCS. Bomb numbers are contained in JCS 1952/11, 10 February 1950, CCS 373 (10–23–48) Bulky Package, JCS.

33. JCS 2056/7, 12 August 1950, with Decision, 15 August 1950, CCS 373.11 (12–14–48) Sec. 2, JCS; letter, Bernard Brodie to David A. Rosenberg, August 22, 1977; author's interview with Bernard Brodie, Chicago, April 29, 1977; Brodie, *War and Politics*, 64; entry, General LeMay's Diary, 23 January 1951, Diary No. 3, 1951 Folder, Box B–64, Curtis E. LeMay Papers, LC; Poole, *The JCS and National Policy, Vol. IV*, 165–66.

34. JCS 1496/3, 19 September 1945 and JCS 1518, 19 September 1945, CCS 381 (5–13–45) Sec. 2, JCS; JCS 1805, 23 September 1947; JCS 1691/10, 29 December 1947; and JCS 1805/21, 26 June 1950, with Decision, 7 August 1950, CCS 471.6 (10–16–45) Sec. 9, Parts 1, 2, and 3 respectively, JCS.

35. JCS 1823/14, 27 May 1949, CCS 471.6 (8–15–45) Sec. 15; JSPC 877/120, 26 June 1950; and JCS 2143, 12 July 1950, CCS 381 (1–26–50) Sec. 2 and 3 respectively, all JCS.

36. Letter, Brodie to Rosenberg, August 22, 1977.

37. Entry, General LeMay's Diary, 23 January 1951.

38. Letter, Brodie to Rosenberg, August 22, 1977; JCS 2056/16, 18 June 1951, with decision on 16 July 1951, CCS 373.11 (12–14–48) Sec. 4, JCS; Poole, *The JCS and National Policy, Vol. IV*, 165–67.

39. JCS 2056/4, 19 January 1950, with decision on 18 April 1950, CCS 373.11 (12–14–48) Sec. 1, JCS; Little, *Organizing for Strategic Planning*, 44–46; Poole, *The JCS and National Policy, Vol. IV*, 166n.; JCS 2056/47, 13 May 1953, with decision on 27 May 1953, ccs 373.11 (12–14–48) Sec. 11, JCS. The debates over target intelligence organization are described in papers in the JCS 2056 series of between June 1952 and May 1953 in Sections 7 through 11 of *ibid*.

40. "Notes for Discussion with General Vandenberg," 4 November 1948, Diary Folder, Box B–64, LeMay Papers, LC; General Curtis E. LeMay with MacKinley Kantor, *Mission with LeMay, My Story* (Garden City, N.Y.: Doubleday, 1965), 429–47. See also Harry Borowski, *A Hollow Threat, Containment and Strategic Air Power Before Korea* (Westport, Conn.: Greenwood Press, 1982), 162–84, and letter, Hoyt E. Vandenberg to Commanding General, Strategic Air Command, 27 October 1949, Subject: Priority in Preparation for Atomic Warfare, appended to letter, LeMay to General Nathan F. Twining, 6 February 1951, Twining Folder, Box B–60, LeMay Papers, LC.

41. "Briefing on Exercise 'Dualism' Conducted by Colonel John A. Armstrong," 9 December 1948, A/AE (1948) 354.2 Exercise Dualism, CSAF; Rosenberg, "U.S. Nuclear Stockpile, 1945 to 1950," 29–30. On SAC problems, see, in particular, letter, Charles A. Lindbergh to Secretary of the Air Force Thomas K. Finletter, 8 June 1950, in Office of the Administrative Assistant, Correspondence Control Division, Special Interest File, 1950, Record Group 340, Papers of the Secretary of the Air Force, Modern Military Branch, National Archives; letter, LeMay to Vandenberg, 21 September 1950, Vandenberg Folder, Box B–61, discussing B–29 and B–50 engine problems, and paper "Major Deficiencies in the B–47 Aircraft," 26 October 1950, Command Papers, Box B–98, both in LeMay Papers, LC; "Strategic Air Command Progress Analysis, 1 November 1948 to 31 October 1953," Box B–100, LeMay Papers, LC, 11–12.

42. For contrasting views of the B–36 and U.S. strategic capabilities, see the rather pessimistic remarks in "Aircraft and Weapons Board Proceedings, 29 December 1948–6 January 1949," Vol. I, pp. 54–141, in Executive Office, House Investigation, August–October 1949, CSAF; and the confident predictions of General Vandenberg in JCS 1952/1, 21 December 1948, CCS 373 (10–23–48) Sec. 1, JCS. For a useful overview of Air Force thinking, see John T. Greenwood, "The Emergence of the Postwar Strategic Air Force, 1945–1953," in Alfred F. Hurley and Robert C. Ehrhardt (eds.), *Air Power and Warfare: The Proceedings of the 8th Military History Symposium, U.S. Air Force Academy, October 18–20, 1978* (Washingotn, D.C.: 1979), 215–44.

43. "Strategic Air Command Project Analysis, 1948–1953," 37–38, 44–50; "Strategic Air Command Project Analysis, 1 November 1948–31 December 1956," 28–30, 65–83, Box B–100, LeMay Papers, LC; Document One: Memorandum, Op–36C to Op–36, Subject: Briefing given to the representatives of all services at SAC Headquarters, Offutt Air Force Base, Omaha, on 15 March, 1954, in David Alan Rosenberg, "A Smoking Radiating Ruin at the End of Two Hours: Documents of American Plans for Nuclear War with the Soviet Union, 1954–1955," *International Security*, 6 (Winter 1981–82), 3–38.

44. "Headquarters, Strategic Air Command, Report: Springfield Radar Bombing Evaluation," 7 July 1952, Box B–106; "Strategic Air Command Progress Analysis, 1948–1953,"

27–29, Box B–100; Letter, Curtis LeMay to Major General Frank A. Armstrong, 9 July 1953, Armstrong Folder, Box B–49; and Info for Vice Commander, D/Ops, on Location of Airfields from Radar Photos, Commanders Diary No. 5 Folder, 1953, Box B–64, all LeMay Papers, LC.

45. Special Electronic Airborne Search Operations are described in Memoranda, General Omar Bradley to Secretary of Defense Louis Johnson, 5 May and 22 July 1950, and Johnson to the President, 24 May 1950, all in Omar N. Bradley Folder, General File, PSF, HSTL. President Truman's approval of flights is noted on the 5 May letter. "Strategic Air Command Progress Analysis, 1948–1953," 39–50. Letter, Curtis E. LeMay to Professor Harland Moulton, ca. December 1980, copy courtesy Professor Moulton. Prados, *The Soviet Estimate*, 24–30.

46. Peer DeSilva, *Sub Rosa: The CIA and the Uses of Intelligence* (New York: Times Books, 1978), 58–61; Prados, *The Soviet Estimate*, 29–30. The "balloon operation" is also mentioned in A. J. Goodpaster, MCP, February 10, 1956, in Joint Chiefs of Staff, January–April 1956, Folder 2, Subject Series, Defense Department Sub Series, Box 4, WHO-SS, DDEL.

47. Alfred Goldberg (ed.), *History of Headquarters, USAF, 1 July 1950 to 30 June 1951* (Washington, D.C.: Department of the Air Force, 1955), 7; James M. Erdmann, "The WRINGER in Postwar Germany: Its Impact on United States–German Relations and Defense Policies," Clifford L. Egan and Alexander W. Knott, *Essays in Twentieth Century Diplomatic History Dedicated to Professor Daniel M. Smith* (Washington, D.C.: University Press of America, 1982), 159–91.

48. Department of State, *FRUS, 1949, Vol. I: National Security Affairs, Foreign Economic Policy* (Washington, D.C.: 1976), 481–82; Rosenberg, "American Atomic Strategy and the Hydrogen Bomb Decision," 75–79; James S. Lay, Jr., Memorandum for the President, October 2, 1950, summarizing report of Special Committee of the National Security Council, with President's Approval, October 9, 1950, noted, Expansion of the Fissionable Material Folder, NSC-Atomic File, PSF, HSTL.

49. JCS 1800/164, 6 September 1951, CCS 370 (8–19–45) Sec. 34, JCS. See also Memorandum for the Chief of Staff, by TKF (Thomas K. Finletter Memorandum for the Secretary of Defense, 16 July 1951, all in Folder 2A, Memos Re 138 Wings, Box 83, Hoyt S. Vandenberg Papers, LC.

50. Memorandum for the President, January 17, 1952, summarizing meeting of NSC Special Committee on Atomic Energy with the President, January 16, 1952, and President's approval on Memo, James S. Lay, Jr., to the President, January 16, 1952. The amount of increase is discussed in Memorandum Robert A. Lovett to Executive Secretary, National Security Council, 11 December 1951, Subject: Secretary of Defense Comment on Expansion Program, all in Expansion of the Fissionable Material Folder, NSC-Atomic File, PSF, HSTL.

51. Soviet atomic capability is described in JCS 2101/75, 25 October 1952, Appendix C to Enclosure A, CCS 381, US (1–31–50) Sec. 20, JCS, and N.I.E. 64, Part I, Soviet Bloc Capabilities through Mid-1953, 12 November 1952, National Intelligence Estimates, 64–66 Folder, Box 254, Intelligence File, PSF, HSTL. The bootstrapping dynamic was described in author's interview with Mr. John P. Coyle, veteran Navy operations analyst, Washington, D.C., 29 March 1978.

52. Nuclear production facilities are listed in Richard G. Hewlett and Francis Duncan, *History of the United States Atomic Energy Commission, Vol. II: Atomic Shield, 1947–1952* (University Park: Pennsylvania State University Press, 1969), 669; Stockpile size is estimated in Rosenberg, "A Smoking Radiating Ruin," 7–8; William M. Arkin, Thomas B. Cochran, and Milton M. Hoenig, "The U.S. Nuclear Stockpile," *Arms Control Today, 12* (April 1982), 1–2; and is estimated for 1952–54 in Memorandum, 2 November 1951, with page with figures labeled "Atomic Conf. Finletter's Office 11/2/51," in Diary Notes Folder, Dan A. Kimball Papers, Box 2, HSTL.

53. Information on nuclear weapons design is drawn from the following sources: Rosenberg, "U.S. Nuclear Stockpile, 1945 to 1950," 27–28; Office of Public Affairs, U.S. Depart-

ment of Energy, Nevada Operations *Office, Announced United States Nuclear Tests, July 1945 through December 1981* NVO–209 (Rev. 2), January 1982; JCS 1823/8, 6 November 1948, JCS 1823/11, 20 December 1948, and JCS 1823/35, 30 November 1950, CCS 471.6 (8–15–45) Sec. 13 and 20, JCS (declassified, with deletions, December 1976 and August 1980); Lee Bowen, *History of the Air Force Atomic Energy Program, Vol. IV; The Development of Weapons* (Washington, D.C.: U.S. Air Force Historical Division History, 1955, declassified with deletions, June 1981), 1–143; Table appended in letter, Robert H. Duff, Office of Classification, U.S. Department of Energy, to David A. Rosenberg, December 4, 1980; Herbert York, *The Advisors, Oppenheimer, Teller, and the Superbomb* (San Francisco: W. H. Freeman, 1976); Affidavit, Dimitri A. Rotow, May 3, 1979, in *United States of America vs. The Progressive, Inc.* (copy courtesy of Aaron Meyers, Esq.); and Charles Hansen, "U.S. Nuclear Bombs," *Replica in Scale, 3* (January 1976), 154–59.

54. Bowen, *Air Force Atomic Energy, Vol. IV*, 174–233; JCS 1823/35; York, *The Advisors*, 82–87. Yield possibilities in boosted weapons are discussed in David Holloway, "Research Note, Soviet Thermonuclear Development," *International Security, 4* (Winter 1979–80), 192–97; and in JCS 1823/34, 1 November 1950, CCS 471.6 (8–15–45) Sec. 20, JCS.

55. Rosenberg, "American Atomic Strategy and the Hydrogen Bomb Decision," 81; JCS 1823/35; Memorandum, David Driggs to Hoyt S. Vandenberg, Subject: The Drastic Implications of BUSTER Air Blast Measurements, 17 December 1951, Folder No. 8, Buster Data, Box 88, Vandenberg Papers, LC; JCS 1953/11, 28 May 1952, CCS 373 (10–23–48) Sec. 7, JCS; Poole, *The JCS and National Policy, Vol. IV*, 167.

56. Poole, *The JCS and National Policy, Vol. IV*, 175–77; JCS Policy Memo 84, 14 July 1952.

57. NSC-68, "United States Objectives and Programs for National Security," April 14, 1950, Department of State, *FRUS, 1950, Vol. I: National Security Affairs; Foreign Economic Policy* (Washington, D.C.: 1977), 281–82; NSC 114/3, Report to the National Security Council on United States Programs for National Security, June 5, 1952, NSC Meeting, 105 Folder, Box 215, Subject File, PSF, HSTL.

58. Study, June 11, 1952, appended to Memorandum, Everett Gleason to the President, October 23, 1952, NSC–Atomic Weapons—Procedures for Use Folder, NSC Atomic File, PSF, HSTL. See also the other documents in this folder. The process began with a draft memo by R. Gordon Arneson for Secretary of State Acheson, April 24, 1951, in *FRUS, 1950, Vol. I: National Security Affairs; Foreign Economic Policy* (Washington, D.C.: 1979), 820–26. See also Hewlett and Duncan, *Atomic Shield*, 539.

59. "The President's Farewell Address to the American People, January 15, 1953," *Public Papers of the Presidents: Harry S. Truman, 1952–1953* (Washington, D.C.: 1966), 1197–1202; letter, Truman to Murray, January 19, 1953; and letter Murray to Truman, January 16, 1953, both in Atomic Bomb Folder, General File, PSF, HSTL.

60. On Eisenhower's nuclear background, see in particular, Rosenberg, "U.S. Nuclear Stockpile, 1945 to 1950," 27–28; JCS 1725/2, 12 March 1947, CCS 004.04 (11–4–46) Sec. 3, JCS; Letter, Major General K. D. Nichols USA (Ret.) to David A. Rosenberg, October 27, 1980; Oral History, General Lauris Norstad, Interview by Dr. Thomas Soapes, 11 November 1976, DDEL, 6–29, 39–42; Senior Officers Debriefing Program, Conversations between General Andrew J. Goodpaster and Colonel William D. Johnson and Lt. Colonel James C. Ferguson, 29 January 1976, 56–57; 25 February 1976, 6–14; U.S. Army Military History Research Collection, U.S. Army Military History Institute, Carlisle Barracks, Pa. (hereafter USAMHI).

61. Emmet John Hughes, *The Ordeal of Power* (New York: Dell Books, 1964), 88; Oral History, General Andrew J. Goodpaster, Interview by Dr. Thomas Soapes, January 16, 1978, DDEL, 104–6.

62. Memo, C. E. Wilson, to Chairman, JCS, Subject: Transfer and Deployment of Atomic Weapons, 24 June 1953, in JCS 2019/62, 25 June 1953, CCS 471.6 (8–15–45) Sec. 39, JCS. The original JCS request for custody is in Memo, William M. Fechteler for the Joint Chiefs of Staff to the Secretary of Defense, Subject: Custody of Atomic Weapons, 11 March 1953,

in Atomic Energy-miscellaneous 1953–54 Folder No. 2, NSC Series, Subject Subseries, Box 1, White House Office, Special Assistant, National Security Affairs (hereafter WHO-SANSA), DDEL. The record of JCS discussions and presidential decisions through 1953 is in the JCS 2019 series, CCS 471.6 (8–15–45) from 1949 on, and the Folders: "NSC-Atomic Weapons, Agreed Concepts," "NSC-Atomic Weapons, Non-Nuclear Components," and "NSC-Atomic Weapons, Department of Defense," all in NSC-Atomic File, PSF, HSTL.

63. Andrew J. Goodpaster, MCP, January 13, 1961, dated January 17, 1961, in AEC, December 1960–January 1961, Vol. III, Folder No. 6, Subject Series, Alphabetical Subseries, WHO-SS, DDEL. Eisenhower's philosophy on dispersal is explored in A. J. Goodpaster, Notes on Meeting with the President, 1 December 1954, with Letter, Secretary of State to the President, December 1, 1954, and Letter, Eisenhower to Lewis L. Strauss, 1 December 1954, Atomic Energy Commission, 1953–1954, Folder 2, Administration Series ACWF, EPP, DDEL.

64. Diary entry, January 22, 1952, in Robert H. Ferrell, *The Eisenhower Diaries* (New York: Norton, 1981), 209; the multilevel process is best documented in John Lewis Gaddis, *Strategies of Containment: A Critical Appraisal of Postwar American National Security Policy* (New York: Oxford University Press, 1982), 127–63; Douglas Kinnard, *President Eisenhower and Strategy Management*, 1–36; Glenn H. Snyder, "The New Look of 1953," in Warner R. Schilling *et al., Strategy, Politics, and Defense Budgets* (New York: Columbia University Press, 1962), 379–524; and Samuel F. Wells, Jr., "The Origins of Massive Retaliation," *Political Science Quarterly, 96* (Spring 1981), 31–52.

65. NSC 162/2, Review of Basic National Security Policy, October 30, 1953, NSC Papers, Modern Military Branch, National Archives (hereafter NSC-MMB). These statements are also contained in NSC 162, September 30, 1982, and NSC 162/1, October 19, 1953, *ibid.*

66. Strategic Air Command Progress Analysis, 1948–53," 1–25. The nature of "offensive Striking Power" is discussed in JCS Info Memo 922, 10 February 1954, CCS 381 U.S. (1–31–50) Sec. 35, JCS.

67. L. A. Minnich, Jr., Legislative Leadership Meeting, May 12, 1953, Supplementary Notes, Staff Notes, January-December 1953, DDE Diary, Box 4, ACWF-EPP, DDEL. The controversy over Air Force Budget cuts is recounted in E. Bruce Geelhoed, *Charles E. Wilson and Controversy at the Pentagon, 1953 to 1957* (Detroit: Wayne State University Press, 1979), 59–80; Alfred Goldberg (ed.), *A History of the United States Air Force, 1907–1957* (Princeton, N.J.: Van Nostrand, 1957), 117.

68. JCS 2220/4, 31 January 1952, with SM–271–52, 28 January 1952 appended, CCS 471.6 (4–18–49) Sec. 7, JCS. Preparations for tactical nuclear planning are well documented in a series of "Red Line" Messages between Lauris Norstad and Hoyt Vandenberg from March through December 1951, in Box 86, Vandenberg Papers, LC; in Norstad Oral History, DDEL, 6–42; and in Goodpaster Conversations, February 1976, USAMHI, 6–14.

69. Final Report, Project VISTA, A Study of Ground and Air Tactical Warfare with Especial Reference to the Defense of Western Europe (Pasadena, California Institute of Technology, 4 February 1952), Modern Military Branch, National Archives, xxi-vi; Red Line Message, Personal to Vandenberg from Norstad, 7 December 1951, Red Line Messages, 1 May–31 December 1951 Folder, Box 86, Vandenberg Papers, LC. See also Charles J. V. Murphy, "The Hidden Struggle for the H-Bomb," *Fortune*, May 1953, 109–10, 230; VISTA Final Report, xxi-viii, 138–42, 165–92.

70. Information on the size and capabilities of smaller nuclear weapons came from the source cited in notes 72 and 73. Undated list, Los Alamos Stockpiled Nuclear Weapon Designs, Los Alamos Scientific Laboratory (copy courtesy Thomas B. Cochran); and documents in the JCS 2012 series through 1954, CCS 471.6 (5–31–44), JCS.

71. Memorandum, Kirkpatrick to Admiral Radford, 7 November 1955, Subject: Review of Events Leading Up to JCS Action of 10 December 1953 concerning "Military Strategy and Posture," CJCS 381, Military Strategy and Posture; Memorandum for Admiral Radford by "W," 11 September 1954, CJCS 381 (Continental Defense) January-December 1954; and

Memorandum, E. H. J. Carns to Admiral Radford *et al.*, Subject: Estimate of Military Risk, SM–1721–53, 16 October 1954, CCS 381 U.S. (1–31–50) Sec. 30, all JCS.

72. NSC 162, 30 September 1953, NSC-MMB, 26; JCS 2101/113, 9 December 1953, with decision, 10 December 1953, CCS 381 U.S. (1–31–50) Sec. 31, JCS; copy also in Charles E. Wilson, Secretary of Defense 1953, Folder No. 2, Box 44, Administration Series, ACWF-EPP, DDEL.

73. For example, see Message CINCLANT to JCS, 14 January 1959, Subject: Fiscal Year 1960 Weapons Requirements, CCS 4614 (Allocation) 6 January 1959; JCS 1844/299, 19 November 1959, and SM–1207–59, H. L. Hillyard to Chief, Defense Atomic Support Agency, 27 November 1959, Subject: Allocations of Atomic Weapons, CCS 4614 (Allocation) 20 April 1959, Group 2, all JCS.

74. Presentation to the National Security Council, 1 February 1950, "Need of Defense Measures Against Increasing Threat of Atomic Attack Against the Continental United States," appended to Memorandum, Alfred M. Gruenther to the Deputy Secretary of Defense, 31 January 1950, CD–22–2–2, Record Group 330, Papers of the Office of the Secretary of Defense, Modern Military Branch, National Archives.

75. NSC-139, An Early Warning System, December 31, 1952, NSC Memoranda Approvals, Box 193, Subject File, PSF, HSTL. NSC-140, January 19, 1953, and NSC-140/1, May 18, 1953, both listed with titles in Annotated List of Serially Numbered National Security Council Documents, appended to Memo by James S. Lay, Jr., for the NSC, February 17, 1959, in Folder: Subject Filing of NSC Papers, Subject Series, Alphabetical Subseries, Box 20, WHO-SS, DDEL.

76. NSC-159, Report of the Continental Defense Committee, July 22, 1953, quoted in NSC -5408, Continental Defense, February 11, 1954, NSC-MMB; NSC-153/1, June 10, 1953, quoted in *ibid.*

77. David Holloway, "Soviet Thermonuclear Development," 192–97; National Intelligence Estimates 11–3–55, Soviet Capabilities and Probable Courses of Action through 1960, 17 May 1955, in Folder, same title, NSC File, Subject File, Box 10, WHO-SANSA, DDEL, 24–25; NSC-5423, June 23, 1954; NSC-5511, February 14, 1955; NSC-5605, May 24, 1956; NSC-5728, December 24, 1957; NSC 5816, July 1, 1958, all contain directives to the Net Evaluation Subcommittee. Annotated List of Serially Numbered NSC Documents, February 17, 1959.

78. NSC-5408; NSC 5606, Continental Defense, June 5, 1956; NSC-5707/4, Review of Basic National Security Policy: Military and Non-Military Aspects of Continental Defense, March 26, 1957; NSC 5802, Continental Defense, February 3, 1958; and NSC 5802/1, February 19, 1958, in Boxes 6, 9, 17, 20, and 23 of NSC Series, Policy Papers Subseries; and Department of Defense Progress Report on Status of Military Continental Subseries; and Department of Defense Progress Report on Status of Military Continental Defense Programs, 1 June 1954, Study of Continental Defense by R. Sprague 1953–54, Folder No. 6, NSC Series, Subject Subseries, all WHO-SANSA, DDEL. See also papers in the JCS 1899 and 1851 series, CCS 381 U.S. (5–23–46) through 1958, and 3210 Air Defense Operations, by date, thereafter; the JCS 2084 Series, CCS 373.24 U.S. (9–8–49) through 1958, all JCS; and discussions of Operation ALERT in Cabinet Meeting Minutes in the DDE Diary, ACWF-EPP, DDEL.

79. Glen Snyder, "The New Look of 1953," 407–9; Major General Robert M. Lee, USAF, Memorandum for the Chief of Staff, U.S. Air Force, 21 August 1953, Subject: The Coming National Crisis, Top Secret File (1), 1952–1957, Subject File, Box 121, Nathan F. Twining Papers, LC.

80. Memorandum, Eisenhower to Dulles, September 8, 1953, DDE Diary, August-September 1953, Folder 2, DDE Diary, Box 3, ACWF-EPP, DDEL.

81. NSC 5410, United States War Objectives, 19 February 1954, and NSC 5410/1, 29 March 1954, in NSC 5410/1 U.S. War Objectives Folder, Box 9, NSC Series, Policy Papers Subseries, WHO-SANSA, DDEL. See also Rosenberg, "A Smoking Radiating Ruin," 29n; General Mathhew B. Ridgway, Memorandum for the Record, 17 May 1954, Historical Record, 15 January to 30 June 1954 Folder, Box 30, Matthew B. Ridgway Papers, USAMHI.

82. NSC 5440/1, December 28, 1954; approved as Basic National Security Policy in NSC

5501, January 6, 1955, NSC-MMB, Paragraph 35. See also M. B. Ridgway, Memo for the Special Assistant to the President for National Security Affairs, Subject: Review of Basic National Security Policy, 22 November 1954, Historical Record Folder, Box 30, Ridgway Papers, USAMHI.

83. Draft Special N.I.E., 11–8–54: Probable Warning of Soviet Attack on the U.S. Through Mid-1957, 10 September 1954, SNIE 11–8–54 Folder, Box 47, WHO-SANSA, DDEL; L. A. Minnich, Minutes, BiPartisan Legislative Meeting, January 5, 1954, Staff Notes, January-December 1954 Folder, Box 4, DDE Diary, ACWF-EPP, DDEL; A. J. Goodpaster, MCP, 22 December 1954, ACW Diary December 1954 (2) Folder, ACW Diary Series, Box 3, ACWF-EFF, DDEL.

84. Document One in Rosenberg, "A Smoking Radiating Ruin," 18, 27; Letter, Nathan Twining to LeMay, 17 June 1954, Twining Folder, Box B-60, LeMay Papers, LC.

85. Document One in Rosenberg, "A Smoking Radiating Ruin," 24–26; Historical Division, Headquarters, Strategic Air Command, "Historical Study 73A, SAC Targeting Concepts" (April 1959, extracts only declassified, 1980), 2, 3, 5–7; George F. Lemmer, *The Air Force and Strategic Deterrence*, 21–23; A. W. Radford, Memorandum for Mr. John Foster Dulles, 13 October 1953, CJCS 040 Atomic Energy Commission, JCS.

86. L. L. L. (Lyman L. Lemnitzer) to General Ridgway, 21 June 1954, Historical Record, January to 30 June 1954 Folder, Box 30, Ridgway Papers, USAMHI. For a different report of the President's statement by Press Secretary James Hagerty, see John Gaddis, *Strategies of Containment*, 135n.

87. Brodie, *War and Politics*, 394n. This edisode is also discussed in Norman Moss, *Men Who Play God: The Story of the Hydrogen Bomb* (New York: Harper and Row, 1969; Penguin Books reprint with revisions, 1972), 58–60.

88. Alfred Goldberg, *A Brief Survey of the Evolution of Ideas About Counterforce* (Santa Monica: Rand Corporation, Memorandum RM–5431–PR, October 1967, Revised March 1981), 8–12; George F. Lemmer, *The Air Force and Strategic Deterrence*, 55–57.

89. Paper, no author, "Comments on WSEG No. 10 for General Twining," n.d. (ca. early 1954), Ready File, General Twining (1954), Box 120, Nathan Twining Papers. The tasking of WSEG No. 10, Evaluation of the Effects of the Mid-1954 First Phase Atomic Offensive Against Fixed Industrial Targets in the Soviet Bloc, is in CCS 373 (10–23–48) Sec. 6, 7, and 8, JCS; *Announced U.S. Nuclear Tests*, 4; Entry, April 5, 1954, Phone Calls, January-May 1954—1, DDE Diary, Box 5, ACWF-EPP, DDEL. Even before this test, the JCS had increased their request for thermonuclear weapons production. See JCS 2096/19, 18 January 1954, with Decision, 19 January 1954, CCS 471.6 (12–14–49) Sec. 4, JCS.

90. Robert F. Futrell, *Ideas, Concepts, Doctrine, Vol. II*, 551–52; Office of the Historian, Headquarters, Strategic Air Command, *Development of Strategic Air Command* (Omaha, Neb.: Office of the Historian, Headquarters, Strategic Air Commmand, 1976), 43–53, 77. B-52 capabilities are described in Walter Boyne, *Boeing B-52: A Documentary History* (New York: Jane's Publ. Co., 1981), 135–37, 147.

91. Letter, Nathan Twining to Curtis LeMay, 9 June 1955; LeMay to Twining, 18 June 1955; and Twining to LeMay, 22 July 1955, Twining Folder, Box B-60, LeMay Papers, LC; CSAFM 284–55, 7 October 1955, appended to JCS 2057/32, 7 October 1955, CCS 381 (12-1-47) Sec. 5, JCS; JCS 2057/47, 18 October 1954, CCS 373.11 (12-14-48) Sec. 20, JCS.

92. JCS 2056/71, 12 April 1955, forwarding Ridgway Memo of 9 April 1955, *ibid.*, Sec. 23; JCS 2056/75, 10 November 1955, with Decision, 18 November 1955, *ibid.*, Sec. 24; "Strategic Air Command Progress Analysis, 1948–56," 65–69.

93. James R. Killian, Jr., *Sputniks, Scientists, and Eisenhower* (Cambridge: MIT Press, 1977) 68–71; "Meeting the Threat of Surprise Attack," Report to the President by the Technological Capabilities Panel of the Science Advisory Committee, Office of Defense Mobilization, February 14, 1955, Technological Capabilities Panel of the S.A.C., Report to the President, February 14, 1955 Folder, Subject Series, Alphabetical Subseries, Box 11, WHO-SS, DDEL, Vol. I, 10–22, 31–46; Vol. II, 50–71, 73–111.

94. *Ibid.*, 17. See also Killian, *Sputniks, Scientists, and Eisenhower*, 71–93.

95. Briefing of WSEG Report No. 12, "Evaluation of an Atomic Offensive in Support of the Joint Strategic Capabilities Plan," April 8, 1955, Document Two, in Rosenberg, "A Smoking Radiating Ruin," 29–38. WSEG-12's summary report was completed February 28, 1955, according to John Ponturo, *Analytical Support for the Joint Chiefs of Staff: The WSEG Experience, 1948–1976* (Arlington, Va.: Institute for Defense Analyses, Study S-507, July 1979), 101.

96. N.I.E. 11–3–55, 17 May 1955, 30–31; Prados, *The Soviet Estimate*, 38–47; David Holloway, "Soviet Thermonuclear Development," 192–97; Rear Admiral Edwin T. Layton, Memorandum for Chairman, Joint Chiefs of Staff, Subject: Implications of Soviet Armaments Programs and Increasing Military Capabilities, 9 December 1955, CJCS 091 Russia, 1953–55, JCS.

97. Memorandum, by S. Everett Gleason, Subject: Discussion at the 272nd Meeting of the National Security Council, January 12, 13, 1956, 272nd Meeting of the NSC Folder, NSC Series, Box 7, ACWF-EPP, DDEL; diary entry, January 23, 1956, Robert Ferrell (ed.), *The Eisenhower Diaries*, 311–12.

98. A. J. Goodpaster, MCP, February 10, 1956; Eisenhower's reactions to the Bomber Gap are recounted in Prados, *The Soviet Estimate*, 43–50; Department of Defense, *Semi Annual Report of the Secretary of Defense, January 1 to June 30, 1957* (Washington, D.C.: 1957), 8.

99. The "New Look" debates are chronicled by Stephen Jurika, Jr. (ed.), *From Pearl Harbor to Vietnam: The Memoirs of Admiral Arthur W. Radford* (Stanford: Hoover Institution Press, 1980), 327–30; and papers in the JCS 2101 series, CCS 381 U.S. (1–31–50) Secs. 26 through 32, JCS. Later debates are covered in the CJCS 381 (Military Strategy and Posture) files of JCS Chairman Radford's Office Files, JCS; and exemplified by JSCP debates in JSPC 877/299, 23 November 1955, CCS 381 (11–29–49) Sec. 27. See also Matthew W. Ridgway, with Harold H. Martin, *Soldier* (New York: Harper and Row, 1956), 266–322; and General Maxwell D. Taylor, *The Uncertain Trumpet* (New York: Harper and Row, 1959), 23–46.

100. Memorandum, C. E. Wilson to Chairman, JCS, 27 January 1956, Subject: Military Strategy and Posture, and Memorandum, Lt. Colonel C. J. George to Wilson, February 6, 1956, CJCS 381 (Military Strategy and Posture) 1956, JCS. The Wilson memo is also in Military Planning 1956–57, Folder 2, Subject Series, Defense Department Subseries, Box 6, WHO-SS, DDEL. Significantly, this copy, declassified in 1980 vice 1978 for the copy in the JCS files, has the section on nuclear weapons use quoted here deleted.

101. NSC 5602/1, Basic National Security Policy, March 15, 1956, NSC 5602/1, Basic National Security Policy Folder, NSC Series, Policy Papers Subseries, Box 17, WHO-SANSA, DDEL, 1–11; A. J. Goodpaster, MCP, March 30, 1956, dated April 2, 1956, April 1956—Goodpaster Folder, DDE Diaries, Box 15, ACWF-EPP, DDEL; Arleigh Burke, Memorandum for the Record, Subject: Conversation with the President, 30 March 1956, Originator's File, AAB, NHC.

102. A. J. Goodpaster, MCP, May 24, 1956, May 1956—Goodpaster Folder, DDE Diaries, Box 15, ACWF-EPP, DDEL.

103. The record of JSCP/JSOP debates and their resolution may be found in CJCS (Military Strategy and Posture) and in CCS 381 (11–29–49) Sec. 30, JCS. The approved strategic concepts are in SM-423-56, 23 May 1956, in *ibid.*, and SM-763-56, 19 Sept. 1956, CCS 381 U.S. (1–31–50) Sec. 66, JCS. "Pentomic" reorganization is recounted in A. J. Goodpaster, MCP, October 11, 1956, Diary—Staff Memos, October 1956, DDE Diary, Box 19, ACWF-EPP, DDEL.

104. A. J. Goodpaster, MCP, February 10, 1956; MB-1 Genie deployment is noted in Naval Message, Basegram, from Admiral H. D. Felt, 192309Z February 1957, CCS 471.6 (8–15–45) Sec. 90, JCS. Genie yield is based on information in Tom Compere, ed., *The Air Force Blue Book, 1961, Vol. II* (New York: Military Publishing Institute, 1960), 341, and *Announced U.S. Nuclear Tests*, 6. Deployment of Nike Hercules with nuclear warheads is noted in letter, Neil McElroy to the President, January 12, 1958, Neil McElroy, Secretary of Defense 1959, Folder 4, Administration Series, Box 28, ACWF-EPP, DDEL; and list,

Los Alamos Stockpiled Nuclear Weapons Designs; and U.S. Army Antiaircraft Artillery and Guided Missile School, Fort Bliss, Texas, Joint Doctrine, Army Surface to Air Atomic Fires in Air Defense, January 8, 1957, File No. AAGMS, SAAF, JD, USAMHI.

105. A. J. Goodpaster, Memorandum for Admiral Arthur W. Radford, February 29, 1956, Joint Chiefs of Staff, January-April 1956, Folder 2, Subject Series, Defense Department, Box 4, WHO-SS, DDEL.

106. The best sources on ballistic missiles are Edmund Beard, *Developing the ICBM: A Study in Bureaucratic Politics* (New York: Columbia University Press, 1976); Ernest G. Schwiebert, *A History of the U.S. Air Force Ballistic Missiles* (New York: Praeger, 1965); Nathan F. Twining, *Neither Liberty Nor Safety* (New York: Holt, Rinehart and Winston, 1966), 299–309; Michael A. Armacost, *The Politics of Weapons Innovation, The Thor-Jupiter Controversy* (New York: Columbia University Press, 1969); Lemmer, *The Air Force and Strategic Deterrence*, 11–19, 40–46; Max Rosenberg, *The Air Force and the National Guided Missile Program, 1944–1950* (Washington, D.C.: USAF Historical Division Liaison Office, June 1964, declassified 1981); and Robert L. Perry, *The Ballistic Missile Decisions* (Santa Monica: Rand Corporation, Paper P-3686, October 1967).

107. Decision on AFC 12/8, Subject: USAF Strategic Missile Program, 6 May 1954, Air Force Council Decisions, Vol. I, Box 103, Nathan Twining Papers, LC; Beard, *Developing the ICBM*, 142–87; Schwiebert, *USAF Ballistic Missiles*, 67–85, 217–19; Technological Capabilities Panel Report, 38–39, 63–65; James S. Lay, Jr., Memorandum for the National Security Council, Subject: Recommendations of the Report to the President by the Technological Capabilities Panel of the Science Advisory Committee, ODM, Continental Defense, Study of, by R. Sprague, 1955, Folder 8, NSC Series, Subject Subseries, Box 1, WHO-SANSA, DDEL.

108. A. J. Goodpaster, MCP, December 19, 1956, dated December 20, 1956, December 1956 Diary—Staff Memos Folder, DDE Diary, Box 20, ACWF-EPP, DDEL. A similar comment may be found in A. J. Goodpaster, MCP, March 15, 1956, dated March 16, 1956, Joint Chiefs of Staff, January-April 1956 Folder 2, Subject Series, Defense Department Subseries, Box 4, WHO-SS, DDEL.

109. Decision on AFC 22/4a, Subject: Vulnerability of the USAF Strategic Striking Complex, 10 March 1953, Air Force Council Decisions, Vol. I, Box 103, Nathan Twining Papers, LC. See also A. J. Wohlstetter, *et al.*, *Selection and Use of Strategic Air Bases* (Santa Monica: Rand Corporation, Report R-266, April 1954).

110. Staff Report, *Protecting U.S. Power to Strike Back in the 1950s and 1960s* (Santa Monica: Rand Corporation, Report R-290, Contract No. AF 18 (600)-1600, September 1, 1956); *Development of Strategic Air Command*, 58–60; "Strategic Air Command Progress Analysis, 1948–1956," Foreword, 117–35; Decision on AFC 20/7, 6 March 1956, Subject: Strategic Plan of Operations, Air Force Council Decisions, Vol. I, Box 103, Nathan Twining Papers, LC.

111. Robert Cutler, *No Time for Rest* (Boston: Atlantic–Little Brown, 1956), 347–61; Prados, *The Soviet Estimate*, 51–75.

112. A. J. Goodpaster, MCP, November 4, 1957, dated November 6, 1957, Science Advisory Committee, November 1957-April 1958, Folder 3, Subject Series, Alphabetical Subseries, Box 23, WHO-SS, DDEL; NSC 5724, "Deterrence and Survival in the Nuclear Age," Report to the President by the Security Resources Panel of the Science Advisory Committee, 7 November 1957, in Gaither Report, November 1957–January 1958, Folder 2, *ibid.*, Box 13; Appointments, November 9, 1957, November 1957, Folder 2, ACW Diary, Box 9, ACWF-EPP, DDEL.

113. Appointments, November 9, 1957; A. J. Goodpaster, MCP, November 4, 7, 1957, following NSC Meeting, Military Planning, 1958–61, Folder 3, Subject Series, Defense Department Subseries, Box 6, WHO-SS, DDEL; Robert Cutler, Memorandum for the President, Subject: SAC Concentration in U.S. and Reaction Time, October 25, 1957, Robert Cutler 1956–57, Folder 1, Administration Series, Box 11, ACWF-EPP, DDEL.

114. A. J. Goodpaster, MCP, February 4, 1958, dated February 6, 1958, Missiles and

Satellites, Vol. II, January-February 1958, Folder II, Subject Series, Defense Department Subseries, WHO-SS, DDEL; anticipated Soviet ICBM deployments are laid out in JCS 1899/ 523, 20 October 1959, CCS 3340, Strategic Air And ICBM Operations, 10 September 1959, JCS; Prados, *The Soviet Estimate*, 75–126.

115. Lemmer, *The Air Force and Strategic Deterrence*, 45–51; Office of the Director, Defense Research and Engineering, Report No. 10, Military Space Projects, March-April-May 1960, Folder, same title, Subject Series, Defense Department Subseries, Box 9, WHO-SS, DDEL. JCS discussions of the Gaither report's implications for continental defense are in the JCS 2101 series, CCS 381 U.S. (1-31-50) Sec. 74–79; while those pertaining to SAC vulnerability are in the JCS 1899 series, CCS 381 U.S. (5–23–46) Secs. 94–98, both JCS.

116. The documentary evidence on advance authorization is fragmentary. This statement is based on B. L. Austin, Memorandum for Chairman, JCS, DM–93–58, 27 March 1958, Subject: Status of the "Instructions for the Expenditure of Nuclear Weapons under Special Circumstances," CCS 471.6 (8-15-45) Sec. 111, JCS; Memoranda, James S. Lay, Jr. to the Secretaries of State and Defense, Subject: Policy Regarding Use of Atomic Weapons, March 19, April 2, April 9, and April 23, 1958; Memorandum, Gordon Gray to General Goodpaster, December 15, 1958, on proposed Executive Order; undated page containing chronology of developments regarding Instructions for the Expenditure of Nuclear Weapons from February 17, 1959, through May 18, 1960; and letter of Thomas S. Gates to the President, June 5, 1959, all in AEC-Policy on Use of Atomic Weapons Folder, Box 9, WHO, Project Cleanup, DDEL. Withdrawal sheet of documents in *ibid*. Withdrawal sheets of documents on Atomic Weapons, Presidential Approval annd Instructions for Use Of, Folders 1–5; Atomic Weapons, Correspondence and Background for Presidential Approval, Policy re Use, Folders 2–6, both in NSC Series, Subject Subseries, Box 1, WHO-SANSA, DDEL. Instructions to Commanders, Folders 1–5, Subject Series, Alphabetical Subseries, Box 14, WHO-SS, DDEL.

117. *Development of Strategic Air Command*, 67–77; Special Report on SAC in Aviation Week and Space Technology, 72 (June 20, 1960), 101–44; WSEG Staff Study No. 77, The Feasibility, Cost and Effectiveness of Dual Runways at SAC Bomber Bases, 20 July 1959, CCS 4960, Air Bases, 27 July 1959, JCS.

118. Memo, Chief of Staff, USAF to the JCS, on Launching of the Strategic Air Command Alert Force, CSAF M–72–58, 10 March 1958, enclosed in JCS 1899/398, 10 March 1958, in CCS 381 U.S. (5-23-46) Sec. 95, JCS; JCS deliberations on Airborne Alert are in CCS 3340, Strategic Air and ICBM Operations, 10 September 1959, JCS; Robert F. Futrell, *Ideas, Concepts, Doctrine*, 578–82.

119. Briefing for the President, SAC Operations with Sealed Pit Weapons, in Defense Department, Vol. II, Folder 9, July 1958, Box 1, Defense Department Subseries; and A. J. Goodpaster, MCP, August 27, 1958, dated August 29, 1958, in Atomic Energy Commission, Vol. VII, Folder 4, August-September 1958, Box 3, Alphabetical Subseries, both in Subject Series, WHO-SS, DDEL; Message, DA, WASH DC, to USCINCEUR, Paris, France, 29 May 1958, Subject: Optimized, Sealed Pit Weapons, CCS 471.6 (8–15–45) Sec. 115, JCS.

120. *Development of Strategic Air Command*, 75; Bill Gunston, *Bombers of theWest* (New York: Scribner's, 1973), 183–213, 236–61; Strategic Air Command Progress Analysis, 1948–56, 65–66; Robert F. Futrell, *Ideas, Concepts, Doctrine*, 224–25; Prados, *The Soviet Estimate*, 30–37, 96–110; Oral History Interview, Richard M. Bissell, Jr., November 9, 1976, by Dr. Thomas Soapes, DDEL, 3–10.

121. Interview with John P. Coyle, 29 March 1978. Coyle was a major Navy analyst on Project Budapest. Budapest is also mentioned in Coyle's brief unclassified 1978 paper, "Biography of a Strategic Concept," courtesy John Coyle. JCS concerns on large nuclear weapons are noted in DM–221–57, 9 July 1957, Memo for General Eddleman, *el al*; Subject: Use of Large Weapons, CCS 471.6 (8–15–45) Sec. 9C, JCS; and Memo, Nathan Twining to Chairman, JCS, 8 May 1957, Subject: Studies of Large Yield Weapons, Subject File, Top Secret File, 1952–57, Folder 4, Box 122, Nathan Twining Papers, LC. The date of Budapest is noted in Chairman, JCS, Daily Log, 29 August 1957, Diary of CJCS Notebook, 8/15/57–12/31/57, Box 6, *ibid*.

122. For background on Navy thinking on nuclear strategy, see David Alan Rosenberg, "American Postwar Air Doctrine and Organization: The Navy Experience," Hurley and Ehrhart, eds., *Air Power and Warfare*, 245–78; Berend D. Bruins, *Navy Bombardment Missiles to 1960* (unpublished Ph.D. dissertation, Columbia University, 1981). For an example of one counterproposal to optimize the Navy's carriers for an all-out nuclear exchange, see Memorandum, Rear Admiral W. M. Beakley to the Chief of Naval Operations, Serial 0049P60, 2 November 1956, Subject: Comments on letter from Capt. J. T. Hayward, 12 September 1956, with First Endorsement, by Vice Admiral R. E. Libby, Serial 00132PO6, 3 November 1956, A–16–1 Folder, 1956, Strategic Plans Division Files, NHC.

123. On Polaris development, see David Alan Rosenberg, "Arleigh Albert Burke," in Robert William Love, Jr., *The Chiefs of Naval Operations* (Annapolis: Naval Institute Press, 1980), 263–319; Richard G. Hewlett and Francis Duncan, *Nuclear Navy, 1946–1962* (Chicago: University of Chicago Press, 1974), 220–70; and Harvey M. Sapolsky, *The Polaris System Development: Bureaucratic and Programmatic Success in Government* (Cambridge: Harvard University Press, 1972).

124. Vice Admiral R. E. Libbyk, First Endorsement, Beakley Memo, 3 November 1956; Captain W. T. Kinsella, Memorandum for the Record, Subject: Minutes of VCNO Meeting, 1045, 17 June 1957, Folder Conferences and Symposiums, 1957, Box 76, Guided Missile Division Papers, Accession No. 38–76–81, Washington National Records Center (hereafter GMDP). This concept is based on the conclusions of Naval Warfare Analysis Group Study 1, Introduction of the Fleet Ballistic Missile into Service, forwarded by Rear Admiral Roy L. Johnson to the Chief of Naval Operations, Serial 007 P93, 30 January 1957, and written by John P. Coyle. NAVWAG 1 was declassified March 1980 by the Office of the Chief of Naval Operations.

125. Rear Admimral Roy L. Johnson, Memorandum for the Chief of Naval Operations, Subject: Preliminary Views on POLARIS in Relation to Recent Events, Serial 0083 P93, 24 October 1957, Ballistic Missiles, October-November Folder, Box 74, GMDP. See also Navy Augmentation plans for Polaris in JCS 1620/175, 6 February 1958, CCS 471.6 (5–31–44) Sec. 14, JCS; and Rosenberg, "Arleigh Albert Burke," 279–86.

126. SM–12–58, 4 January 1958, Memorandum for General Twining, *et al*; Subject: SM–910–57 of 19 December 1957, and Army Flimsy, 26 December 1957, Subject: JCS 1844/242, Atomic Annex to the Joint Strategic Capabilities Plan, both in CCS 373.11 (12–14–48) Sec. 38, JCS. Information on the "Alternative Undertaking" is also based on other documents in *ibid*.; JCS 1844/242, 2 December 1957, declassified with many deletions by the Directorate of Freedom of Information and Security Review, Office of the Secretary of Defense (hereafter OSDFOI); and interview with John P. Coyle, 29 March 1978.

127. Coyle interview, *ibid*. The JSCP Annex C was approved 9 April 1958, DM–136–58, 23 April 1958, Memorandum for General Eddleman, *et al*; Subject: Operational Implications of the Use of Surface Burst Nuclear Weapons, CCS 471.6 (10–16–46) Sec. 24, JCS.

128. Rosenberg, "Arleigh Albert Burke," 291–92; Taylor, *Uncertain Trumpet*, 57–65; S. Everett Gleason, Memorandum, May 2, 1958, Subject: Discussion at the 364th Meeting of the National Security Council, Thursday, May 1, 1958, 364th Meeting, NSC Folder, Box 10, NSC Series, ACWF-EPP, DDEL. See also NSC 5810/1, Basic National Security Policy, May 5, 1958, NSC 5810/1 BNSP Folder, NSC Series, Policy Paper Subseries, Box 25, WHO-SANSA, DDEL.

129. NSC 5816, A Net Evaluation Subcommittee, July 1, 1958, NSC 5816, A Net Evaluation Subcommittee Folder, *ibid*.; Gordon Gray, Memorandum of Conversation with the President, Wednesday, November 19, 1958, dated 22 November 1958. Meetings with the President, 1958, Folder 1, Special Assistant Series, Presidential Subseries, Box 3, WHO-SANSA, DDEL. This study may have been sparked by Captian John Morse, USN, (Navy Observer to the AEC), Memorandum to General Cutler, Subject: Massive Deterrent, March 8, 1958, Nuclear Policy Folder, Box 12, WHO-Project Cleanup, DDEL.

130. Gordon Gray, Memo of Conversation with the President, 19 November 1958; NSC Action no. 2009, Record of Action by the National Security Council at its 387th Meeting,

held on November 20, 1958 (approved by the President on December 1, 1958), declassified copy provided by National Security Council, 1980.

131. John S. D. Eisenhower, MCP, December 16, 1958, dated December 22, 1958, Intelligence Matters, Folder 7, December 1958, Subject Series, Alphabetical Subseries, Box 15, WHO-SS, DDEL; A. J. Goodpaster, MCP, January 16, 1959, dated January 20, 1959, Staff Notes, January 1959, Folder 2, DDE Diary, WHO-SS, DDEL.

132. Gordon Gray, Memoranda of conversation with the President, Monday, February 16, 1959, dated February 18, 1959, and Thursday, February 26, 1959, dated February 28, 1959, Meetings with the President, 1959, Folder 6, Special Assistant Series, Presidential Subseries, Box 4, WHO-SANSA,, DDEL. The Hickey committee tasking is contained in General Nathan F. Twining, Memorandum for Lt. General Thomas F. Hickey, Net Evaluation Sub Committee, CM–305–59, 20 February 1959, Subject: Approval of Relative Merits from the Point of View of Effective Deterrence of Alternative Retaliatory Efforts, CCS 3070 Grand Strategy, 20 February 1959, JCS debates on these taskings are contained in *ibid*.

133. Arleigh Burke, CNO Personal Letter No. 5 to Retired Flag Officers, Subject: Pertinent Information, Summary of Major Strategic Considerations for the 1960-70 ERA, Navy Folder, Box 28, Thomas D. White Papers, LC. Burke's thinking was built on papers such as Rear Admiral Roy L. Johnson, Memo for the Distribution List, Subject: Adaptation of a National Military Posture to the Era of Nuclear Parity: A Suggested Navy Posture, Serial 0008 P93, 3 December 1957, with paper, same subject, appended, A-16-10 Folder, 1957, Strategic Plans Division Papers, NHC. See also Rosenberg, "Arleigh Albert Burke," 292-95.

134. JCS 2056/143, 22 December 1959, containing Navy Memo, 30 September 1959, declassified with deletions, August 1980, 3205, Target Systems (17 August 1959); Memorandum, James S. Russell to the Secretary of Defense, Subject: Statement of Navy Views on the Concept of Employment and Command Structure for the Polaris Weapons System, Serial 000182 P60, 5 May 1959, CCS 4720 Intermediate Range (5 January 1959) Group II, both JCS.

135. "Polaris" Chronology, C. A. Haskins, 2/10/60, Defense Department, Vol. IV, Folder 3, March-April 1960, Subject Series, Defense Department Subseries, Box 2, WHO-SS, DDEL.

136. Curtis E. LeMay, Memorandum for the Chief of Staff, USAF, March 2, 1959, Subject: Rand Briefing on Polaris, Air Force Council Folder, Box 25, Thomas D. White Papers, LC; E. P. Oliver *Polaris Weapon System* (Santa Monica: Rand Corporation, U.S. Air Force Project RAND Research Memorandum RM-2311, October 28, 1958), extracts declassified, September 1982.

137. Thomas D. White, Memorandum for DCS/Plans and Programs, 30 March 1959, Chief of Staff "Signed Memos" Folder, Box 26; and Letter, White to General Laurence S. Kuter, 3 March 1959, Chief of Staff, 1959, Top Secret General File, Box 29, both Thomas D. White Papers, LC.

138. Curtis E. LeMay, Memorandum for the Chief of Staff, USAF, Subject: USAF Tasks and Objective Force Structure (1959–70), 5 May 1959, with Tabs A through E appended, approved by the Chief of Staff, May 12, 1959, Air Force Council Folder; and Jacob E. Smart, Decision, Subject: USAF Tasks and Objective Force Structure (1959–70), 15 May 1959, Air Force Council Decisions, 1959, Notebook, both Box 25, Thomas D. White Papers, LC.

139. Herbert Goldhamer and Andrew W. Marshall, with the assistance of Nathan Leites, *The Deterrence and Strategy of Total War, 1959–1961: A Method of Analysis* (Santa Monica: Rand Corporation, U.S. Air Force Project RAND Research Memorandum RM-2301, April 30, 1959), 191.

140. Richard F. Fryklund, *One Hundred Million Lives, Maximum Survival in a Nuclear War* (New York: Macmillan, 1962), 1–30; Goldberg, *Survey of Ideas about Counterforce*, 13–21. See also Desmond Ball, *Politics and Force Levels: The Strategic Missile Program and the Kennedy Administration* (Berkeley; University of California Press, 1980), 31–34.

141. Curtis E. LeMay, Memorandum to the Chief of Staff, USAF, Subject: The Threat, March 2, 1960, with paper enclosed, approved by General White, March 2, 1960, Air Force Council No. 1 Folder, January-June 1960, Box 36, Thomas D. White Papers, LC.

142. JCS 1620/250, 28 April 1959, CCS 4720 Intermediate Range (5 January 1959) Group II, JCS; Arleigh Burke, Memorandum for All DCNOs, Subject: SAC Control of the FBM, Op-00 Memo 0529-58, 8 December 1958, Originator's File, AAB, NHC; *The Washington Star*, April 17, 1959.

143. JCS 1620/254, 2 May 1959, CCS 4720 Intermediate Range (5 January 1959) Group II, JCS. See also Rosenberg, "Arleigh Albert Burke," 302–4.

144. JCS 2056/124, 1 June 1959, CCS 3205 Target Systems (29 May 1959) JCS; JCS 2056/129, 23 July 1959; JCS 2056/130, 12 August 1959; JCS 2056/138, 20 October 1959, with Note to the Control Division, 27 October 1959, and Notes by the Secretaries to the Holders of JCS 2056/138, 1 February 1961 and 13 March 1961, all in CCS 3205 Target Systems (29 May 1959) JCS. The impasse this caused was partially responsible for the establishment of the Defense Intelligence Agency. Ball, *Politics and Force Levels*, 95.

145. JCS 2056/131, 20 August 1959, declassified with deletions, 1980, CCS 3205 Target Systems (17 August 1959), JCS. See also *JSTPS History, SIOP-62*, 6–11.

146. Brief Summary of Comparative Data, NESC 2009 and NTSDBs, dated 29 August and 7 September 1960, Memos and Letters (NSTL) AAB, NHC; Transcript, Admiral Burke's Conversation with Admiral Russell, November 11, 1960; A. J. Goodpaster, MCP, February 12, 1960, dated February 18, 1960, Staff Notes, February 1960, Folder 1, DDE Diary, Box 47, ACWF-EPP, DDEL; Tab B to Thomas Gates, draft memo to the JCS, appended to letter, Gates to Goodpaster, 10 August 1960.

147. A. J. Goodpaster, MCP, November 21, 1959, dated January 2, 1960, Defense Department, Vol. IV, Folder 1, January 1960, Subject Series, Defense Department Subseries, Box 2, WHO-SS, DDEL. See also A. J. Goodpaster, MCP, November 5, 1959, dated November 6, 1959, Staff Notes, November 1959, Folder 3, DDE Diary, Box 45, ACWF-EPP, DDEL; A. J. Goodpaster, MCP, January 25, 1960, dated January 26, 1960, Staff Notes, January 1960, Folder 1, DDE Diary, Box 47, ACWF-EPP, DDEL.

148. A. J. Goodpaster, MCP, 16 November 1959, dated December 2, 1959, Budget, Military, FY 62, Folder 2, Subject Series, Defense Department Subseries, Box 3, WHO-SS, DDEL. This comment was repeated five days later. See MCP, November 21, 1959. A. J. Goodpaster, MCP, May 5, 1960, dated May 7, 1960, Joint Chiefs of Staff, Folder 8, September 1959–May 1960, Subject Series, Defense Department Subseries, Box 4, WHO-SS, DDEL.

149. A. J. Goodpaster, MCP, April 6, 1960, Defense Department, Vol. IV, Folder 3, March-April 1960, Subject Series, Defense Department Subseries, Box 2, WHO-SS, DDEL. See also the President's comments on Polaris in A. J. Goodpaster, MCP, March 18, 1960, dated March 26, 1960, *ibid*.

150. A. J. Goodpaster, MCP, May 4, 1960, dated May 7, 1960, Dr. Kistiakowsky, Folder 3, April-June 1960, Subject Series, Alphabetical Subseries, Box 16, WHO-SS, DDEL.

151. Briefing Sheet for the Chairman, JCS, 7 December 1959, Subject: Joint Strategic Objectives Plan for 1 July 1963, with Enclosure, CCS 3130, JSOP (25 November 1959) JCS. NSC 5904/1, 17 March 1959, is listed without title in Annotated List of Serially Numbered NSC Documents, February 17, 1959 (updated to December 1960), but its title is listed in Memorandum by Chief of Staff of the Air Force on JSCP Definitions, CSAFM 84–60, 29 February 1960, CCS 3120, JSCP (24 August 1959), JCS. Questions on U.S. War Objectives are contained in James S. Lay, Jr., Memorandum for the NSC, January 7, 1959, Subject: Review of NSC5410/1, with discussion paper enclosed. Folder NSC 5410/1, U.S. War Objectives, NSC Series, Policy Papers Subseries, Box 9, WHO-SANSA, DDEL.

152. A. J. Goodpaster, MCP, January 25, 1960.

153. A. J. Goodpaster, MCP, July 6, 1960, Staff Notes, July 1960 Folder, DDE Diaries, Box 51, ACWF-EPP, DDEL.

154. Message, CNO to CINCPACFLT, CINCLANTFLT, CINCUSNAVEUR, 0051/06 November 1960; Arleigh Burke, Memorandum for the Record, Subject: Conversation with Mr. Gates on the Preparation of the NSTL and SIOP, 15 August 1960, Op-00 Memo Serial 000469-60, 15 August 1960; and Arleigh Burke, Memo for the Record, Subject: Preparation

of Basic National Target List and a Single Integrated Operational Plan, 15 August 1960, both in NSTL/SIOP Briefing Folder, AAB, NHC.

155. The Navy plans for dealing with the SIOP are laid out in Transcript, Admiral Burke's Conversation with Captain [F.A.] Bardshar, 22 August 1960, Transcripts & Phone Cons Folder, AAB, NHC; and in Rear Admiral Paul Blackburn, Memo for the Record, Subject: Comments on the Questions, 12 October 1960. Navy frustrations with the Army are indicated in Arleigh Burke, Memorandum for Op-06C, Subject: Army Participation in the NSTL/ SIOP, Op-00 Memo 00638-60, 3 November 1960, Memos & Letters Folder (NSTL), AAB, NHC; Memo, Burke to Lemnitzer, 22 November 1960.

156. L. R. Geis, Memo for the Record, Subject: NSTL-SIOP, Op-00 Memo, 000691-60, 28 November 1960, discussing Admiral Burke's conversations with Captain Aurand, Memos & Letters (NSTL) Folder, AAB, NHC; Special Edition, Flag Officers' Dope, 4 December 1960, discusses Burke's doubts and pressures for approval.

157. Special Edition, Flag Officers' Dope, 4 December 1960: A. J. Goodpaster, Memorandum for the Secretary of Defense, January 12, 1961, Department of Defense, Vol. IV, Folder 10, December 1960–January 1961, Subject Series, Department of Defense Subseries, Box 2, WHO-SS, DDEL; Kistiakowsky, *A Scientist at the White House*, 421.

158. *Development of Strategic Air Command*, 79–81; Ball, *Politics and Force Levels*, 43– 53, 116–17; Lemmer, *The Air Force and Strategic Deterrence*, 44; Futrell, *Ideas, Concepts, Doctrine*, 576–82.

159. Gordon Gray, Memorandum of Meeting with the President, Wednesday, August 24, 1960, dated August 25, 1960, Subject: Report of Panel of President's Science Advisory Committee on Weapons Technology for Limited Warfare, Staff Notes, August 1960, Folder 1, DDE Diary, Box 51, ACWF-EPP, DDEL. See also Eisenhower's comments in MCP, November 21, 1959; Arkin, Cochran, and Hoenig, "The U.S. Nuclear Stockpile," 1–2.

160. WSEG Report No. 50, Evaluation of Strategic Offensive Weapons Systems, 27 December 1960, Appendix E to Enclosure A, The Feasibility of Achievement of Counterforce Objectives, 64–81, OSDFOI; John K. Gerhart, Memo to AFCCS, Subject: Analysis of the Problem of Finding and Striking Soviet Mobile Missiles, 7 November 1960, Folder 4–5, Missiles/Space/Nuclear, Box 36, Thomas D. White Papers, LC.

161. Air Staff Summary Sheet, Major General David A. Burchinal to General White, Subject: Reply to CINCSAC Message on RAND "Counterforce" Briefing, 1 March 1961, with message for General Power from General White, 7 March 1961, appended, Top Secret 1961 Folder, Box 48, Thomas D. White Papers, LC.

162. Message, Vice Admiral E. B. Parker to Admiral Burke, 052100Z February 1961, NSTL/SIOP Messages, AAB, NHC; Ball, *Politics and Force Levels*, 119–20, 186–90; Message, CNO to CINCPACFLT, CINCLANTFLT, CINCUSNAVEUR, 191635Z May 1961, NSTL/ SIOP Messages, AAB, NHC; Draft, Appendix 1 to the Memorandum for the President, September 23, 1961, Subject: Recommended Long Range Nuclear Delivery Forces, OSDFOI. THe new Hickey study estimated 1,200 to 1,700 "aim points" for 1965, and 1,350 to 2,200 for 1967.

163. Draft, Memo for the President, September 23, 1961.

164. Ball, *Politics and Force Levels*, 190–92; Henry S. Rowen, "Formulating Strategic Doctrine," Part III of Vol. 4, Appendix K to *The Report of the Commission on the Organization of the Government for the Conduct of Foreign Policy* (Washington, D.C.: GPO, 1975), 220–34; Captain Mark D. Mariska, USA, "The Single Integrated Operational Plan," *Military Review, 52* (March 1972), 32–39.

165. SM-833-59, 25 August 1959 (updated through 30 March 1964), Memorandum for Chief of Staff, U.S. Army, *et al.*, Subject: Uniform Readiness Conditions, appended to JCS 1968/50, CCS 3180, Emergency Readiness Plan (20 April 1959), JCS.

166. Air Force report quoted in Draft Memorandum for the President, November 21, 1962, Subject: Recommended FY 1964–FY 1968 Strategic Retaliatory Forces, OSDFOI. See also Futrell, *Ideas, Concepts, Doctrine*, 623–27; and Conversations between General David A. Burchinal, USAF (Ret.) and Colonel Jack Schmidt and Lt. Colonel Jack Strater, 11 April

1975, Senior Officers Debriefing Program, USAMHI, 108–12; Rowen, "Formulating Strategic Doctrine," 227–32.

167. General L. L. Lemnitzer, Chairman, JCS, Memorandum for Secretary McNamara, CM-190-61, 18 April 1961, Subject: "Doctrine" on Thermonuclear Attack, OSDFOI.

168. JCS 1920/6, 2 October 1956, with Note to Holders, 12 October 1956; and SM-781-57, 6 November 1957, Brig. General R. D. Wentworth, to Chief of Staff, U.S. Army, *et al.*, enclosing Joint Long Range Strategic Estimate, (JCS 1920/8 as amended), CCS 381 USSR (3-2-46) Secs. 73 and 74 respectively, JCS. The last preceding paper in this series had been JCS 1920/5, 19 December 1949, Draft Long Range War Plan DROPSHOT, in Bulky Package, Sec. 3 of *ibid*.

169. Arleigh Burke, CNO Speech–Discussion, Defense Policy Seminar, Harvard University, 24 March 1960, AAB, NHC, 9–10.

THE BUREAUCRATIC AND
POLITICAL ENVIRONMENT

5
Civil-Military Relations:
The President and the General

DOUGLAS KINNARD

American civil-military relations—the issue of civilian supremacy over the military, which so occupied the founding fathers at Philadelphia and other political thinkers through the last century—was no longer a serious political or constitutional issue in the post–World War II period.[1] Prior to the Second World War, threats to American security were few and distant. As a result, military forces were small and the integration of diplomacy and military planning almost nonexistent, except in time of war. After World War II this changed drastically, and national security considerations became central to American political thinking. These considerations focused on the perceived Soviet threat, along with the need for the United States to provide leadership to the Western nations in meeting that threat. Quite obviously, this new role required the United States to support substantial military forces, and it necessitated a sustained and active involvement in the political/strategic aspects of world affairs not previously part of the American experience. Given this new situation—the manner in which foreign and security problems were conceived, and the processes by which policies were developed and implemented to meet these problems, would be different from previous arrangements.

From 1945 to 1947 organizational options for conceptualizing and executing national security policy were proffered, debated, and finally articulated in the National Security Act of 1947. Among other things, the act established a National Security Council to advise the President on foreign and defense matters; a National Military Establishment headed by a secretary of defense supervising (initially in a kind of federalized arrangement) the military departments, including the new Department of Air Force; and a statutory Joint Chiefs of Staff. The central issue faced by those whose task it was to implement the new law was how to reconcile the resources required by America's new world role with competing and growing demands for social programs, and at the same time to promote a viable economy. It is in this context that civil-military relations evolved in the postwar period.

One part of the 1947 act established the position of secretary of defense. It gave this official, who was in effect the President's deputy for national security affairs, only limited authority. Early experiences with the office—most notably those of James Forrestal, its first incumbent—led to 1949 amendments that increased the secretary's authority and created a chairman of the Joint Chiefs of Staff. Both changes were designed to improve civilian control over the military.

Although the 1949 amendments strengthened the authority of the Secretary of Defense, they did not solve the underlying interservice divergencies that had caused the problems in the first place. These problems, though normally articulated in doctrinal terms, in reality arose out of the competition among the services for the shares of the fairly austere military budgets of that period. After the beginning of the Korean war in 1950, the accompanying larger budgets removed much of the impetus for interservice competition, at least for the duration of that conflict.

Eisenhower—who, shortly after taking office in January 1953, terminated the Korean war—faced the problem of establishing new civil-military relations in a peacetime environment and of setting the direction these relations would take for the remainder of the 1950s. This chapter will examine civil-military relations during the Eisenhower administration with particular attention to budgetary-strategic doctrine and the processes which Eisenhower established to control the substantive outcomes.

The Eisenhower presidency fell into two related but somewhat different periods. During the first, 1953 and 1954, the President established his strategic doctrine and budgetary priorities. In the second period, beginning in 1955, he struggled to hold the line against those who would change the direction of his strategic and budgetary approach. This chapter focuses, in the main, on the second period, not only because of its importance in its own right but also because the Eisenhower experience considerably influenced civil-military relations in the next decade, that of the Vietnam war. General Maxwell Taylor, Army Chief of Staff from 1955 to 1959, can be considered the major military counterpoint to President Eisenhower. Although other senior military leaders at the time may have played important roles, the Army's challenge to the President seems most pointed. In addition, it was the Army's doctrinal challenge that was to provide the basis for a new strategic approach in the 1960s. This gives it the relevance that goes beyond the Eisenhower period.

I

When Maxwell Taylor arrived in Washington in the early summer of 1955 to become Army Chief of Staff, the Eisenhower administration had been in place for two and one-half years. Eisenhower's own strategic policies and budgetary goals were well established, and he had superimposed his own ideas on the process employed for conducting national security affairs. During the 1952 campaign Eisenhower had made two major promises: to end the Korean war, which had been stalemated for a year, and to reduce the budget. There was a direct relationship between the two. Ending the war, which he did within six months after taking office, was a necessary prelude to reducing the budget, but he needed to do more. To cut the overall budget from $74 billion for the fiscal year in which he took office, to $70 billion the next year, and to $60 billion the following, meant a further paring of the defense budget. This, in turn, would necessitate a close look at the kind of strategy the United States was going to pursue in the post-Korean war period.

Before discussing Eisenhower's strategic concepts at the time he assumed office, it might be well to stress that his conservative economic views were central to his thinking on all issues, including national security. These views were genuine and of long-standing. His strategic concepts on assuming office, he set forth in his memoirs: to rely on deterrence and to rule out preventive war; to stress the role of nuclear technology, reducing reliance on United States conventional forces; to place heavy reliance on allied land forces around the Soviet periphery; to stress economic strength, especially through reduced defense budgets; and to prepare for a continued struggle with the U.S.S.R. over decades. Eisenhower's problem was to blend these strategic views into a credible strategy that he could implement at a fairly low cost and sell both to the American people and to the nation's allies. To accomplish this objective, the President used organizational means, careful selection of key appointees,[2] his own large experience in handling bureaucracies, and his great rapport with the American people.

At the apex of the defense and foreign policy process, Eisenhower established a refurbished National Security Council (NSC), which had been rather loosely structured under Truman. He transformed it into a highly structured system that incorporated these changes: wider representation at the meetings to include the Secretary of the Treasury and the Budget Director; a planning board that prepared papers for council consideration; and an operations coordinating board that monitored the follow-through on presidential decisions. The restructured NSC was a formal organization, but Eisenhower balanced this with informal procedure. In fact, he placed even more emphasis on informal meetings and briefings on defense-related matters. The number of such meetings was substantial.[3] At least one well-placed observer, who was present at nearly all the National Security Council meetings during the last 27 months of the administration, believed that the informal office meetings were much more important than the council sessions.[4]

By July 1953 Eisenhower concluded that the time had come for the newly appointed service chiefs to undertake a reexamination of United States strategic policy.[5] Since the Korean armistice was about to be signed, the President wished to develop a defense posture that the country could sustain for the indefinite future. He wanted the new chiefs, before they were caught up in their office duties, to produce the agreed-on evaluation of overall defense policy. Their report was the first step in what subsequently became known as the "New Look," which the President later defined as

> first a reallocation of resources among the five categories of forces, and second, the placing of greater emphasis than formerly on the deterrent and destructive power of improved nuclear weapons, better means of delivery, and effective air-defense units.[6]

The Chiefs of Staff were able to agree on a basic paper of strategic premises and guidelines; they faced greater difficulty in translating these generalities into the specifics for the fiscal year 1955 defense budget. After some deliberation, the Joint Chiefs concluded that they could make no substantial changes in the defense budget of $42 billion. They reasoned that there was no change in the perceived threat, no change in alliance commitments, and no new guidance on the employment of nuclear weapons.

Defense Secretary Charles Wilson presented this problem to an NSC meeting on October 13, 1953. The reaction of Treasury Secretary George Humphrey (who expected a defense budget of $36 billion) and of Budget Director Joseph M. Dodge was what one source called "horrified." It fell to Joint Chiefs of Staff Chairman Arthur W. Radford to defend the Joint Chiefs' premises. He centered his discussion on the nature of presidential guidance for employment of nuclear weapons. In his message, which was to have very significant results, he argued that if the administration accepted the use of nuclear weapons from the outset of a conflict as a planning premise, then it could develop a less costly force structure. This premise led to a subsequent NSC session on October 29 at which the President approved NSC 162/2, the policy basis of the New Look. Picking up Radford's suggestion of October 13, NSC 162/2 placed maximum reliance on nuclear weapons from the outset of a conflict. Radford's talk of October 13 had been entirely his own; that is, neither the Army nor the Navy agreed with the new NSC policy on nuclear war. Nevertheless, Secretary Wilson, with Radford's help, was able to obtain qualified agreement from Army Chief Matthew B. Ridgway and Navy Chief Robert B. Carney, and to use the new policy to reduce the defense budget to a level acceptable to Eisenhower and Humphrey.

The President's public announcements about the New Look came mostly in three messages to Congress: State of the Union, Budget, and that accompanying the Economic Report. Throughout the fall and winter of 1953, high-level administration spokesmen worked at selling it to the public. Of all the speeches made to explain the new defense policy, only one is now remembered: John Foster Dulles's "massive retaliation" speech before the New York Council on Foreign Relations on January 12, 1954. This speech, which was surely one of the great moments in the history of cold war rhetoric, caused such an uproar that Dulles published in the April issue of *Foreign Affairs* an article stressing that there were wider options than nuclear weapons. By autumn the immediate flurry of criticism and clarification brought on by the speech was over; still, for many years thereafter, analysts and writers continued to criticize United States defense policy. Some doubters concentrated on alternative deterrence strategies; others focused on the notion of limited war.[7]

Congress examined the New Look during the hearings of the fiscal year 1955 defense budget; these debates offered no challenge to the concept and almost none to the particulars. The administration's image of unanimity on the Eisenhower strategy remained intact during the hearings. Ridgway's misgivings about the administration's lack of emphasis on land forces were more implied than actual. Floor debate was more active in the Senate than in the House, but in neither case was it systematic or informed. With the clearing of the defense appropriation, Eisenhower had gained his strategic policy.[8]

Although the main interaction between the military and the President over his strategy and budgetary constraints still lay ahead, Ridgway began to challenge the Army's share of the budget directly. Ridgway expressed his views at length when the National Security Council met on December 3, 1954. Five days later, in a small meeting in the President's office, Treasury Secretary Humphrey told Eisenhower that he was puzzled by Ridgway's presentation. The President explained that he wished Ridgway to have an opportunity to express his criticisms at the highest level. Such a course was espcially desirable since budgetary action was to be taken with which Ridgway would probably not agree.[9]

Several weeks later the Secretary of Defense and the service chiefs had a final session with the President about the 1956 defense budget. Although he still faced opposition, especially on the part of Ridgway and the Army, the President had a message for those present. As commander-in-chief, he said, he was entitled to loyal support for his position, and he expected to have it. He had read and considered the differences that the Army and Navy chiefs had set forth. But now he had made the decision, and all must follow it.[10]

II

Ridgway's years as Chief of Staff were difficult, given his and the Army's misgivings concerning the Eisenhower strategy and his inability to secure any changes in the President's program. By early 1955 Eisenhower had made the decision to replace Ridgway that summer. The leading candidate was General Maxwell Taylor, then commander of the armed forces in the Far East.[11] The President summoned Taylor home, without revealing the purpose, to enable the General to discuss his prospective appointment with him and with Secretary of Defense Wilson.

When Taylor met with the President on February 24, Eisenhower issued two demands. The new Chief of Staff would have to "wholeheartedly accept that his primary responsibility relates to his joint duties," and he must "hold views as to doctrine, basic principles, and relationships which are in accord with those of the President. Loyalty in spirit as well as in letter is essential." Taylor's reply "indicated complete understanding and acceptance of these views of the President."[12]

Eisenhower's first point with Taylor—his duties as a member of the Joint Chiefs of Staff—was a subject of considerable interest to the commander-in-chief. Between Taylor's February interview and his June arrival in Washington, the President had become concerned about the need to prevent members of the Joint Chiefs from voicing opposition to his policies when they were testifying before Congress. Welcoming Taylor to his new duties on June 29, Eisenhower indicated that what he wanted especially from Taylor was "teamwork."[13]

Taylor and the other chiefs were to hear more on this subject from the President. They subsequently requested through General Andrew Goodpaster of the White House staff some explanation of Eisenhower's concept of the Joint Chiefs. Goodpaster's summary of Eisenhower's views is instructive and worth repeating:

> While each is the head of his own service, his main task is—or should be—as one of the Joint Chiefs of Staff. The President does not consider them as advocates for the Army, Navy, etc. Though each has a particular service background, they should think and act as a body. . . . He thought great harm had been done on past occasions when the Chiefs of Staff were called upon to speak out on individual policy views without regard to announced Administration policy. . . . He would agree that there are of course, great service pressures on the individual Chiefs of Staff, even more in peacetime than in War. Subordinates in the services may advance service interests very strongly. The Chief of Staff will be acutely aware of these pressures and sensitive to them, but he must shape them into the larger purpose.[14]

During the spring of 1956 Eisenhower was troubled by the appearance of former Army Chief Ridgway's publications critical of the President's policies.[15] The President indicated that he was "thinking of asking for a new type of oath to be taken by all military and civilian officials who serve in the Pentagon . . . that on termination of their duty they will disclose nothing which the Department of Defense determines to be security information."[16] A few days later, in a conversation with Defense Secretary Wilson, the President commented that he was "inclined to think that the Chiefs of Staff system . . . has failed." He was astonished at the actions of "one or two" of the chiefs "that I have known all my life."[17]

In his first year as Army chief, Taylor became involved with strategic issues of a doctrinal nature, which were eventually to bring him into a conflict with the President. While awaiting his return to Washington during the spring of 1955, Taylor received a copy of the administration's 1955 Basic National Security Policy (BNSP) paper.[18] In examining the document, he was "struck by the breadth of its language and the degree of departure from the dogma of Massive Retaliation."[19] Accordingly, he decided to develop his own "National Military Program" more in keeping with the Army viewpoint and yet, as he saw it, in keeping with the guidance contained in the BNSP. The National Military Program went through several refinements during Taylor's early months in Washington and was the basis of what eventually became his proposed strategy of flexible response.

Taylor's program stressed the need for the deterrence and defeat of local aggression in addition to the deterrence of general war emphasized in Eisenhower's New Look strategy. What this meant in terms of resources was an increased commitment to conventional forces, together with the mobility and logistical support necessary to permit and sustain their intervention wherever required. Additionally, as Taylor saw it, these forces needed the capability to employ tactical atomic weapons, the technical feasibility of which was still uncertain.

By the late winter of 1956, Secretary Wilson thought that it was time to assemble the military chiefs and to reexamine the basic strategic issues. He set up a meeting for them in Puerto Rico and joined them at its conclusion. Taylor felt that this would be a good opportunity to introduce his National Military Program into the Joint arena; but, as he tells it, "My colleagues read this Army study politely and then quietly put it to one side."[20] This was not a surprising reaction, for Taylor's program would mean additional budgetary resources for the Army, presumably at the expense of the other services if Eisenhower was to hold the lid on the budget. As a result of the meeting, the chiefs called for an overall increase in budgetary outlays from the earlier target of $34 billion up to $40 billion by 1960, but this did not involve any basic changes in the New Look strategy.

A few days after the meeting ended, Wilson called on the President with a draft memorandum on the thinking of the Joint Chiefs. The tenor of the memorandum bothered Eisenhower. "The memorandum seemed to say that the U.S. military position has worsened in the last three years," and with that he would not agree. Specifically, the President could not understand why manpower could not be cut, given America's technological superiority. Wilson agreed and opined that more military strength over the past three years "would not have bettered us in our international position."[21] Taylor's new program was off to a bad start.

In the same month of March, 1956, the drafting of the new Joint Strategic Objectives Plan (JSOP) presented Taylor another occasion for questioning a basic premise of Eisenhower's strategy. Increasing costs of defense had convinced Chairman Radford that economies at the expense of conventional (primarily army) forces were in order. The issue focused on early use of atomic weapons. Taylor proposed language in the new JSOP that would place some limitations on the use of atomics in the initial stages of a conflict with the U.S.S.R. Radford and the other chiefs opposed this change, arguing from the basic premise of the New Look strategy.[22] The issue required a series of meetings that spring between the President and his military advisers.

In late March, Radford brought the chiefs to the White House and opened the meeting with the President by saying "that unless brought under control, a situation may develop in which the Services will become involved in increasing public disagreement among themselves. Also, in the last four or five months," he added, "quite a large number of 'split' issues had to be taken to Secretary Wilson." The most troublesome concerned the use of atomic weapons. The President agreed that the subject was one that "required great care in discussion"; however, he was clear in his own mind that "in any war with the Soviets we would use them." While he had the chiefs there, the President went on to tell them that he wanted it understood "that any of them who wished could always come along with Radford to see him."[23]

Two months later Taylor accepted the President's offer. He and Radford appeared at Eisenhower's office to discuss the use of atomics, again in the context of the JSOP, which was by now before the chiefs for decision. The chairman and the Air Force and Navy chiefs took the view, said Taylor, that all strategic planning must be based on the use of atomic weapons. Taylor, on the other hand, argued that, given the concept of nuclear deterrence, the most likely contingency would be small wars not requiring the use of atomic weapons. The President held the contrary view—that the U.S.S.R would use atomic weapons "at once," should they decide to go to war; further, our own thinking should be based on such use. It was, he said, "fatuous to think that the U.S. and USSR would be locked into a life and death struggle without using such weapons." On the question of local wars, the President declared that "the tactical use of atomic weapons against military targets would be no more likely to trigger off a big war than the use of twenty-ton block busters."[24] All in all, it was a frustrating first year for the new Army Chief of Staff and his National Military Program.

In addition to promoting his views in conversations with the other chiefs, the Defense Secretary, and the President, General Taylor was very active in granting interviews to magazines, journals, and newspapers, and especially in addressing audiences outside Washington.[25] He presented one of his speeches, "A National Military Program," off the record to the New York Council on Foreign Relations in May 1956. The message, though somewhat broader in context, was essentially a summary of his established views.

Hamilton Fish Armstrong, editor of the Council's journal, *Foreign Affairs*, was impressed and invited Taylor to write an article for the journal. Taylor was happy to accept because many influential people in the private sector who read the journal were interested in foreign policy and security issues. Taylor's article, entitled "Security Through Deterrence," ran into clearance problems in the departments of Defense and State as well as with the JSC chairman; it was never published. The Defense Department declined clearance, with the argument that Taylor's views were in conflict with approved policy and that the disagreement should not be carried into the public forum. The department had not forgotten Eisenhower's reaction to Ridgway's post-retirement pronouncements on the New Look. Although President Eisenhower was always willing to discuss the doctrinal aspects of his strategic policy, he resisted any direct challenge to his budgetary ceilings, particularly when it came from within the Defense Department.

In the spring of 1956 the major assault on the budget came not from the Army but from the service that was getting the largest share of the defense budget—the Air Force. The trouble began with new congressional pressure for higher levels of defense expenditures. The Air Force submitted its request for additional funds by demanding a larger strategic bomber force. Senator Stuart Symington, an Air Force proponent, scheduled airpower hearings before his subcommittee of the Senate Armed Services Committee. Eisenhower met with Defense Secretary Wilson and Chairman Radford to counter the congressional probes and possible Air Force testimony; however, his message to the senior military went beyond the immediate question of the Air Force budget. The President maintained that "a Chief of Staff of one service should not present just the picture of his own service . . . each man testifying must think of what other services contribute. If he can't bring himself to do this, he doesn't belong in the position he holds."[26]

III

By the summer of 1956, Taylor felt the need to give the Army a place in the atomic sun—in effect, to project an image of an army armed with the most modern weapons and willing to experiment. Without time for extensive analysis, the Army undertook the atomic approach with zeal. Under the rubric of PENTANA (pentagonal atomic-nonatomic army), the Army developed something called the Pentomic Division. This was a small division designed to fight in either atomic or conventional war.[27] Without changing his basic belief that the United States needed additional conventional forces, Taylor believed that something new and atomic would assist the army in the budget battle. In October, Taylor briefed the President, Secretary Wilson, and Army Secretary Wilbur Brucker at the White House. After explaining the principles on which the new organization was based, Taylor pointed out that the new organization would require new kinds of equipment that was still being developed. Taylor hoped to establish the groundwork for future expansion of the Army budget.

The President, although interested in the presentation, countered with some points of his own. Sensitive to the services' media appeals for gaining support of their budget efforts, Eisenhower opposed a publicity campaign in behalf of the new division; the Army, said the President, should regard it simply as experimental. When Secretary Wilson interjected a question about personnel requirements, the President opined that the new division based on a fuller use of modern firepower would make possible overall personnel reductions.[28] It was Taylor's and the Army's view that a tactical nuclear battlefield required more, not fewer, people, but no one was listening.

Undoubtedly Eisenhower spent much of his time on national security matters. His secretary, Ann C. Whitman, who thought that he spent too much time on such matters, once commented:

> I can't always see why some of the inter-service problems can't be resolved before they come to the president. . . . Budget, manpower, etc. take an enormous length of time, either with the Chiefs of Staff, or with their civilian superiors.[29]

The President was interested in defense not only because of his background but especially because all major defense decisions ultimately showed up in the defense budget. Controlling the size of the defense budget was the centerpiece of Eisenhower's overall budgetary effort and economic program. Another President and another Secretary of Defense, less concerned with the budget, might have delegated such decisions. Eisenhower chose Wilson, who sorely tried him at times,[30] for his managerial qualities (which the former head of General Motors presumably had developed in his long executive experience).

Since the President's perception of the role of the Secretary of Defense conditioned the manner in which Wilson carried out his duties, and in turn influenced the nature of civil-military relations, Eisenhower's views on Wilson were relevant to his conduct of national security affairs. Early in his presidency, Eisenhower dictated a memorandum for his files on his principal associates, including Wilson. "In his field," Eisenhower said, "he is a really competent man. . . . I have no doubt that . . . he will produce the maximum security for this country at minimum or near minimum cost." The latter part of this assessment is no doubt the principal reason for the President's selection of Wilson. The former supreme commander did not want a strategist to handle the Pentagon; he would be his own strategist. What he wanted was a manager who would keep the lid on the Pentagon budget.

Late in 1956 Eisenhower turned to the fiscal year 1958 defense budget. Still mindful of the successful efforts of the Air Force and its supporters to increase the previous budget, Eisenhower summoned all the principals, including the Joint Chiefs, to assemble in his office on December 19 to discuss the new budget. In spending money for defense, he noted, one approached a point of "lessening returns or even of net loss." In the end, he said, this could "weaken the country's overall position." Whereas he realized that some members of the Joint Chiefs might doubt the wisdom of the defense budget, in the end it was a matter of presidential decision.[31]

Ten days later an unusual meeting took place in the Pentagon, a follow-through of the December 19 meeting. Jerry Persons, Andrew Goodpaster, and Bryce Harlow came over from the White House; Secretary Wilson and Admiral Radford were the principals from the Defense Department. The subject was the "solidity" of the chiefs' commitment to Eisenhower's defense budget. Wilson and Radford declared that the chiefs had accepted the President's program. Goodpaster pointed out that this was not the impression that the group had left in their meeting with the President. Radford agreed that the chiefs had not spoken up in the session with the President. One of the defense officials present observed that at least one of the services was organizing an "end run" to Congress and seemed determined not to let "the President get in the way."[32] Nothing much came of this threat. Secretary of Treasury George Humphrey's news conference of January 15, 1957, in which he predicted a "depression that will curl your hair," had galvanized congressional efforts to join the President in holding down the defense budget for fiscal 1958.

IV

By the summer of 1957 Maxwell Taylor had completed two frustrating years as army Chief of Staff. His National Military Program had made little headway; in fact, that summer there was a serious challenge to Army manpower authorization in the fiscal year 1959 defense budget.[33] Specifically, the defense department planned a reduction in Army strength from 900,000 to 700,000 over several years, with an initial drop of 50,000 as part of the new budget. Although the Army leadership did not become aware of this planned strength reduction until July 22, Taylor met it head-on at a meeting of the National Security Council on July 25.

After the Defense Department had explained the manpower cuts, Taylor stressed the strategic implications of the reduction. He listed the varieties of possible wars (as set forth in current strategic appraisals): cold war; conflicts short of general war; and general war, with little likelihood of that occurring by surprise. Taylor pointed out that forces based on the new manpower goals were structured toward the least likely possibility. He concluded that

> the constant downward trend in certain types of forces may lead to the abandonment of a forward strategy . . . we will lose still further the ability to react swiftly and effectively to the most likely form of military challenge—limited war—and run the hazard of . . . backing into the general war we are seeking to avoid.[34]

There is no evidence that Taylor's logic persuaded any of the others at the NSC meeting, but outside assistance came along in the fall of 1957 in the form of the Soviet satellite *Sputnik*. One reaction was a small increase in the army budget for fiscal year 1959 and, as a result, a smaller cut in army manpower than the Defense Department had programmed.

Obviously, the orbiting *Sputnik* in October would exert pressure for a larger defense budget.[35] The President, however, was not one to overreact, especially when it came to defense spending. On October 30 he met with the new Secretary of Defense, Neil McElroy,[36] to discuss the budget. To be certain that McElroy was properly oriented, the President delivered the brief talk that the others had heard before: "If the budget is too high, inflation occurs, which in effect cuts down the value of the dollar, so that nothing is gained, and the process is self-defeating." It was the President's intention to cut manpower, and the army's Pentomic Division would help him do that. This was not exactly what Taylor had in mind when he approved the new division for the atomic battlefield.

A few weeks after he became Secretary of Defense, McElroy sought the President's guidance on the fiscal 1959 defense budget which would soon be reaching the point of final executive decision. The President launched into a discussion of the need for restraint on the part of the services in setting forth their requirements. He reminded McElroy that "the individual chiefs tend to be caught up in demands for more for each separate service, and are unable to review the matter in terms of their responsibility." McElroy suggested that he bring the chiefs in to obtain the President's views. Eisenhower countered with a proposal to invite them to a stag dinner on the following Monday evening.[37]

After that dinner the President opened the discussion by saying that in the course of three meetings that day, several people had expressed concern over the rivalry among the military services. He went on to state his belief that the Joint Chiefs "must be above narrow service considerations." Each one "should try to approach problems from a national standpoint. . . . It is wrong," he continued, "to stress or simply to press for, Army, Navy, and other service interests." Perhaps, he said, "the members of the JCS should turn over the executive direction of their service to their deputy, and concentrate on their joint responsibilities."

Disagreeing with certain aspects of the President's proposal, Chief of Naval Operations Arleigh Burke stressed the desirability of diverse views, based on individual backgrounds. Taylor observed that the problem was really budgetary and, further, that the President's proposal concerning the vice chiefs would require an organizational overhaul. Deputy Defense Secretary Donald Quarles, although agreeing that the budget issue was central, thought the solution would be a single defense appropriation that the department could, in turn, apportion out to the services. Bringing the session to a close, Eisenhower said it was "essential that the group stay close together. They must stand firmly behind [the budget]. . . . Once they have agreed to it [although it may not meet their individual desires], they should say this is what we believe."[38]

Evidently Eisenhower was convinced that the Defense Department needed some additional reorganization.[39] He had received several suggestions from various individuals and groups and spent many hours himself thinking about possible reorganization plans. McElroy had established his own group to examine the problem; Eisenhower met with them in the Pentagon on one occasion in January 1958. After listening to the group, the President said he thought they were "too eager to support the status quo." The Defense Secretary, said Eisenhower, should take the position that the primary duty of the chiefs was their JCS role. "Their greatest task," he went on, "was to work corporately in support of the president and secretary of defense."[40]

On April 3 and 16, 1958, Eisenhower submitted messages to Congress containing his proposals for reorganization of the defense department. Certain of these proposals were actions he could take as President, such as (1) establishing unified commands under the Secretary of Defense, who would operate them through the JCS; (2) strengthening the secretary's authority over the budget; and (3) making the Joint Staff a truly operational staff. Other presidential proposals required legislative action. They included (1) repeal of the authority of JCS members and the service chiefs to present recommendations to the Congress on their own initiative; and (2) authorization for chiefs to delegate duties to vice chiefs.

The President's struggle with Congress over the reorganization continued through the spring and early summer. In the end the President received most of what he wanted but lost on two important items designed to reduce meaningful interaction between the military departments and Congress: JSC members retained the right to present recommendations to Congress on their own initiative, as did the service secretaries. Notwithstanding these losses, Eisenhower's proposals increased the authority of the secretary of defense. The new law provided all the legal authority Robert McNamara was to need to gain true secretarial control of the Pentagon during the next administration.

Meanwhile, having made little headway by 1958 in his efforts to increase budgetary resources allocated to the Army, Taylor returned to his earlier doctrinal approach. He saw his opening in an article that John Foster Dulles had published in the October 1957 issue of *Foreign Affairs*. The Secretary of State's article expressed the hope that in the decade ahead low-yield atomic weapons would permit less reliance on the country's "vast retaliatory power." In April 1958 there was an extraordinary meeting in McElroy's office on this subject. Secretary Dulles was present, along with the Deputy Secretary of Defense, the service secretaries, the Joint Chiefs of Staff, and others. McElroy said that he had brought the group together at President Eisenhower's request to consider a matter Dulles had raised with Eisenhower a few days earlier concerning overall national strategy.[41]

Dulles explained that for some years he had been a supporter of the massive retaliation concept. Now he wondered whether tactical atomic weapons provided a supplementary concept that would make United States strategic policy more credible. Others began to inject their own thoughts. Chairman Nathan Twining stated that, although smaller weapons were being developed, they could not stop a large-scale attack. Taylor pointed out that tactical nuclear weapons offered major possibilities for strategic innovation, but the number of such weapons in the inventory was not sufficient. Deputy Defense Secretary Quarles interjected the notion that the country could not escape its reliance on massive retaliation. And so it went, an interesting and inconclusive session; still, Taylor could assume that Dulles would side with him when the matter arose again.

Several months later the question of strategy came before the NSC. At issue was the 1958 revision of the Basic National Security Policy (BNSP). This time Taylor and the army received the support of the Navy and Marines in emphasizing the need for improving America's limited war capability. Acting as the spokesman for those who favored such capability, Taylor made a strong presentation. He expected support from Dulles, but the Secretary remained silent.[42] This forum differed from that in McElroy's office in one important respect: Eisenhower, architect and still proponent of a nuclear-heavy strategy, was present.[43] After hearing the air force position, that is, to retain the status quo, he made the decision that there would be no revision in the BNSP that year.

V

The practical effect of the status quo stance, as Taylor saw it, was that the fiscal year 1960 defense budget would be designed in a manner similar to the previous budget. He was correct. In his memoirs Eisenhower expressed his determination to gain a balanced budget in fiscal year 1960. As he recalled:

> I planned to let the Congress know that if it materially added to the budget, I would respond with a veto. . . . In preparing the budget, the giant military demands gave us, as usual, the gigantic headaches. No major item budgeted in each of the Armed Services was approved for inclusion unless the question "why" was answered to my satisfaction.[44]

As the preparation of the fiscal year 1960 defense budget reached its final stages, the President on November 28, 1958, met in his office with his civilian defense advisers and the chairman of the Joint Chiefs. In the Defense Department's presentation, McElroy developed the major issues and pointed out that he had reduced the service estimates by almost $1 billion. Director of the Budget Maurice Stans agreed that the defense department had made substantial cuts, but said more cuts were needed—in the vicinity of $3 to $4 billion. The President asked McElroy to look over the budget again to see what cuts could be made. Meanwhile, Eisenhower thought it wise to have a stag dinner, to include the Joint Chiefs, prior to a formal NSC meeting on the reworked Defense Department budget.[45]

Taylor described the session as follows: "We Chiefs had been given to understand that the purpose of the meeting was to allow us to discuss the problems of the new budget with the President. However it turned out to be quite otherwise. . . . After receiving something in the nature of a 'pep talk,' the Chiefs were allowed to respond."[46] The White House record of the meeting stated that President Eisenhower asked each of the chiefs to express his views in light of the "vital necessity of maintaining both an adequate defense and a national economy not impaired by inflation, loss of confidence, or run on the dollar." The paragraph summarizing Taylor's reply to the President and the latter's rejoinder is instructive:

> General Taylor, who spoke first, questioned the division of Defense funds among the services, indicating that the decision to carry forward the same percentage division this year as existed in previous years was arbitrary and failed to take into account the completing of the Air Force re-equipment phase and the rising need for army modernization. As to the broad point concerning consideration of a sound economy, he said that he as a military man respected this consideration but felt that it lay outside his responsibility. The President contested this view, pointing out that at our military colleges a major subject of inquiry is the economy and industrial base of popular adversaries; if these considerations have military significance for our adversaries, they have military significance for ourselves.[47]

Within a few days after the stag dinner McElroy pressed the chiefs for their written endorsement of the new budget, although as a group they had limited time to consider the document. Finally on January 19, 1959, the chiefs gave the budget what Taylor called "rather tepid support." Nonetheless McElroy presented the budget to Congress.[48] The major reservation of the chiefs was not on the overall dollar total of the defense budget, but rather on the way the individual services were funded.[49]

By 1959 the climate was right for Congress to intervene more fully in defense matters. Technology was in a state of flux, raising many technical and strategic questions; few people seemed certain of the answers. The services were sufficiently far apart in their objectives that it was not difficult to find points of conflict between them or between a service and the administration. Finally, the political climate caused by the Democratic sweep of 1958 and the presidential election on the horizon encouraged Congress to challenge the administration.

Committees in the House and Senate asked the usual questions about hardware and strategy, and the more unusual question about who had played what part in the development of the defense budget, including the guidelines on which it was based. In these hearings the senior military revealed in public their lack of consensus regarding the particulars of the defense budget. Still the most spectacular hearings that spring were not those related directly to the appropriations process, but rather those conducted by Senator Lyndon Johnson's Preparedness Subcommittee,[50] which was interested in exactly how the Eisenhower defense budget had been developed. Johnson focused on the use of budgetary ceilings and the role of the bureau of the budget.

The memorandum of support for the budget, solicited by McElroy from the chiefs, proved to be the catalyst for the Johnson subcommittee hearings. The chairman summoned the chiefs before the committee to express their views under oath and, subsequently, to file written statements concerning their reservations on the budget. These hearings provided an open break between the administration and the chiefs, especially Taylor,[51] on both strategic and budgetary issues. Taylor summed up his own view of the importance of these hearings as follows:

> This open testimony of the Chiefs of Staff before the Johnson Subcommittee had a country-wide impact. Along with their testimony released from closed hearings before other Congressional committees, it revealed for the first time the extent of the schism within the Joint Chiefs of Staff and the division in their views on Massive Retaliation and related matters of strategy. This revelation profoundly disturbed many members of Congress as well as thoughtful citizens generally.[52]

The *New York Times* of March 9, 1959, carried the story of the chiefs' testimony before Johnson's subcommittee, as well as the written texts of their memorandums.[53] Meeting that same morning with JCS Chairman Twining, President Eisenhower brought up the article, which he himself had read. The President instructed Twining "to caution the Joint Chiefs that the military in this country is a tool and not a policy-making body; the Joint Chiefs are not responsible for high-level political decisions." As the meeting came to a close, "the President philosophized briefly on the difficulties of a democracy running a military establishment in peacetime."[54]

The hearings were politically embarrassing to the administration, and undoubtedly they were so designed. There was no question, either, of the breakdown in consensus within the administration, which had begun earlier that year with the testimony of the Army and Navy leaders at appropriation hearings. In retrospect, however, these hearings had little effect on the Eisenhower strategy and defense budget. Probably the primary motivation for the hearings was the 1960 presidential campaign. The hearings may have been successful in setting the stage for the defense debate during that campaign.

Taylor's departure from military service at the end of June 1959 brought forth a flurry of newspaper articles on his views of the inadequacy of the country's defenses. Much of this followed his remarks before the National Press Club in Washington about a week before he retired. His more permanent critique of Eisenhower's defense policies came in the form of a book, *The Uncertain Trumpet*, published in January 1960, shortly before the opening of the new congressional session and, as it turned out, in time to be of some use in the campaign of John Fitzgerald Kennedy.

As for Eisenhower, his strategic views remained unchanged. In the days after Taylor's departure he held a series of White House meetings over the wording of the 1959 version of the Basic National Security Policy (BNSP) paper. McElroy reminded the President that the Army, Navy, and Marines felt that there should be more reliance on conventional forces. Christian Herter, Dulles's replacement as Secretary of State, argued for a greater conventional capability and for the use of nuclear weapons only as a last resort. Eisenhower thought this too cautious a view. In the end the President had no interest in any significant revision of his strategy.[55]

VI

As he indicated in his memoirs, President Eisenhower brought to his office what he called "logical guidelines for designing and employing a security establishment." How could it be otherwise, given his long experience in the military? His design, based on a technologically heavy strategy, can be understood only in the context of his strongly held belief that the nation's strength and security depended on a fine balance between its economy, and its military capabilities. In imposing and retaining his views, Eisenhower ran into increasing opposition, which included the senior officers, over whom he managed to prevail by employing various leadership techniques and organizational processes. His basic power lay in his wide public support and, as pertains to defense issues, the perception by the American public that he was the most important military figure in the country. His success in making this power effective lay in part in the considerable time he spent as President on military matters—not merely because they interested him, which they did, but because he perceived them to be a vital element in carrying out his overall presidential goals.

One of Eisenhower's successful approaches to leadership (which came through clearly in many episodes) might be termed avoidance of public confrontation. Specifically, he sought prior agreement on issues to prevent their becoming matters of public debate. In particular, his key political and military appointees had to undergo some form of loyalty test to convince him of their willingness to support his policies. This is one reason why Eisenhower permitted vigorous debate in the NSC forum and still expected support for his decisions. These decisions had, in numerous cases, already been made in smaller, informal meetings. The NSC served the function of simultaneously widening the base of support for his decisions while clarifying his rationale to his key appointees. Eisenhower's employment of organizational process can be understood only in the context of an interplay between formal and small informal groups.

One of the principal issues confronting Eisenhower was control of the policy-fiscal dialogue between the senior military and key civilian appointees. Eisenhower solved this problem through his predilection for being, in effect, his own Secretary of Defense. He accomplished this operationally by dealing directly with the chairman of the Joint Chiefs of Staff on strategic matters and, as is normal, with the Secretary of Defense on budgetary matters. Thus, President Eisenhower became the first civilian official to deal with all aspects of strategy and management. Eisenhower kept his Defense secretaries—especially Wilson—on a fairly short leash. He perceived their major role as being managers of the Pentagon, especially in keeping the lid on defense budgets. Eisenhower did, however, through the 1953 and 1958 reorganizations of Defense, considerably strengthen the legal powers of the secretary over the military departments. This was especially true of the 1958 reorganization, which came in response to the wide range of problems raised by service disagreements. It should be noted, parenthetically, that the full range of powers provided the secretary by the 1958 legislation were not exploited until McNamara assumed that office in the Kennedy administration.

In dealing with the military, either directly or through the Secretary of Defense, Eisenhower's basic goal was to gain their support on both strategic policy and budgetary constraints. To achieve this purpose, he employed techniques that conditioned the nature of civil-military relations during his presidency. There was careful selection of senior military appointees, followed by his conveying to them the role he expected them to play—particularly the requirement for public loyalty to his strategic and fiscal policies. President Truman had needed military leaders with prestige to provide effective public advocacy of his decisions. Eisenhower, on the other hand, already had the public image to be his own advocate in strategic matters.[56]

Eisenhower viewed the joint role of the service chiefs as their most important function. In the model he conceived—but never succeeded in establishing—the chiefs would delegate their service functions to their vice chiefs. He wanted the chiefs to think in broader categories than purely military considerations. In particular, he constantly stressed the need for them to view the condition of the nation's economy as a pillar of American security and, further, that they take this consideration into account in setting forth military requirements.[57]

General Maxwell Taylor, the military counterpoint to the President in this chapter,[58] arrived in Washington in the summer of 1955 with a very extensive military background, but his Washington experience, although ample, was not extensive.[59] His outlook on budgetary and strategic issues could be described as highly professional, with unusual emphasis on the Army perspective. His purpose was to modify the Eisenhower military strategy rather extensively. This goal, if it were to succeed, would be a direct threat to the budgetary underpinning of Eisenhower's overall presidential goals. Taylor approached his task in a rational manner, developing a National Military Program that set forth his strategic views, and he subsequently introduced this paper into the Joint arena. His colleagues on the Joint Chiefs of Staff were not impressed. Whatever the logic of his argument, its acceptance would pose a direct threat, especially in the case of the Air Force, to their own more advantageous budgetary positions.

Soon thereafter, Taylor confronted the problem from what might be described as an organizational-psychological approach. The Army, to create a forward-looking image, embraced the new technology in the sense of organizing its divisions to fight on an atomic battlefield. Perhaps this would secure greater presidential support for the Army's efforts and loosen up the budgetary restrictions. The President thought the idea a good one, especially since he perceived that personnel savings could result—quite the opposite of what Taylor had in mind. Taylor's efforts to secure bureaucratic allies eventually succeeded to a limited extent in the case of the Navy and at lower levels of the State Department. None of this had any real influence on Eisenhower or his programs.

Taylor's efforts outside the administration met with some success, most notably with Congress in 1959. His influence here was not in securing additional budgetary resources for the Army, but rather in helping to set the stage for the 1960 presidential campaign in which defense issues played a prominent part. His final effort after leaving office—the publication of *The Uncertain Trumpet*—also played a part in the 1960 campaign. Moreover, it helped bring about his return to office in a much more influential role in the Kennedy administration.

In conclusion, civil-military relations in the Eisenhower administration were characterized by a President superbly equipped—in fact and in the public mind—to deal with military matters and who thoroughly dominated the relationship; a continued strengthening, through reorganization and practice, of the civilian hand, thus setting the stage for an all-powerful secretary of defense in the next administration; and a declining influence of senior military spokesmen on major policy decisions, the beginning of a trend which was to continue during the next decade and beyond.[60]

Notes

1. The most recent paper of significance on the overall subject of American civil-military relations is Allan R. Millett, *The American Political System and Civilian Control of the Military: A Historical Perspective* (Mershon Center Position Papers in the Policy Sciences, No. 4, April 1979, Mershon Center, Ohio State University). The paper contains extensive notes that provide an excellent listing of the literature, both explicit and implicit. I found the following also to be most useful on the subject of American civil-military relations: Richard K. Betts, *Soldiers, Statesmen, and Cold War Crises* (Cambridge: Harvard University Press, 1977); Bernard Brodie, *War and Politics* (New York: Macmillan, 1973); Charles L. Cochran, ed., *Civil-Military Relations* (New York: Free Press, 1974); A. A. Ekirch, *The Civilian and the Military* (New York: Oxford University Press, 1956); Robert G. Gard, "The Military and American Society," *Foreign Affairs, 49* (April 1971), 698–710; Robert N. Ginsburgh, "The Challenge to Military Professionalism," *Foreign Affairs, 42* (July 1964), 255–68; Andrew J. Goodpaster and Samuel P. Huntington, *Civil-Military Relations* (Washington, D.C.: American Enterprise Institute, 1977); Samuel P. Huntington, *The Soldier and the State* (Cambridge: Harvard University Press, 1957); Morris Janowitz, *The Professional Soldier* (New York: Free Press, 1960); John P. Lovell and Philip S. Kronenberg, *New Civil-Military Relations* (New Brunswick: Transaction Books, 1974); Gene M. Lyons, "The New Civil-Military Relations," *American Political Science Review, 55* (March 1961), 53–63; Ernest R. May, *The Ultimate Decision* (New York: Braziller, 1960); Walter Millis, Harvey C. Mansfield, and Harold Stein, *Arms and the State* (New York: Twentieth Century Fund, 1958); Louis Smith, *American Democracy and Military Power* (Chicago: University of Chicago Press, 1951); John W. Spanier, *The Truman-MacArthur Controversy and the Korean War* (Cambridge: Harvard University Press, 1959).

2. Key appointments were John Foster Dulles as secretary of state, George Humphrey as secretary of the treasury, Charles Wilson as secretary of defense, and Arthur Radford as JCS chairman. He also appointed new service chiefs shortly after taking office: General Matthew B. Ridgway, Army; General Nathan B. Twining, Air Force; and Admiral Robert B. Carney, Navy.

3. Andrew J. Goodpaster transcript, Columbia Oral History Project. Goodpaster, then a brigadier general, was staff secretary and Defense liaison officer.

4. John S. D. Eisenhower, unpublished manuscript, 1972.

5. Previously senior officials had begun reviewing the basic principles of American foreign policy in an exercise known as Operation Solarium.

6. The five categories of forces were (1) nuclear retaliatory; (2) land and air forces overseas; (3) naval and marine forces at sea; (4) continental air defense units; (5) strategic reserve forces in the United States. Dwight D. Eisenhower, *Mandate for Change, 1953–1956* (Garden City, N.Y.: Doubleday, 1963), 449–51.

7. This remarkable body of literature, most of which was produced from 1956 to 1960, was largely the work of academics. Since the logical fallacies of massive retaliation were too obvious to be overlooked, its opponents included about every strategic thinker of any importance. Some of the better known were Brodie, Kaufmann, Kissinger, Morgenstern, Osgood, and Wohlstetter. Early emphasis was on limited war; toward the end of the period, stable deterrence was emphasized. In aggregate, the argument was for a wider spectrum of options than massive retaliation seemed to allow. There is no evidence that Eisenhower paid

any attention to all of this, but the literature did provide theoretical support for his opponents in the bureaucracy and in Congress. Subsequently, it was the basis for the Kennedy defense platform and later for the McNamara strategic approach.

8. NATO still had to be brought on board, and this was accomplished at the ministerial meeting in December 1954, when the NATO Council approved MC 48, which made the primary strategy of NATO dependent on nuclear weapons. Since the Allies, like the United States, perceived that they needed economies, they accommodated to the new strategy.

9. Memorandum of Conference with the President (hereafter cited as MCP and occasionally Memorandum for Record, MR), December 8, 1954. Entries such as these refer to meetings with the President on which notes were taken by his staff. The notes were subsequently converted into documents now on file in the Dwight D. Eisenhower Library in Abilene, Kansas. My opportunity to examine the documents was provided elsewhere. Eisenhower's comments about allowing Ridgway his day in court is a good example of his sense of leadership in dealing with his subordinates. In this case he gave Ridgway the consideration of listening to his views, although they were opposite to his. Presumably having had his say, Ridgway would be prepared to support the President's decision publicly.

10. MCP, December 22, 1954.

11. Subsequently, for a short time he was also Far Eastern Commander.

12. MR of Taylor's meeting with the President, February 24, 1955. Taylor tells the story in somewhat more general terms, which has Wilson questioning him on his loyalty to civilian leadership. Maxwell Taylor, *The Uncertain Trumpet* (New York: Harper, 1959, 1960), 28, 29. In view of later events, I find the two versions significantly different.

13. MCP, June 29, 1955.

14. Memorandum to the Joint Chiefs of Staff, February 14, 1956. These were not new views for Eisenhower. In a long memorandum written on his final day as Army Chief of Staff (February 7, 1948) to James Forrestal, then secretary of defense, Eisenhower discussed this matter, among others. His suggestion to Forrestal was to wean the service chiefs from working to make their services more independent of one another, toward accepting greater integration both through formal procedures and through the secretary's leadership.

15. Matthew Ridgway, "My Battles in War and Peace. . . . ," *Saturday Evening Post*, January 21, 1956; and Ridgway, *Soldier* (New York: Harper, 1956).

16. MCP, May 14, 1956.

17. MCP, May 18, 1956.

18. Theoretically, the annual BNSP was the most important strategic policy paper emanating from the Eisenhower NSC system. Rather broad in nature, the document defined United States interests and objectives, covering political, economic, and military elements. There is evidence that Eisenhower was skeptical of the validity of doctrinal papers of this type, at least as to their utility in defining strategic concepts with any degree of precision. Douglas Kinnard, *President Eisenhower and Strategy Management* (Lexington: University Press of Kentucky, 1977), 114–16.

19. Taylor, *Uncertain Trumpet*, 29, 30.

20. *Ibid.*, 37.

21. MCP, March 13, 1956.

22. Taylor, *Uncertain Trumpet*, 38, 39.

23. MCP, March 30, 1956.

24. MCP, May 24, 1956.

25. Taylor in his first half-year as Chief of Staff in 1955 made 20 speeches; in 1956, 47; in 1957, 34; in 1958, 34; and in 1957, his last half-year as chief, 22.

26. MCP, April 5, 1956. The pressure by the air force and its supporters did have some success in securing an increase in the air force budget for fiscal year 1957 by about $800 million above the President's request—largely for accelerated aircraft procurement. The army's efforts that spring were longer range and abortive. This was the so-called revolt of the colonels (without Taylor's supervision but apparently with his knowledge), which involved releases of material to the press; specifically, position papers that were critical of the air force

("A Decade of Insecurity Through Global Air Power" was the title of one paper) and advocated a greater role for the Army. On May 21, 1956, Wilson called a press conference that included the service secretaries and members of the JCS. Reading from a prepared statement, Wilson let everyone know his extreme displeasure with the activities of "partisan service representatives." The "colonels" were reassigned out of Washington, and army tactics of this kind ceased. E. Bruce Geelhoed, *Charles E. Wilson and Controversy at the Pentagon* (Detroit: Wayne State University Press, 1979), 136–38.

27. This division proved to be unworkable, and not many years after Taylor retired from the Army, it was discarded, the divisions being reorganized along more traditional lines.

28. MCP, October 11, 1956.

29. Ann Whitman to Milton Eisenhower, August 28, 1956, Whitman File, Eisenhower Library, Abilene, Kansas.

30. I refer here to matters other than Wilson's incurable case of "foot in mouth disease" whether at a press conference or before a congressional committee. Particularly annoying to Eisenhower was Wilson's tendency to bring to the commander-in-chief many detailed Pentagon problems. For example, meeting with Eisenhower just before the presidential election of 1956, Wilson indicated that he had a number of unresolved disputes that needed to be settled before the fiscal year 1958 budget could be put in final form. Eisenhower suggested that Wilson return just after the election. When the meeting did take place, Wilson presented a summary of a number of issues. After Eisenhower looked over the summary, he commented that "the questions" were largely technical and would require his getting "into the whole atmosphere of military planning." This he was reluctant to do. On the other hand, Eisenhower expected to be consulted on all major defense issues. Since Wilson sometimes could not separate the two categories, he was in a difficult position. This was understandable since, from time to time, Eisenhower could not suppress a strong interest in military problems that really were details. For example, the high ratio of Army colonels and Navy captains to lower ranks was the subject of a letter from the commander-in-chief to Wilson in late 1953.

31. MCP, December 19, 1956. Although he was concerned at this point with getting his fiscal year 1958 budget through Congress, the President was not unmindful of future budgets. Not long after this meeting, he stated in connection with an NSC action that he did not intend to go above $39 billion for defense in any fiscal year during his remaining term in office. Subsequently he told a small group of his civilian advisers that this was a measure to help Wilson in his further dealings with the military by avoiding excessive initial budget estimates on their part. MCP, January 12, 1957.

32. MR (December 29 meeting in Pentagon), dated January 12, 1957.

33. Manpower is an area where budget cuts can be realized rather dramatically and hence always has a high appeal to budget cutters. The previous summer Chairman Radford had led a major effort to cut the strength of the military, especially the army, rather drastically. Fortunately for the army the story was leaked and published in the *New York Times*. Since the cuts would have impacted severely on American forces in Europe, there was a strong reaction there, especially in West Germany by Chancellor Adenauer. As a result of the adverse publicity, Radford's proposal was withdrawn.

34. Statement contained in Taylor Papers, National Defense University Archives, Fort McNair, Washington, D.C.

35. In addition to the pressures from the services for increased resources, and the overall psychological impact of *Sputnik* (which seemed to require additional defense outlays by the United States), Eisenhower had to contend at the same time with the Gaither committee. This committee, made up of private citizens, had been formed to study problems of continental defense, especially shelter programs. Like many such panels, they decided to broaden their interests to include the entire range of United States defense programs. Coming on the heels of *Sputnik*, this would have been a disruptive force to Eisenhower's budgetary goals, as the Gaither panel proposed increased defense programs that would have been very expensive. After giving them a hearing in his office and at the NSC meeting, the President thanked its members and sent them on their way. Despite enormous pressures from Congress and else-

where to release the report, Eisenhower refused to do so, although portions of the report were leaked to the press. Eisenhower would not permit a committee, which he had established, to push him into increased defense spending when he was not convinced of the need.

36. Charles Wilson's tour as secretary of defense had lasted almost five years. His successor, Neil McElroy, apparently was surprised at being selected for the job and accepted it on the basis that he would serve no more than two years. His background with Procter and Gamble— most recently as president of that firm—was less relevant to defense activities than Wilson's at General Motors had been. Like Wilson, he can be regarded as a nonstrategist and a functionalist in his approach to the secretary's role. A few months previously, Admiral Arthur Radford had retired from the JCS chairmanship. For four years Radford had been an able advocate of the administration's position on defense matters. Highly effective and respected by the President and his principal civilian advisers (Dulles, Humphrey, and Wilson), he had the difficult task of working routinely with the service chiefs. Only one of these did he consider cooperative: Air Force Chief Nathan Twining, who succeeded him as chairman. Taylor was, of course, Radford's chief military adversary on doctrinal and budgetary issues.

37. MCP, October 30, 1957. The Eisenhower papers have dozens of guest lists for stag dinners of various types. Sometimes these would be executive branch officials, as this one was, sometimes party leaders, sometimes those outside of government, and sometimes combinations of the foregoing. Typically, after dinner the group would gather for discussion in the White House living area. Eisenhower consistently directed the conversation toward matters of interest to him, either to obtain information or to convince others of the validity of his own views. The latter objective was the essential purpose of the stag dinners with senior defense officials.

38. MR of stag dinner, November 4, 1957.

39. The National Security Act of 1947, as amended in 1949, was the legal basis for the department of defense organization. During the course of the Korean war, relatively little attention was paid to the department's organization. Truman's last secretary of defense, Robert Lovett, analyzed the shortcomings of the defense department at Truman's request shortly before leaving office. Early in his term of office Secretary Wilson appointed a committee on department of defense organization headed by Nelson A. Rockefeller. The committee, which had the advantage of Lovett's views, made its report to Wilson, who subsequently forwarded it to Eisenhower. In April 1953 the President endorsed the suggestions made by the Rockefeller committee and transmitted his own recommendations to Congress as Reorganization Plan No. 6. The reorganization became effective on June 30, 1953. The plan abolished certain boards and agencies concerned with defense matters and incorporated them in the department of defense. It also gave increased powers to the chairman of the Joint Chiefs of Staff over the Joint Staff.

40. MR, January 25, 1958.

41. MR, April 7, 1958.

42. Taylor, *Uncertain Trumpet*, 59–65. Gerard Smith, who was present, confirms that the secretary of state failed to support Taylor on this occasion. Gerard Smith transcript, Dulles Oral History Project, Firestone Library, Princeton University.

43. Dulles does not emerge as the major figure in strategic policy development that he is sometimes held out to be. In *President Eisenhower and Strategy Management*, I summarize my argument (128, 129) on this issue as follows: "Dulles had great rapport with Eisenhower. Yet, except for the early days of the administration . . . there is no evidence that his influence was great on matters of strategic policy. For one thing he stayed out of the military infighting by choice. Also he apparently did not want to weaken his power base with the president by challenging directly what he knew was a strategy to which Eisenhower was committed. Dulles never really asked the big questions about defense policies, which were, however, a large component of the administration's foreign policies."

44. Dwight D. Eisenhower, *Waging Peace, 1956–1961* (Garden City, N.Y.: Doubleday, 1965), 252.

45. MCP, November 28, 1958.

46. Taylor, *Uncertain Trumpet*, 70, 71.

47. MR, December 3, 1958. As for Taylor's point that the economy lay outside his responsibility, and by implication outside his official interest, this is the opposite of the position he was to take in the early 1960s when Kennedy was President. JFK asked the chiefs to consider broader political and economic factors when making major military decisions. Taylor was then supportive of such an approach.

48. After six years in office, and with Congress heavily controlled by the Democrats, Eisenhower was well aware of the need for carefully thought-out legislative tactics. Apropos of this, an informal body of rules had been developed by this point to guide executive leaders appearing before congressional committees. These were designed to convey the impression of a united administration and to prevent executive personnel from providing gratuitous information to Congress. No testimony was allowed on matters under consideration by the administration but not yet resolved or released; how particular determinations had been given the President, MR, March 7, 1958.

49. Taylor, *Uncertain Trumpet*, 72, 73.

50. An interesting perspective on LBJ's revitalization and use of this subcommittee commencing with *Sputnik* is contained in George Reedy, *The Twilight of the Presidency* (Boston: Houghton Mifflin, 1973), 52ff.

51. Taylor's decision to retire at the end of four years as Army Chief of Staff was confirmed at about that time. There had been some possibility of his eventually succeeding General Lauris Norstad as Supreme Allied Commander in Europe after a year or so of understudy as deputy U.S. commander (to Norstad). Taylor advised McElroy that he did not wish to continue on duty to do this, and McElroy so informed the President on March 6, 1959. MCP, March 6, 1959.

52. Taylor, *Uncertain Trumpet*, 78.

53. *New York Times*, March 9, 1959, 1. "Four Military Chiefs List Objections to Budget Limits," the story was headed. Farther down was the following: "Gen. Maxwell D. Taylor, the Army's Chief of Staff, was most vehement in his comments."

54. MCP, March 9, 1959. A complicating factor at the time and in the discussion with Twining that day was the Berlin crisis of 1958–59. The crisis originated with an announcement by Khrushchev on November 10, 1958, followed by an ultimatum to the United States, Great Britain, and France, setting a deadline of May 27, 1959, for negotiating an agreement over Berlin. There are many explanations for the Soviet action; however, of main interest here is the internal Washington debate as to what actions to take, military and otherwise. One thing Eisenhower wished to avoid was any "crash military measures" that would have an impact on his budget plans. His judgment proved correct as the crisis faded in the spring of 1959.

55. MCPs, July 2, 14, 27, 1959. In addition to the arguments within and without government for improved conventional capabilities and a more flexible strategy, Eisenhower by this time was plagued by those who thought he had not done enough in developing the nation's strategic forces. *Sputnik* had dramatized the technological gains of the Soviet Union and led to a claim by some congressmen, academics, and writers that the American strategic advantage was being nullified. For their part, the Russians soon claimed ICBMs were in production and shortly thereafter claimed an operational capability in ICBMs. Russian claims were increasingly debated in the press and during the 1958 congressional elections. The debate continued on into 1959 and eventually became a major issue in the 1960 presidential campaign—Kennedy himself raising the so-called "missile gap" issue no less than nine times in campaign speeches. Eisenhower, through U-2 photography, was well aware of Soviet capabilities and knew that there was no missile gap. After taking office in 1961 the Kennedy administration "discovered" that no such gap existed.

56. Both Presidents in their own way were attempting to politicize the chiefs. In assessing the efficacy of this, one must be both realistic and cautious. It is not possible to remove national security issues entirely from the political arena. The notion of pure military professionalism at the highest level is, I would submit, nonsense. On the other hand, there are

important reasons for caution in this regard. A service chief remains in effective control of his service only so long as he maintains its confidence, and nothing can cause the loss of such confidence more than the perception by members of his service that the chief has abandoned his role as service spokesman.

57. To help implement Eisenhower's views, Secretary Wilson published a directive in the summer of 1954 ordering the chiefs to "avail themselves of military, scientific, industrial, and economic points of view." Department of Defense Directive No. 5158.1, July 26, 1954.

58. It would not be appropriate to choose Admiral Arthur W. Radford, Eisenhower's chairman of the Joint Chiefs (from August 1953 to July 1957) because his role as chairman was not typical of the senior military, although his experiences as chairman could give some insights on civil-military relations of a different kind. Radford, as can be surmised from discussion in the body of the chapter, was operating under ideal conditions because of his rapport with the President and Wilson. In this respect he had two specific advantages: his strategic and economic views were in harmony with the President's, and he worked for a functionalist defense secretary who had little strategic understanding. It is true that Radford, as all chairmen, was at a disadvantage in having no real role in the budgetary process. He made up for that, however, by his influence over Wilson, through which he sometimes played an unofficial role in development of Defense's budget.

59. From July 1941 until July 1942, Taylor was an assistant secretary of the Army General Staff in the ranks of major, lieutenant colonel, and colonel. He served on the Army General Staff from February 1951 through July 1951 as assistant chief of staff G-3 (Operations), and from August 1951 until February 1953 as deputy chief of staff for operations and administration in the ranks of major general and lieutenant general respectively.

60. As one unfortunate legacy, importnat decisions of the 1960s regarding Vietnam were made without full and open military participation at the presidential level. Kennedy and Johnson were not Eisenhower; and Johnson, in particular, needed some realistic military advice that an all-powerful secretary of defense and his civilian helpers could not provide. Participation by senior military officials in Vietnam decision-making was not adequate. Perhaps this could be cited as an example of civilian overcontrol.

6
The Presidency and National Security Organization

I. M. DESTLER

Given the choice, few Americans would not choose the international situation in January 1961 over the one that prevailed in 1982. The world position of the United States was preeminent; the country had achieved something close to "peace with strength," notwithstanding perceived threats in Berlin, Cuba, Laos, and Vietnam. In that same month also Dwight David Eisenhower handed down to John Fitzgerald Kennedy an elaborate, sophisticated system for national security policy management. On the formal side was the National Security Council (NSC) chaired by the President, which met faithfully almost every Thursday morning to review broad policy issues. But the NSC was only the most exalted of a broad network of interagency committees—including the NSC Planning Board and the Operations Coordinating Board—backed by a substantial supporting staff. Informally, there was Brigadier General Andrew J. Goodpaster, quietly overseeing the President's day-to-day national security business from his desk down the hall from the Oval Office. And out front, until his death in early 1959, there was Secretary of State John Foster Dulles, who had taken a strong public lead while, in fact, deferring assiduously to his presidential patron.

John F. Kennedy was having none of this. Of the world situation he inherited, he could declare before the end of January: "No man entering upon this office . . . could fail to be staggered upon learning . . . the harsh enormity of the trials through which we must pass in the next four years. Each day the crises multiply. Each day the solution grows more difficult. Each day we draw nearer the hour of maximum danger. . . ."[1] As for Eisenhower's policymaking system, Kennedy basically dismantled it. He continued to hold NSC meetings, but fewer and fewer of them. He abolished the Operations Coordinating Board less than a month after taking office, replacing it with an open, free-wheeling process overseen by McGeorge Bundy. And, it should be emphasized, foreign policy experts generally endorsed both Kennedy's assessment of the world and his treatment of the Eisenhower policy system.

Twenty-one years later Eisenhower looked much better. So did his system. So did our world position in 1961. How do we explain why Kennedy responded so negatively? The Eisenhower people had two answers to this question. One was, as Dillon Anderson wrote to Robert Cutler and Gordon Gray in 1968, that "the young and inexperienced Kennedy washed out the system" because he didn't know any better. The second was the "politically motivated" attack mounted by Democrats on Eisenhower—especially the reports of Senator Henry Jackson's Subcommittee on National Policy Machinery—an attack against both Eisenhower's national security policies and his national security institutions.[2]

Both explanations had some validity. Kennedy was inexperienced in executive management, and unlikely to draw much on Eisenhower's expertise. He complained to one aide after his meeting with Eisenhower on December 6, 1960, "He treated me like a 2nd lieutenant." Moreover, as a President who had campaigned against his predecessor's record, Kennedy had a political stake in beginning anew, changing things, making a fresh start. He had won the election, whereas Eisenhower, as well as Nixon, had lost. But it was not merely Kennedy and partisan Democrats who rejected the Eisenhower legacy. The missile gap charge reflected a broad consensus among defense experts, one that had been gaining force ever since the Gaither Committee Report of 1957. The Jackson Subcommittee reports reflected the most sophisticated academic thinking on organizational issues. If these attacks were so far off-base, why were they so successful? It will be argued here that a partial answer lies in the limits of the Eisenhower system itself—both in how it operated and how it presented itself to the public.

I

The story begins with the end of World War II: an America triumphant and preeminent, yet uncertain and disorganized with respect to the world struggle that lay ahead. Wartime statesmen, notably Secretary of the Navy James Forrestal, saw a need for a National Security Council, headed by the President, to coordinate military and diplomatic policy. History records that Forrestal sought—and failed—to use this proposal to prevent creation of a unified Department of Defense—which Navy had opposed. Thereafter, when he was given the consolation prize of serving as the country's first Secretary of Defense, he sought unsuccessfully to have the NSC staffed from the Pentagon. And after President Harry S. Truman located it firmly in the Executive Office of the President, it came to be dominated not by Defense but, in its initial years, by the Department of State.

One reason that Forrestal failed was that Truman had obtained strong counter-recommendations about the NSC from his Budget Director, James Webb. The Budget Bureau urged Truman to view the NSC as a "further enlargement of the Presidential staff," with its executive secretary a new administrative assistant—in contrast to Forrestal's view of it as "an integral part of the national defense setup." Following Budget's recommendation that he avoid permitting the new Council to encumber his freedom of action, he presided over the first meeting and then stayed away for the next ten months, returning only to coordinate specifics of the Berlin airlift after he had made, outside the Council, the decision to proceed. Two years later, he decided outside the NSC to resist North Korean aggression, and then met regularly with the Council to implement this decision.[3]

A more important reason why the NSC's role was limited was Truman's extraordinary confidence in his last two secretaries of state, George Marshall (1947–49) and Dean Acheson (1949–53). His trust in them minimized the possibility that the Council might prove the vehicle for either enhanced military influence on foreign policy, on the one hand, or a powerful new White House adviser on the other. In any case, Truman's first NSC executive secretary, Admiral Sidney Souers, held scrupulously to the policy-neutral, anonymous role called for in ascendant public administration doctrine. A Missouri insurance executive who had been involved in wartime intelligence, Souers saw himself as a "non-political confidant of the President" who was to forgo "publicity and personal aggrandizement." He stayed away from the morning meetings of Truman's regular, political staff, seeing the President privately thereafter; he limited those working for him to a small secretariat, with the main NSC studies and the substantive preparation for NSC meetings handled by committees of departmental officials, typically led by State. Partly because of his low profile and his deference to Marshall and Acheson, Souers did succeed in playing a useful senior coordinating role, more effectively than did his successor James Lay. But as Richard Neustadt later put it, "The gap between the White House staff, as a politically oriented, totally Presidential entity, and the neutral secretariat of NSC was never bridged in Truman's time on any systematic basis."[4]

If Truman hesitantly and gradually employed the National Security Council when it suited his purposes, Eisenhower put on a very different public face. In his campaign he had denounced Truman's refusal to let it become more than a "shadow agency." In office he effusively embraced the NSC. While retaining Lay as executive secretary, and retaining also the concept of a policy-neutral, career NSC staff, he created a new position, Special Assistant to the President for National Security Affairs, to bridge the gap which Neustadt described, and to increase presidential influence over the Council's work. He named an energetic Boston banker, Robert Cutler, to fill this position. Cutler established the first independent analytic unit within the NSC, bringing Bromley Smith over from State to head it. Building on processes already begun under Truman, Cutler and his successors—Dillon Anderson, William Jackson, and Gordon Gray—organized and administered a system of comprehensive policy-planning unlike any this country had seen before or since. The Council held 346 regular meetings in eight years—compared with 128 meetings in somewhat over five years under Truman.[5] Two-and-a-half hours was a typical duration, with Eisenhower himself presiding about 90 percent of the time. The Council typically considered policy papers carefully prepared by the NSC Planning Board, an interagency committee which developed comprehensive "basic national security policy," area policies, and functional policies. Under Eisenhower NSC approved a total of 187 serially numbered NSC policy documents, 67 of them still current on January 29, 1961. There was also, as mentioned, an Operations Coordinating Board to oversee policy implementations. In one of the most comprehensive descriptions of the process, Cutler wrote in *Foreign Affairs:*[6]

Assume that the National Security Council sits at the top of policy hill. On one side of this hill, policy recommendations travel upward through the Planning Board to the Council, where they are thrashed out and submitted to the President. When the President has approved a policy recommendation, it travels down the other side of policy hill to the departments and agencies responsible for its execution. Each department or agency with a function to perform under such approved policy must prepare its program to carry out its responsibility. Part way down this side of the hill is the Operations Coordinating Board, to which the President refers an approved national security policy as its authority to advise with the relevant departments and agencies as to their detailed operational planning and as to coordinating the interdepartmental aspects of their respective programs.

Cutler's description of NSC procedures was careful and very thorough—no administration since has made anthing like the effort Eisenhower's did to explain its processes, and only the early Nixon administration even tried. And certainly a prodigious effort went into developing, maintaining, and implementing formal NSC policies. But Cutler's "policy hill" metaphor was also monumentally misleading. The clear implication was that it was this planning process, these NSC meetings, that Eisenhower employed directly for making his major policy decisions. Eisenhower seems to have encouraged this impression, to his later regret. While final judgment awaits a broadened declassification of documents, the evidence that exists suggests overwhelmingly that this was not the case at all.

The emphasis on the NSC was misleading on two grounds. First, it overstressed the importance of the formal meetings and the policy documents drafted and adopted therein, compared with the informal communication that was their byproduct. The overall policies reached after laborious interagency negotiations seem to have been frequently, and inevitably, too general to have much operational usefulness. As reported in one of few NSC minutes yet declassified, Eisenhower listened on August 30, 1956, to Dulles and JCS chairman Arthur W. Radford as they argued over language in an NSC planning document: whether the United States should limit military aid to formal allies, as Radford argued, or establish a more flexible rule, as favored by Dulles, allowing such aid to go, on occasion, to countries such as India and Burma. The debate was sharp and simplistic and neatly resolved when Eisenhower accepted a compromise formulation: as a "general rule" allies would be favored, but exceptions would be made when they "were in the strategic interests of the United States." In other words, the United States would aid the countries that it wanted to aid. The administration hardly needed an elaborate planning process to decide that.[7]

Any examination of selcted available documents reveals their limitations. They tended to accentuate, rather than challenge, the conventional wisdom of the time, however wrong-headed hindsight makes it appear. A December 1953 paper on Southeast Asia was elaborate in laying out United States policy goals, military options, and dilemmas—particularly in a closely guarded appendix discussing what to do if France gave up the battle. But it was positively Manichean in its division of the world ("the Communist and non-Communist worlds clearly confront one another on the field of battle"). It said virtually nothing about local or regional political forces and rivalries, and it put forward a primitive version of the domino theory to justify the conclusion that a Communist victory in Southeast Asia would "critically endanger" United

States security interests. A November 1953 paper on United States policy toward Communist China was, surprisingly, more sophisticated. It recognized the regime's greater independence vis-à-vis the Soviet Union, when compared with the European satellites. But it dismissed out of hand any American initiatives that might capitalize on this situation. To some critics it may appear strange that a process aimed at broad policy analysis should produce such narrow results, but it seems a likely result of any procedure that sought, above all, to set down on paper an agreed statement of policy, "splits" notwithstanding.[8]

There is evidence that Eisenhower grew bored with discussion of NSC documents. In talking with Cutler on April 2, 1958, he "expressed a strong preference that future Council meetings should focus *less* on discussion of papers and *more* on discussion of issues." Even when accepting this instruction Cutler felt compelled to contest this matter, substantiating staff member Robert H. Johnson's later observation that Cutler "had a passion for neatness and order which must surely have equalled or surpassed Eisenhower's own."[9]

But Eisenhower did apparently find NSC meetings useful for other purposes. They gave his senior officials continuing exposure to him, one another, and the policy issues the administration was facing—what Gordon Gray has called "the President in Council." The time investment was enormous, but all those Thursday mornings did no doubt contribute to the sense that there was a team, and a regular discussion-and-review process to which all responsible agencies had access. The same was true at the sub-Cabinet level. Cutler once stressed to Eisenhower the nature of "the great annual struggle" in the Planning Board to revise the Basic National Security Policy: "As President you see only the end-product . . . the *text* of the paper. . . . But far greater value inheres in the tremendous interagency intellectual effort that goes into preparation of the integrated text." Bromley Smith reached a similar conclusion about the Operations Coordinating Board. Its most important feature was the informal luncheons that often led to corrective action or implementation without the elaborate paperwork for which the OCB was criticized. Gordon Gray may have agreed, to judge from a somewhat oblique reference to the Board's "less tangible and little known" contribution in his 1961 letter of resignation and summation. More generally, Johnson wrote several years later, "the process, more than the formal product" was often "the most valuable aspect of the Council's work—the process of coordination, planning, discussing, educating, and creating a network of relationships which constituted a national security community." This was no mean accomplishment. But it did not mean that the plans themselves were decisive, though the credibility of the process may have required, to some degree, that this fiction be maintained.[10]

II

The more important way that the emphasis on the NSC was misleading, however, was the impression—encouraged by Cutler and his successors—that it was the overriding policymaking body of the Eisenhower administration, rather than one component of a broader system. One would have assumed, from reading the Cutler *Foreign Affairs* article, that NSC meetings were the chief advisory channel for the key Eisenhower decisions—on Dienbienphu, or Suez, or Lebanon, or initiatives vis-à-vis the Soviet Union. This was not true. One NSC-administered effort, the famous "Project Solarium," did seem to make an important contribution to one key early choice: to retreat from campaign rhetoric about "liberation" of Communist countries and continue what was essentially the Truman containment policy. Many other NSC discussions and documents doubtless influenced policy at the margins. And Eisenhower's national security assistants did acquire the primary staff responsibility for overseeing most covert operations. But the findings of scholars on most specific issues suggest overwhelmingly that Eisenhower made his major policy choices as all other Presidents have made them—after informally organized, Oval Office consultations with those members of his administration whom he trusted personally and/or whose involvement was critical to these specific issues.

General Douglas Kinnard found, in his study of Eisenhower's strategic management, "few instances when the key decisions on strategic policy were not made by the President in small informal meetings," not in the Cabinet Room but in the Oval Office. Richard Neustadt found that in the Suez crisis of 1956 Eisenhower kept operational control through careful day-to-day dealings with Secretary of State Dulles. In crises such as Indochina, the Formosa Straits, and Lebanon, Eisenhower generally made his decisions after informal meetings. On major new policy initiatives, he frequently employed White House "idea men" such as C. D. Jackson or Nelson Rockefeller, whose energy and persistence he found valuable in balancing the caution of Dulles. And the key policy vehicle for public announcements was frequently a presidential speech.[11]

Two individuals were particularly crucial to Eisenhower's managment of day-to-day policy decisions. Secretary Dulles was determinded, strongminded, and yet scrupulous in cultivating Eisenhower and in responding to his instructions. He was clearly the junior partner in a much-misunderstood relationship, although the President did frequently defer to him on matters of both policy and prerogative. Dulles accepted responsibility for policies that were less than successful, such as Suez, allowing Eisenhower to reserve his visibility for more positive enterprises and outcomes. Dulles fought relentlessly with White House-based advisers, especially Rockefeller and disarmament negotiator Harold Stassen, whom he saw as threats to his primacy as a presidential adviser. He worked comfortably, however, with Eisenhower's national security assistants, who kept, in the main, to the role of managers and maintained a policy-neutral, honest-broker stance on public issues.

If Eisenhower's use of Dulles was his most visible exercise in foreign policy management, of considerable importance also was the nearly invisible role played by his staff secretary, Andrew J. Goodpaster, whose official position was that of White House super-clerk. The staff secretary position was created in 1953, as Goodpaster tells it, "when some paperwork got crossed up—someone had done something unaware that another line of activity had begun." Eisenhower raised the issue of creating a special staff position when he commented: "I look to my staff to keep such things straightened out. I should not have to be my own sergeant major." The audience of White House staff civilians were uncertain as to what a sergeant-major was, so they went to General Paul ("Pete") Carroll, Eisenhower's aide for national security and intelligence liaison. Carroll enlightened them. "About ten days later," wrote Carroll, "the same thing happened again, and [Eisenhower] called the chief people of the staff and said, 'I told you I don't plan to be my own sergeant major, and I don't. I want to have a staff secretary and General Paul Carroll, you're going to be the staff secretary right now.' "[12] A year later, when Carroll suffered a fatal heart attack, Goodpaster—who had worked for Eisenhower in Europe—was called in to succeed him.

Staff secretary was Goodpaster's formal title, and he had overall supervisory responsibility for White House paperwork and broader administrative operations. But unknown to almost everybody outside government, he spent the bulk of his time on intelligence and national security liaison. This meant not only serving as information channel but also assuming broad operational coordination responsibility. For example, Goodpaster watched over the very sensitive U-2 operations. He organized and took notes for Eisenhower's many Oval Office meetings on national security, and he initiated follow-up action as appropriate. "Tending the door and handling urgent messages silently—a wise and good man"—that is how McGeorge Bundy described Goodpaster and his role in a memo of January 24, 1961, to John F. Kennedy.

But Goodpaster did far more than pass messages. In fact, the more one reviews the record, the more one comes to think of Goodpaster as the first man who played the role made visible by Bundy and his successors—that of presidential national security coordinator for current, day-to-day business. Cutler, Anderson, and Gray managed the formal planning system and its less-formal spinoffs. Goodpaster served Eisenhower on matters here-and-now.[13]

Goodpaster's role appears to have grown between 1954 and 1960. In the early days he seems (from a reading of selected documents now available) to have been a distinctly junior participant in the process, scrupulously anonymous, and deferential to Dulles ("Mr. Secretary," not "Foster") in particular. This contrasted with the senior status that Cutler enjoyed from the start. By the time that Christian Herter became Secretary of State, Goodpaster had emerged much more as a senior player, a near-equal advising on how to deal with Eisenhower, although his fidelity to the staff role remained that of anonymity and a determination to use that role to reinforce, not undercut, complementary aides such as Gordon Gray. He played an expanding role as facilitator of the relationship between President and Secretary of State. Dulles began by insisting on meeting with Eisenhower alone. This helped buttress his personal ties with the President, but it caused problems for everyone else. As his trust in Goodpaster grew, the Secretary would sometimes ask that he join them, or even request that Goodpaster raise certain matters with the President himself and save Dulles the trip from Foggy Bottom. When Herter became Secretary, Goodpaster and his deputy, John Eisenhower, "began monitoring all meetings between Herter and the Boss, even private ones." Herter acquiesced. Indeed, he often found this useful, since he was hard-of-hearing and the President sometimes spoke rather indirectly, in allusions. Herter could ask Goodpaster, after the meeting, what Eisenhower had actually said or meant.[14] Goodpaster's position did not involve independent substantive analysis or advice in the manner of Bundy and his successors. But he sat in a main-floor West Wing office; he saw and briefed the President an average of once or twice a day; he was well-linked to, and trusted by, all the senior departmental and White House officials involved.

III

How did all these people and processes come together to address a live issue of front-rank importance, such as the Anglo-French military intervention at Suez in 1956? A full analysis is beyond the scope of this chapter, but Eisenhower Library documents add something to the picture available from published accounts. The President decided very early that Egypt's July 26 nationalization of the Canal was not a cause for war. He instructed Dulles that his task was to find a peaceful formula for resolving the crisis. By July 31 the Secretary was en route to London, carrying an Eisenhower letter to Prime Minister Anthony Eden stressing "the unwisdom even of contemplating the use of military force at this moment."[15]

The National Security Council did not hold its regular meeting that week, or the next. An August 6 memorandum of a Dulles telephone call from Dillon Anderson, Special Assistant for National Security Affairs, included the following:

> A. said he talked with the President re NSC discussion on the ME. The Sec. said he understood it would be brought up Thursday. . . . They agreed Defense is anxious to have a meeting to present their point of view. The secretary thinks thay feel left out. . . . A. said the President seemed to have in mind that necessary studies in various departments should be underway on an urgent basis. He did not contemplate any decisions. The Secretary does not think any are called for unless it develops some papers are obsolete. A. will have Lay run a check on that.

The NSC did meet on Thursday, August 9, with the Suez Canal the last agenda item. It was also on the agenda at most of the subsequent meetings between that date and the end of October.[16]

On October 29 and 30, Eisenhower discussed the Israeli invasion and Anglo-French invasion by telephone with Dulles and in at least three small Oval Office meetings involving Dulles and a few others, with Goodpaster taking notes. At these Eisenhower decided, consistent with the line he had followed since summer, to stand strongly and visibly against the surprise British-French-Israeli actions. Discussion turned mainly on intelligence—figuring out what was happening—and the details of the United States response, cabling Eden, and introducing a UN Security Council resolution. The group spent October in preparing a prime-time Presidential "report to the nation" on Suez and Hungary, with speechwriter Emmet John Hughes putting the text together in literally the final minutes, after the rejection of a Dulles draft.[17]

On November 1, at 9:00 a.m., Eisenhower opened the regular NSC meeting (labeled simply "a meeting in my office" in *Waging Peace*) by saying he wanted to concentrate discussion on the Middle East. The opening intelligence briefing was followed by an extensive and impassioned Dulles description of the last few days' events, concluding with a strong condemnation of the British-French action. Discussion turned to the highly operational question of what to do at the United Nations, with Treasury Secretary George Humphrey and disarmament assistant Harold Stassen attempting to soften the Eisenhower-Dulles position that the United States needed to take a clear position against what Britain and France and Israel had done. To the reader of a santized transcript a quarter-century later, the discussion seems much more general, much less sensitive to the specifics of the past and the current situation, than the transcripts of phone conversations or Oval Office discussions. Also, no one refers specifically to any existing formal NSC policy, whether global or regional, as a possible guide to current action. Still, the meeting did address a real choice—what to do in New York. Eisenhower clarified matters by pointing out that, in fact, "the Secretary was asking for a mild U.S. resolution in the Nations. . . . [Eisenhower] couldn't agree more. Do we need to do anything beyond this? Secretary Dulles replied that he though the best thing was for him to go back to the State Department and work in quiet on a draft."[18] By 11:05 a.m. Dulles was, in fact, back at State and on the telephone with Eisenhower discussing the draft of the resolution. Eisenhower stressed that "it has to be understood that a cease fire will require withdrawal to their own shores," not just stopping in place. That afternoon Dulles flew to New York, at Eisenhower's urging, to help win a 65–5 approval of the United States resolution in the General Assembly.[19]

What do these specifics illustrate? They are insufficient to permit a conclusion as to which policy forum or process contributed precisely and to what degree to Eisenhower's decisions and those of his administration. But they do suggest a rather sophisticated and flexible policymaking system, and a very human one. They suggest the sort of normal tension one would expect between the managers and participants in the formal NSC, on the one hand, who tried to expand its scope, and those like Dulles, on the other, with good informal ties to Eisenhower, who sought to limit it. They suggest a President with multiple channels of information, very much in command of the substance, drawing a clear policy line (against resort to arms) and in close touch with his Secretary of State, even though he did not dictate every Dullesian maneuver.

The mystery, then, is why the Eisenhower administration allowed, even encouraged, people to believe otherwise. Why did its public face, and its propaganda, reinforce the impression of a President who presided over long, sterile, formalized NSC meetings while, in practice, John Foster Dulles was running the show? If, as Douglas Kinnard argued persuasively, "The [deinstitutionalized, humanized] NSC that C. D. Jackson wanted was already at work in the Oval Office," staffed by Goodpaster, why did nobody know it?[20] To the degree that sophisticated outside observers talked of the President as a figurehead, who reigned but did not rule, Eisenhower clearly did not like it. Still, the view that he was a passive leader resulted in large measure from consistent practices which reflected strong organizational convictions. Eisenhower wanted to be visibly in charge on the inside, and to cultivate the sense of having an administration team of senior officials who worked together, and yet also to reinforce the public standing of his Cabinet officers, who were supposed to be in the forefront, acting, making decisions, not referring all matters to him. Regular National Security Council (and Cabinet) meetings served the first two of these goals; allowing Dulles the public spotlight served the third. Eisenhower seems also to have liked the *political cover* which his practices provided him. He could insulate himself from some of the inevitable foreign policy controversy, yet maintain his public standing, his flexibility, and his capacity to intervene in any specific decision when he so desired. And the system—plus his extensive communications with other advisers, most importantly his brother Milton—helped him keep abreast of issues and emerging developments. He liked, however, to maintain a public impression of detachment, one reason why John F. Kennedy did not see him as an appropriate model to follow.

Thus Eisenhower's "hidden hand" style of leadership, as Fred Greenstein has labeled it, had considerable sophistication. It was ultimately successful on some very important matters—avoiding heavy United States intervention in Indochina, and facilitating the decline of Senator Joseph McCarthy. But there were significant costs to this leadership style as well. It seems no accident, for example, that as a sympathetic recent book by Robert Divine puts it, "nearly all of Eisenhower's foreign policy achievements were negative in nature," such as averting war over Indochina or Quemoy and Matsu. Such issues were destined to come to him, and on these he could draw clear lines, exploiting his prestige and expertise. On issues where a more sustained, overt, purposeful, continuing engagement was required, the results were less impressive.[21]

IV

From his April 1953 address to the American Society of Newspaper Editors to the downing of the U-2 seven years later, Eisenhower regularly sought an easing of the cold war, a more manageable relationship with the Soviet Union. The death of Stalin and the rise of Khrushchev offered unusual opportunities for success. The strategic preeminence of the United States limited the risks involved. Yet despite a number of initiatives—atoms for peace, the Geneva summit, the Khrushchev visit to the United States, a suspension of nuclear testing—he achieved no enduring breakthroughs. The difficulties involved were substantial, of course, and he might have enjoyed some success had not the U-2 incident intervened. But the fact that the possibilities for détente had taken so long to develop seems a product, in part, of a lack of presidential persistence earlier. Instead of sustained, direct personal engagement, he seems to have stood semi-detached as aide after aide— Emmet John Hughes, C. D. Jackson, Nelson Rockefeller, Harold Stassen—did battle with the skeptical John Foster Dulles. And each, in turn, was vanquished. Only after Dulles died did the administration seem truly liberated for this aspect of "waging peace."[22]

Another high priority for the President was the withdrawal of some American troops from Europe and the shifting of the burden there in greater measure to the Western allies. Aides such as Dulles and Goodpaster had no doubt that this was a deep personal goal, for Eisenhower pressed it on them repeatedly. But this goal remained buried in a general United States policy providing for such troop withdrawal only if tensions were eased and the existing East-West force balance retained.

Finally, Eisenhower sought to hand down a legacy of moderate, sustainable defense spending, of adequacy and restraint in American military forces. But by 1959 and 1960 his administration was overwhelmingly on the defensive in the national security debate. The attacks came not only from the Democrats but also from others, such as the Rockefeller Brothers Panel, including the former White House aide who now governed New York. To give one modest personal illustration, when this author was enrolled in Henry Kissinger's Harvard undergraduate lecture course in the spring of 1960, the future Secretary would frequently hold court, responding to questions. He was asked one day what he thought of the Eisenhower defense program. He replied in a conclusive tone that no "expert" of whom he knew thought it adequate. Scarcely a year later, the alleged missile gap disappeared. Eisenhower was proved correct, the experts and critics wrong. But how was it that Eisenhower, with his enormous public prestige, his military reputation, and his presidential platform, was placed so badly on the defensive in the public debate?

Visible leadership on the outside, persistent and continuing presidential pressure on the inside—these might have destroyed the missile gap idea in 1959 or 1960 and accomplished something more lasting with the Soviet Union. But this was not the way Eisenhower operated. His approach was successful in maintaining his public popularity and in retaining the loyalty and respect of senior officials within the government. It prevented, presumably, any number of unwise actions. It contributed, however, to his administration's disappointing conclusion.

Eisenhower might have engaged in and won a public national security debate. Instead, his administration at the end of 1960 was on the defensive. Its imperfect but useful national security policymaking institutions failed also to gain the respect which they deserved from officials of the new Kennedy administration. Confronted by the critiques of the Jackson Subcommittee concerning the cumbersomeness of the Eisenhower process—overcrowded meetings, too much paper, often-sterile discussions—the outgoing officials did not acknowledge that these were serious problems which they, too, pesistently addressed. Still less did they place the NSC in broader context by showing how it related to other decision-making procedures used by the President and his top aides. Instead, they took refuge in almost loving descriptions of the committee apparatus and how it operated, interrupted only briefly by some *pro forma* recognition, such as (to select from one Cutler statement) "the President may—and does—use from time to time other procedures and mechanisms for particular national security matters." In the end, through their overemphasis on the formal National Security Council, Eisenhower's aides unwittingly "supported the conclusions of their critics," as George Washington University historian Anna Nelson has perceptively observed. These critics "knew"that government could not work this formally. What they did not comprehend was that Eisenhower knew it too.[23]

The old and new administrations were like ships passing in the night. Following Eisenhower's instructions "to leave things in your area in apple pie order for my successor," Gray recounts, "I broke my pick. We brought up to date every NSC paper except one I think." The administration approved no less than eighteen updated policies in its last month. On January 13, in his long letter of resignation to Eisenhower, Gray could follow three proud pages of organizational history with the confident assertion that, thanks to the President's strong participation, "there is in existence a well-established organizational structure readily adapted to the particular needs of the next President."[24]

The heirs apparent were not interested. Rather their attention focused on what the Eisenhower people had consciously downplayed—day-to-day national security staffing. Transition aide Richard Neustadt stressed repeatedly, from October 30, the need for "a Personal Assistant to the Commander-in-Chief-Elect" to handle duties that "roughly correspond to (and expand upon) the work now done for Eisenhower by General Goodpaster." When Kennedy saw the President on December 6, he extracted Eisenhower's reluctant assent to Goodpaster's staying on for a month after inauguration day, deferring his transfer to the active-duty post that Eisenhower was instrumental in holding for him. On January 3, Neustadt wrote a memo for formal transition representative Clark Clifford entitled "Introducing McGeorge Bundy to General Persons." It declared that Bundy, as Special Assistant to Kennedy, would be doing the jobs of no less than five Eisenhower aides— Gordon Gray, Karl Harr, Clarence Randall, James Lay, and Bromley Smith. And Neustadt certainly had in mind Goodpaster also, whose name he unaccountably omitted. In any case, this rather summary dismissal of the elaborate Eisenhower staff structure suggested that the Kennedy approach to foreign policymaking would be far less formal, and far less organized, than Eisenhower's had been.[25]

When he met with Bundy on Januaray 11, 1961, Gray urged him to look before leaping. He anticipated Bundy's operational role by suggesting "it would be desirable that he maintain his office in the White House itself . . . at the end of 'the buzzer' " rather than in the Old Executive Office Building where Gray was housed. But much of this discussion involved Gray's description and defense of NSC processes and his repeated injunction to avoid any "hasty decision." Regarding the Operations Coordinating Board, Gray noted that its functions "were vital in government and that it did not make sense . . . to abolish the agency and then find it necessary to recreate it." But on February 19, Kennedy did in fact abolish the OCB without adequately arranging for alternative coordination methods. The speed and imprecision surprised even Neustadt, who later remarked that his critique—and that of the Jackson Subcommittee—"aimed at Eisenhower and hit Kennedy." Certainly the untidiness of the transition created disorganization in Kennedy's early months, which was one important contributor to the Bay of Pigs disaster the following April.[26]

Thereafter, of course, Kennedy and Bundy created a new presidential national security coordinating system, one which has lasted, with variations, to the present day. It was built on day-to-day presidential business. Thus it followed the Goodpaster precedent more than the NSC of Cutler, Anderson, and Gray. It involved an activist staff, electronic access to overseas cable traffic, an office within the White House. It was more satisfactory to Kennedy and his successors, more responsive to their needs for immediate engagement, but also more dangerous becauase it lacked the balancing institutions present under the Eisenhower system. In particular, it risked elevating the role of the national security assistant beyond what was wise. But that is another subject.

This chapter ends by repeating two conclusions: that the Eisenhower system was sophisticated and useful, and that it failed to survive the presidential transition of 1960–61. That failure flowed in large measure from Eisenhower's tendency to minimize, even to conceal, the crucial, informal elements of his administration's foreign policymaking system—those which made it complete and placed Eisenhower squarely at its center.

Notes

This chapter draws upon published accounts, personal interviews with several officials involved in the Eisenhower administration and in the Eisenhower-Kennedy transition, and some documentary materials, as cited, from Presidential libraries.

1. Annual Message to the Congress on the State of the Union, January 30, 1961, in *Public Papers of the President*, 1961, 22.

2. Anderson to Cutler and Gray, January 24, 1968, Dwight D. Eisenhower Library (DDEL), Gordon Gray Papers, Box 1; Anna Kasten Nelson, "National Security I: Inventing a Process (1945–1960)," in Hugh Heclo and Lester Salamon, eds., *The Illusion of the Presidency* (Boulder, Colo.: Westview Press (for the National Academy of Public Administration), 1981), 255.

3. Nelson, "National Security I," 234–45; Walter Millis, ed., *The Forrestal Diaries* (New York: Viking, 1951), 316.

4. Untitled description of role of NSC Executive Secretary, n.d., Truman Library, Sidney Souers Papers, Box 1; Richard E. Neustadt, in Francis H. Heller, ed., *The Truman White House: The Administration of the Presidency 1945–1953*.

5. DDEL, Index to NSC Series, Ann Whitman File.

6. Robert Cutler, "The Development of the National Security Council," *Foreign Affairs* (April 1956); George Weber to Bundy and Rostow, "The Output of the NSC in the Eight Years of the Eisenhower Administration," January 27, 1961, John F. Kennedy Library (JFKL), National Security Files, Box 283.

7. Summary of Discussion at 295th Meeting of the National Security Council, August 30, 1956, DDEL, Ann Whitman File, National Security Series, Box 8.

8. NSC 177 of December 30, 1953; NSC 166 of November 6, 1953.

9. Cutler, "Guidance from President on Conduct of Council Meetings," April 2, 1958, DDEL, Whitman File, Administration Series; Cutler to Eisenhower, April 7, 1958, *ibid.*; Robert H. Johnson, "The National Security Council: The Relevance of Its Past to Its Future," *Orbis*, 13 (Fall 1969), 715.

10. Gordon Gray, group oral interview on Eisenhower administration policymaking, June 11, 1980, National Academy of Public Administration (NAPA), 67; Cutler to Eisenhower, April 7, 1958; Gray to Eisenhower, January 13, 1961, DDEL; Johnson, "The National Security Council," 729.

11. Douglas Kinnard, *President Eisenhower and Strategic Management* (Lexington: University of Press of Kentucky, 1977), 134–35; Richard E. Neustadt, *Alliance Politics* (New York: Columbia University Press, 1970), 103–6; William Bragg Ewald, Jr., *Eisenhower the President* (Englewood Cliffs, N. J.: Prentice-Hall, 1981), 223–40; Richard H. Immerman, "Eisenhower and Dulles: Who Made the Decisions," *Political Psychology*, 1 (Autumn 1979), 21–38.

12. Oral History of Andrew J. Goodpaster, Columbia Oral History Collection, quoted with permission, as supplemented by personal interview of January 18, 1982.

13. Bundy to Kennedy, January 24, 1961, "The Use of the National Security Council," JFKL, National Security Files, Box 283.

14. John S. D. Eisenhower, *Strictly Personal* (Garden City, N. Y.: Doubleday, 1974), 234;

Goodpaster in NAPA group oral interview, 39–40. This paragraph also draws upon telephone transcripts and correspondence in the John Foster Dulles papers, Princeton University Library, and the Eisenhower Library.

15. Dwight D. Eisenhower, *Waging Peace 1956–1961* (Garden City, N. Y.: Doubleday, 1965), 34–41, 664; Townsend Hoopes, *The Devil and John Foster Dulles* (Boston: Atlantic–Little, Brown, 1973), 345–51.

16. "Telephone Call from Dillon Anderson," August 6, 1956, 10:23 a.m., in Eisenhower Library—John Foster Dulles Files at the Princeton University Library (DDEL-JFDF), Telephone Conversation Memoranda, White House Subseries, Box 10; DDEL, Index to NSC Series, Ann Whitman File.

17. Telephone memcons of Eisenhower-Dulles conversations of October 29 (8:00 a.m.) and October 30 (11:37 a.m., 2:17, 3:40, 3:50, 4:54, and 5:23 p.m.), DDEL-JFDF, Telephone Conversation Memoranda, White House Subseries, Box 11; Memoranda of Conferences with the President, October 29 (7:15 and 8:15 p.m.) and October 30, 1956, DDEL-JFDF, White House Memoranda Series, White House Correspondence/Meetings with the President, 1956, Box 4; Emmet John Hughes, *The Ordeal of Power* (New York: Atheneum, 1963), 218–22; Ewald, *Eisenhower the President*, 231–32.

18. Eisenhower, *Waging Peace*, 82–83; Summary of Discussion at the 302nd Meeting of the National Security Council, Thursday, November 1, 1946, DDEL, Ann Whitman File, National Security Series, Box 8.

19. Telephone memcon, Dulles to Eisenhower, November 1, 1956, DDEL-JFDF, Telephone Conversation Memoranda, White House Subseries, Box 11; Hoopes, *The Devil and John Foster Dulles*, 378–80.

20. Kinnard, *Eisenhower and Strategic Management*, 134.

21. Fred I. Greenstein, *The Hidden Hand Presidency: Eisenhower as Leader* (New York: Basic Books, 1982); Robert A. Divine, *Eisenhower and the Cold War* (New York: Oxford University Press, 1981), 154.

22. On Eisenhower's love-hate relationship with certain of these advisers, see Ewald, *Eisenhower the President*, 223–40.

23. Robert Cutler, statement to the [Jackson] Subcommittee on National Policy Machinery, Senate Committee on Government Operations, May 24, 1960, in *Organizing for National Security*, Vol. I: Hearings, 1961, 579; Nelson, "National Security I," 256.

24. Gray in NAPA group oral interview, 24; Weber to Bundy and Rostow, "The Output of the NSC"; Gray to Eisenhower, January 13, 1961.

25. Richard E. Neustadt, "Memorandum on Staffing the President-Elect," October 30, 1960, Meeting with President-Elect Kennedy," in *Waging Peace*, 715–16; Neustadt to Clifford, "Introducing McGeorge Bundy to General Persons," January 3, 1961, copy provided by Neustadt. See also Neustadt, "The National Security Council: First Steps," December 8, 1960, JFKL, Presidential Office Files, Box 64.

26. Gordon Gray, "Memorandum for the Record," January 17, 1961, DDEL, Ann Whitman File, Transition Series, Box 1; Oral History Interview with Bromley Smith, Johnson Library.

7
The Domestic Politics of National Security

GARY W. REICHARD

Cold war literature has focused chiefly on diplomatic and national security subjects, but has produced as well a number of generalizations about the domestic political environment in which national leaders attempted to meet the country's external challenges during the Truman and Eisenhower administrations. Certain of these generalizations, without much systematic examination, have come to be accepted as conventional wisdom. These generalizations assert primarily

1. that a monolithic "cold war mentality," productive of virtually indistinguishable views on foreign policy, prevailed in the two major parties during the period of 1945–60; or, to emphasize the operational side of policy, that "bipartisanship" became the norm in foreign policy-making after World War II;
2. that, in a reversal of trends toward strong presidential government begun during the Democratic administrations of Franklin D. Roosevelt and Harry S. Truman, the administration of Dwight D. Eisenhower was marked by relative passivity toward Congress, and consequently the 1950s saw a cooperation of more or less equals between the White House and Congress; put another way, that Eisenhower's "Whiggish" view of the presidency led him to consult frequently and respectfully with Congress—a practice which reinforced the "cold war consensus" on foreign policy and national security matters; and
3. that the formal security and intelligence machinery which matured in the decade and a half after World War II—in particular, the Central Intelligence Agency and the National Security Council, two vital organs of the "National Security state"—grew without challenge because they were immune to partisan criticisms and, hence, to legislative control.

The purpose of this chapter is to present evidence which at least calls into question the accuracy of these generalizations.

Historians have seemed to agree that there was consensus on cold war policy between the two major parties, and that policies in the period 1945–60 were therefore "bipartisan"—with the notable exception of the years 1949–52, when the Truman administration was under attack from Republicans. Still, any argument on these points turns on semantic differences. Most would not deny that there were some party divisions over policy. At the same time, consensus of the most general sort certainly existed in the two parties: that the Soviet Union, harboring an aggressive ideology inimical to Western values, endangered Western security through its control not only of a powerful military structure but also of the world Communist movement through which it could extend its power and influence merely by supporting revolutionary movements. It assumed, additionally, that the United States bore the world's major responsibility for checking that threat. But if "consensus" is defined as interparty agreement on the specific shape and nature of the threat to American security, and on specific policies to be followed, it is difficult to maintain that true consensus existed during the period.

As for "bipartisanship"—the conduct of foreign policy by an administration of one party in consultation with, and cooperation of, opposition leaders in Congress—the term can be applied with accuracy only to the brief period between March 1947 (the Truman Doctrine) and the election of 1948—and then only on matters related to Europe.[1] Beginning in 1949, perhaps excepting a very brief "honeymoon" following Eisenhower's election, bipartisanship was not characteristic of American national security and foreign policy-making.

Bipartisanship was a tactic born of political expediency as Harry Truman tried to work with Republicans to obtain consensus on foreign policy in and after 1947. Yet there were always political arguments against it, as well as for it. Even before the administration began its quest for bipartisanship, a Democratic adviser urged Truman against any attempt to gain agreement on his policies from congressional Republicans. "Once having acceded to this proposition of joint responsibility," wrote James Rowe, Jr., "the President is then unable to resort to his public forum without the accusation that he violated his pledge to cooperate. . . . But more important . . . is the simple fact that [bipartisan mechanisms] just won't work under the American two-party system. For 'cooperation' is a one way street. The President can discipline the Executive Branch . . . [and] force it to cooperate. The Republican leaders may agree to have co-equal responsibility for executing the agreements reached on policy but they do not have co-equal power 'to deliver.' "[2]

In 1947 and 1948, confronted by the need to ship unprecedented quantities of American aid abroad, President Truman disregarded this advice and, together with Secretary of State George C. Marshall and Undersecretary of State Dean Acheson, carefully cultivated congressional Republicans—especially Senate Foreign Relations Committee chairman Arthur Vandenberg—to encourage their support for important matters such as aid to Greece and Turkey and the European Recovery Program. With equal success the Truman leadership secured Republican approval of the Vandenberg Resolution, a measure authorizing the administration to negotiate American membership in a peacetime collective security agreement with several European nations. The administration's bipartisan tactics worked; Republicans, led by Vandenberg, generally supported aid to Europe. By another yardstick, however, it is clear that even at the high point of bipartisan cooperation, the Republican party was sharply divided. Of 51 Republican Senators voting, thirteen consistently opposed Truman on aid to Greece and Turkey and the Marshall Plan, while eight others (including Senator Robert A. Taft of Ohio) could be classified as "unreliable." Opposition levels were about the same, and sometimes higher, among House Republicans. In short, 40 percent of Republicans were not a part of the alleged bipartisan consensus in 1947–48.[3] A number of influential Republicans resented Vandenberg, and anti-administration figures such as Taft and Senator Kenneth S. Wherry of Nebraska often commanded as much support on major foreign policy roll-calls as did Vandenberg.

Admittedly bipartisanship, even in its heyday, was an uneven partnership. As William S. White wrote in 1953, "The endless salutes to 'bipartisanism' that became part of the national folklore actually were salutes that the Democrats thmeselves cannily set off. . . . This cheering tended . . . wholly to obscure the fundamental power relationship between the two parties."[4] Consultation between the administration and opposition leaders was not so frequent as is sometimes pictured, nor did it usually precede the formulation of policies. In fact, Truman regularly resorted to "crisis diplomacy" with congressional Republicans, presenting them with policies already in place and selling those policies on the basis of impending calamity abroad. Even Vandenberg complained about this tendency. In March 1947 he wrote angrily to a Republican colleague: "The trouble is that these 'crises' never reach Congress until they have developed to a point where Congressional discretion is pathetically restricted."[5]

Truman's lack of commitment to bipartisanship was evident in the

1948 campaign, when he and the Democratic platform ignored the contributions of Republicans to postwar American foreign policy. In opting for this partisan strategy, Truman followed the advice of his chief political adviser, Clark Clifford. Since "the President is responsible for foreign policy" and "the people will make their judgment" on that basis, Clifford reasoned in a pre-campaign memorandum to the President, Truman should avoid giving any credit to the Republicans.[6] That the administration's Republican supporters might resent this tactic did not seem to matter.

After Truman's victory at the polls in 1948, there was even less evidence of bipartisanship. As Taft later wrote, thereafter the President "never consulted the Republicans," attempting to "go it alone in every way."[7] Moreover, once again in control of Congress, the Democrats quickly moved to secure over-representation (and dominance) on the Senate Foreign Relations Committee. Also in early 1949, Truman nominated Dean G. Acheson, "a thoroughly partisan Truman Democrat," to succeed George C. Marshall at the State Department. Acheson's nomination presented problems even for Vandenberg, who liked him well enough personally; many Republicans were outraged.[8] It is not surprising, then, that one year later, when the administration was vulnerable because of its policy failures in China, Acheson was the target of bitter partisan attacks in the Senate.

The so-called "fall" of China to Communist forces in 1949 served as a catalyst for an open break by Republicans from administration foreign policy. So intense were partisan feelings that Senate Republicans voted by a five-to-one margin against confirmatioin of a State Department China specialist, who Truman had nominated for an Assistant Secretary of State position.[9] But however united they were in opposing Truman-Acheson policies in Asia, the Republicans were slow to develop a policy of their own. Taft's sentiments were typical. "There is no subject which puzzles me so much," he wrote to a colleague at the end of 1949. "I know we should not be in the mess that we are in, but it is difficult to see how we can get out of it."[10] Soon, however, Republicans closed ranks. Shortly after, in January 1950, Truman announced that no further "military aid or advice" would be provided to Chiang Kai-shek on Formosa, and Acheson, one week later, delivered his famous "defensive perimeter" speech, both Taft and former President Herbert Hoover delivered major addresses of their own that signaled their move from "non-interventionism" to the ranks of the "Asia firsters," who had been urging assistance to Chiang. Thus in the early months of 1950 the division among Republicans between "isolationists" and "internationalists"—in principle, the split between the Taft-Wherry forces and those who had followed Vandenberg—closed appreciably. Virtually at the same time, Senator Joseph McCarthy, a wavering follower of the bipartisan course in 1947 and 1948, launched his crusade against alleged Communists in the State Department. Republicans also took out after Acheson in the spring of 1950, their motives being deeper than merely to secure his removal. The attack on the Secretary, observed one liberal journalist, was simply "the surface expression of the deeper drive in Congress to seize power which the Constitution had given to the President."[11]

In this highly partisan climate the Korean war afforded Republicans expanded opportunities to snipe at the Truman administration. Although their public reactions were muted in the immediate aftermath of the President's decision to intervene in Korea, the political truce did not last long. Truman missed an important chance to coopt Republican critics by securing a joint resolution authorizing the American police action; without doubt he could have obtained bipartisan support for such a measure. According to White House aide George Elsey, a draft resolution circulated in the administration but went nowhere.[12] Instead, Truman relied on two speeches of July 19, 1950—one to the public, the other to Congress—to rally support. His strategy failed. Taft wrote to Chicago *Tribune* publisher Robert McCormick that he believed Truman lacked the "constitutional authority" to send troops to Korea, while numerous congressional Republicans revived their harsh criticisms of Trumn's new foreign-aid program and the administration's "futile" policies in Asia. The war in Korea, they claimed, had been caused by American "betrayal" of the Chinese Nationalists.[13] The G.O.P. wasted no time in making Korea, and Asian policy generally, an issue in the 1950 congressional elections, as the Republican National Committee issued a lengthy campaign document rehashing their charges against the administration.[14] The course of Republican criticisms during the war was directly related to the changing prospects for military success. A high point of partisan tension occurred with Truman's firing of General Douglas A. MacArthur from the Korean command in the spring of 1951.

By that time, the so-called "Great Debate" on Europe had run its tempestuous course in the Senate. What touched off that brouhaha was Truman's announcement in December 1950 that he would send troops to Europe to participate in the newly formed Western European defense force under the auspices of NATO, which the Senate had ratified just a year earlier. Combined with events in Korea, this unilateral presidential action was too much for Republicans. Following opening shots by former President Hoover and Senator Taft, most congressional Republicans united behind a resolution proposed by Senate Minority Leader Wherry, a longtime foe of the Truman line, that would bar the despatch of troops abroad before Congress had determined "a policy on that matter."[15] In three months of debate, the Republicans—led by Taft, Wherry, Homer Capehart of Indiana, Harry Cain of Washington, and James Kem of Missouri—repeatedly raised both constitutional and substantive objections to administration policies. Only a handful of erstwhile followers of bipartisanship (including Vandenberg, Thomas E. Dewey, John Foster Dulles, Harold Stassen, and Wayne Morse) argued publicly against the intrusion of partisan politics into this sensitive issue.[16] By hauling out its big military guns, including General Dwight D. Eisenhower, newly appointed to head the NATO forces in Europe, the administration was able to win at least a qualified victory in the "Great Debate" and to send the proposed four divisions to Europe. Still, discussion and voting on the various roll calls involved showed a hardening of party lines on foreign policy; on the eleven most crucial roll-calls on the troop question, Democrats and Republicans consistently voted against each other.[17]

During the last two years of the Truman administration, the Republican party was still divided internally on the degree of its enthusiasm for United States participation in collective security ventures. But the party's attack on administration policies was incessant, focusing on constitutional issues as well as on policy substance. Basic to Republican criticisms was the charge that the administration had been misinformed and derelict (if not traitorous) in failing to shore up Chiang Kai-shek's forces in China and had, as a corollary to its dereliction in Asia, spent too much effort and money on European nations unwilling to contribute adequately to their own defense.

I

These burgeoning partisan conflicts over foreign policy dominated the 1952 presidential election. As the Truman administration prepared a massive published defense of its actions abroad, pre-convention activities intensified foreign policy differences within the Republican party. With Senator Taft, the front-runner for the nomination in early 1952, it appeared that the party forces most critical of the Truman-Acheson policies were increasing their hold over the party. A pamphlet issued in February by the Senate Minority Policy Committee presaged the likely Republican campaign: "The Republican party recognizes that the United States cannot live in isolation. . . . But our party also recognizes that foreign friends cannot be won by intermeddling nor bought with

American money."[18] Differences over collective security in the G.O.P. were real in 1952, but Taft tried during his pre-convention campaign to moderate his image as a "go-it-aloner" in foreign policy. His whole effort proved unsuccessful, largely because by spring the internationalist camp had a formidable candidate of its own in Dwight D. Eisenhower. As the personification of post-1945 American commitment to collective security, particularly in Europe, General Eisenhower had decided to run because he feared, apparently, that Taft's election would lead to repudiation of the whole collective security effort, including NATO.[19]

Eisenhower's nomination by the Republicans is usually regarded as the triumph of the internationalist (or bipartisan) point of view within the G.O.P. This conclusion is accurate enough, but only in the long run. As President, Eisenhower did in fact produce a significant conversion of mainstream Republicans from a stance critical of internationalism (specifically, foreign aid and reciprocal trade policies and American participation in collective security arrangements) to support for those policies. But that came later. The General's victories in 1952—both in the Republican convention and in the general election—had more to do with his personal appeal than with his views on foreign policy; and the foreign policy planks in the 1952 party platform, framed by John Foster Dulles to fit either a Taft or Eisenhower candidacy, certainly reflected the broad spirit of Republican criticisms of the Truman-Acheson program.[20] Insofar as foreign policy was important to the voters in 1952, Eisenhower's image of being able to handle the Korean war probably helped him more than any other specific issue. Congressional Republicans, meanwhile, remained until the advent of the Eisenhower administration much as they had been in 1949 and 1950: suspicious of expensive commitments abroad and generally irritable about too-generous U.S. policies toward Europe, even while taking, with questionable consistency, an increasingly hard-line posture toward Soviet expansion abroad.[21] Beginning in 1953, Eisenhower was able to exploit the internal inconsistencies in these policy views to his own advantage, so that by the end of the decade the party was clearly identified with the Eisenhower-Dulles foreign policy approach. Perhaps it was equally true that the Eisenhower policies enjoyed a solid Republican consensus because they embodied many of the party's internal inconsistencies.

It is not accurate to label Eisenhower's policies as simply internationalist. As he had asserted during his 1952 campaign, "isolationism in America [was] dead as a political issue."[22] No party or candidate could take an isolationist line in 1952, let alone at the end of the decade; and virtually no party leader did. This did not mean, however, that Republican and Democratic views on foreign policy converged during the Eisenhower years. Even though Eisenhower moved his party toward a more explicit acceptance of internationalist policies, divisions opened up between Democrats and Republicans on new dimensions. Just as new international realities had shifted partisan disagreements over foreign policy in the period 1949–52, the same occurred in the period 1953–60. Bipartisanship no more characterized the Eisenhower years than it did the last years of Harry Truman's presidency.

Since Eisenhower and his fellow Republicans had sharply attacked Democratic foreign policies in the 1952 campaign, prospects for inter-party cooperation during the new administration were at best mixed. Congressional Democrats, though naturally resentful, faced a dilemma: if they failed to cooperate, they would need to offer constructive policies of their own or risk sounding like the "nay-sayers" they had accused Republicans of being. During the Truman years, they had come to believe—or at least so they proclaimed—that the President ought to control foreign policy. Consequently, leading Democratic spokesmen, including defeated presidential candiate Adlai Stevenson, spoke in cautious, conciliatory tones at the onset of the new administration.[23] The appearance of harmony was reinforced when Democrats and administration forces worked without rancor on the confirmation of Charles E. Bohlen as ambassador to the Soviet Union and on the shelving of a proposed, controversial resolution condemning the Yalta accords of 1945.[24]

In the area of defense, however, Democratic opposition appeared early. Eisenhower's "New Look," unveiled in two stages during 1953, produced varying criticisms from Democrats. In April, acting to reduce overall defense spending, President Eisenhower announced cutbacks of over $5 billion in funds for the Air Force. This brought howls from Democratic airpower advocates—notably Senators Stuart Symington of Missouri, Henry Jackson of Washington, Richard B. Russell of Georgia, and John Stennis of Mississippi, as well as Representatives John McCormack of Massachusetts, George Mahon of Texas, and Melvin Price of Illinois. Foreshadowing later, more extensive Democratic charges that Eisenhower's defense policies were inadequate, these critics predicted specifically that a dangerous airpower "gap" would open up between the Soviet Union and the United States.[25]

When Eisenhower announced the second stage of the "New Look" in late 1953, it became obvious that the cutbacks would affect conventional forces more than the nation's strategic air arm. This revelation predictably evoked a different sort of protest from defense-minded Democrats, who had enthusiastically shared the Truman administration's post-1950 commitment to high levels of defense spending, as called for in the document NSC 68. Air enthusiasts continued to complain about absolute reductions in spending for airpower, but other Democrats (such as Senators Hubert Humphrey in Minnesota, Albert Gore of Tennessee, Herbert Lehman of New York, and Mike Mansfield of Montana) argued that the "New Look" represented an unwise overemphasis on strategic airpower that would prove inflexible, and hence not credible, in certain kinds of crises.[26]

As in the Truman years, the basic differences between Democrats and Republicans over defense policy reflected the different fiscal views characterizing the two parties. Democrats were more willing to spend to maintain a strong defense. Roll calls on defense measures in 1953 and 1954, at least in the Senate, revealed that Democrats strongly supported both increased airpower and larger conventional forces. Still, during Eisenhower's first term the essentially different tacks taken by the airpower advocates and those predominantly concerned about over-all cutbacks kept Democrats divided and thus relatively ineffective as an opposition to administration defense policies. Even Secretary of State John Foster Dulles's presentation of the concept of "massive retaliation" in early 1954 did not evoke a unified Democratic response. Analyses of Dulles's remarks by Democrats Dean Acheson and Chester Bowles, both published in the *New York Times Magazine*, revealed continuing divisions in the party. Acheson, the "realist," criticized the administration posture as likely to fail because it was impractical for most situations; Bowles, taking a "moralist" position, emphasized the consciencelessness of the policy and despaired of chances for international disarmament in the light of such a policy.[27] This cleavage between "idealism" and "realism" plagued the Democratic party for much of the Eisenhower years, although its importance can be exaggerated.

II

Democrats in Congress began early in the Eisenhower years to stake out identifiable positions on substantive foreign policy matters. Although subsequent national involvement in Vietnam under Democratic presidents in the 1960s has obscured the fact, Democratic leaders exercised a crucial restraining influence on those in the Republican administration who wanted to intervene in Indochina at the time of the Dienbienphu disaster in the spring of 1954.[28] Speeches on the floor of Congress pointed up some emerging differences of viewpoint between Democratic critics and the administration. Notable were Senator John F. Kennedy's objection that United States intervention would ignore the important issue of colonialism involved in the French-Indochinese struggle, and Hubert Humphrey's admonition against turning the conflict into "one of white man versus Asiatic." Outside Congress, Adlai Stevenson and Chester Bowles echoed Kennedy's statements about colonialism. Although even some of those taking up anticolonialist arguments, such as Kennedy and Mansfield, occasionally lapsed into the rhetoric of cold war militancy, on balance the Democratic position in the crisis was one of restraint.[29]

The significance of this early lack of enthusiasm among Democrats for a major American commitment in Vietnam was somewhat eroded by the obvious willingness (even initiative) of key party spokesmen and officials to support the regime of Ngo Dinh Diem during the mid-1950s, when American policies were solidifying. Even so, their language was often different from the administration's, suggesting a greater interest in effecting basic social changes in Vietnam. The objective, Senator Kennedy remarked in 1956, should be to "offer them a revolution . . . far superior to anything the Communists can offer." More importantly, by 1957 some Senate Democrats were again voicing tentative reservations about the apparently growing American commitment; Senator Mansfield, for example—a longtime supporter of Diem—raised solemn and troubling warnings about the difficulties that might be building in Vietnam.[30] Before the end of the decade, Senate Democrats were also vociferously criticizing scandals in the Vietnam foreign aid program, although the party's criticisms still fell far short of altering administration policy, or even questioning it in a comprehensive or concerted way.

If Democratic positions on Vietnam remained ill-defined, however, at least part of the reason was that the administration's policies were themselves imprecise and its methods and actions largely covert. Whether the failure to present clear-cut policy alternatives in such circumstances represents "consensus" in any meaningful sense is at least open to question. Clearly, whatever the 1960s were to bring, there existed—in the mid-1950s, at least—shades of difference between Democrats and the Eisenhower administration on the nature of the challenge posed by Vietnam. Those differences seemed to recede with the apparent success of the Eisenhower policies in Southeast Asia.

Opposition criticisms of the administration's China policies arose even earlier and took a clearer form. Beginning with expressions of concern about the administration's bellicose spirit in backing Chiang Kai-shek during the Formosa crisis of 1954–55, leading Democrats steadily pressed for less rigid commitments to the Nationalist regime. Although party members voted overwhelmingly for the "blank check" Formosa

Resolution requested by Eisenhower in early 1955, the limited debate over the measure revealed the depth of reservations within the party. Acquiescence in policy was not the same as bipartisan agreement. As Humphrey remarked in executive session of the Foreign Relations Committee, there was "a remarkable difference of opinion in the Senate" on China policy, "way beyond the difference shown by the vote on the resolution. . . ."[31]

Easy passage by Congress of the three major Asia-related measures of 1954–55—the SEATO treaty, the Formosa Resolution, and a mutual security treaty with the Nationalist Chinese government—reflected an important political reality of the 1950s: the considerable muscle of a voluble, visible Democratic congressional leadership which usually supported administration initiatives. These cooperationist leaders—notably, Senate Majority Leader Lyndon B. Johnson, Speaker Sam Rayburn, and Senators Walter George and Richard Russell—were powerful, articulate, and often victorious within their party. But the success of their strong-arm tactics should not be equated with the existence of a bipartisan consensus. "It made me most unhappy," complained Senator Morse after the Asia-related votes had been taken, "to find out that so many members of the Senate were willing to admit in cloakroom discussions that they simply had to go along with the Democratic leadership."[32]

Morse and fellow dissidents picked up large numbers of allies in their opposition to administration China policy in the fall of 1958 when another Formosa crisis developed, again over Communist Chinese shelling of the offshore islands. When Secretary of State Dulles reacted to the renewed shelling with strong statements of support for Chiang and implications of military assistance if the islands of Quemoy and Matsu came under attack, Democrats of virtually every stripe spoke out in opposition. Joining longtime administration critics like Wayne Morse and Chester Bowles, for example, were former Truman administration officials Dean Acheson and Thomas Finletter. "We seem to be drifting . . . toward war with China," warned Acheson in a public statement during the crisis, "a war without friends or allies. . . . The decision seems now to have been made to defend Quemoy, even though it leads to World War." Labeling this decision "horrendous," Acheson charged that the Eisenhower administration had

> most unwisely maneuvered itself, with the help of Chiang Kai-shek, into a situation of which it [had] lost control. . . . The attitude of the Administration is that nothing will be done to extricate ourselves from this position during

periods of quiet, and that nothing can be done about it in times of crisis. This is an attitude which cannot be tolerated.[33]

Finletter was equally outspoken in a letter to the *New York Times*, asserting that it was time to "stop the . . . unilateral assumption of power and responsibility by the United States with respect to the whole Formosa group of islands." Even the normally cooperative Senator Russell agreed, writing privately of the administration's "folly" in trying to defend the islands "to the limit" against the best military advice.[34] Perhaps these critics would have been surprised to learn that the President shared their doubts.

Democrats who had, in Morse's words, "whooped through" the Formosa Resolution three years earlier, now scrambled to back away from it. Charging that Eisenhower was "misreading" the meaning of the "bipartisan understanding" of 1955, Senator Kennedy told constituents that the "fundamental reason why many Senators voted for the resolution was not out of an affirmative belief that the off-shore islands must be defended . . . but out of a conviction that it would be unwise to repudiate the President's public request."[35] Still, for a time Dulles pressed on with the administration line, assuring one influential audience that "the stakes involved are not just some square miles of real estate. . . . The offshore islands, including Quemoy and Matsu, have, for the Republic of China, a great significance, comparable to the significance of Berlin to the West." Republican congressional leaders, meanwhile, steadfastly backed the Eisenhower-Dulles policy.[36]

The administration could not hold out long in the face of a united Democratic opposition. When the party rallied behind Senator Theodore F. Green in his public dispute with Eisenhower over the administration's implied willingness to use troops to defend Quemoy and Matsu, Dulles for the first time softened his stance.[37] A demand from several liberal Democrats for a special session of Congress to deal with the crisis went unheeded, but in mid-October the administration took advantage of a lull in the shelling to cool its rhetoric. Eventually the crisis atmosphere subsided,[38] but despite the Democratic criticism the administration's commitment to Chiang continued unchanged.

Opposing this commitment to the Chinese Nationalists did not amount to a policy per se, but the thrust of Democratic policy toward China was becoming clearer. More than a year before the crisis of 1958, Senator Fulbright had contemplated calling for a study mission to consider "whether or not negotiations looking toward recognition [of the People's Republic] should be opened"; but, citing the State Department's "rabid" opposition to the idea, he had given up.[39] In May 1958, however, the liberal Americans for Democratic Action publicly reversed its past position by adopting a resolution calling for negotiations aimed at possible recognition of the PRC. Then, after the Formosa crisis, Fulbright and his Democratic colleagues on the Senate Foreign Relations Committee became more aggressive, undertaking a full-scale investigation of foreign policy developments during the Eisenhower administration. "United States Foreign Policy in Asia," a 15-page report issued by the committee in October 1959, recommended that American policy should be based on the assumption that "the Chinese Communist Government will have a lengthy tenure"; consequently, there should be further exploration as to the best policy.[40] Although again stopping short of a call for outright reversal of existing China policy, the Democrats, more unified than ever, were clearly moving away from the Eisenhower-Dulles position. Events of the 1960s precluded any significant progress toward a new China policy under Democratic administrations, but formal talks with PRC emissaries during the Johnson administration were a precursor of the change that would eventually come.[41]

Democratic assertiveness also received a boost from the crisis mood that followed the Soviets' launching of *Sputnik* in lake 1957. The diffusion of viewpoints in the party on defense issues, which had been gradually diminishing since 1953, cleared after *Sputnik*, as party spokesmen merged their calls for "flexible response" capability and for closure of the "missile gap" into a united offensive for greater preparedness for all military eventualities. Virtually every leading Democrat—especially the several interested in the party's 1960 presidential nomination—associated himself in some way with the drive for increased defense capabilities. Party members consistently voted for higher military spending than the administration requested.

But if the Democrats took a militant stand on defense matters, on the issue of foreign aid they were less disposed toward military spending than was the administration. Almost from the beginning of Eisenhower's presidency, congressional Democrats objected to the overemphasis on military aid to other nations at the expense of economic aid.[42] On roll calls, they consistently voted for relatively greater economic assistance, while often supporting cutbacks on the military side. The Foreign Relations Committee, and particularly Fulbright, exerted leadership on this issue. A comprehensive committee study of the overall aid program, begun in 1956, charged that the administration's approach was "confused," and urged reductions in military aid. It also called for converting much of the program to a loan basis—a recommendation which eventually led to establishment of the Development Loan Fund in 1957.[43]

Democrats also evinced growing concern about the special needs of developing nations during the 1950s. Party spokesmen were critical of the administration's tendency to make aid dependent on a recipient nation's friendliness to the United States. "We should . . . recognize," wrote Averell Harriman in 1954, "that political attitudes do change . . . and that with respect to certain countries we must proceed in the hope and expectation that fundamental interests will assert themselves and bring about more favorable attitudes." Indeed, the challenge posed to United States policy by the growth of neutralism, and the idea that a bipolar concept of the world was no longer accurate, became increasingly common in Democratic rhetoric. "Much as we see the world as fractured in two, as a dualism between the United States and the U.S.S.R.," noted John F. Kennedy in November 1957, "the truth is becoming ever enlarged that there is no such simple counterpoint any longer. . . . There are other states which cannot be ignored. . . ."[44]

The Democratic Advisory Council played an important role in presenting party alternatives in national security affairs and foreign policy in the late 1950s. The DAC, formed by the party's National Committee in December 1956, was made up of advisory committees focusing on several discrete policy areas. This foreign policy advisory committee was broadly representataive of Democratic criticisms of Eisenhower-Dulles policies. Headed by Acheson, it also included Bowles, Benjamin Cohen, former Senator Herbert H. Lehman, Professor Hans Morgenthau of the University of Chicago, and Paul Nitze, among others.[45] Most Democratic congressional leaders declined membership on DAC committees, but—aside from Johnson, Samuel Rayburn, and a few others—their decision to do so was probably not so much because they disagreed with DAC policies as because they felt that joining the body and co-authoring its statements would make them appear to be assuming an inappropriate role as unsanctioned party leaders. Acheson's prominent role in the DAC foreign policy group ensured that the panel's statements used aggressive cold war rhetoric, and some Democrats—for example, Hubert Humphrey—were offended by their tone. Overall, however, the documents captured the essence of Democratic criticisms of Eisenhower's policies and probably exercised an influence on many congressional Democrats.[46]

Despite the apparent convergence of Democratic arguments, party members did not vote as a bloc against the policies of the Eisenhower administration. The forceful leadership of Lyndon Johnson and Sam Rayburn, especially, remained an important restraint on would-be dissidents. Also, by the end of the decade many Southern Democrats had moved to a position opposing foreign aid in general, largely out of considerations of fiscal conservatism.[47] These factors, along with some lingering resistance to Eisenhower's policies within the Republican party, actually produced a decrease in the intensity of interparty differences in roll-call voting over the decade; measured statistically, those differences remained consistent, but were less substantial in the late 1950s than they had been earlier.[48]

It is necessary, then, to qualify arguments that the Democrats developed foreign policy alternatives to the positions taken by the Eisenhower administration. Admittedly, party members did not vote as a bloc in Congress, as intraparty divisions over defense policy and foreign aid persisted throughout the decade. Nonetheless, voting records as well as the rhetoric of leading party spokesmen indicated a shift in the central tendency among Democrats to differ with certain key administration policies: to favor a less rigid China policy and relatively greater emphasis on economic (as opposed to military) foreign aid, to be aware of the issue of anticolonialism in dealing with developing nations, and to support increased military preparedness. If the Democrats failed to frame their alternative policies in a clear or comprehensive manner, that failure was at least partially the result of the fact that the Eisenhower administration itself never set forth an overall security policy which clearly linked means to ends, or was generally applicable around the globe. But interparty differences were real and pervasive. If the Democrats, after returning to power in the 1960s, did not proceed in all of the directions they came to advocate during the later Eisenhower years, that should not negate the fact that the alleged "cold war consensus" never included many Democrats both inside and outside Congress.

III

In the spate of literature lately on the growth of presidential power in recent decades, the presidency of Dwight Eisenhower is generally viewed as an exception. Arthur M. Schlesinger, Jr., in *The Imperial Presidency* (1973), for example, notes some gains in executive influence during the 1950s, but accepts the traditional view of Eisenhower as a weak President. "Eisenhower had come to the White House as a Whig," writes Schlesinger. "He was therefore reluctant . . . to get into contention with the legislative branch."[49]

As much of the recent scholarly work on Eisenhower indicates, this view of Eisenhower as a "Whig" is questionable. To be sure, he cultivated the image, speaking frequently about the proper boundaries of authority between the two branches, and always acting deferentially toward congressional prerogatives. Eisenhower's efforts were persuasive not only to commentators on the presidency, but to the public as a whole. A 1959 poll by the Survey Research Center found that, even though 61 percent of the individuals questioned believed the President was in a better position than Congress to know what the country needed, only 10 percent thought—in the second to last year of Eisenhower's presidency—that the Chief Executive actually had "the most . . . say" in the conduct of policy; 52 percent believed Congress was dominant in the decision-making process.[50]

By sucessfully maintaining the appearance that he deferred to Congress and held a limited view of the powers of his office, Eisenhower amassed great power virtually unnoticed. That his increased power was invisible increased it further. Samuel Huntington described this "paradox of power" in *American Politics: The Promise of Disharmony* (1981):

> Power revealed is power reduced; power concealed is power enhanced. . . . In general, if it becomes widely accepted that the Presidency lacks extensive power and that its occupant is readily checked by other officials and groups, this fact in itself is evidence of support for presidential power and hence the existence of presidential power. If, on the other hand, people believe that the President is extremely powerful, this in itself is evidence . . . that the President is not so powerful or that his power is declining. When presidential power is really great, public opinion never considers it to be too great; when presidential power is fading, public opinion considers it inordinate.[51]

Eisenhower's tactics in dealing with Congress were consistent throughout his presidency. His specific style, in the words of Fred Greenstein, was "hidden hand leadership"—behind-the-scenes, informal manipulation.[52] But there was a more general consistency in Eisenhower's approach. Fiercely resistant to legislative intrusions when he regarded them inappropriate (which he felt especially true in matters of foreign policy and national security), he avoided confrontational rhetoric, stressing instead the need for unity in the face of cold war dangers. In this way he averted unnecessary tensions with members of Congress, while working to persuade them to go his way. This line of approach characterized Eisenhower's actions in the three major episodes of his presidency which most clearly related to the issue of executive power: the Bricker Amendment, the Formosa Resolution, and the Middle East Resolution.

The Bricker Amendment was originally a Republican-sponsored initiative aimed at constricting the powers of a Democratic President, Harry S. Truman. Specifically, Ohio Republican John Bricker had introduced his proposed amendment to limit the treaty-making (and executive agreement) power in 1951. As part of the assault on presidential autonomy in external affairs connected with the Great Debate, it had obvious partisan and substantive content. Not surprisingly, it made no headway in the Democratic-controlled Congress during the last two years of Truman's presidency.

The story of the amendment's defeat in early 1954 need not be presented in detail here, since it did not involve national security issues per se. But the methods by which the Eisenhower administration overcame Senator Bricker and his supporters are significant because they were to be repeated by the administration later. Although President Eisenhower fumed privately about the amendment (calling it a "stupid, blind violation of [the] Constitution" at one point), he was discreet in public, avoiding the constitutional issue and calling instead for maneuvering room in his efforts to lead the nation in the cold war.[53]

Eisenhower's victory on the Bricker Amendment issue marked the beginning of a successful offensive which, by the end of the 1950s, left the executive branch clearly in control of foreign policy. The major milestones in this expansion of presidential authority were the "area resolutions," which Eisenhower obtained in 1955 and 1957, giving him advance authorization for unspecified future actions in the area of Formosa and in the Middle East, respectively. The Formosa and Middle East Resolutions, both drafted with guidance from the White House, were the first instances of this new device. One could read into the area resolutions whatever one wanted, a fact which suited Eisenhower's purposes admirably. Both were perfectly designed to reinforce his leadership image: contemporary observers, including many members of Congress, viewed the resolutions as proof that Eisenhower accepted the necessity to ask Congress for any powers not clearly granted to the President in the Constitution. It is clear that the President himself, on the other hand, saw them as a way to avert later congressional criticism if events should go awry.

In requesting the Formosa Resolution in January 1955, Eisenhower repeated Truman's practice of presenting an "essential" foreign policy measure to Congress in an atmosphere of crisis, without prior consultation with congressional leaders. As in the struggle over the Bricker Amendment, he avoided taking on the constitutional issue directly. In the special message transmitting the request, he referred to "the authority that may be accorded by Congress. . . ," and Secretary of State Dulles was equally deferential before the Senate Foreign Relations

Committee, telling members that there was "at least doubt as to whether or not the President could, without Congressional authorization, take the kind of action" implied by the resolution. "[But] even if there was no doubt about the legal position," he said, "I believe it would be indispensable that the Congress should indicate its concurrence in it as a matter of policy. . . . "⁵⁴

Congress responded as Eisenhower wanted. A small number of Democrats opposed the resolution as a dangerous "blank check," but most, regardless of party, believed it was innocuous because unnecessary—the very conclusion Eisenhower and Dulles had hoped to inspire. Most members of Congress felt reassured that the President had asked for their consent. As one Republican Congressman put it, "President Eisenhower has certainly shown consideration of Congress and his deep adherence to the principles of constitutional government. . . . "⁵⁵ Congress endorsed the Formosa Resolution overwhelmingly, recording three dissenting votes in each house.

Almost two years later, in the face of an escalating crisis over the Suez, the administration set out to duplicate its strategic coup with a second area resolution applicable to the Middle East. Since the new request included provisions for potentially costly foreign aid, fiscal conservatives were apprehensive about it. And many Democrats, frustrated by Eisenhower's smashing re-election in 1956 and conscious of the need for the party to build a foreign policy record, were especially critical. Some, such as Fulbright, raised the constitutional issue, protesting against giving such sweeping powers to the President. "It would not . . . ," said Fulbright, "be a proper discharge of our duty as Senators to give him a blank check ahead of time and say, 'Whatever you do is all right.' "⁵⁶ But the opposition was no more effective than in the case of the Formosa Resolution. In hearings Dulles again purposely clouded the constitutional issue, specifically noting that the issue of how the resolution would be terminated was "a matter which would be fully discussable with the President. . . ." Dulles invoked the by-now familiar image of Eisenhower as a prestigious and credible leader of the Free World. It was up to Congress, he said, "to decide whether or not they wish to respond, whether they prefer to take the responsibility of saying they know more about the conduct of foreign affairs than the President does. . . ."⁵⁷ The Middle East Resolution was adopted easily, and with only inconsequential amendments. By securing a second area resolution in two years, Eisenhower had in effect institutionalized the technique of coopting Congress through pre-authorization of actions unspecified. This pattern, of course, would be followed by President Lyndon Johnson in the 1960s.

Aside from illuminating the growth of Eisenhower's control over foreign policy, the stories of these three legislative episodes illustrate an important feature of national security politics in the 1950s: the use of constitutional arguments by the congressional opposition as surrogates for policy alternatives. Senator Bricker and his supporters, in proposing their amendment during the Truman administration, and Democrats who spoke out against the Formosa and Middle East resolutions, all emphasized constitutional issues but were motivated in large part by disapproval of particular foreign policies. In neutralizing the constitutional objections of the opposition, Eisenhower also deflected their implicit criticisms of substantive policy.

IV

The role of intelligence, surveillance, and government-by-secrecy greatly increased in the period after World War II. Shielded from direct congressional scrutiny from the time of their inception in 1947, the Central Intelligence Agency and National Security Council were the prime institutional embodiments of this trend toward non-accountable, subterranean policymaking and security operations.

President Truman took the initiative in establishing a centralized intelligence agency by executive order in early 1946, but that body—the Central Intelligence Group—drew its funds from the War, Navy, and State departments, to which it also reported. Consequently, it lacked autonomy. Truman was nonetheless reluctant to request statutory authorization for an independent intelligence agency with its own budget. In mid-1946, however, presidential aide Clark Clifford met with CIG officials about the matter; this meeting produced agreement that the agency should not remain "a small planning staff," but should become "a legally established, fairly sizeable, operating agency." After Truman approved the idea in early 1947, its outlines were included in the National Security Act of 1947, which established both the Central Intelligence Agency (CIA) and the National Security Council.[58] These agencies came to epitomize what Daniel Yergin has labeled the "national security state."[59]

Under the 1947 statute the functions of the CIA were left deliberately vague. It was the clear intention of Congress that the agency be limited to intelligence-gathering functions only, rather than engaging in operational activities, but the last of its five specified functions was sufficiently broad as to open the way for later trouble: the new body was empowered "to perform such other functions and duties related to intelligence affecting the national security as the National Security Council will from time to time direct."[60]

The CIA took a giant step towards total autonomy with passage of the 1949 Central Intelligence Act. That legislation exempted the agency from normal federal requirements of "publication or disclosure of the organization, functions, names, official titles, salaries, or numbers of personnel employed by it." It stipulated that there should be no financial accounting of the agency's activities to Congress. Unaudited funds could be spent, the act provided, "for objects of a confidential, extraordinary, or emergency nature."[61] Despite this latitude, there is little evidence that President Truman either sought or encouraged covert operations by the agency. It remained during his administration what it had been originally intended to be: an agency for the gathering and reporting of intelligence. But in fact, Truman responded to pressures from Republican critics in at least one action concerning the CIA. In 1950, to counter attacks by McCarthy's followers and such "non-political" critics as General MacArthur and J. Edgar Hoover, the President appointed General Walter Bedell Smith, Eisenhower's wartime chief of staff and a zealous anti-Communist, to head the agency. Thereafter, the CIA showed greater aggressiveness in intelligence-gathering and more interest in the possibilities of conducting covert operations.[62] During the Eisenhower years, under the leadership of Allen Dulles, this potential was realized, as the CIA, its funds and operations legitimately concealed from congressional scrutiny, became an important operational arm of Eisenhower-Dulles foreign policies.

The CIA steadily expanded its sphere of operations in the 1950s. As Harry Howe Ransom has noted,

> The real operating constitution of the CIA is not so much the statutory authority given by Congress in 1947 and 1949, but a score or so of super-secret National Security Council Intelligence directives which only a few high government officials have ever seen. These directives, after accumulating for a dozen years, were "codified" in 1959. . . .[63]

Though Eisenhower avoided advertising his reliance on the CIA, he aided Allen Dulles in the latter's efforts to shield the agency from attempts by Congress to increase its oversight of the agency's operations. Simultaneously, of course, the administration knew the CIA to be deeply involved in covert operations in a number of countries, including Iran, Guatemala, Egypt, Indonesia, and Laos as the decade progressed.[64]

At first Eisenhower tied his protection of the CIA to his general defense of executive authority against McCarthy's onslaught, telling two Republican congressmen in early 1954 that a proposed bill to set up a joint congressional oversight committee would pass only "over his dead body," because he feared such a committee "would end up being dominated by Senator McCarthy. . . ." But it was not merely McCarthy's potential influence that Eisenhower feared. Renewed efforts by Senator Mike Mansfield (certainly no supporter of McCarthy) to establish an oversight committee also met administration resistance. Despite its thirty-two cosponsors in the Senate in 1955 (including thirteen Republicans) and its recommendation by an eight-to-one vote by the Senate Committee on Rules and Administration, the Mansfield bill went down to defeat. Eloquent attacks on the growth of executive secrecy by Senators Morse and Mansfield were not enough to counter strong opposition. On the final vote of 59–27 against the bill, fourteen of the original cosponsors, all but one a Republican, reversed their positions and opposed it; the twenty-seven supporters included mainly liberal Democrats, although eight Republicans (mostly former supporters of McCarthy) also voted for it.[65]

In response to these congressional pressures, Eisenhower took steps to ensure periodic review of the government's intelligence activities, establishing in early 1956 a high-level, eight-member advisory committee headed by James R. Killian, president of the Massachusetts Institute of Technology. The President did not, however, follow a number of recommendations offered by that committee. Although he complained in early 1957 at a meeting of the National Security Council that intelligence had become a billion-dollar-a-year operation that perhaps ought to be cut back, the CIA continued as an active operational arm of American policy throughout the decade and, despite growing suspicions in the ranks of congressional Democrats, particularly more junior members, it remained immune to congressional scrutiny or control.[66]

Near the end of Eisenhower's second term, in the form of the U-2 incident in May 1960, critics of CIA operations were presented with an unexpected opportunity to further their cause. After the Soviets shot down the American surveillance plane and terminated the June Paris summit meeting, congressional Democrats merged their complaints about the administration's foreign policies and excessive secrecy in the conduct of those policies. Leading the critics was Senator Fulbright, now chairman of the Foreign Relations Committee, who called for a full investigation of the incident by the committee. Even Lyndon Johnson supported Fulbright's actions. As usual, Fulbright disclaimed any partisan motives. Predictably, he stressed the constitutional aspects of the issue, implying a need for Congress to assert itself in scrutinizing this obvious intelligence failure. "We hope," he remarked at the beginning of the committee hearings, "that the procedures we have set up for the conduct of these hearings will make it possible for representatives of the Executive Branch to be candid and complete because unless there is such candor it is most difficult for the Senate to discharge its responsibilities in the field of foreign policy."[67]

In the course of the closed-session hearings, several liberal Democrats expressed displeasure with the administration's handling of the U-2 matter. "I must say," said Senator Albert Gore, long a critic of Eisenhower's policies, "that I never knew until this incident came up that cover stories went so far as to become . . . falsehood. . . . I do not condone an official falsehood at any level of government. . . ." Committee Republicans, on the other hand, defended not only administration policies, but the secrecy surrounding them. "Where do we go from here now?" Alexander Wiley asked Fulbright at one point during the hearings. "Are we going . . . to try to ball up the agency that got the information, that has done such a tremendous job . . . ?" Fulbright denied that the hearings were intended to "ball up anything," and in fact their results on policy were minimal.[68] The U-2 incident and its aftermath led to the airing of Democratic grievances with certain administration policies and intensified foreign policy issues in the unfolding 1960 presidential campaign, but they had no immediate impact on procedures concerning the CIA.

In the last years of Eisenhower's presidency, no doubt emboldened by the greater vulnerability of the administration after the launching of *Sputnik* in 1957, congressional Democrats directed their attention toward the National Security Council. Created by the same 1947 statute which established the CIA, the NSC symbolized executive autonomy in national security policy. Once again Fulbright, stimulated by the chief of staff of the Foreign Relations Committee, Carl Marcy, took the initiative, writing to Majority Leader Lyndon Johnson to request the establishment of a temporary Senate Committee on National Security, its functions to include keeping "under *constant surveillance* [italics in original] the domestic, foreign policy and military activities and programs of the Executive Branch designed to promote the national security . . . ." Johnson, who had already announced the beginning of "a searching inquiry" into the nation's missile and satellite programs by his own Preparedness Subcommittee of the Senate Armed Services Committee, responded noncommittally to Fulbright's request.[69]

Senator Henry Jackson, a member of the Senate Committee on Government Operations, renewed the idea of such a study in the spring of

1959. In a major speech at the National War College, he criticized existing NSC operations, claiming they were not producing "clearly defined and purposeful strategy for the 'cold war.' " After posing a number of questions implying inadequate and tardy national security planning over the previous decade, Jackson asserted that the United States was "losing the cold war when we could be winning it. . . . I think our fundamental problem is that we do not have a national strategy for victory in the contest with world communism."[70] Although Jackson insisted in his speech and afterward that the proposed study would be nonpartisan and not directed toward the substance of policy, the language in his public salvo at the War College reflected the partisan origins of the proposal.

The White House was not fooled. Former presidential security adviser Robert Cutler, charged by the President to analyze Jackson's speech, described it as "in the nature of a vigorous polemic." Jackson disagreed "with the Administration's basic security policy," Cutler wrote, and had confused "the mechanism's effectiveness with the abilities of its operators." As the Senate prepared to take up the Jackson resolution in June, White House Special Assistant Gordon Gray echoed Cutler's sentiments, recommending to the President "that all reasonable efforts be made to avoid the adoption of the Resolution."[71] General Wilton B. Persons, Sherman Adams's successor as Assistant to the President, led efforts to block what Eisenhower privately termed Jackson's "unconscionable scramble for publicity" by attempting to work through Senators Styles Bridges and Richard Russell.[72]

Efforts to defeat Jackson's proposal revealed as much about internal rivalries in the Democratic party as about the conflict between Democrats and Republicans. Differing presidential aspirations and jurisdictional jealousies both had impact, as Senators Johnson, Russell, and Fulbright met with Eisenhower, Gordon Gray, and Bryce Harlow to develop a counter-strategy. Russell and Fulbright (who was already directing the Foreign Relations Committee's "non-partisan" investigation of foreign policy and obviously did not want competition) assured the President they had tried to dissuade Jackson from his course during the spring. Johnson explained that he had postponed taking the resolution to the Democratic Policy Committee for a month and had tried to get Republican Senators Karl Mundt and Everett Dirksen to lead the opposition to it, but that it could no longer be kept from the Senate floor. President Eisenhower repeated his negative view, warning that, if adopted, the resolution would "harmfully affect matters now going fairly well." The group decided that the best strategy was for Eisenhower to write a letter to Majority Leader Johnson explaining his opposition to the proposed investigation. The President did so the next day. "Senate Resolution 115," he wrote to Johnson on June 25,

> . . . raises considerations so significant to our country that I feel I must call it to your attention in the hope that it can be withdrawn or further action withheld.
>
> . . . This resolution would inescapably thrust Congressional investigative activities deeply into the Nation's highest national security and foreign policy deliberative processes which traditionally as well as Constitutionally have remained within the province of the Chief Executive. . . . It would thrust the Executive and Legislative Branches into needless controversy over jurisdictional issues which have been argued throughout our history and cannot now be resolved without either Congressional or Executive concessions which over the years neither has been willing to make.
>
> . . . Aside from such general considerations as these, I should remind you that the National Security Council, though a statutory body, has only an advisory function. . . . I would regret very much to see any arm of the Congress so impinge upon this process as to incline me or any of my successors to avoid its use. . . .[73]

These efforts were not enough in the heatedly partisan atmosphere of the late 1950s. On July 14, the Senate adopted S. Res. 115 by voice vote. Four days later Jackson, named to head the subcommittee, made public a letter from Eisenhower pledging cooperation. The President retreated gracefully but without surrendering unconditionally. "The bounds contemplated [in the investigation]," he wrote Jackson, "seem to me to be generally satisfactory, it being my understanding that insofar as the National Security Council is concerned your study is directed to procedures and machinery and not to substance. . . ."[74] The hearings, which began in late 1959 and lasted into the succeeding Congress (and thus the Kennedy administration), actually proved to be less partisan in tone than many expected, but the administration continued throughout 1960 to provide material to sympathetic Republican senators to help correct "some of the erroneous implications growing out of testimony . . . before [the] subcommittee." The interim reports issued by the subcommittee in late 1960 actually served, according to Jackson's later assessment, as a "task-force study" for President-elect Kennedy. Carefully nonpartisan in language, they contained a number of recommendations implicitly critical of practices in the Eisenhower administration, notably including a call for "better ways to relate military power more closely to foreign-policy requirements."[75] That statement seemed to sum up the thrust of Democratic criticisms of Eisenhower's policies that had been evolving since the early days of the "New Look."

V

Close examination of the politics of national security and foreign policy in the period 1945–60 reveals that important partisan differences over policy were the rule rather than the exception. Aside from the years 1947 and 1948 and a brief honeymoon period at the outset of the Eisenhower administration, true bipartisanship did not exist. Nor, except in the most general sense, did a monoliothic "cold war consensus" prevail. Just as the Republican opposition lambasted Truman and Acheson on foreign policy issues after 1949, the Democrats criticized, albeit more sedately and without charges of willful wrongdoing, the policies of Eisenhower and Dulles throughout the 1950s.

Yet opposition forces generally failed to alter the substance of national security policy and foreign policy in the period, or even to increase congressional influence in the formulation of those policies. This was not for want of effort. Involvement in the Korean War made it difficult for Republicans to succeed in their attacks on Truman, and during the Eisenhower administration the Democrats experienced particular frustrations, even after overcoming their internal divisions, because of the President's reputation for expertise in national security matters and his skill in manipulating the executive-congressional balance. Eisenhower was also greatly helped by the cooperative attitude of visible and powerful Democratic leaders such as Johnson, Rayburn, and Russell.

If the congressional opposition failed to shape policy in these years, it also failed to propose clearly articulated alternatives to administration programs in matters of national security and foreign policy. This was so, at least in part, because administration policies themselves were in such flux throughout the period. Although the Truman administration devised fairly clear policies with respect to Europe (and these were at least generally followed by the Eisenhower administration), neither administration developed a coherent set of policies applicable in a global sense that might in turn be countered by a coherent set of alternative policies. Within the nation a minority of writers and critics offered analyses of world trends which proved to be unerringly accurate. However, leaders of both parties, with few exceptions, were reluctant in the 1950s to break from the cold war assumptions and adopt the prescriptions that flowed from the critical writers of the decade.

Events of these years also demonstrated the limitations that seemed to characterize the role of a congressional opposition in the area of national security policy. So constrained did legislators feel, because of public sentiment favoring the President's control of security policy and because they feared themselves that they lacked necessary information, that they nearly always cloaked objections to substantive policy in the rhetoric of institutional, or constitutional, arguments. Thus, during the Truman and Eisenhower years, the major debates over foreign policy and national security policy occurred, usually in veiled terms, over such "constitutional" issues as the sending of troops to Europe, the Bricker Amendment, the Formosa and Middle East resolutions, and proposals to scrutinize the activities of the CIA and the NSC.

If members of opposition parties differed with administration policies in the 1945–60 period, they seemed to effect little change in those policies once their parties came to enjoy *both* majority status in Congress and control of the White House (the Republicans in 1953–54 and the Democrats after 1960). Underlying the national outlook of the Truman, Eisenhower, and Kennedy years was the assumption of a dangerous world. Moving into the White House seemed to firm up the "anti-Communist" impulse of the elected President. Certainly this proved true for Kennedy, who in the 1950s had shared the views of many of his Democratic colleagues in Congress, yet, as President, failed to implement most of them. As for congressional Democrats in the 1960s, party loyalty seemed to overtake ideological and institutional considerations, and it was not until the Vietnam War began to go sour in the latter part of the decade that themes that they had presented earlier resurfaced.

The period 1945–60, then, should not be viewed as a time of consensus when bipartisanship became the norm in matters of national security and foreign policy. Politicians of the time differed, sometimes sharply, even if they smoothed over those differences by employing the rhetoric of "bipartisanship" or "nonpartisanship." Their reasons for such tactics apply equally to other periods, including the present: they feared that open opposition to administration policies would, at worst, brand them as disloyal and, at the least, require them to propose a well-developed set of alternatives. The result—throughout the cold war era—was a short-circuiting of democratic processes and of a whole system of shared powers delineated by the Constitution. Administration policy-makers were not unaware of the benefits of keeping the congressional opposition in line through appeals to the norm of bipartisanship. Perhaps Dean Acheson, late in his life, put it best:

> Bipartisan foreign policy is ideal for the executive because you cannot run this damned country any other way except by fixing the whole organization so it doesn't work the way it is supposed to work. Now the best way to do

that is to say politics stops at the seaboard. . . . If people will swallow that, then you're off to the races.[76]

Notes

1. Norman Graebner extended the period of bipartisanship to early 1950, but focused attention on the Republican leadership of Senator Arthur M. Vandenberg. See Norman A. Graebner, *The New Isolationism: A Study in Politics and Foreign Policy Since 1950* (New York: Ronald Press, 1956), 17–18.

2. James Rowe, Jr., memorandum, "Cooperation—or Conflict?—The President's relationships with an opposition Congress," December 1946, Clark Clifford Papers, Box 4, Harry S. Truman Library, Independence, Missouri.

3. The thirteen opponents were Brooks (Ill.), Butler (Neb.), Bushfield (S. D.), Dworshak (Idaho), Hawkes (N. J.), Kem (Mo.), Langer (N. D.), Malone (Nev.), Moore (Okla.) Revercomb (W. Va.), Wherry (Neb.), Williams (Del.), and Wilson (Iowa). The eight "unreliables" were Brewster (Me.), Bricker (Ohio), Buck (Del.), Martin (Pa.), McCarthy (Wis.), Robertson (Wyo.), Taft (Ohio), and Watkins (Utah).

4. W. L. White, "Report on the 'New Nationalism,' " *New York Times Magazine*, June 28, 1953, 8.

5. Vandenberg to Bruce Barton, March 24, 1947, quoted in Thomas G. Paterson, "Presidential Foreign Policy, Public Opinion, and Congress: The Truman Years," *Diplomatic History, 3* (Winter 1979), 15. See also Arthur M. Schlesinger, Jr., *The Imperial Presidency* (Boston: Houghton Mifflin, 1973), 129; and Henry W. Berger, "Bipartisanship, Senator Taft, and the Truman Administration," *Political Science Quarterly, 90* (Summer 1975), 224.

6. Clifford to Truman, November 19, 1947, Clifford Papers, Box 21; see also "L" to Clifford, October 5, 1948, *ibid.*, Box 20.

7. Arthur H. Vandenberg, Jr., and Joe Alex Morris, eds., *The Private Papers of Senator Vandenberg* (Boston: Houghton Mifflin, 1952), 462; Taft to Henry J. Mahady, July 12, 1951, Robert A. Taft Papers, Box 874, Library of Congress.

8. Surprisingly, only six Republicans (Bridges, Capehart, Jenner, Knowland, Langer, and Wherry) voted against Acheson's confirmation. See Vandenberg and Morris, *Vandenberg Papers*, 468–70; and H. Bradford Westerfield, *Foreign Policy and Party Politics: Pearl Harbor to Korea* (New Haven: Yale University Press, 1955), 327.

9. On the nomination of W. Walton Butterworth, Republicans divided 5 for, 27 against.

10. Taft to H. Alexander Smith, December 12, 1949, Taft Papers, Box 811.

11. Irving Brant, "531 Secretaries of State," *The New Republic*, March 13, 1950, p. 13.

12. Elsey to Beverly Smith, July 16, 1951, George Elsey Papers, Box 71, Truman Library; see draft resolution dated July 3, 1950, apparently authored by Frank Pace of the Defense Department, *ibid.*

13. Taft to Robert McCormick, July 25, 1950, Taft Papers, Box 822; Ronald J. Caridi, *The Korean War and American Politics: The Republican Party as a Case Study* (Philadelphia: University of Pennsylvania Press, 1968), 56–57; Westerfield, *Foreign Policy and Party Politics*, 369; Ross Y. Koen, *The China Lobby in American Politics*, ed. by Richard C. Kagan (New York: Harper & Row, 1974), 83–169.

14. See Republican National Committee, "Background to Korea" [August 1950], Elsey Papers, Box 77. The best coverage of 1950 campaign issues and results is Richard M. Fried, *Men Against McCarthy* (New York: Columbia University Press, 1976), 95–140. See also Fried, "Electoral Politics and McCarthyism: The 1950 Campaign," in Robert Griffith and Athan Theoharis, eds., *The Specter: Original Essays on the Cold War and the Origins of McCarthyism* (New York: New Viewpoints, 1974), 190–222; Caridi, *Korean War and American Politics*, 100–102; and Blair Bolles, "Will Election Results Modify U.S. Foreign Policy?", *Foreign Policy Bulletin, 30* (November 17, 1950), 1–2.

15. See Hoover's speech in *Vital Speeches of the Day, 17* (January 1, 1951), 165–66, and Taft's speech in *Congressional Record*, 82d Cong., 1st sess., 1951, I, 54–61. Wherry introduced his resolution, S. Res. 8, on January 8, 1951.

16. *Congressional Quarterly Almanac, 7* (Washington, D.C.: Congressional Quarterly, Inc., 1951), 222; John Foster Dulles to Arthur Vandenberg, January 8, 1951, and Vandenberg to Dulles, January 23, 1951, John Foster Dulles Papers, Box 143, Series I, Princeton University Library; telegram, Vandenberg to Kenneth Wherry, February 2, 1951, in Vandenberg and Morris, *Vandenberg Papers*, 567; *New York Times*, February 28, 1951, p. 16; Stassen speech of January 15, 1951, in *Vital Speeches of the Day, 17* (February 1, 1951), 229.

17. Of the eleven key roll calls, 34 of the 49 Democrats (69.4 percent) voted for the administration position on nine or more; of the 46 Republicans voting, only seven voted in support that often, while thirty-one (67.4 percent) supported Truman's position on fewer than three roll calls.

18. Office of Senate Minority Policy Committee, "Materials for Reports to the People in Lincoln Day Speeches and Other Addresses," February 5, 1952, Taft Papers, Box 632. For the administration-sponsored defense, see U. S. Senate, Committee on Foreign Relations, *Review of Bipartisan Foreign Policy Consultations Since World War II, Sen. Doc. 87*, 82d Cong., 1st sess., 1952.

19. Taft to Herbert Hoover, February 5, 1952, Taft Papers, Box 995; James T. Patterson, *Mr. Republican: A Biography of Robert A. Taft* (Boston: Houghton Mifflin, 1972), 529–30; Robert A. Divine, *Foreign Policy and U. S. Presidential Elections, 1952–1960* (New York: New Viewpoints, 1974), 30; Dwight D. Eisenhower memorandum on his decision to run in 1952 (undated), Eisenhower Diaries, Dwight D. Eisenhower Papers, Box 29, Dwight D. Eisenhower Library, Abilene, Kansas; James C. Hagerty diary entry, January 4, 1954, James C. Hagerty Papers, Eisenhower Library.

20. On Dulles's role in drafting the plans, see Dulles to Eisenhower, May 20, 1952, Dulles Papers, Box 144, Series II; Eisenhower to Dulles, June 20, 1952, *ibid.*, Box 483, Series X; "Platform Draft (June 20, 1952)," *ibid.*, Box 483, Series X; Townsend Hoopes, *The Devil and John Foster Dulles* (Boston: Atlantic–Little, Brown, 1973), 129–30; and Divine, *Foreign Policy and . . . Elections*, 27, 31–34.

21. A content analysis of the campaigns of several victorious Republican candidates for the House and Senate in 1952 reveals that they were highly critical of Democratic foreign policy. However, while two outspoken Senate foes of bipartisanship and collective security (Zales Ecton and James Kem) were defeated for re-election, some of the party's most strident opponents of internationalism were re-elected (including Bricker, Jenner, Malone, Edward Martin, McCarthy, Watkins, and Williams). See Gary W. Reichard, *The Reaffirmation of Republicanism: Eisenhower and the Eighty-third Congress* (Knoxville: University of Tennessee Press, 1975), 16–17, 23.

22. Eisenhower speech at Chicago on October 31, 1952, *New York Times*, November 1, 1952.

23. See Adlai Stevenson to James E. Doyle, December, 1952, in Walter Johnson, ed., *The Papers of Adlai E. Stevenson* (Boston: Little, Brown, 1974), IV, 219; remarks by Walter George and John Sparkman in spring 1953, *Congressional Record*, 83d Cong., 1st sess., 1953, 921, A1979–80; Hubert H. Humphrey, "Statement on Bipartisan Foreign Policy . . . February 1953," Hubert H. Humphrey Papers, Box 93, Minnesota State Historical Society, St. Paul.

24. See Reichard, *Reaffirmation of Republicanism*, 52–58, and James N. Rosenau, *The Nomination of "Chip" Bohlen* (New York: McGraw-Hill, 1960).

25. *Congressional Record*, 83d Cong., 1st sess., 1953, 7803–55, 7932–79, 9452 ff. Also John F. Kennedy speech of May 14, 1953, John F. Kennedy Pre-Presidential Papers, Box 287, John F. Kennedy Library, Waltham, Mass.; Thomas C. Hennings to M. L. Stephenson, July 23, 1953, Thomas C. Hennings, Jr., Papers, Box 153, University of Missouri Library, Columbia; *Congressional Quarterly Weekly Reports, 10* (May 22, 1953), 685; *ibid., 10* (June 26, 1953), 850; *ibid., 10* (June 2, 1953), 726; Eric Sevareid to Adlai Stevenson, September 5, 1953, Adlai E. Stevenson Papers, Box 378, Princeton University Library.

26. See Symington and Russell comments in *Congressional Quarterly Weekly Reports, 12* (January 15, 1954), 65; also Thomas K. Finletter, *Power and Policy: U. S. Foreign and Military Power in the Hydrogen Age* (New York: Harcourt, Brace., 1954), esp. 3, 21, 23–24.

27. Dean Acheson, "Instant Retaliation: The Debate Continued," *New York Times Magazine*, March 28, 1954, 78; Chester Bowles, "A Plea for Another Great Debate," *ibid.*, February 28, 1954, 24–25.

28. Senators Lyndon Johnson and Earle Clements, asking the most probing questions at an emergency bipartisan leaders' meeting on the crisis held in early April, undoubtedly contributed to Eisenhower's decision not to intervene. See Charlmers M. Roberts, "The Day We Didn't Go to War," *Reporter*, September 14, 1954, 31–32.

29. See Ronald J. Nurse, "America Must Not Sleep: The Development of John F. Kennedy's Foreign Policy Attitudes, 1947–1960," Ph.D. dissertation, Michigan State University, 1971, 80–81, 83–84, 108, 132–33; also Lee P. Marvin to Priscilla Johnson, April 17, 1953, and John F. Kennedy to John Foster Dulles, May 7, 1953, Kennedy Pre-Presidential Papers, Box 290; Stevenson, "Report by Adlai Stevenson," *Look*, June 2, 1953, 38; Chester Bowles to Stevenson, June 5, 1953, Stevenson Papers, Box 374; Hubert H. Humphrey To Carl S. Hagemayer, March 1, 1954, Humphrey Papers, Box 106.

30. Ronald A. Goldberg, "The Senate and Vietnam: A Study in Acquiescence," Ph.D. dissertation, University of Georgia, 1972, 109–10.

31. U. S. Senate, Committee on Foreign Relations, *Hearings on Mutual Defense Treaty with Republic of China* (Executive Session), 84th Cong., 1st sess., 78–79, RG 46, National Archives.

32. Wayne Morse to Benjamin H. Kizer, February 14, 1955, Wayne L. Morse Papers, Box 45, University of Oregon Library, Eugene.

33. Acheson press release, September 6, 1958, Dean G. Acheson Papers, Box 139, Truman Library.

34. Thomas Finletter, letter to editor, *New York Times*, September 6, 1958, in Stevenson Papers, Box 748; Russell to M. H. Barnett, September 10, 1958, Richard B. Russell Papers, Box J-6, Series I, University of Georgia. The only notable exception was former President Truman, who publicly called upon his party colleagues to avoid "partisan attacks in the field of international relations," in *New York Times*, October 14, 1958.

35. Morse to William Benton, October 31, 1958, Morse Papers, Box 13, Series A; Kennedy form letter reply [September 1958], Kennedy Pre-Presidential Papers, Box 484-A.

36. Dulles speech to Far East–America Council of Commerce and Industry, Inc., September 25, 1958, Dulles Papers, Princeton, Box 45, Series I. See Styles Bridges press release, September 30, 1958, OF 168-B-1 (2), Eisenhower Papers.

37. Erwin L. Levine, *Theodore Francis Green: The Washington Years, 1937–1960* (Providence, R. I.: Brown University Press, 1971), 143–44; Bernard G. Browne, "The Foreign Policy of the Democratic Party During the Eisenhower Administration," Ph.D. dissertation, University of Notre Dame, 1968, 295; Green speech draft, September 28, 1958, Records of Senate Committee on Foreign Relations, File 85 A-F-7, National Archives.

38. See Charles Blatnik, et al., to Dwight Eisenhower, October 3, 1958, and Eisenhower reply, October 8, 1958, Eisenhower Papers, OF 168-B-1 (2). See also draft of Dulles statement before Senate Committee on Foreign Relations, with Eisenhower's penciled suggestions, October 13, 1958, John Foster Dulles Papers, Box 7, White House Memoranda Series, Eisenhower Library.

39. Fulbright to Carl Marcy, June 24, 1957, James William Fulbright Papers, BCN 113, University of Arkansas Library, Fayetteville.

40. Stanley D. Bachrack, *The Committee of One Million: "China Lobby" Politics, 1953–1971* (New York: Columbia University Press, 1976), 145, 152–56.

41. See Kenneth T. Young, *Negotiating With the Chinese Communists: The United States Experience, 1953–1967* (New York: McGraw-Hill, 1968), esp. 276–98.

42. Browne, "Foreign Policy of the Democratic Party," 60–61.

43. *Congressional Quarterly Weekly Reports, 14* (May 4, 1956), 504; *ibid., 14* (July 6,

1956), 789–90; and *ibid., 14* (December 28, 1956), 1467–68; Burton I. Kaufman, "The United States Response to the Soviet Economic Offensive of the 1950s," *Diplomatic History, 2* (Spring 1978), 153, 159; James Robinson, *Congress and Foreign Policy-Making: A Study in Legislative Influence and Initiative* (Homewood, Ill.: Dorsey Press, 1967), 57–58.

44. Averell Harriman, "Leadership in World Affairs," *Foreign Affairs, 32* (July 1954), 537; draft of John F. Kennedy speech, November 19, 1957, Fred Holborn Files, Box 53, Kennedy Pre-Presidential Papers; Fulbright to Ronald B. McCallum, April 3, 1956, Fulbright Papers, BXN 105; and Chester Bowles, *The New Dimensions of Peace* (New York: Harper & Brothers, 1955), passim.

45. Herbert S. Parmet, *The Democrats: The Years After FDR* (New York: Macmillan, 1976), 154. For lists of the membership of the foreign policy committee at different times in the late 1950s, see Paul Butler Papers, Boxes 59 and 61, University of Notre Dame Library, Notre Dame, Indiana.

46. David B. Truman, *The Congressional Party: A Case Study* (New York: John Wiley, 1959), 301; Browne, "Foreign Policy of the Democratic Party," 25. On Humphrey's lukewarm response to an early statement on foreign policy by the DAC, see Humphrey to Norman Thomas, October 29, 1957, Humphrey Papers, Box 138.

47. Malcolm Jewell, "Evaluating the Decline of Southern Internationalism through Senatorial Roll Call Votes," *Journal of Politics, 21* (November 1959), 631–37; Browne, "Foreign Policy of the Democratic Party," 10–11, 162–63.

48. The correlation coefficient *phi* (ϕ) can be employed to assess the strength of association between difference in party membership and disagreement on an individual roll call; ϕ ranges from 0 to 1, equaling 0 when members of both parties divide in exactly the same way, and equaling 1 when all members of one party disagree with all members of the other party. Computation of ϕ for all contested foreign policy roll-calls (those on which the minority position was favored by more than 10 percent of all legislators whose views were recorded) in both houses for the Eighty-second through Eighty-sixth Congresses yields the following results:

Congress	Average ϕ (House)	Average ϕ (Senate)
82nd	.481	.531
83rd	.314	.347
84th	.291	.287
85th	.243	.330
86th	.195	.256

49. Schlesinger, *Imperial Presidency*, 152–153.

50. Roberta S. Sigel, "Image of the American Presidency: Part II of an Exploration into Popular Views of Presidential Power," *Midwest Journal of Political Science, 10* (February 1966), 128.

51. Samuel P. Huntington, *American Politics: The Promise of Disharmony* (Cambridge, Mass.: Harvard University Press, 1981), 76.

52. Fred I. Greenstein, "Eisenhower as an Activist President: A Look at New Evidence," *Political Science Quarterly, 94* (Winter 1979–80), 584–86.

53. For detailed treatment of Eisenhower's handling of the Bricker Amendment, see Gary W. Reichard, "Eisenhower and the Bricker Amendment," *Prologue: The Journal of the National Archives, 6* (Summer 1974), 88–99. Eisenhower quotation in James C. Hagerty diary entry, January 14, 1954, Hagerty Diaries, Eisenhower Papers.

54. U.S. President, *Public Papers of the Presidents: Dwight D. Eisenhower, 1955* (Washington, D. C.: GPO, 1960), 209; U. S. Senate, Committees on Armed Services and Foreign Relations, *Hearings on Resolution Authorizing the President to Employ the Armed Forces of the United States for Protecting the Security of Formosa, the Pescadores and Related Positions and Territories of that Area* (Executive Session; 2 vols.), 84th Cong., 1st sess., 1955, I, 46, 47, Records of the Senate Committee on Foreign Relations.

55. *Congressional Record*, 84th Cong., 1st sess., 1955, CI, 677. (Comment is by Rep. Laurence Curtis of Massachusetts.)

56. *Congressional Quarterly Weekly Reports, 15* (January 11, 1957), 41; Democratic Advisory Committee, "The Democratic Task During the Next Two Years," C. Estes Kefauver Papers, Box 2, Series IV-F, University of Tennessee Library, Knoxville; U. S. Senate, Committees on Armed Services and Foreign Relations, *Hearings on S. J. Res. 19, Authority for Economic and Military Cooperation with Nations in the Middle East* (Executive Session), 85th Cong., 1st sess., 1957, 1133–34.

57. *Hearings on S. J. Res. 19* (Executive Session), 9, 10, 16, 57.

58. See George Elsey, memorandum for file, July 17, 1946, and memorandum of conversation, Clark Clifford and Hoyt Vandenberg, January 9, 1947, Elsey Papers, Box 56; Stephen E. Ambrose, with Richard Immerman, *Ike's Spies: Eisenhower and the Espionage Establishment* (Garden City, N. Y.: Doubleday, 1981), 165. The act, also known as the Armed Forces Unification Act, established in addition a permanent Joint Chiefs of Staff and a unified Department of Defense.

59. Daniel Yergin, *Shattered Peace: The Origins of the Cold War and the National Security State* (Boston: Houghton Mifflin, 1977).

60. Harry H. Ransom, *The Intelligence Establishment* (Cambridge, Mass.: Harvard University Press, 1970), 83, 85, 87.

61. *Ibid.*, 87; J. Malcolm Smith and Cornelius P. Cotter, *Powers of the President During Crises* (Washington, D. C.: Public Affairs Press, 1960), 15, 79–80.

62. Ambrose, *Ike's Spies*, 170–71.

63. Ransom, *Intelligence Establishment*, 89.

64. Ambrose, *Ike's Spies*, 175–76. For treatment of CIA operations in Iran and Guatemala, see *ibid.*, 189–251, and Richard Immerman, "Guatemala as Cold War History," *Political Science Quarterly, 95* (Winter 1980–81), 629–53.

65. Ambrose, *Ike's Spies*, 187–88; Ransom, *Intelligence Establishment*, 164–67; *Congressional Quarterly Weekly Reports, 14* (February 10, 1956), 154, and *ibid., 15* (April 13, 1956), 431; *Congressional Record*, 84th Cong., 2d sess., 1956, CII, pt. 5, 5923–24, 5926.

66. Ambrose, *Ike's Spies*, 242–43; *Congressional Quarterly Weekly Reports, 14* (January 20, 1956), 79.

67. U. S. Senate, Committee on Foreign Relations, *Hearings Regarding Summit Conference of May 1960 and Incidents Relating Thereto* (Executive Session, 4 vols.), 86th Cong., 2d sess., 1960, I, 2, Records of Senate Foreign Relations Committee. See Johnson's statement, transcript of comments on "Face the Nation" television program, May 22, 1960, Fulbright Papers, BCN 147; also statement of Democratic Advisory Committee, May 22, 1960, Butler Papers, Box 25.

68. Gore comments in *Hearings Regarding Summit Conference . . . 1960*, III, 627; Wiley-Fulbright exchange in *ibid.*, I-A, 194.

69. See Fulbright to Johnson, November 26, 1957, Marcy memorandum to Fulbright, November 18, 1957, and Johnson to Fulbright, November 29, 1957, in Fulbright Papers, BCN 121. On Johnson's announcement of Preparedness hearings, see *Congressional Quarterly Weekly Reports, 15* (November 8, 1957), 1240.

70. *New York Times*, April 17, 1959, 1–2.

71. Memorandum, Robert Cutler to Wilton B. Persons, June 4, 1959, and Gordon Gray to Dwight D. Eisenhower, June 11, 1959, Bryce N. Harlow Files, Eisenhower Papers, Box 17.

72. Eisenhower's handwritten comment on unsigned "Memorandum for the President," June 12, 1959, Eisenhower Diary Series, Eisenhower Papers, Box 26.

73. Bryce Harlow memorandum of meeting in White House, June 24, 1959, dated June 29, 1959, Eisenhower Diary Series, Box 26; Eisenhower to Lyndon B. Johnson, June 25, 1959, Harlow Files, Box 17. On Fulbright's early efforts to block Jackson, see Jackson to Fulbright, May 19, 1959, Fulbright Papers, BCN 135.

74. Henry M. Jackson press release, July 19, 1959, and Eisenhower to Jackson, July 10, 1959, Harlow Files, Box 17.

75. Henry M. Jackson, ed., *The National Security Council: Jackson Subcommittee Papers*

on Policy-Making at the Presidential Level (New York: Praeger, 1965), xiii, 27–28, 39. On changes in NSC procedures initiated by Kennedy, see especially Roger Hilsman, *To Move a Nation: The Politics of Foreign Policy in the Administration of John F. Kennedy* (New York: Dell, 1967), 22–24.

76. Quoted in Theodore A. Wilson and Richard D. McKinzie, "White House Versus Congress: Conflict or Collusion? The Marshall Plan as a Case Study," paper presented at the 66th annual meeting of the Organization of American Historians, Chicago, April 1973, 2.

Conclusion: The Limits of Nuclear Strategy

NORMAN A. GRAEBNER

Through eight generally peaceful years the Eisenhower presidency built a strategic edifice for the United States on foundations designed by the Truman administration. President Dwight D. Eisenhower himself, as the contributors to this volume agree, stood at the center of Washington's decision-making process, at least in defense matters, throughout his years in the White House. The Eisenhower record, revealed in detail in the private and presidential papers housed in the Eisenhower Library as well as in the President's own two-volume memoir, *Mandate for Change* (1963) and *Waging Peace* (1965), suggest that Eisenhower was indeed an active President, leaving little to chance, directly or indirectly determining all the basic decisions of government. As President, Eisenhower seemed to possess a remarkable knowledge of the ways of the world, an essential moderation, and a self-assurance that enabled him to dominate his administration, not least the defense establishment. What simplified Eisenhower's task in dealing with the nation's highest ranking officers was the special prestige he carried from his role as wartime commander of all allied forces in western Europe and, later, as Chief of Staff. If he had commanded the generals when on active duty, he would continue to do so as President. Moreover, the challenge of defining a wise and coherent strategy for successful coexistence with a turbulent and revolutionary world demanded the determined efforts of any President.

Eisenhower's extensive involvement in the affairs of state sought a working arrangement whereby the administration could fulfill its campaign pledge of tax reduction and still answer the charge that the government was neglecting the country's defense. The chapters of Richard Challener, I.M. Destler, and Douglas Kinnard delineate the President's role in managing the National Security Council and his quest for a defense structure that would not strain the federal budget or produce large deficits. To gain greater efficiency in procurement, and thereby bring the country additional defense at less cost, he brought Charles E. Wilson and Roger Kyes of General Motors into his administration as Secretary and Deputy Secretary of Defense, respectively.[1]

To achieve his basic objective—an optimum balance between costs and defense—Eisenhower quickly adopted a nuclear strategy, based on an effective air delivery system, as the country's surest guarantee against unwanted attack and an accumulating national debt. He held to this strategy despite the countering arguments of generals Matthew Ridgway and Maxwell Taylor, who advocated a more flexible defense structure with larger conventional forces.[2] Rejecting the dominant views of the administration—that any war with the Soviet Union would escalate quickly to a nuclear exchange—Ridgway and Taylor predicted that future wars would tend to remain too limited in scope and purpose to permit the use of the nuclear arsenal. If the President could control the nature of the defense structure, however, he seemed unable to limit its size, for the Strategic Air Command (SAC) presented its perceptions of need with remarkable success. Even when the President, as David Rosenberg reveals, repeatedly questioned the growth of the nuclear arsenal, as well as the proliferation and redundancy in the targeting of Soviet nuclear installations, airfields, and urban centers, he could not deter SAC from reaching overkill. If the plateau of defense expenditures under Eisenhower was sufficient to produce an arsenal which even he regarded excessive, it was far below what it might have been.

What matters in any judgment of the Eisenhower administration's decision-making processes, or even the President's own procedures to govern those processes, is not the nature of the system but the quality of the decisions that it produced. How well did those decisions serve the short-term and long-term interests of the United States? In large measure the lack of restraint in building the American nuclear arsenal assumed a possible attack from the U.S.S.R. Whatever the cost, Washington insisted, the United States would be prepared. But power of even such magnitude would not, as could the far more limited power of earlier centuries, shield cities and populations from attack. There was no assurance that the defense of urban areas against missiles or long-range aircraft would be any more successful in the future than it was in the recent European war. Defense against the nuclear destruction of the United States and its allies required policies that would either eliminate or effectively discourage any such attack. It was not strange, therefore, that some military leaders after 1950 advocated preventive war as one total defense against nuclear destruction. The rapid expansion of the Soviet nuclear arsenal after the mid-1950s destroyed the appeal of the preventive war arguments. The actuality of coexistence and the absence of direct security threats, moreover, permitted no occasion for attacking the Soviet Union. Nor could national leaders, whatever their fears of the Kremlin, base their decisions on the assumption that Soviet-American antagonism would terminate in war. Undoubtedly the planners of the Eisenhower years would have ultimately agreed with the advice that Bismarck offered his king during the war crisis of 1875: "I would . . . never advise your Majesty to declare war forthwith, simply because it appeared that our opponent would begin hostilities in the near future. One can never anticipate the way of divine providence securely enough for that."[3] Such a prescription alone ruled out even a preemptive strike in the event of a war crisis.

With the doctrine of "massive retaliation," John Foster Dulles, Secretary of State after January 1953, announced a far more acceptable formula for protecting the nation from nuclear attack. The doctrine was inherent in the Eisenhower decision of 1953 to concentrate the nation's defense efforts on nuclear power. What made the Dulles formula especially attractive was its promise to prevent aggression against friends and allies no less than assaults on the United States itself. *"There is one solution and only one,"* Dulles wrote in May 1952, *"that is for the free world to develop the will to organize the means to retaliate instantly against open aggression by Red armies, so that if it occurred anywhere, we could and would strike back where it hurts, by means of our own choosing."*[4] Dulles repeated this formula in his speech before the New York Council on Foreign Relations on January 12, 1954. The new strategy, which now became the official orientation of American defense policy, would prevent future losses to communist influence by assuring aggressors that United States retaliatory power would reduce their urban centers to rubble.[5] Critics noted that the doctrine of massive retaliation, by placing major reliance on nuclear rather than conventional power, would limit American options, in the event of war with the U.S.S.R., to capitulation or annihilation.[6] Dulles's successive modifications of the doctrine admitted the need for additional choices, but the administration's continuing commitment to American and European security rested, fundamentally, on the nuclear deterrent as the surest guarantee against war.

Few questioned the appropriateness of massive retaliation as a defense of the United States itself, especially since the country was not in danger of armed invasion. Europe as well opted for the nuclear defense because it, like the United States, sought a maximum of protection at minimum cost. European leaders concluded that their inability to fight a successful conventional war enforced the nuclear deterrent by assuring the Kremlin that any Soviet invasion of western Europe would inevitably terminate in a full-scale nuclear exchange. Always at the core of NATO's strength, unity, and effectiveness was the American commitment to Western defense. Without the steady conviction that the United States would fulfill its obligation to the NATO members, the alliance would cease to exist. This essential guarantee Washington sought to sustain. Secretary Dulles, at a news conference of October 16, 1957, declared that the United States was prepared to use its Strategic Air Command in defense of its European allies, including Turkey. President Eisenhower repeated that assurance at Paris in December. "Speaking for my own country," he said, "I assure you in the most solemn terms that the United States would come, at once and with all appropriate force, to the assistance of any NATO nation subjected to armed attack. This is the resolve of the United States—of all parts and all parties."[7] Two factors, perhaps reinforcing each other, sustained the peace of Europe: the remoteness of vital interests in conflict and the fear of mutual extinction. Washington, emphasizing the deterrent effect of nuclear arsenals, preferred to entrust Western security to the nation's retaliatory power.

Despite his concern for budgetary restraints, his willingness to accept sufficiency rather than superiority in nuclear weapons and, thus, accept also a relative increase in Soviet power, Eisenhower could not escape the momentum of the warfare state. He had appointed a leading industrialist to impose some order on the military services and streamline the military-industrial relationship. He hoped, furthermore, to appoint officers to the Joint Chiefs of Staff who would discard their service loyalties and promote a broad, cooperative approach to national defense. At the end Eisenhower and his business appointees failed to eliminate the special pleading of the Service chiefs. Each branch, he once complained, acted as if it alone were responsible for the country's security. Eventually Eisenhower concluded that the defense contractors themselves exerted an inordinate influence over the military budget. He accepted John J. McCloy's conclusion that "the inter-service game extends right down through the corporations, depending upon which branch their contracts flow from and it even goes into the academic institutions depending from where their research grants flow."[8] Arms expenditures even at the level that Eisenhower would permit simply created too many vested interests. In his farewell address Eisenhower recognized "the conjunction of an immense military establishment and a large arms industry," a relationship new to the American experience. He warned the nation against "the acquisition of unwarranted influence, whether sought or unsought, by the military-industrial complex."[9]

Unfortunately the country's unprecedented level of destructive power could never dispel the nation's mood of insecurity because that power could not eliminate the sources of danger that demanded it. Nuclear weapons might deter an attack on the United States and its allies; additionally, they might enable the United States, either through a preemptive or an effective second strike, to save some American cities and populations in a general war. In any lesser confrontation the sheer destructiveness of nuclear power would quickly elminate its legitimate use. War, Carl von Clausewitz wrote, is not ruled by laws of its own, but is "simply a continuation of political intercourse, with the addition of other means. . . . The main lines along which military events progress, and to which they are restricted, are political lines that continue throughout the war and into the subsequent peace." If war cannot be divorced from political life, then to destroy the links between politics and war through the excessive use of force would leave us, in Clausewitz's words, "with something pointless and devoid of sense."[10] For that reason the country's nuclear arsenal would not recover the lost world of Versailles or undo the changes in world politics wrought by war and revolution in the 1940s. Nor would it give the United States the means to command the stage in any regional crisis and permit it to force others to adjust their goals and policies. In short, the nuclear arsenal, even while it underwrote the country's international leadership and prestige, would not in itself give the United States the initiative it sought, or sustain the predominant position it enjoyed during the Truman-Eisenhower era.

The perennial effort to gain the initiative through nuclear power had the effect of stimulating an arms race with the U.S.S.R. Herbert F. York described the Soviet-American interaction in his book, *Race to Oblivion: A Participant's View of the Arms Race* (1970):

Our unilateral decisions have set the rate and scale for most of the individual steps in the strategic-arms race. In many cases we started development before they did and we easily established a large and long-lasting lead in terms of deployed numbers and types. Examples include the A-bomb itself, intercontinental bombers, submarine-launched ballistic missiles, the MIRV. In other instances, the first development steps were taken by the two sides at about the same time, but immediately afterward our program ran well ahead of theirs both in the development of further types and applications in the deployment of large numbers. Such cases include the mighty H-bomb and, very probably, military space applications. In some cases, to be sure, they started development work ahead of us and arrived first at the stage where they were able to commence deployment. But we usually reacted so strongly that our deployments and capabilities soon ran far ahead of theirs and we, in effect, even here, determined the final size of the operation. Such cases include the intercontinental ballistic missile and, though it is not strictly a military matter, manned space flight.[11]

Although American leaders understood clearly that their technological advances would produce an arms race, they pursued policies that caused the weapons competition to escalate at a faster pace than the nation's security required. The arms race came not because the Eisenhower administration was insensitive to the dangers or uniquely aggressive, but because American science and technology, being more dynamic, generated a profusion of ideas and inventions, including more and more powerful and efficient weapons of mass destruction. The problem, York concluded, was "a sort of technological exuberance that . . . overwhelmed the other factors that go into the making of overall national policy."[12]

I

Despite the inapplicability of nuclear power to limited-war conflicts, the Eisenhower administration applied its formulations of massive retaliation to Asia no less than to Europe. Indeed, the country's long-standing purpose of protecting the Afro-Asian world against Communist aggression reached its most elaborate form in Dulles's proclamations. The formula assumed that the United States, because of the destructive power at its command, could manage or eliminate unwanted change in the immediately critical regions of East and Southeast Asia simply by threatening to use atomic weapons. The added assumption that the dangers emanated from the Kremlin enhanced the credibility of the deterrent; a major force would take the threat of nuclear retaliation more seriously than would a minor one. That major force had allegedly driven Chiang Kai-shek into exile on the island of Formosa and had brought aggression to Korea; by 1953 it threatened to overrun Indochina as well. Vice President Richard Nixon described the ongoing struggle in Southeast Asia as a simple matter of Communist imperialism on French soil. Dulles himself attributed the threat to the "mighty land power of the Communist world."[13] The Eisenhower administration was not prepared to resist such power in another war on Asian soil. Thus it had no choice but to witness further expansion of Communist influence in Asia or prevent it with the deterrent of massive retaliatory power. If Dulles's formulations of massive retaliation provided an effective and fundamentally risk-free program for preventing unwanted aggression in Asia, they comprised a rejection of the entire American involvement in Korea. Massive retaliation, if effective at all, would have rendered that war unnecessary.

During the spring of 1953 Eisenhower faced the challenge of ending the Korean war. The prolonged negotiations had produced some agreements on prisoner exchanges, but the long-sought truce remained elusive. Stalin's death in March apparently eroded much of the Chinese confidence in the Kremlin. Thereafter Peking appeared more willing to accept the American demands that all Chinese prisoners of war receive the choice to remain in exile rather than return to China. Still the record suggests that Eisenhower broke the diplomatic impasse of mid-May 1953 by hinting that the United States might use atomic weapons if the Chinese did not accept the truce. American purpose in Korea enjoyed the official support of the United Nations and much of the non-Communist world. European and Asian leaders, however, had made clear their opposition to any use of nuclear weapons in Korea. Earlier, Democratic officials had contemplated the conventional bombing of Manchurian targets and a naval blockade of the Chinese coast. Eisenhower might well have threatened China with destruction by American air and naval forces; only with extreme difficulty could he have explained to a troubled world that the nation's interest in terminating its three-year involvement in Korea required the destruction of millions of Chinese lives. At any rate, Dulles could later claim that the administration's success in obtaining the July 1953 truce in Korea demonstrated the effectiveness of atomic diplomacy.[14]

Dulles formal announcement of the doctrine of massive retaliation in January 1954 suggested that the administration had Indochina in mind. That spring Eisenhower hesitated to commit American ground forces to prevent a French collapse. "The jungles of Indochina," he explained, ". . . would have swallowed up division after division of United States troops, who, unaccustomed to this kind of warfare, would have sustained heavy casualties until they had learned to live in a new environment."[15] The President feared, moreover, that the country could not sustain the high cost of wartime defense spending without suffering economic disaster or unwanted governmental intervention. He hoped especially to avoid another limited war on the Eurasian continent, where the United States would fight at a disadvantage. Secretary of the Treasury George M. Humphrey spoke for the administration when he insisted that the United States had "no business getting into little wars. If a situation comes up where our interests justify intervention," he said, "let's intervene decisively with all we have got or stay out."[16] To avoid a limited war in Asia, Washington had either to resist the temptation to elevate local pressures into matters of vital concern or rely on threats of massive retaliation to prevent unwanted change.

Eisenhower desired to avoid war in Indochina; still he feared any further Communist gains in Southeast Asia. As he warned Winston Churchill: "We failed to halt Hirohito, Mussolini and Hitler by not acting in unity and in time. This marked the beginning of many years of stark tragedy and desperate peril. May it not be that our nations have learned something from that lesson?"[17] Eisenhower assured Churchill early in April 1954, however, that under no circumstance would the defense of Southeast Asia require British and American ground forces. Later that month the President informed his aides: "If we, without allies, should ever find ourselves fighting at various places all over the region, and if Red Chinese aggressive participation were clearly identified, then we could scarcely avoid . . . considering the necessity of striking directly at the head instead of the tail of the snake, Red China itself."[18] In early June, Dulles indeed threatened the Chinese with massive retaliation if they moved southward.[19] Soon thereafter the Geneva Conference terminated the immediate struggle for Indochina by dividing the former French colony into three independent states, assigning only that portion of the state of Vietnam north of the seventeenth parallel to the victorious Ho Chi Minh. Again Dulles attributed the post-Geneva peace of Southeast Asia to the administration's art of brinksmanship.[20]

In September 1954 the mainland Chinese shelled the offshore islands of Quemoy and Matsu, both under the control of the Nationalist regime on Formosa, with the apparent intent of seizing them by force. At the outbreak of the shelling the Joint Chiefs agreed that the offshore islands were not essential for the defense of Formosa, more than one hundred miles off the China coast, and that the Chinese Nationalists could not hold them without American assistance. Eisenhower cautioned Admiral Arthur W. Radford, the chairman of the Joint Chiefs, who advocated a decisive American response: "We're not talking now about a limited, brush-fire war. We're talking about going to the threshold of World War III. If we attack China, we're not going to impose limits on our military actions, as in Korea. Moreover . . . if we get into a general war, the logical enemy will be Russia, not China, and we'll have to strike there."[21] Thereafter Eisenhower, as Richard Challener notes, saw little reason for the United States to become involved in the defense of the offshore islands. Dulles responded to the crisis by assuring Chiang that the Nationalists on Formosa would not stand alone against an invasion from the mainland.

What quickly subjected the Eisenhower administration to open criticism throughout the non-Communist world was the doubtful posture it assumed on the question of the offshore islands. Any assult on those islands would have left the United States only two impossible alternatives. If American forces rushed to the aid of Chiang's exposed position, the country would be involved in another open conflict with China on Asian soil; the resort to atomic bombs, as Dulles warned, might shortly involve the United States in a general war. If, on the other hand, Washington backed down and deserted Chiang, it would suffer a tremendous loss of prestige. Few Americans or Europeans regarded the United States commitment to the defense of Formosa unreasonable or particularly dangerous, but they questioned the wisdom of any commitment to the offshore islands. Except for the assumption that Chiang, to avoid the disintegration of his regime, required the offshore islands as symbolic stepping-stones for his return to the mainland, the American involvement in the Formosa Strait had no apparent purpose. Walter Lippmann detected danger in this assumption. "If, as a matter of fact," he wrote, "the internal strength of Nationalist China rests on the fantasy that Chiang Kai-shek will some day return to China, we are headed for trouble."

In the Formosa Resolution of late January 1955, Congress authorized the President to resist any effort to capture the offshore islands if it appeared that the assault was an initial move against Formosa itself. "Clearly, this existing and developing situation," the President warned, "poses a serious danger to the security of our country and the entire Pacific area and indeed to the peace of the world."[22] The President promised to use United States forces only in situations which he could recognize as part of a general assault on Formosa itself. His purpose, he said, was to demonstrate American determination to maintain its commitment to the defense of Formosa. When newsmen questioned Eisenhower in March 1955 on his apparent decision to employ nuclear weapons in defense of the offshore islands, the President responded: "Now in any combat where these things can be used on strictly military targets and for strictly military purposes, I see no reason why they shouldn't be used just exactly as you would use a bullet or anything else."[23] Analysts observed that even the tactical use of such weapons around Amoy would have killed an estimated 12 to 14 million Chinese civilians. Eisenhower escaped the crisis by resisting the appeals of Radford, Dulles, and others for stronger responses to the Chinese shelling while still avoiding the charges of appeasement.[24]

II

In August 1958 the Chinese created another major crisis when they resumed the shelling of Quemoy. Dulles looked on in disbelief. Certainly, he declared, the Chinese would not attempt to take the islands. On September 4 Dulles traveled to Newport, Rhode Island, where Eisenhower was vacationing, with a well-prepared statement which represented the views of the Pentagon, the CIA, and his advisers in the State Department. The document assumed that the United States faced a major threat to its security in the Pacific. Dulles predicted that the loss of Quemoy would lead to the loss of Formosa; this, in turn, would expose the entire anti-Communist barrier in the western Pacific to destruction. Clearly the United States had no choice but to defend Quemoy. To that end Dulles recommended that the United States, if it could not persuade the mainland Chinese to abandon their goals, prepare for the use of nuclear weapons. The world might object, but a swift, total victory would soon cause it to forget. After suggesting a few minor changes in the text, Eisenhower accepted the Dulles proposal and authorized the secretary to release it to the press.[25]

Again Washington had embarked on a unilateral policy in Asia which had little or no support among the European allies. Soviet leader Nikita Khrushchev warned the President in a letter of September 7, 1958: An attack upon the People's Republic of China . . . is an attack upon the Soviet Union." Two weeks later he threatened to use nuclear weapons against any country that used them against China.[26] Still the President defended his uncompromising stand on the offshore islands and the concommitant threat to use nuclear weapons in their defense. When on September 29, Senator Theodore F. Green, chairman of the Foreign Relations Committee, questioned the importance of Quemoy to the defense of Formosa and the United States, the President responded that a successful attack on Formosa would drive the United States from the western Pacific. To prevent that, the country had no choice but to protect the status of Quemoy and Matsu. "We must not forget," Eisenhower concluded, "that the whole Formosa Straits situation is intimately connected with the security of the United States and the free world."[27] Fortunately, China's leaders ordered no assault on the offshore islands. Perhaps for them also the struggle over the islands was not worth the price. The Peking regime shared with Formosa the dream of a united China, one that bound Formosa to the mainland. The mainland Chinese had as much reason as the Nationalists to keep the Chinese struggle alive, exerting pressure on Formosa by threatening, not capturing, the offshore islands.

Inasmuch as no country other than the Republic of China supported Washington's commitment to the offshore islands, any American war fought with nuclear weapons in their defense would have produced a worldwide revulsion of incalculable proportions. For the mainland Chinese this fact alone, if they actually perceived a clear nuclear threat, must have made the inclination to call the bluff compelling indeed. Had the Chinese done so, the President would have faced the choice between an ignominious retreat and the unleashing of a massive war, one that could easily have degenerated into disaster—all over the defense of two tiny islands hugging the China coast and of little strategic value to anyone. Such choices, inherent in the nature of bluffs, explain why all the world's masters of diplomacy abhorred such devices. Bluffs have the simple purpose of obtaining something for nothing, and success in diplomacy is seldom that cost-free. Nor should it be, for a peaceful diplomatic settlement always assumes some quid pro quo. Moreover, no government can keep an antagonist guessing without keeping its own people and its allies in doubt as well. One conclusion is certain: the American people would never have supported a major war on the Asian mainland for the defense of Quemoy and Matsu.

President Eisenhower did not contemplate the destruction of the Communist enemy in Asia in a series of successful wars; rather he sought the prevention of unwanted change through the absolute assurance that any aggression would ultimately face the full might of the United States. Indeed, what rendered the doctrine of massive retaliation so acceptable to Americans generally was its assurance of Afro-Asian stability without the necessity of fighting. To counter a limited aggression in the critical region of Southeast Asia, the Eisenhower administration had formed the Southeast Asia Treaty Organization (SEATO). At the organization's initial meeting in Manila during September 1954, Dulles warned the allies that the United States, because of its global commitments, would not engage in another conventional war on the Asian mainland. The United States, he said, would grant logistical, naval, and air support; beyond that it would resort to weapons of massive destruction. To create an American conventional force in Asia, the Secretary later informed the United States Congress, would be "an injudicious overextension of our military power. We do not have the adequate forces to do it," he explained, "and I believe that if there should be an open armed attack in that area the most effective step would be to strike at the source of the aggression rather than to try to rush American manpower into the area to try to fight a ground war."[28] Dulles's formula left the United States with the unfortunate prospect of either accepting what its Asian allies could achieve or resorting to nuclear weapons. As late as 1960 spokesmen of the administration could recall years of American success in containing Communist expansion in Asia without resorting to war.

In Indochina, Ho Chi Minh had already demonstrated that the Dulles formula actually offered no defense at all. After eliminating the French from Southeast Asia in 1954, Ho never permitted the Geneva settlement to weaken his determination to unite Vietnam under his leadership. His subsequent guerrilla war against the United States–backed regime in Saigon exposed the hollowness of the nuclear deterrent as a controlling element in the politics of Asia, especially when any revolutionary movement had an interest in defying it. By 1960, long before South Vietnam had experienced the full impact of either Communist-led subversion or North Vietnamese infiltration, the Saigon government controlled only half of South Vietnam.[29] Hanoi had long demonstrated its capacity to counter whatever force Saigon or America's allies in Asia could mount against it. It was equally apparent that the Eisenhower administration did not contemplate a war against Hanoi to underwrite its pervading commitment to South Vietnam. Thus the United States one day would accept Ho's domination of all Vietnam or would attempt to prevent it belatedly with a direct employment of its conventional, not its nuclear, power.

Why global containment, as demonstrated even in the late 1950s, met only limited success was clear enough: *The power to destroy is not the power to control.* The effective threat of retaliation, whether nuclear or conventional, demanded the existence of universally recognized national interests of sufficient magnitude to rationalize the destruction as well as the risk of escalation. Despite the language of world aggression, United States officials could never convince either the North Vietnamese, the people of Europe and Asia, or much of the American populace that American security interests were universal. Through the logic of history and geography the United States had written into the record its vital concern for what occurred in Europe and in the Western Hemisphere. Where its interests were primary the nation faced no direct challenge to its policies of containment. But the world generally—and Asians particularly—refused to recognize a body of established American security interests in Asia. Here United States concerns were secondary. This fact, added to the weakening effect of distance, invited repeated defiance of an entire spectrum of clearly stated American preferences. The United States could not, whatever its threats of countering violence, dispose of revolution, political turmoil, subversion, guerrilla warfare, and all the other enemies of peaceful change and self-determination that existed in Asia. For in the defense of any commitment there must be a clear relation between the price of destruction and the gain to national security. In the turbulent Afro-Asian world that relationship remained agonizingly elusive.

III

Power, even nuclear power, is a means, not an end. The essential factor in any country's foreign relations is the body of interests that it pursues, not the means whereby it intends to protect them. The quality of a nation's external policies hinges on the precision whereby it determines its interests amid the dangers and possibilities of a competing world. From the outset the Eisenhower administration defined the security interests of the United States so broadly that the American people could have little knowledge of what Washington might ask them to defend. The United States by 1960, despite the size of its nuclear arsenal, was more fearful, more extended militarily, and less inclined to come to terms with the Communist world as an inescapable necessity than it had been at mid-century. Indeed, the fears and purposes that drove American policy could find no answer in the nation's burgeoning nuclear arsenal. Perhaps the rhetorical effort, begun under Truman, to eliminate nothing from America's official concern had a reasonable purpose: to keep all potential aggressors in doubt as to the country's intentions and thereby discourage unwanted assaults on the status quo everywhere. Unfortunately the attempt to manage world affairs by dwelling on global perceptions of danger and the need to oppose them embraced objectives that the country could never achieve and discounted the powerful role of other nations in maintaining the necessary international equilibrium.

President Eisenhower accepted the basic suppositions of the times when he warned the nation early in 1953 that it stood in greater peril than at any time in its history. On January 27, six days after he assumed his new office, Secretary Dulles informed a national radio and television audience: "Already our proclaimed enemies control one-third of all the people of the world. . . . At the end of the Second World War, only a little over seven years ago, [the Soviets] only controlled about 200 million people. Today, they control 800 million people and they're hard at work to get control of other parts of the world."[30] Even as the administration mounted a defense based on massive retaliation the fears continued to mount. In June 1957 Walter S. Robertson, Assistant Secretary of State for Far Eastern Affairs, could tell the nation: "Starting from zero in our generation, the international Communists now hold in a grip of ruthless power 16 nations, 900 million people—a circumstance recently described by the Secretary of State as 'the most frightening fact history records.' "[31] The clear assumption that the Communist world was monolithic and expansive decreed that the United States not only contain it but also seek its destruction.

Dulles, like Acheson, assumed that the U.S.S.R. could not, in the long run, survive the pressures of Western containment. Upon taking office he proclaimed American purpose toward the Soviet bloc as that of creating "in other peoples such a love of freedom that they can never really be absorbed by the despotism, the totalitarian dictatorships, of the Communist world."[32] The new strategy of instant retaliation, he informed the nation in January 1954, would permit time and the human desire for freedom to work their destruction on the Communist enemy. "If we persist in the course I outline," he promised the nation, "we shall confront dictatorship with a task that is, in the long run, beyond its strength. . . . If the dictators persist in their present course, then it is they who will be limited to superficial successes, while their foundations crumble under the treads of their iron boots. . . ."[33] For the Eisenhower administration the Communist control of both Eastern Europe and China was at once too dangerous and too ephemeral to merit its recognition by the United States.

After mid-century Washington rationalized its burgeoning defense effort as a prerequisite for successful negotiations with the U.S.S.R. By 1953 it seemed clear that the Marshall Plan and NATO, backed by the economic power and atomic supremacy of the United States, had halted the threatened landslide into disaster. Convinced that Western power vis-à-vis the Soviet Union would never be greater than it was at that moment, Western leaders and analysts, such as Winston Churchill and Anthony Eden, argued that the time had arrived to begin the arduous task of negotiating a general European settlement. Washington officials who commanded Western policy, however, concluded that Western gains after mid-century warranted further delay to enable Western diplomats to approach the Kremlin with total military superiority. Some warned indeed that Winston Churchill's widely publicized demand for a Big Four meeting merely injured Western unity and encouraged a dangerous euphoria in the democracies.[34] Unfortunately Washington's minimum requirements, enhanced by the Eisenhower administration's inflexible rejection of Soviet gains in East-Central Europe, demanded no less than diplomatic capitulation. It was not strange that Eisenhower and Dulles saw little point in East-West diplomacy.

For Dulles the goal of liberating Eastern Europe, proclaimed without restraint during the 1952 presidential campaign, became a logical and necessary extension of the policy of containment. In his appearance before the Senate Foreign Relations Committee on January 15, 1953,

Dulles commented on the limited objectives of past containment policy. He warned the committee:

[W]e shall never have a secure peace or a happy world so long as Soviet Communism dominates one-third of all the peoples that there are. . . . These people who are enslaved are people who deserve to be free . . . and ought to be free because if they are the servile instruments of aggressive despotism, they will eventually be welded into a force which will be highly dangerous to ourselves and to all the free world. Therefore, we must always have in mind the liberation of these captive peoples. . . . Liberation can be accomplished by processes short of war.[35]

Dulles reaffirmed the need of liberation when he addressed the American Society of Newspaper Editors in April 1953: "It is of utmost importance that we should make clear to the captive peoples that we do not accept their captivity as a permanent fact of history. If they thought otherwise and became hopeless, we would unwittingly have become partners to the forging of a hostile power so vast that it could encompass our destruction." Unless the United States reduced the Soviet presence in Eastern Europe, Dulles warned repeatedly, not even the established lines of demarcation would hold. Still, Eisenhower informed his administration at the outset that he would seek containment, not liberation, under the assumption that a long-term evolution toward self-determination would achieve United States objectives in Europe without the risk of war.

President Eisenhower, in his first State of the Union message, February 2, 1953, condemned the wartime agreements, which, Republicans insisted, had brought Russian dominance to millions of Europeans. He would ask Congress, he said, to join in "an appropriate resolution making clear that this Government recognizes no kind of commitments contained in secret accords which condoned enslavement." Dulles explained the resolution before the House Foreign Affairs Committee on February 26. "The aim," he said, "is to make totally clear the integrity of this Nation's purpose in relation to the millions of enslaved peoples in Europe and Asia."[36] The proposed resolution condemned Soviet behavior rather than Franklin D. Roosevelt's alleged sell-out at Yalta; Senate Republicans rejected it. Thereafter they demended that the administration fulfill its promise to free the captive peoples of Europe. Unfortunately, liberation required the withdrawal of Soviet military power and political influence from Eastern Europe. As *The Economist* (London) observed on August 30, 1952: "Unhappily 'liberation' applied to Eastern Europe. . . means either the risk of war or it means nothing. . . . 'Liberation' entails no risk of war only when it means nothing."

Dulles assumed that he could weaken the Soviet Union by denying it the moral respectability and needed resources of the Western World. Following Stalin's death in March 1953, his successor, Georgi Malenkov, argued for peaceful coexistence and new measures to guarantee the peace. When Eisenhower advocated a hopeful and positive response to the Soviet overtures, Dulles made clear his displeasure. ". . . I think there's some real danger of our just seeming to fall in with these Soviet overtures," he cautioned. "It's obvious that what they are doing is because of outside pressures, and I don't know anything better we can do than to keep up these pressures right now." The East German riots of June 1953, followed in July by the execution of Lavrenti Beria, notorious head of the Soviet secret police, convinced Dulles that the Soviet empire was seething with discontent and that greater Western pressure could break Soviet control of East-Central Europe completely. "This is the kind of time when we ought to be *doubling* our bets, not reducing them—as all the Western parliaments want to do," he informed the Cabinet on July 10. "This is the time to *crowd* the enemy—and maybe *finish* him, once and for all." At the same time Dulles assured the nation: "[T]he Communist structure is over-extended, over-rigid and ill-founded." As oppressed populations demonstrated their spirit of independence, the Secretary continued, the Kremlin "would come to recognize the futility of trying to hold captive so many peoples who, by their faith and their patriotism, can never really be consolidated into a Soviet Communist world."[37]

Eventually American revisionism focused on the issue of German reunification; anything less would upset West Germany's internal stability and would trouble, especially, the millions of refugees from the East residing in that country. For political reasons alone the Bonn government would not accept as permanent the Soviet subjugation of 17 million East Germans. If the West could not satisfy this German interest, some Americans feared, Bonn might eventually negotiate with the Kremlin on its own. As early as July 1953, Eisenhower declared that an honorable European peace would require the reemergence of a united German republic, dedicated to the welfare of its own people and to the peace of Europe. "The continued partition of Germany," Dulles declared more forcefully in September, "is a scandal. It is more than that. It is a crime. . . . [I]t is not only wrong to the Germans; it is a menace to the peace."[38] Certainly the subsequent incorporation of West Germany into NATO was a net gain. But Dulles never explained how a rearmed West German state, tightly integrated into the Western alliance, could achieve reunification without Soviet approval. Eisenhower on many occasions, especially at the Geneva Summit of July

1955, demonstrated his desire to improve United States–Soviet relations. But the goal of liberation, exceeding the possibilities of any diplomatic settlement, demanded its price in the prolongation of East-West tensions across the heart of Europe.[39]

IV

Similarly the Eisenhower administration refused to come to terms with the Communist-led government of China. What rendered the Peking regime diplomatically unacceptable was its alleged subservience to Kremlin-directed international communism. Ambassador Karl Lott Rankin in Taipei detected the essential role of the presumed monolith in United States–Chinese relations. He reminded Ambassador George V. Allen in India in July 1953 that the United States could maintain its anti-Peking posture only by denying that Mao Tse-tung enjoyed any independence from Moscow. Whether or not this was true, wrote Rankin, the Chinese Nationalists feared that Washington might accept it as true and thereafter follow the course of Britain and India. "Only so long as they are persuaded that Americans continue to regard Mao simply as a Soviet tool," ran Rankin's warning, "will they feel reasonably assured as to our China policy."[40] For official Washington, Soviet control of China was merely the initial stage in a process that would eventually destroy all national entities in Asia and create one vast community under Communist domination. Nationalism was the Asiatic agent for the new universalism. "The Soviet leaders, in mapping their strategy for world conquest," Dulles warned in November 1953, "hit upon nationalism as a device for absorbing the colonial peoples."[41] The danger, continued Dulles, rested in the ability of Communist agitators to aggravate the nationalist aspirations of a people so that it would rebel violently against the existing order. Before a new stability appeared, the Communists would gain control of the nation and convey it into the Soviet orbit.

Chiang's supporters across the country, as well as the China bloc in Congress, declared emphatically that Eisenhower's election was a mandate that the administration abrogate Truman's limited commitment to the Nationalist cause and give all possible assistance to the Republic of China. For them, coexistence with the mainland regime was tantamount to surrender. "There can be no American policy for the Pacific," Indiana's William Jenner warned the Senate, "if the Communists are allowed to retain the heartland of Asia. . . . All American policy must start from a firm decision to reestablish the legitimate anti-Communist government on the China mainland."[42] Senator William F. Knowland of California emerged as Chiang's leading spokesman in the Senate; Congressman Walter Judd of Minnesota assumed command of the House's powerful Nationalist China bloc. These Republican stalwarts committed the Eisenhower administration to the indefinite nonrecognition of the Peking regime. This would, they assumed, prevent China's new leadership from consolidating its power.

Eisenhower had little interest in the Republican party's anti-Peking crusade; as Richard Challener noted, the President resented the persistent pressures which the Nationalist China group exerted on the administration. Indeed, early in his administration the President, in meetings with his staff, expressed uneasiness over the United States commitment to the Nationalist regime. Robert J. Donovan, who attended such meetings in preparation of his semi-official history of the administration, *Eisenhower: The Inside Story* (1956), recorded the President's views in the following passage: "The President was not convinced that the vital interests of the United States were best served by prolonged nonrecognition of China. He had serious doubts as to whether Russia and China were natural allies. . . . Therefore, he asked, would it not be the best policy in the long run for the United States to try to pull China away from Russia rather than drive the Chinese ever deeper into an unnatural alliance unfriendly to the United States?"[43] Officially, however, Eisenhower remained committed to Chiang Kai-shek as the legitimate ruler of all China.

Conscious of the abuse that former Secretary of State Dean Acheson and other Truman officials had suffered at the hands of Chiang's supporters in Congress, the new administration was not inclined to challenge them. The transcripts of Dulles's telephone conversations reveal that Knowland and Judd reported every rumor or newspaper report that suggested a softening of official policy toward China. Dulles invariably reassured them that there had not been and never would be any change in the administration's posture toward the mainland government of China.[44] Eisenhower established a liaison with the China bloc by appointing Walter S. Robertson, a staunch friend of Chiang, to the position of Assistant Secretary of State for Far Eastern Affairs. In naming Admiral Arthur W. Radford as chairman of the Joint Chiefs of Staff, the President placed in a high advisory post another powerful member of the Nationalist China bloc. Radford made no secret of his belief that the Peking regime must be eliminated even if it required a fifty-year war. These men, joined by Knowland, Judd, and others in Congress and the press, possessed the power to bind the United States inflexibly to the Nationalist cause, but little more. Nothing revealed the emptiness of the Eisenhower posture toward China more than did the "unleashing" of Chiang Kai-shek in February 1953, when the President, in a dramatic gesture of reversing Truman's Korean war order to the Seventh Fleet to defend Formosa, announced that the fleet would no longer protect the mainland.[45] Beyond this gesture the administration had no plan to return Chiang to the mainland.

Gradually the official antagonism toward China became so pervading that China often replaced Russia in official speeches as the dominant threat to Asian stability. Whatever the changing perceptions of Chinese power and subservience, nonrecognition demanded a perennial denial that the mainland regime represented the Chinese people. Washington officials continued to accuse Peking of imposing an alien minority rule on the intimidated Chinese populace and of flouting every Chinese treaty obligation and every principle of the United Nations. As late as March 1959, Walter Robertson reminded a Canadian audience: "Let no one say that representation is being denied to 600 million mainland Chinese. The fanatical Marxists of Peiping come no closer to representing the will and aspirations of the Chinese people than the puppet regime of Budapest comes to representing the will and aspirations of the Hungarian people or William Z. Foster comes to representing the will and aspirations of the American people."[46]

This denial of Peking's legitimacy enabled Washington to maintain its allegiance to Nationalist China as an essential element in the containment of Communist expansion. "Many an Asian has told me," reported Walter P. McConaughy, Director of the Office of Chinese Affairs, in January 1954, "that American nonrecognition of the Communist regime in Peiping has had much to do with checking the impetus of the Communist advance in Asia."[47] Conversely, recognition of the Peking dictatorship, declared McConaughy, whould comprise "the hardest psychological blow against the will to resist the further spread of communism that could be devised." Recognition, Dulles warned an Australian audience in March 1957, would encourage influences hostile to the United States and its allies and further imperial countries whose independence strengthened American peace and security.[48] Shortly thereafter William J. Sebald, the ambassador to Australia, observed, "A change in the status of Free China would, I believe, have a chain-reaction effect which would seriously weaken the free world." Robertson declared even more dramatically in March 1959:

If the United States were to abandon its commitments to the Republic of China in order to appease the threatening Red Chinese, no country in Asia could feel that it could any longer rely upon the protection of the United States against the Communist threat. These comparatively weak nations

would have no alternative but to come to terms—the best they could get—
with the Peiping colossus.[49]

Beyond containment, nonrecognition sustained the hope of China's
eventual liberation. Unlike other countries suffering under Communist
tyranny, observed Ambassador Rankin, China had its Formosa as "a
bastion and rallying point where hope is being kept alive and preparations made for a better future."[50] One day, Rankin predicted, Formosa might prove to be the Achilles heel of communism in Asia. During
March 1957 Rankin acknowledged that the United States had done
much for the Republic of China. But, he noted, the government in
Taipei remained "as far as ever from its great objective of bringing
about the liberation of mainland China from Red tyranny." The dis-
parity between the two protagonists in total military and economic
strength, he added, was increasing at an accelerated pace to Free
China's disadvantage; continued drift would end in disaster, leaving
but one China.[51] For Dulles, however, nonrecognition still carried the
assurance of liberation. As he declared in his noted San Francisco
speech of June 1957: "We can confidently assume that international
communism's rule of strict conformity is, in China as elsewhere, a
passing and not a perpetual phase. We owe it to ourselves, our allies,
and the Chinese people to do all we can to contribute to that passing."[52]
What troubled Chiang and his supporters everywhere, however, was
the realization that beyond nonrecognition the United States had no
policy of liberation. The status of China, like that of Eastern Europe,
had long ceased to be a matter of strategic interest.

V

President Eisenhower rejected Europe's traditional colonialism as a
condition without moral or political justification. He recognized as well
the power and intensity of postwar nationalism throughout the Afro-
Asian world. He reminded Secretary of the Treasury George Humphrey
in March 1957 that the "*protection of our own interests and our own
system* demands . . . that we . . . understand that the spirit of nationalism, coupled with a deep hunger for some betterment in physical
conditions and living standards, creates a critical situation in the underdeveloped areas of the world."[53] At the same time Eisenhower rejected
the notion that self-determination gave revolutionaries the right to choose
a radical road to state-building. Nor would he distinguish between the
Communist-led revolution in Indochina and the presumed expansionism of Russia and China in Southeast Asia. Secretary Dulles described

the administration's official view of the Asian danger as early as February 1953: "The Soviet Russians," he told the nation, "are making a drive to get Japan, not only through what they are doing in Korea but also through what they are doing in Indochina. If they could get this peninsula of Indochina, Siam, Burma, and Malaya, they would have what is called the rice bowl of Asia. . . . [I]f the Soviet Union had control of the rice bowl of Asia, that would be another weapon which would tend to expand their control into Japan and into India."[54] Vice President Nixon elaborated on the danger in December: "If Indochina falls, Thailand is put in an almost impossible position. The same is true of Malaya with its rubber and tin. The same is true for Indonesia. . . . That indicates . . . why it is vitally important that Indochina not go behind the Iron Curtain."[55]

Despite such official perceptions of danger, Eisenhower did not support the French at Dienbienphu in the spring of 1954. He explained to his close friend, Everett Hazlett, that he failed to obtain "the conditions under which I felt the United States could properly intervene to protect its own interests."[56] Eisenhower was determined, however, to hold the line in Southeast Asia, defined that summer by the Geneva Accords. The Pacific, he said, would remain an American lake. After the French withdrawal from Indochina he committed the United States not only to the support of Ngo Dinh Diem's new Saigon regime, in control of all Vietnam south of the seventeenth parallel, but also to the eventual elimination of Ho Chi Minh's control of North Vietnam. Washington's single-minded support of Diem as the legitimate inheritor of French authority throughout Vietnam seemed to overlook a variety of inescapable factors: that Ho Chi Minh had secured the independence of all Indochina from French rule, including that portion of the former French colony now ruled from Saigon; that Ho's cause had not been the cause of Russian or Chinese expansionism but the cause of Indochinese independence; that as an Indochinese nationalist he was fiercely independent of all external control; that in achieving victory he had defeated a good French army, administering 175,000 casualties with 92,000 dead; and that his military power would only increase with the passage of time. How could the United States build into the Saigon regime the unity and power—which the French had failed to achieve in eight years of bitter struggle—sufficient to achieve a political and military victory over the forces of Ho Chi Minh? From the beginning American purpose in Southeast Asia carried the seeds of possible disaster.

After 1954 Ngo Dinh Diem shouldered the chief responsibility for defending his own and America's interests in Southeast Asia. Diem's political and military success remained the only barrier to an uncertain future of chaos and war. Having rendered itself hostage to Diem, Washington was powerless to control his regime or to desert it. In response to official warnings that Diem's fortunes were not promising, the Eisenhower administration surfeited him with aid, advisers, and praise; it offered renewed commitments to the survival of his regime. Walter Robertson observed at a meeting of the American Friends of Vietnam, in Washington, during June 1956, that Diem was "a truly worthy leader whose integrity and devotion to his country's welfare have become generally recognized among his people."[57] During Diem's official visit to Washington in May 1957, President Eisenhower lauded the Vietnamese leader publicly at the airport for bringing to the task of organizing his country "the greatest of courage, the greatest of statesmanship. . . ." Diem, in return, thanked the President for the "unselfish American aid which has accomplished a miracle of Viet-Nam."[58] When Diem departed Washington on May 11, the two presidents issued a joint communiqué which "looked forward to an end of the unhappy division of the Vietnamese people and confirmed the determination of the two Governments to work together to seek suitable means to bring about the peaceful unification of Viet-Nam in freedom."[59]

Until the end of the decade Washington predicted disaster if containment at the seventeenth parallel should fail. Eisenhower explained his fears to a Gettysburg College audience in April 1959:

> Strategically, South Viet-Nam's capture by the Communists would bring their power several hundred miles into a hitherto free region. The remaining countries of Southeast Asia would be menaced by a great flanking movement. . . . The loss of South Viet-Nam would set in motion a crumbling process that could, as it progressed, have grave consequences for us and for freedom.[60]

Even as Eisenhower left office his commitment to the future of the Saigon regime remained firm. On October 26, 1960, the fifth anniversary of the founding of the Republic of Vietnam, the President explained to Diem what long observation of Vietnam's struggle had taught him:

> I sense how deeply the Vietnamese value their country's independence and strength and I know how well you used your boldness when you led your countrymen in winning it. I also know that your determination has been a vital factor in guarding that independence while steadily advancing the economic development of your country. I am confident that these same qualities of determination and boldness will meet the renewed threat as well as the needs and desires of your countrymen for further progress on all fronts.

As in Vietnam, every action or threatened action of the Eisenhower years in Asia, the Middle East, Africa, and Latin America was taken in the name of containing Soviet expansionism. In 1953 and 1954 the President authorized the CIA to overthrow the governments of Iran and Guatemala, both devoted to social reform but neither Communist-controlled or tied to the Soviet Union. Premier Muhammad Mossadegh endangered Western interests in Iran when, in May 1951, he seized the British-owned Anglo-Iranian Oil Company and threatened to carry out a nationwide social revolution. When Eisenhower entered office he agreed with the British on the necessity of removing Mossadegh from power, especially when the premier forced the pro-Western Shah to flee the country. As in Vietnam, the President did not distinguish between radical nationalism and Soviet communism. While State Department pronouncements linked Mossadegh to Communism, the CIA organized a successful coup against the premier and arranged for the return of the Shah.[61]

Washington's identification of Jacobo Arbenz's democratically elected and reform-minded government of Guatemala with international Communism was even more pervading. Arbenz, in carrying out his land reform program, nationalized only unused lands and thus left Guatemala's basic power structure intact. But when, by 1953, he had appointed known Communists to high office and appeared to threaten the vast land holdings of American-owned United Fruit Company, John M. Cabot, Assistant Secretary of State for Inter-American Affairs, accused Guatemala of having "a regime which is openly playing the Communist game. . . ."[62] To terminate this alleged Soviet-directed conspiracy in Central America, Eisenhower ordered Arbenz's overthrow. Shortly after the liberal government's collapse in June 1954 under internal as well as external pressures, Eisenhower accepted the credentials of the ambassador of Guatemala's new military regime of Carlos Castillo Armas with these words: "The people of Guatemala, in a magnificent effort, have liberated themselves from the shackles of international Communist direction, and reclaimed their right of self-determination."[63]

Even in the Middle East, where Israeli, British, and French action against Egypt sparked the Suez crisis, Eisenhower defined the subsequent American commitment to Middle Eastern stability as an effort to prevent the onrush of Soviet influence in the region. The Eisenhower Doctrine, adopted by Congress in March 1957, declared in part that the United States was "prepared to use armed force to assist any [Middle Eastern] nation or group of nations requesting assistance against armed aggression from any country *controlled by international communism.*

. . ." In response, Cairo's *Akher Saa* declared Soviet aggression in the Arab world imaginary. On February 1, 1958, Syria and Egypt announced their union in the United Arab Republic. Several days later State Department officer William M. Rountree assured the Senate Foreign Relations Committee that the U.S.S.R. had not converted any Middle Eastern country into a satellite, but it had, through deception, "succeeded in exploiting the mistaken belief of some of those countries that they can deal closely with the Soviet Union without risking subversion and ultimate loss of independence."[64] This defined the Soviet problem. In Africa as well the Eisenhower administration saw the political evolution of the 1950s in cold war terms. Following Ghana's independence celebration Vice President Nixon reported that African development "could well prove to be the decisive factor in the conflict between the forces of freedom and international communism."[65]

In its repeated, often ruthless, responses to foreign challenges, the Eisenhower administration, operating as it did from a position of predominant power, managed generally to have its way. This was especially true in Iran, Guatemala, the Middle East, Korea, and China's offshore islands where others had no intention or power to retaliate. But the days when the United States could dispose of every unwanted Third World condition with such limited displays of power were numbered. Nor did the successful pursuit of counter-revolutionary or status quo policies necessarily demonstrate proper ends. As Daniel Graham wrote of the American involvement in Guatemala in May 1955: "Deep down everyone in Guatemala knows that Communism was not the issue. Feudalism was the issue, and those who profited from feudalism won."[66]

VI

With the inauguration of John F. Kennedy in January 1961 the Eisenhower administration passed into history. Its external purposes did not. Through eight years the Eisenhower administration never acknowledged any vital interest, one meriting the resort to force, in liberating either Eastern Europe or China. Still it left office with such goals intact. Eisenhower's statesmanship often lay in his refusal to follow the advice of the hard-liners in his administration, especially those who advocated the elimination of the Peking regime of China. Even when they challenged the President's efforts to avoid high risks or miscalculation, such advisers as Dulles, Radford, and Robertson served the administration's interests admirably. Eisenhower was as determined to maintain an image of inflexible anti-Communism as he was to project an image of moderation. By any political measurement the President's effort to bridge the nation's foreign policy spectrum was remarkably successful. If the proclaimed objectives of his administration often defied the creation of policy, they reassured the governments of Taipei and Saigon, as well as their supporters everywhere, that the United States would defend them against Communist-led aggression. At home the promises of liberation built a powerful consensus, broad enough to encompass the entire Republican party, both inside and outside the government, and most Democrats. The voices of criticism in Congress were scarcely audible. Gary Reichard has demonstrated clearly that not all Democrats agreed with the Eisenhower policies, but he also observed that even the Democrats who chose to object could never mount an effective assault on the assumptions and declared purposes of the administration. Much of the media refused to question the administration's rhetorical pursuit of the unachievable. This permitted the Eisenhower leadership to reap untold political advantage from its promises of liberation even when the promises remained unfulfilled. The government's power to dispose of its critics with such apparent success was simply a measure of the overwhelming consensus which its purely anti-Communist objectives enjoyed. Not since the 1920s had the country's foreign policies achieved such broad public approval.

Unfortunately, the Eisenhower consensus on matters of Eastern Europe and China, built and sustained with astonishing energy and determination, was incompatible with the nation's need to accept forthrightly what it could not avoid. In time the country would assign liberation to the realm of lost causes, but until then it would make little progress in its negotiations with Moscow or Peking. The avoidance of diplomatic accommodation settled nothing; but the administration's devotion to liberation, if only at the level of words, was all that remained of its promise to create a more dynamic, successful foreign policy than that which it inherited from the Truman years. Governments are always free to escape their verbal, even their diplomatic, commitments when national purposes exceed the bounds of acceptable policy. The world never makes that escape easy or palatable. To the extent that the language of liberation held the administration's potential cold war critics in line, to that same extent the administration would bear charges of retreat and failure if it permitted its anti-Communist purposes to falter under the pressure of events.

Fortunately for President Eisenhower, he faced no need to modify his administration's declared goals in Europe or China. In both regions the United States confronted conditions that were essentially stable. The issues raised by these two major areas of conflict would drift toward solutions of their own. Indirectly, the administration's rejection of the

Peking regime demanded a special price. As an official position it was untouchable and thus contributed immeasurably to the public approbation that the administration enjoyed. But non-recognition and the extravagant language that underwrote it sustained the notion that the Chinese government was the creation of an international Communist conspiracy. This aggravated the fears of Asian revolution. By refusing to allay the nation's anti-Chinese sentiments, the President compelled the nation to strengthen its commitments to all pro-Western regimes in the Far East. The administration posture toward China turned out to be meaningless rather than dangerous, but the conviction that China underwrote the Communist expansionism of Southeast Asia ultimately reinforced the American resolve to meet the challenge of revolutionary Indochina.[67]

Southeast Asia presented a dynamic rather than a static problem. Here the United States would meet another successful assault on its containment policies or it would engage in war to prevent it. For a minority of Americans not converted to falling dominoes, any decision to reduce the American commitment to Vietnam would have been welcome indeed. Perhaps President Eisenhower himself never intended that the United States should fight in Vietnam.[68] Still, he did nothing to reduce the American commitment to Ngo Dinh Diem or prepare an avenue of escape from a war in Saigon's defense. Whatever the President's personal intentions in Southeast Asia, his repeated predictions of disaster, should Saigon fall, made retreat even for him almost impossible. Any administration that permitted Ho Chi Minh to triumph in his purpose of uniting North and South Vietnam would face the charge that it was exposing all Asia to a Moscow-Peking global conspiracy. Were the United States, moreover, unwilling to support Saigon in a crisis, the screams of anguish and the accusations of duplicity would reach Washington in such volume that only with the greatest of difficulty could an administration have avoided the moral and political pressure. Ultimately, the government would have been held responsible for what it said as well as what it did.

For the moment the probable tragedy of American policy in Southeast Asia mattered little. As long as the proclaimed triumphs of the South Vietnamese government and the SEATO alliance guaranteed successful containment at little cost, the Eisenhower administration faced no demands for an explicit explanation of its intentions. Still the intellectual and policy dilemmas of the future were already clear. The ends of policy assumed a global danger of which Ho's Hanoi government comprised only a minor segment; yet the means of policy, as they evolved during the Eisenhower years, did not include even a sure defense against Hanoi, much less against Russia and China. If the latter two nations constituted the essential danger to American security interests in Asia, policies aimed at the disposal of Ho's national ambitions, whatever their success, would not touch, much less resolve, the dangers posed by the two leading Communist powers. If, on the other hand, the challenge to United States security lay in Hanoi, then the rhetoric of a Soviet-based global danger had no meaning. Washington directed its efforts against North Vietnam; it did not contemplate war with China or Russia to settle the question of Communism in Southeast Asia.

For Americans generally the country's world role in the 1950s had been satisfactory. Behind the progress toward relative stability had been the outpouring of American dollars to underwrite both the country's massive defense establishment and the unprecedented prosperity of the Western world. Yet, tragically, fear still comprised the most powerful force in the nation's foreign policy. Fear stimulated the endless quest for security; at the same time the very imprecision of the factors that sustained the insecurity never permitted the nation to discover when it had achieved an adequate level of defense. The nation's declared purposes, whether strategic or moral, always exceeded what any military structure could achieve. Containment of Communist power in Europe and China had sought massive changes in a fundamentally stable environment; elsewhere containment tended to oppose change in a fundamentally unstable environment. Thus, in both Europe and the Third World, the United States stood at odds with the basic tendencies in world politics. In refusing to recognize legitimacy either in the Kremlin's continuing effort to assure pro-Soviet policies in Eastern Europe or in China's Peking regime, Washington neglected to exercise the limited options before it. Maurice Duverger reminded the U.S. administration in *Le Monde* on April 27, 1954, that it was defying the basic rules of traditional diplomacy:

> The entire diplomatic tradition of Europe rests on two unwritten principles: recognition of reality on the one hand, compromise on the other. If the devil himself should be installed at the head of a nation's government, his neighbors could adopt only two attitudes: either try to destroy him by war or negotiate with him a modus vivendi. The first attitude is military; the second is diplomatic; there is no third. . . . One can almost define the diplomacy of the United States as principles opposed to those which have just been set forth: on the one hand, refusal to recognize disagreeable situations, on the other hand a desire to obtain capitulation pure and simple.

If the nation's security and self-image as world leader demanded that it hold the line against Communist-led encroachments wherever they might occur, the means of achieving that goal seemed promising enough. Throughout the Third World, but especially in South Korea, Formosa, the Philippines, Thailand, Pakistan, Iran, Turkey, Israel, Saudi Arabia, and various Latin American states, pro-Western governments appeared willing, even anxious, to join the United States in bilateral and multilateral defense pacts, to provide military bases, or to accept economic and military aid under arrangements designed to assure their capacity to resist Communist pressures and thus aid the United States in its determination to contain Soviet power and influence. Unfortunately the defense lines which marked the periphery of the Communist world moved outside the borders of Russia and China into regions where Communist-directed sabotage, insurgency, and guerrilla warfare rendered interests and the means to defend them ambiguous. Throughout the Third World, moreover, intensely nationalistic, anti-Western revolutionary movements already endangered some of the elitest governments bound to the United States. How would American leaders adjust national purposes to the Third World's burgeoning assertiveness and the country's limited interest and influence in opposing it? The challenge of coming to terms with unwanted change in Asia, Africa, and Latin America required less a nuclear strategy than a recognition of the power of nationalism as a force for stability as well as change, a precise definition of national interests with the will and capacity to defend them, and a willingness to coexist with a sometimes troublesome world that otherwise served the nation's interests admirably.

Notes

1. Norman A. Graebner, *The New Isolationism: A Study of Politics and Foreign Policy Since 1950* (New York: Ronald Press, 1956), 130–31.

2. For the military views of Matthew Ridgway and Maxwell Taylor, see Matthew B. Ridgway, *Soldier: The Memoirs of Matthew B. Ridgway* (New York: Harper & Brothers, 1956), 295–321; and Maxwell D. Taylor, *The Uncertain Trumpet* (New York: Harper & Brothers, 1960), 1–79.

3. Bismarck quoted in Bernard Brodie, *Strategy in the Missile Age* (Princeton: Princeton University Press, 1959), 234.

4. John Foster Dulles, "A Policy of Boldness," *Life, 32* (May 19, 1952), 150.

5. Dulles's speech before the Council on Foreign Relations, New York, January 12, 1954, *Department of State Bulletin, 30* (January 25, 1954), 107–8.

6. Graebner, *The New Isolationism*, 132–33.

7. "NATO Talks on Disarmament," *Manchester Guardian, 77* (December 19, 1957), 3; Statement of President Eisenhower, December 16, 1957, *Department of State Bulletin*, 38 (January 6, 1958), 7.

8. Robert Griffith, "Dwight D. Eisenhower and the Corporate Commonwealth," *American Historical Review, 87* (February, 1982), 120.

9. Eisenhower's Farewell Address, January 17, 1961, *Public Papers of the Presidents of the United States: Dwight D. Eisenhower, 1960–1961* (Washington: GPO, 1961), 1038.

10. Carl von Clausewitz, *On War*, eds. Michael Howard and Peter Paret (Princeton: Princeton University Press, 1976), 605.

11. Herbert F. York, *Race to Oblivion, A Participant's View of the Arms Race* (New York: Simon & Schuster, 1970), 230–31.

12. Herbert F. York, *The Advisors: Oppenheimer, Teller, and the Superbomb* (San Francisco: W. H. Freeman, 1976), ix.

13. Graebner, *The New Isolationism*, 162–63.

14. James Shepley, "How Dulles Averted War," *Life, 40* (January 16, 1956), 71.

15. William Bragg Ewald, Jr., *Eisenhower the President: Crucial Days, 1951–1960* (Englewood Cliffs, N.J.: Prentice-Hall, 1981), 119.

16. Graebner, *The New Isolationism*, 132.

17. Dwight D. Eisenhower, *Mandate for Change, 1953–1956: The White House Years* (Garden City, N.Y.: Doubleday, 1963), 347.

18. *Ibid.*, 354.

19. Robert A. Divine, *Eisenhower and the Cold War* (New York: Oxford University Press, 1981), 51.

20. Shepley, "How Dulles Averted War," 72.

21. Eisenhower, *Mandate for Change*, 463–64.

22. President Eisenhower to Congress on Defense of Formosa, January 24, 1955, Russell D. Buhite, ed., *The Dynamics of World Power: A Documentary History of United States Foreign Policy, 1945–1973, Vol. IV: The Far East* (New York: Chelsea House, 1973), 211.

23. A. M. Rosenthal in the *New York Times*, February 13, 1955.

24. Eisenhower, *Mandate for Change*, 483.

25. Dwight D. Eisenhower, *Waging Peace, 1956–1961: The White House Years* (Garden City, N.Y.: Doubleday, 1965), 299–300. For the September 4 memorandum in full, see *ibid.*, 691–693.

26. Brodie, *Strategy in the Missile Age*, 256n–257n.

27. Eisenhower to Senator Green, October 2, 1958, Buhite, *The Far East*, 253.

28. *Department of State Bulletin, 34* (May 14, 1956), 788; Department of State, *American Foreign Policy: Current Documents, 1956* (Washington: GPO, 1959), 779.

29. See, for example, Robert Shaplen, *The Lost Revolution: The U.S. in Vietnam, 1946–1966* (New York: Harper & Row, 1966), 140–43; George McTurnan Kahin and John W. Lewis, *The United States in Vietnam* (New York: Dell, 1969), 99–120.

30. Dulles's address to the nation, January 27, 1953, *Department of State Bulletin, 28* (February 9, 1953), 212–13.

31. Walter S. Robertson, "America's Responsibilities in the Far East," June 3, 1957, *ibid., 36* (June 24, 1957), 997.

32. *Ibid., 28* (February 9, 1953), 215.

33. Speech before the Council on Foreign Relations, New York, January 12, 1954, *ibid., 30* (January 25, 1954), 110.

34. For the debate on the proper timing of negotiations see C. L. Sulzberger in the *New York Times*, November 1, 1953. Anthony Eden favored early talks. See the *Des Moines Register*, December 1, 1953.

35. *Hearings before the Committee on Foreign Relations, United States Senate, Eighty-third Congress, First Session, on the Nomination of John Foster Dulles, Secretary of State-Designate, January 15, 1953* (Washington: GPO, 1953), 5–6.

36. The resolution appears in Department of State, *American Foreign Policy: Basic Documents, 1950–1955* (Washington: GPO, 1957), II, 1958–59; Dulles's statement, February 26, 1953, *ibid.*, 1959.

37. Emmet John Hughes, *The Ordeal of Power: A Political Memoir of the Eisenhower Years* (New York: Dell, 1964), 95–96, 120; *American Foreign Policy, 1950–1955*, II, 1746.

38. *American Foreign Policy, 1950–1955*, II, 1747–48, 1843–44.

39. For George Kennan's well-known critique of the sharp military division of Europe and

the neglect of diplomacy to resolve the issue of Germany can be found in Kennan, *Russia, the Atom and the West* (New York: Harper & Brothers, 1957), passim.

40. Karl Lott Rankin, *China Assignment* (Seattle: University Washington Press, 1964), 173.

41. "The Moral Initiative," speech before the CIO, Cleveland, November 18, 1953, *The Department of State Bulletin, 29* (November 30, 1953), 742.

42. William Jenner in the *Congressional Record*, 83d Cong., 1st Sess., Vol. 99, Pt. 8, 11000-11001.

43. Robert J. Donovan, *Eisenhower: The Inside Story* (New York: Harper & Brothers, 1956), 132.

44. Papers of John Foster Dulles, Telephone Calls Series, Dwight D. Eisenhower Library, Abilene, Kansas. Note especially Dulles's conversations with Judd or Knowland for April 9, 1953, August 1, 1953, November 14, 1953, February 27, 1954, February 20, 1954, August 20, 1954, November 20, 1954, January 27, 1955, April 27, 1955, August 1, 1955, and April 2, 1956.

45. Graebner, *The New Isolationism*, 129.

46. Speech before the Canadian Club, Ottawa, March 13, 1959, *Department of State Bulletin, 40* (April 6, 1959), 475.

47. Walter P. McConaughy, "China in the Shadow of Communism," *ibid., 30* (January 11, 1954), 41.

48. Dulles's statement on United States China policy, Canberra, March 12, 1957, *ibid., 36* (April 1, 1957), 531.

49. *Ibid., 40* (April 6, 1969), 474.

50. Rankin, *China Assignment*, 114–15.

51. *Ibid.*, 311, 315, 323.

52. Speech before the convention of Lions International, San Francisco, June 28, 1957, *Department of State Bulletin, 37* (July 15, 1957), 95.

53. Griffith, "Eisenhower and the Corporate Commonwealth," 118.

54. Dulles's survey of foreign policy problems, January 27, 1953, *Department of State Bulletin, 28* (February 9, 1953), 213.

55. Radio and television address, December 23, 1953, *ibid., 30* (January 4, 1954), 12.

56. Griffith, "Eisenhower and the Corporate Commonwealth," 119.

57. Address before the American Friends of Vietnam, Washington, June 1, 1956, *Department of State Bulletin, 34* (June 11, 1956), 972.

58. Meeting at the airport, May 8, 1957, *ibid., 36* (May 27, 1957), 854.

59. Joint statement, May 11, 1957, *ibid.*, 851.

60. Speech at Gettysburg College, April 4, 1959, *ibid., 40* (April 27, 1959), 580–81.

61. For a brief discussion of the Iranian episode, see Richard J. Barnet, *Intervention and Revolution: The United States and the Third World* (New York: The New Library, 1972), 265–67.

62. Speech before the General Federation of Women's Clubs, Washington, October 14, 1953, *Department of State Bulletin, 29* (October 26, 1953), 556.

63. Quoted in Richard H. Immerman, *The CIA in Guatemala: The Foreign Policy of Intervention* (Austin: University of Texas Press, 1982), 5.

64. *Foreign Policy Briefs*, May 30, 1958, 1.

65. Thomas Karis, "United States Policy toward South Africa," Gwendolen M. Carter and Patrick O'Meara, eds., *Southern Africa: The Continuing Crisis* (Bloomington, Ind.: Indiana University Press, 1982), 323.

66. Daniel Graham, "Castillo's Guatemala," *Nation, 180* (May 21, 1955), 440.

67. Kennedy stressed the connection between Chinese expansionism and the problem of Vietnam. See *Public Papers of the Presidents of the United States: John F. Kennedy, 1963* (Washington: GPO, 1964), 243–244, 343, 349, and especially 659.

68. Eisenhower's advisers such as Andrew Goodpaster and Arthur Larson, in conversation with the author, have insisted that Eisenhower would never have led the United States into war in Indochina.

Index